Disposable Passions

Global Exploitation Cinemas

Series Editors
Johnny Walker, Northumbria University, UK
Austin Fisher, Bournemouth University, UK

Editorial Board
Tejaswini Ganti (New York University, USA)
Joan Hawkins (Indiana University, USA)
Kevin Heffernan (Southern Methodist University, USA)
I. Q. Hunter (De Montfort University, UK)
Peter Hutchings (Northumbria University, UK)
Ernest Mathijs (University of British Columbia, Canada)
Constance Penley (University of California, Santa Barbara, USA)
Eric Schaefer (Emerson College, USA)
Dolores Tierney (University of Sussex, UK)
Valerie Wee (National University of Singapore)

Also in the Series:
Grindhouse: Cultural Exchange on 42nd Street, and Beyond

Disposable Passions

Vintage Pornography and the Material Legacies of Adult Cinema

David Church

Bloomsbury Academic
An imprint of Bloomsbury Publishing Inc

B L O O M S B U R Y
NEW YORK • LONDON • OXFORD • NEW DELHI • SYDNEY

Bloomsbury Academic
An imprint of Bloomsbury Publishing Inc

1385 Broadway	50 Bedford Square
New York	London
NY 10018	WC1B 3DP
USA	UK

www.bloomsbury.com

BLOOMSBURY and the Diana logo are trademarks of Bloomsbury Publishing Plc

First published 2016

© David Church, 2016

All rights reserved. No part of this publication may be reproduced or transmitted in any form or by any means, electronic or mechanical, including photocopying, recording, or any information storage or retrieval system, without prior permission in writing from the publishers.

No responsibility for loss caused to any individual or organization acting on or refraining from action as a result of the material in this publication can be accepted by Bloomsbury or the author.

Library of Congress Cataloging-in-Publication Data
Names: David, Church, 1982- author.
Title: Disposable passions : vintage pornography and the material legacies of adult cinema / David Church.
Description: New York : Bloomsbury Academic, 2016. | Series: Global exploitation cinemas | Includes bibliographical references and index.
Identifiers: LCCN 2016005633 (print) | LCCN 2016007906 (ebook) | ISBN 9781501307560 (hardback) | ISBN 9781501307577 (pbk.) | ISBN 9781501307539 (ePDF) | ISBN 9781501307546 (Epub)
Subjects: LCSH: Pornographic films–History and criticism. | Sex in motion pictures. | Pornography–Social aspects. | BISAC: PERFORMING ARTS / Film & Video / History & Criticism. | SOCIAL SCIENCE / Pornography.
Classification: LCC PN1995.9.S45 D38 2016 (print) | LCC PN1995.9.S45 (ebook) | DDC 791.43/6538–dc23
LC record available at http://lccn.loc.gov/2016005633

ISBN: HB: 978-1-5013-0756-0
PB: 978-1-5013-0757-7
ePDF: 978-1-5013-0753-9
Epub: 978-1-5013-0754-6

Series: Global Exploitation Cinemas

Cover design: Seventh Tower Creative Solutions

Typeset by Integra Software Service Pvt. Ltd.

Contents

List of Figures	vi
Acknowledgments	ix
Introduction	1
1 Eroticizing the Degraded Past: Stag Films, Cinephilia, and the Marketing of Necro-erotic Desire	23
2 Ephemerality between Fantasy and Reality: Sexploitation, Fan Magazines, and the Adults-Only Film and Publishing Industries	61
3 "Whatever Happened to Gigi Darlene?" Object Lessons for a Disappearing and Reappearing Corpus	103
4 Preservational Ethics, Cultural Distinctions, and Vintage Pornoisseurship in the Internet Age	151
Conclusion	201
Notes	217
Selected Bibliography	252
Index	265

List of Figures

I.1	A fan-made cover design for a nonexistent Criterion Eclipse box set devoted to Doris Wishman's mid-1960s sexploitation "roughies."	8
I.2	Cover of the short-lived adult film fanzine *Filthy Habits: Hardcore & Sexploitation Fare from the 1960s & 1970s* (2002–2003).	16
1.1	The enchanted stag footage unspools on a domestic projector screen in Radley Metzger's *The Lickerish Quartet* (1970).	23
1.2	Hard-core images from the oft-circulated stag film *The Nun's Story* (ca. early 1950s).	30
1.3	Stag films advertised in late 1950s catalogue for mail-order outfit Saturnalia.	32
1.4	Saturnalia catalogue ad for the 8-mm Melton Viewer, a device originally manufactured and sold as a personal film projector for children and families.	33
1.5	Box cover for *Nostalgia Blue* (1976), released on VHS in 1985 by VCA/Classix Video.	36
1.6	Website for Vintage Classic Porn, one of many niche paysites specializing in "Vintage & Retro Pornography for the True Connoisseur."	38
1.7	Period mise-en-scène in a 1920s-era French stag film.	53
2.1	Ad for paperback pulp novels in adults-only catalogue (ca. 1970) for Central Sales, Ltd.	63
2.2	Dopey men and topless women at a nudist camp in Herschell Gordon Lewis's formulaic nudie-cutie *Goldilocks and the Three Bares* (1963).	67
2.3	Production still taken while filming the trailer for the Western-themed roughie *Hot Spur* (1968), as reproduced on the back cover of *Adult Movies Illustrated*.	73
2.4	Full-page advertisement for 8-mm loops and 35-mm slides from a sexploitation film billed as "too 'unusual' … so we felt it would be better if we sold it directly to the home!"	75

List of Figures

2.5	Cover of *For Love or Money*, a 1968 Olympic Foto-Reader novelization of Don Davis's sexploitation film *For Love and Money* (1968).	77
2.6	Stripper and sexploitation actor Althea Currier in *The Girls on F Street* (1966), a film prominently advertised in *Adam*.	79
2.7	Starkly monochromatic, tightly framed rape scenes from (left) Ingmar Bergman's European art film *The Virgin Spring* (1960) and (right) Lee Frost's American roughie *The Defilers* (1965).	84
2.8	William Rotsler and an unidentified model in a 1974 *Knight* magazine advertisement for *Swingers World*.	97
2.9	Rotsler as the Prince of Verona in Peter Perry's *The Secret Sex Lives of Romeo and Juliet* (1969).	99
2.10	Photo (left) from the "*Astral Trip*" review pictorial, depicting a scene from the nonexistent science-fiction sexploitation comedy; and (right) photo of actor Maria Lease in a whipping scene from the no-longer-extant sexploitation film *You* (1968).	101
3.1	Graffito scrawled on opening credits of Michael and Roberta Findlay's *The Curse of Her Flesh* (1968).	104
3.2	Onset photo of Gigi Darlene being posed by sexploitation filmmaker Lem Amero.	105
3.3	Theatrical poster for *The Orgy at Lil's Place* (1963).	117
3.4	Brief flashes of nudity as Sally poses for future husband Bob's paintings in *The Orgy at Lil's Place*.	119
3.5	The photographer applies lipstick "scourges" to Ann's bare back during the photo session in *The Orgy at Lil's Place*.	120
3.6	Back cover of TVX sales catalogue from 1979.	126
3.7	Constance Money restrained in BDSM-submissive gear in VCA's self-censored version of *Barbara Broadcast* (1977).	134
3.8	A homosexual fellatio scene in *The Story of Joanna* (1975), cut from many video editions.	136
4.1	Front cover for one of Something Weird Video's many *Bucky Beaver's Dragon Art Theatre Triple XXX-Rated Double Feature* DVDs.	160
4.2	Alpha Blue Archives' *The Avon Dynasty: 1980s* DVD box set, featuring cheap and kinky hard-core films made and theatrically screened in New York.	167
4.3	Arthur Morowitz's Video Shack store (ca. 1980) in New York City.	176

List of Figures

4.4	Promotional material for Distribpix's Blu-ray edition of *The Opening of Misty Beethoven* (1976).	179
4.5	The cheap porn film (left) shown playing at the Place Pigalle theater during *Misty Beethoven*'s opening credits. Metzger's opulent cinematography (right) on display during Misty's training.	181
4.6	In *Annie Sprinkle's Herstory of Porn* (1999), the onstage Sprinkle uses a similar vibrator to "masturbate" her on-screen self.	185
4.7	In *Annie Sprinkle's Herstory of Porn*, Sprinkle (left) mimes along to her on-screen analogue; and (right) shushes her younger on-screen self.	185
4.8	Sprinkle describes the once-censored "golden shower" scene during her on-screen commentary track on Distribpix's *Deep Inside Annie Sprinkle* (1981) DVD.	188
4.9	Visually inset during the on-screen DVD commentary track for *Deep Inside Annie Sprinkle*, Sprinkle's position recalls *Annie Sprinkle's Herstory of Porn*.	189
4.10	Interior of Video Shack store in early 1980s.	192
4.11	Vinegar Syndrome cofounder Joe Rubin, director Larry Revene, and star Jane Hamilton at the 2013 "In the Flesh" film series, Anthology Film Archives.	197
C.1	An exhibit at the Erotic Heritage Museum commemorating Distribpix's release of the *Deep Inside Annie Sprinkle* Platinum Elite DVD.	203
C.2	Detail from 1985 Caballero Control Corporation home video catalogue promoting Veronica Hart in *Amanda by Night* (1981).	206
C.3	Darrin Blue (Wade Nichols) and Henrietta Wilde (Georgina Spelvin) performing for the stag movie camera in *Take Off* (1978).	209

Acknowledgments

First of all, my thanks to Austin Fisher and Johnny Walker for the invitation to launch this book within their Global Exploitation Cinemas series. As one of the first books to be published in the series, their guidance and support along the way have been invaluable, as have the comments that I received from the series' editorial board members, including Kevin Heffernan, I. Q. Hunter, and Constance Penley. I also owe a debt of gratitude to Katie Gallof at Bloomsbury Academic for believing in the series and this book's place within it. Likewise, Mary Al-Sayed helped shepherd the manuscript through the publication process.

Joan Hawkins offered patient criticism over multiple drafts of what became the seed of this project, subsequently expanded into my first chapter. The following people also offered fantastic feedback on other chapter drafts in various stages of composition: Peter Alilunas, Will Scheibel, Sean Smalley, and Gregory Waller. I must also thank the formative advice offered by the anonymous peer reviewers for the publications where, as noted below, earlier versions of chapters first appeared.

Other historians, fans, and archivists contributed to the project by providing early drafts of unpublished manuscripts, helpful research tips, specialized knowledge, or even simply productive conversation along the way. Among them, I must particularly thank Peter Alilunas, Michael J. Bowen, Stefan Elnabli, Dan Erdman, Elena Gorfinkel, Mark Hain, Kevin Heffernan, Lucas Hilderbrand, I. Q. Hunter, Austin Miller, Kinohi Nishikawa, Lisa Petrucci Vraney, Ryan Powell, Raymond Rea, Casey Scott, Russell Sheaffer, Sean Smalley, Dan Streible, Whitney Strub, Andy Uhrich, Joshua Vasquez, Tom Waugh, Ashley West, and Linda Williams.

My heartfelt thanks to the various individuals who consented to be interviewed for the last two chapters, including Jane Hamilton, Steven Morowitz, Joe Rubin, Eric Schaefer, Casey Scott, Annie Sprinkle, and several former video industry personnel who wished to remain anonymous. Many of these interviewees also generously offered critical feedback on their relevant chapter sections, but as always, any omissions or oversights are my own.

A special thanks to Jon Vickers, director of the Indiana University Cinema, for inviting me in as the "resident expert" during the accession of a massive shipment of adult/exploitation film prints on behalf of the Kinsey Institute for Research in Sex, Gender, and Reproduction, which was an invaluable glimpse into the early stages of a long archival process. Thanks as well to Russell Sheaffer, Eric Schaefer, and Dan Streible for encouraging one of these formerly "lost" prints, *The Orgy at Lil's Place* (1963), to be digitally preserved by Mike Mashon at the Library of Congress and subsequently screened at the 2013 Orphans Midwest symposium at Indiana University (as I discuss in Chapter 3). The Kinsey Institute's archives proved essential to my research for this book, so I must give an extra-special kudos to librarian Shawn C. Wilson, who put up with innumerable requests for a veritable truckload of materials. DeAnna Berger at the Pacific Northwest Library for Sex-Positive Culture in Seattle was fortunate enough not to be peppered with such requests, but she nevertheless opened up the library's collection and provided plenty of porn-related conversation along the way. The students of my "History of Porn" class, taught through the Seattle International Film Festival, also provided wonderful discussions about the genre's past and future.

Excerpts from this book first appeared in earlier form in several publications. I thank the editors and publishers of these publications for encouraging my work on the topic and granting permission to reprint the following material here:

A much earlier version of Chapter 1 appeared as "Stag Films, Vintage Porn, and the Marketing of Cinecrophilia," in *Cinephilia in the Age of Digital Reproduction, Volume 2*, edited by Scott Balcerzak and Jason Sperb (New York: Wallflower Press, 2012), 48–70. Copyright © Scott Balcerzak and Jason Sperb. Reprinted with permission of Yoram Allon and Columbia University Press.

An earlier version of Chapter 2 appeared as "Between Fantasy and Reality: Sexploitation, Fan Magazines, and William Rotsler's 'Adults-Only' Career," *Film History* 26, no. 3 (2014): 106–43. Thanks to Indiana University Press for permission to reprint it.

Various excerpts from Chapters 3 and 4 appeared in the short articles "Desiring to Merge: Restoring Value in Niche-Interest Adult DVDs," *Film International* 11, no. 3–4 (2013): 11–21; and "Something Weird This Way Comes: Mike Vraney (1957–2014)," *The Moving Image* 14, no. 2 (2014): 51–67. Thanks to Daniel Lindvall and Intellect Books for reprint permission for the former; and to the University of Minnesota Press for the latter.

Finally, my thanks to the various parties who granted permission to reproduce the book's illustrations. Efforts were made to contact all relevant rights holders, but any cases of accidental omission will be corrected in future editions of the book.

Introduction

"I should explain that adult movies—X movies, Triple X, whatever you want to call them—have never particularly aroused me. On the contrary, I found myself drawn to them because of my disenchantment with mainstream films," confesses the narrator in the opening pages of Tim Lucas's novel *Throat Sprockets*, shortly before he becomes obsessed with an erotic horror film, chanced upon during a lunch break spent at a local porn theater. "Adult films also had a peculiar knack for capturing the listlessness I found at the core of real life, better than so-called 'legitimate' films," he continues. "By the time you reach thirty, as I had, you're either just learning to appreciate the anesthetic value of escapism or growing sick of the vapors."[1]

Appropriately enough, this sentiment echoes my own thoughts about sexually explicit cinema in many ways. In their often crude attempts to arouse the audience, their hyperbolic depictions of sexual abandon rendered in oddly mechanistic strokes exude a sort of melancholy admission about cinema's overall powers of mimetic representation, as if to ask, "Is this all there is?" For all of its many paradoxical qualities—it is notoriously hard to define, yet we supposedly "know it when we see it" (to paraphrase U.S. Supreme Court Justice Potter Stewart); it is the most demonized of genres, yet perhaps the most popular in terms of widespread consumption; it is deeply invested in providing documentary evidence of sexual pleasure, yet simultaneously creating fantasies that viewers might seldom live out in actuality—pornographic cinema is perhaps at once the *most* and *least cinematic* of all moving-image genres. While it exemplifies the medium's basic roots in a visual fascination with moving bodies that affectively stimulate the viewer's own body, it can also do so in the virtual absence of conventional standards of narrative, characterization, technical skill, and production values.

In my estimation, adult films from the past are especially adept at encouraging reflection upon such qualities when retrospectively viewed today, for they foreground the cinematic medium's essential physical gulf between spectator and spectacle through a temporal/historical disjuncture between one's present-day self and the films' intended historical audience. With sexually lurid or explicit films in particular, this is precisely because that gulf might be imaginatively reduced through a viewer's acts of autoeroticism surrounding the viewing experience, helping affectively foreclose the apparent distance between here and there, now and then. The historicity of such texts allows one to ruminate on how notions of sexual explicitness and "the pornographic" have or have not changed as social attitudes have shifted over the decades, even as the texts themselves cannot help but still make their original appeals (successfully or not) to latter-day viewers.

Although the primary *intended* uses of pornography may be largely autoerotic, I will illustrate that antiquated pornography also garners the pleasures of collectability, connoisseurship, and historical knowledge that more closely align it with the dynamics of exploitation film fandom than the fandom of most contemporary hard-core pornography. As Laura Kipnis suggests, "There's no reason to assume that pornographic images function any more literally (or produce more literal effects) than other more socially elevated images that we're used to reading for their symbolic and latent meanings—no reason other than class prejudice against 'working photographs' or pure censoriousness against sexual pleasure."[2] Nevertheless, as much as the artifactual qualities of these films may interest historically minded viewers and collectors as surviving curiosities, a large part of their enduring allure cannot be merely reduced to distanced contemplation, instead residing in their present-day capacity to viscerally resonate with viewers. As such, these films' original attempts to affect viewers' bodies can also successfully transcend their bygone production contexts, reminding us of the legacies that early adult films have left—for better or worse—on our cultural landscape.

Furthermore, these various forms of what are today considered "vintage" erotica/pornography/etc. retain their carnal appeal not only *despite* their age, but precisely *because* of it. The archaism and artifactual qualities of these surviving residual texts become framed as potential sources of arousal in their own right, begging the question of how and why *pastness* itself can be eroticized.[3] As Linda Williams argues in her book *Screening Sex*, the history of on-screen sexuality is undergirded by a constant tension between concealment and revelation, which corresponds to an affective tension between the "itch" of a sexual suggestiveness that retains its eroticism through an unfulfilled tease (such as created by censorship restrictions) and the "scratch" of sexual imagery that more viscerally delivers upon its promises through on-screen enactment. Although this dynamic adheres in all manner of films depicting erotic acts, adult films have arguably been the most historically acute nexus of this tension by taking it as their very *raison d'être*. Importantly, though, the march toward greater sexual explicitness as twentieth-century censorship restrictions gradually fell has not necessarily been accompanied by teleological progress from "itch" (prolonged sexual tension) to "scratch" (sexual release). After all, even after hard-core moving imagery showing genital penetration became legally available for public consumption in the United States ca. 1970, cinema in general has not abandoned its representative tension between concealment and revelation, thus allowing the erotic potential and economic marketability of both explicit and nonexplicit sexual imagery to continue unabated.[4]

Building upon Williams's thesis, then, I argue in the coming chapters that the "itch vs. scratch" dynamic between visual strategies of concealment and revelation has become reproduced in the surviving materiality of these otherwise ephemeral texts. That is, at a time when so much sexually explicit imagery is readily available to anyone with an Internet connection, the historical tension between concealment and revelation has become sublimated into more *tactile* questions of cultural neglect vs. cultural visibility. Newer media (e.g., DVD, Blu-ray, and video-on-demand) routinely confer value upon themselves by repurposing the qualities of older media (e.g., photography and film) in their emergent forms.[5] Yet, in the case of vintage erotic texts, these processes of remediation foreground the apparent "promiscuity" of residual texts that still make themselves materially available to the pleasure of anyone who will have them—despite what I will also describe as their retrospective appeal as once-"transgressive" texts that must now be claimed by viewers with the appropriate critical acumen to seek them out. The sheer visibility of these sexual materials in today's marketplace does not necessarily ensure their eroticism, whereas the more metafilmic tension between the *disappearance* and *rediscovery* of these ostensibly ephemeral texts better renews their erotic potential. By reenacting a longtime historical dynamic between what remains cinematically *seen vs. unseen* through archival and affective notions of *tangibility vs. intangibility*, "vintage-ness" becomes marked by the very historicity of past sexual representations that once pushed at the boundaries of legal propriety and "good taste" in their respective historical contexts, but which are now being rediscovered and made newly marketable again.

For viewers today, the erotic potential of such imagery can thereby become retrospectively infused with taste-based notions of subcultural value when the visually and culturally degraded materiality of past adult texts attests to their apparent difference from present-day pornographic materials—a sense of difference echoing the oft-desired nicheness of subcultural investment. In an era when the one-time legal censorship of such texts is now largely (but not wholly) defunct, vintage texts are now effectively "censored" by the logic of the market itself when they fall out of wider popularity and are no longer easily available. As Ramon Lobato observes, the act of distribution—especially in its more *informal* varieties (such as piracy and other forms of unauthorized circulation, as discussed in Chapters 3 and 4)—materially shapes a cinematic text through the accumulation of scratches, pixilation, or other forms of audiovisual degradation. Furthermore, marginalized or peripheral audiences, such as porn viewers, are more likely accustomed to seeing their marginality reflected back to them through viewing such signifiers of cultural neglect.[6]

Yet, as I explain in Chapter 1, for fans of obscure or orphaned films that have fallen into a partial state of cultural obsolescence, such fleeting textual/temporal signifiers of historical marginality can be reclaimed as "oppositional" points of pride. Sarah Thornton's oft-cited concept of *subcultural capital* is important in this regard, since the sense of relative "coolness" rooted in subcultural ideologies and competencies that supposedly mark a subcultural denizen's distinction from the "mainstream" need not be rooted in consumption of the new and cutting edge. Rather, it can also adhere in "lost and almost forgotten" texts that have resisted obsolescence and survived as vintage goods.[7] Nevertheless, the disreputable connotations of autoeroticism can also complicate the supposed "coolness" of the vintage porn aficionado, particularly when these films' uses by past (and present) viewers beyond the present-day fan himself/herself impinge upon one's selective means of remembrance.

Consequently, I argue that *cultural forgetting* fuels the appeal of vintage materials as much as *cultural remembrance*, since value becomes constructed through both processes working in tandem—despite the honorific status so often placed upon remembrance. Cultural memory is inextricable from the practical necessity of cultural forgetting, says Aleida Assmann, but the question of what constitutes a culture's active "working memory" (e.g., history and canons) vs. its passive "reference memory" (e.g., archives) remains a deeply political one. Canons of great works, for example, gain their traditional power as much through the force of exclusion as inclusion, leading to the selective remembrance of a very small percentage of literary/cinematic texts, with the rest consigned to the so-called slaughterhouse of historical neglect. Whereas some forms of cultural forgetting are actively pursued when societies intentionally destroy certain materials (including pornography), *passive* cultural forgetting occurs through more benign forms of neglect and disregard. Archives often house the passively remembered texts comprising a culture's latent memory, which then require the work of historians and critics to recontextualize and raise them to cultural consciousness (and even eventual canonization).[8]

In my estimation, adult films occupy a blurred borderline between passive archival remembrance and both active and passive forms of cultural forgetting, since many of these texts have been persecuted and destroyed as "indecent" and "obscene"; many more have no official homes within archives; and yet some do continue to linger in archives and are only now becoming subject to greater reappraisal. Still, as I will demonstrate in Chapter 3, the archival life of adult films remains contested territory, presenting both obstacles toward rediscovery and emergent pleasures for historians/fans. As Michel Foucault has shown, for instance, active efforts at censorship may paradoxically increase the likely survival of the offending text through the proliferation of discourse against and public curiosity about it[9]—but we should also heed how more *passive* forms of cultural forgetting, such as gradual neglect, may leave far less of a discursive trail. Indeed, forgetting is often seen as a shameful failure while remembering is posited as a virtue—but adult films have been subject to various kinds of forgetting, including forms of forgetting deemed valuable for the public good, over the decades.[10]

In the case of adult films, it thus remains important not to merely denigrate cultural forgetting as a *destructive* form of censorial prudery, but rather to also view forgetting as a *productive* force in the creation of residual cultural/economic value through scarcity or endangerment. Vintage pornography's contemporary appeal relies as much upon our society's apparent need to forget these past films on political and aesthetic grounds as on fans/collectors' desires to sustain their remembrance. Therein lies the importance of vintage pornography's ability to tell certain historical narratives but not others, and its lessons for better understanding the contemporary forms of retrospection invoked by film fandom and historiography alike.

Importantly, however, I must specify at the outset that my argument throughout this book applies to vintage forms of *heterosexual* pornography, which will be my primary focus for several reasons. Lucas Hilderbrand observes that, unlike the relative paucity and marginality of pornography within implicitly heterocentrist archives, specialist archives devoted to gay and lesbian history are practically overflowing with porn, often amassed by private collectors on VHS (and far less commonly on celluloid) before the eventual accession of these idiosyncratic indexes of desire. Whereas heterosexual porn has experienced notable flickers of cultural mainstreaming after hard-core adult cinema's legalization in the early 1970s, the historical coemergence of gay liberation and hard-core cinema meant that porn was always pervasively within the mainstream of gay culture during the years of its most prominent world-making processes, to the point that gay-cultural publications like *The Advocate* largely understood "gay cinema" as synonymous with so-called "all-male" pornographic cinema during the 1970s.[11] The various forms of adult cinema discussed in this book, then, may have once constituted the relatively "mainstream" end of the heterosexual porn market and have only retrospectively become constructed as a special-interest niche, but even the biggest heterosexual porn hits could not approach the sheer centrality of all-male porn in gay culture.

Moreover, in contrast to heterosexual adult cinema's origins in the lowly stag film (discussed in Chapter 1), Ryan Powell observes that the texts constituting gay adult cinema's 1970s "coming out" often self-consciously drew upon the tradition of avant-garde/underground art and theater—thus retrospectively giving gay pornography a more aesthetically redeemable pedigree than most of its straight contemporaries.[12] For both political and aesthetic reasons, then, vintage gay porn's archival life as historical artifacts of cultural pride bears different dynamics than that of vintage heterosexual porn. Whereas vintage gay porn obviously remains more marginalized than vintage heterosexual porn within a dominant heterosexist culture, each corpus bears vastly different valuations within its respective cultural tradition. As such, adequately treating vintage porn's overall sexual diversity is beyond the scope of any one book—although any starting point for a related study on the remediation of vintage gay porn include adult theater owner and film distributor Steven Toushin's company Bijou Video (founded in 1970; rechristened as a video label in 1978), which remains the most prominent video label devoted to circulating vintage gay cinema on DVD, in addition to selling vintage gay ephemera—so I will generally leave discussion of nonheterosexual porn's older forms to historians better versed in that territory.

A note on slippery nomenclature

Another caveat before proceeding: Eric Schaefer offers the instructive suggestion that the overarching term "adult cinema" encompasses a wide swath of cinema that historically targeted adults-only audiences as obscenity standards gradually changed throughout the twentieth century—from classical exploitation films to soft-core sexploitation films to sexually provocative art films to hard-core pornographic films in their various forms.[13] Although I find this a persuasive way to avoid vaguely subjective distinctions between "pornography" and "erotica" and to avoid settling on a threshold for where "the pornographic" begins, I nevertheless retain the politically overdetermined term *pornography* throughout this book, because many of the videos, retailers, and websites under consideration here consciously—and, within the bounds of contemporary obscenity laws, legally—adopt that label as part of their marketing to prospective audiences. In theorizing the retrospective appeal of vintage materials like stag films, for example, my first chapter looks at how contemporary distributors sometimes deliberately avoid the low-cultural connotations of the term "porn" through reference to more legitimate art-historical traditions and active, literate connoisseurship, but such appeals to differing levels of (sub)cultural capital are ultimately rendered unstable by the more explicitly pornographic circulation of the same material by other distributors.

Consequently, I deliberately commingle broad but slippery terms like "porn," "erotica," "adult films," "sex films," and so on as a means of not only reflecting their varied discursive uses today, but also denying the leaky distinctions that some critics have attempted to make between materials of differing explicitness. As David Andrews says, "*pornography, the dominant social concepts*, cannot possibly cover *pornography, the actual aesthetic forms*," since the presence of "pervasive *and* graphic sex" is no more restricted to pornographic films than to art cinema; nor can a filmmaker's artistic intentions be judged as the qualifying factor, since any text can be marketed and distributed for more blatantly "pornographic" uses against its creators' will.[14] Without sacrificing the specificity of discussing historically localized forms (e.g., stag films and sexploitation films), then, I reject the pejorative connotations of the term "pornography" by indicating the historical variability of what is considered pornographic and suggesting how such distinctions reside less in inherent textual qualities than shifts in sexualized discourse over the twentieth century and beyond.

After the hard-core feature film came aboveground around 1970, for instance, the shots of unsimulated genital penetration separating "hard" from "soft" films became a magical line that removed all plausible deniability while seemingly (and arbitrarily) catapulting hard core into a very different register of aesthetic and political implication that continues to this day. That is, this very move from the faked to the undeniably "real" sex act ironically produces more magical thinking among the genre's detractors than adult films remaining safely in the realm of simulation and illusion.[15] Indeed, the very terms "hard-core" and "soft-core," while originally derived from early twentieth-century sociological literature, also evoke penile tumescence in this context, as though the "hard-core" film has more potential to "violate" viewers' sensibilities—a suggestion that antiporn feminists once used in ridiculously equating the production and reception of fictional pornographic representations with literal, real-life acts of rape and subjugation, whereas they could excuse soft-core representations as the realm of politically acceptable "erotica," differentiated from hard-core "pornography" proper. And yet, antiporn feminists have conveniently sidestepped the inconvenient truth (discussed in Chapter 2) that 1960s (soft-core) sexploitation films are far more likely to espouse blatantly misogynistic and politically regressive attitudes (e.g., eroticized representations of rape) than most of the 1970s–1980s hard-core films that followed. Nevertheless, Elena Gorfinkel observes that at the time when hard core came aboveground, this shift also produced instances of critical nostalgia for the earlier sexploitation films whose visual limitations on sexual spectacle bespoke a temporal distance from the far more explicit forms then coming on-scene, prefiguring sexploitation's later take-up as "vintage" texts.[16]

Hard-core films have often been seen as a major factor in the decline of postclassical exploitation cinema—a sort of teleological endpoint in the display of disreputable spectacle—and are sometimes minimized or segregated in fan accounts of exploitation film history.[17] They tend to exist on the periphery of the exploitation film corpus, but are not unambiguously considered a constitutive part of it (unlike, say, the prolific soft-core cycle of sexploitation films). Some directors celebrated by exploitation film fans spent parts of their early or late careers working in the porn industry; other directors actively transitioned between soft-core and hard-core projects in various genres, even recutting the same film for different theaters and audiences. Since the early 1970s, exploitation film distributors might include hard-core inserts (typically filmed with stand-ins for the original actors) depending on the distribution region. After the emergence of theatrically exhibited hard-core material, limited pornographic content could be thus included as yet another source of spectacle in some exploitation films. Meanwhile, some sexploitation films attempted to compete by incorporating less narrative context and featuring extended, increasingly explicit sexual numbers; for example, Bethel Buckalew's *The Pigkeeper's Daughter* (1972) consists of little more than six lengthy, simulated sex scenes, replete with full-frontal male and female nudity, but no clear shots of genital penetration. Meanwhile, some producers of hard-core films outright relied on exploitation film distributors to gain regional and even national placement in theaters. The presence of hard-core inserts in some exploitation films, the simultaneous release of hard-core and soft-core versions of certain exploitation films, the fact that most sexploitation films were released for an adults-only audience, and the coexistence of such films in the same exhibition settings (such as drive-ins, grind houses, and former art theaters), therefore belie any secure dividing line between "exploitation" and "porn" films.

With brief hard-core scenes and long soft-core scenes increasingly appearing in an exploitation marketplace riddled with adults-only screenings, it became far more difficult to separate the appeals to sexual spectacle in soft-core and hard-core films on purely aesthetic or narrative merits than on the films' relative availability as dictated by changing social and legal standards. Today, such overlaps ultimately suggest some degree of shared object choices and reception practices between vintage porn fandom and exploitation film fandom, regardless of the frequent marginalization of the former by the latter. Andrews, for example, notes that as soft-core sexual numbers grow longer and approach the hard-core film's high ratio of sexual numbers to narrative content, fans tend to "diminish or deny" one side of the "narrative-number dichotomy so as to privilege another, a practice that at times verges on textual amputation or mutilation," especially as fans generally attempt to discursively legitimate more "respectable" aspects of the text that are not associated with autoerotic appeals alone.[18] Nevertheless, an early X-rated video buying guide that focuses primarily on hard-core films also includes a number of so-called "soft X" films by directors like Buckalew, Radley Metzger, Russ Meyer, Just Jaeckin, and Doris Wishman (Figure I.1)—all of which are discussed under comparisons to stocking a vintage wine cellar, with discriminating tastes allowing the adult film collector to have appropriate tapes on hand for any mood or occasion.[19]

Figure I.1 A fan-made cover design for a nonexistent Criterion Eclipse box set devoted to Doris Wishman's mid-1960s sexploitation "roughies," claiming her as a worthy contemporary of European art filmmakers while also playing upon the unlikeliness of her inclusion in the tony Criterion Collection catalogue. Parody design by Robert Nishimura/Primolandia Productions.

As adult film writer/director William Rotsler (whose work is discussed in Chapter 2) predicted as early as 1973,

> Some day there will be big fat books on the shelves of booksellers with titles like *Early Porno, The Love Directors, Stars of the Golden Age of Pornopix, The Films of Marilyn Chambers, How "Deep Throat" Was Made*, and perhaps even *The Golden Book of Sex*. […] Precious prints of early porno films will be salvaged and shown at the Museum of Modern Art. Porno-star biographies will be published with a discreet center section of selected photos. Sure, a lot of it will be commercially whipped-up froth, but there *will* be nostalgia periods.[20]

Many of these predictions have indeed come to pass over the past decade, including, as he says, not only retrospective repackagings of older filmic material in new forms but also the collecting of material ephemera like pressbooks, lobby cards, autographed photos, and other artifacts. Such residual materials form the basis of my second chapter, as they echo the ephemerality of commercially minded films that were generally not intended to last, but have nevertheless gained selective cultural remembrance as exemplars of historical change. Discussing the relationship between fan collections and processes of recollection, Amelie Hastie says, "The materiality of these collectibles comments on the historicizing function of objects: they embody both history and fantasy, and they lend a materiality to that history and fantasy."[21] Indeed, as I will subsequently elaborate, the ability for erotic ephemera to conjoin fantasy and reality in affectively stimulating ways has allowed these texts to become all the more arousing for both historians and vintage porn connoisseurs.

Writing amid the initial 1970s boom in theatrically screened hard-core features, Joseph Slade, one of the earliest scholars to study adult films on their own terms, noted in 1977 that, "[v]intage porn offers eroticism aged and layered, lacquered in fading sepia tones of nostalgia. Its age confers a kind of innocence, and blunts its threatening aspects—it seems quaint beside the graphic, convention-lacking celluloid which unreels in the peep-shows of the seventies. And yet the early stags are reminders that sexual fantasies change but little."[22] In the article "Vintage Vamp," published in the glossy sex magazine *High Society* that same year, pseudonymous collector "Richard Merkin" also describes collecting decades-old pornographic material since the late 1960s, but having been put off by the increasing explicitness of early 1970s hard-core forms. Porn lost its "psychological and sexual impact" when it was no longer "charming or even witty," he complains, and its eroticism was "castrated" by easy accessibility. Whereas it had once seemed "a very endangered species" garnering little monetary or sentimental/nostalgic value, "[f]requently now, persons possessing virtually *any* erotic photograph taken prior to the Woodstock Festival are convinced that it is worth a fortune."[23]

For Slade and Merkin, collectors gravitated toward archaic forms for many of the same reasons that so-called vintage porn has become a niche market today—although as Rotsler predicted, early-twentieth-century stag films have since been joined by the feature-length forms that Slade and Merkin—writing for academic and pornographic publications, respectively—then saw as too recent and graphic for nostalgization. In a sense, the sliding scale of historicity has since caught up with 1970s–1980s feature films as the very notion of what constitutes vintage-ness has gradually expanded to envelop a wide range of outdated (but not wholly obsolete) erotic cinema. For the purposes of my study, therefore, I do not merely restrict myself to hard-core texts that explicitly show genital penetration (and which have thus often been positioned as exemplars of "pornography" proper), but instead consider a range of moving images—some more explicit than others—which uneasily coexisted both above and below the oft-hazy legal line of obscenity as adult films gained varying degrees of social visibility.

Past and present "porno chics"

In his historicization of the modern "pornosphere," Brian McNair suggests that pornographic films and other materials have experienced (to date) two waves of mainstreaming and (at least partial) normalization in the United States and Western Europe. An outgrowth of liberalized sexual attitudes in the 1960s and 1970s, the first American wave of "porno chic" (and the one which originally coined the term) coincided with the legal emergence of theatrically exhibited hard-core films like *Boys in the Sand* (1971), *Deep Throat* (1972), and *Behind the Green Door* (1972). Unlike earlier cinematic forms—including the formerly illegal underground trade in hard-core stag films and the legal but adults-only market for soft-core sexploitation films (discussed in Chapters 1 and 2, respectively)—these films rendered hard-core pornography not only publicly visible and accessible but also more culturally acceptable and even "hip" entertainment for ostensibly normative citizens. Such developments did, however, lead to political backlash from right-wing moralists and antiporn feminists during the ensuing "porn wars" and "culture wars" of the 1980s and 1990s. McNair dates the second (and current) wave of "porno chic" from the early 2000s, driven by the diverse proliferation of online pornographies and the playful pastiching or parodying of pornographic tropes in advertising, art, and popular culture. As with the first wave, however, this second wave has faced some lingering antiporn feminism—a curious species of 1970s nostalgia in its own right—in the form of sexual panics over the supposed "pornification" of popular culture.[24]

Nor has past and present pornography been unambiguously "mainstreamed," since adult cinema—especially hard-core cinema—retains its disrepute as a corpus with suspect (autoerotic) uses that are generally not discussed in polite company, and it continues to have something of the folk devil about it in many corners. Despite its considerable moves into the culturally on/scene, then, adult cinema's continuing stigmas still render it a large realm of production and circulation that has received only modest recuperative attention from cultural custodians outside the adult film market itself, remaining little more than a footnote in most official film histories. Indeed, if contemporary antiporn activists make nostalgic claims contrasting today's "destructive" porn to "what had seemed genuinely yet innocently transgressive in the halcyon days of the 1970s,"[25] then the sheer diversity of vintage pornography reveals such claims as profoundly ahistorical. After all, when eroticized rape scenes were far more endemic in 1960s sexploitation films than 1970s–1980s hard-core films, and when once-illicit hard-core forms like pre-1970s stag films are explicitly promoted today as revealing the past to be far less "innocent" than we might now assume, the continued circulation of these historical artifacts as potentially arousing texts belies any facile arguments that newer pornographic videos are "not your daddy's *Playboy*."

With the once-enflamed rhetoric of the porn wars having now died down to smoldering embers, a playfully "hip" repurposing of pornographic clichés within popular culture in general has been joined by much more circumspect analysis within the academy. The recent rise of pornography studies (a subfield, emerging from the scholarship of sex-positive, anticensorship feminists, within which I situate this book as well) has helped counterbalance the genre's long-standing neglect and misunderstanding, while forcefully responding to antiporn critics. Although it remains arguable whether pornography effectively can or should be evaluated on the same political grounds as any less controversial fiction film genre, the legacy of porn's much-debated social impact has at least opened the genre's oft-problematic gender politics to more prevalent ideological scrutiny than the average Hollywood offering, thereby allowing pornography studies to gain an important foothold in the academy.

Meanwhile, the past decade has seen a notable number of adults-only art films incorporating explicit hard-core imagery (e.g., *Anatomy of Hell* [2004], *9 Songs* [2005], *Shortbus* [2006], *Nymphomaniac* [2013], and *Stranger by the Lake* [2013]), which has helped undercut the common presumption that images of genital penetration are automatically "pornographic" and lacking in artistic value. Hence, I would argue that these symptoms of porno chic's second wave have allowed "cultural omnivores"[26] to begin cautiously reevaluating the aesthetic and historical worth of adult films at the other side of the cultural taste spectrum from art cinema, especially in light of our current historical distance from the first porno-chic wave three or four decades ago.

Indeed, a specialist demand for these residual films has grown over the past two decades, concurrent with an emergent broader reappraisal of early adult films, filmmakers, and performers. Whether appearing under adjectives like "classic," "retro," or "vintage," a niche market for pornography made between roughly the 1890s and late 1980s has appeared on various websites and in video retail catalogues, and wider attention to such films has appeared in many realms of popular culture. To some extent, this is a symptom of cultish revival, not unlike the renewed hipness attending many cultural phenomena that have been out of the cultural mainstream for several decades, with the seemingly dated qualities of such films becoming upheld as a source of retro-cool for cultural slummers. Such anachronistic or tactile signifiers of pastness call back to the days when adult cinema seemed more "rebellious" because of its semi-licit status as an excitingly naughty sexual commodity only then coming to cultural visibility as a signifier of so-called sexual revolution.

Yet, this latter-day revivalism also appears invested in a more earnest memorialization of an increasingly passing generation of sexual "pioneers." Since merely the writing of this book began, for example, old age or ill health have claimed famed pin-up photographer Bunny Yeager; burlesque star Blaze Starr; influential adult filmmakers like Mac Ahlberg, Lasse Braun, Jess Franco, David F. Friedman, Martin J. Hodas, Fred J. Lincoln, Harry Novak, Candida Royalle, Joe Sarno, and Kirdy Stevens; soft-core stars Pat Barrington and Sylvia Kristel; 1970s–1980s hard-core stars like Marilyn Chambers, Jamie Gillis, Gloria Leonard, John Leslie, Harry Reems, and Jack Wrangler; and tireless genre promoters like Al Goldstein and Mike Vraney. In another sort of "death," even the once-venerable *Playboy* announced in October 2015 that it would stop publishing nude photos in its pages, citing too much competition from online pornography. Meanwhile, memoirs by past porn stars have joined glossy coffee-table books reproducing adult film posters and photo sets. A spate of recent documentaries and biopics has also appeared in the years since Paul Thomas Anderson's indie hit *Boogie Nights* (1997) fictionalized various true stories from the excesses of the 1970s–1980s porn industry.[27] Within the adult industry itself, remakes like *Misty Beethoven: The Musical!* (2004), *The New Devil in Miss Jones* (2005), and *The New Behind the Green Door* (2013) have paid homage to famed genre classics, while 1980s actor-turned-director Tom Byron's *Seasoned Players* series (2007–2012) lured past stars like Kelly Nichols, Ginger Lynn, and Amber Lynn out of retirement. Blogs, fansites, and podcasts devoted to serious consideration of early adult films have also appeared as grassroots sources of cultural remembrance. Finally, and perhaps most importantly for my purposes, the films themselves have gained accessibility in remediated forms—whether restored and rereleased on DVD and Blu-ray, or made readily available for streaming or download-on-demand from online paysites and free tube sites.

These repurposed media depictions of explicit sexuality have thereby gained their apparent significance by capturing the early historical development of the first pornochic era—a broad period seemingly separated from our second and ongoing pornochic era by the 1980s–1990s political backlash that pornography experienced. Indeed, the so-called "Golden Age of Porn" in the United States was roughly bookended by two politically motivated government reports. The first, the Report of the President's Commission on Obscenity and Pornography (1970), found no evidence linking porn consumption and violent behavior, and recommended lifting federal prohibitions on the availability of sexually explicit material to adults. (Not expecting to receive such panic-free findings, President Nixon and Congress quickly rejected the report.) The second report, from Attorney General Edwin Meese's Commission on Pornography (1986), marked a return to moral panic over porn's supposedly harmful social effects—a less surprising result from a document shaped by Reagan-era religious fundamentalists and antiporn feminists. As materials produced before and during this temporary détente, vintage cinematic forms thus continue to resonate today—both culturally and erotically—as important influences upon the mainstreaming of porn that we are again experiencing with renewed vigor.

Yet, it is difficult to unproblematically reclaim these films as part of our culture's "sexual heritage." After all, if so many of these early films were made for a presumed white, hetero-male viewership, then whose heritage is really being upheld and what are the larger implications of an attendant nostalgia for such texts? This is especially true when we consider that pornography cannot be said to offer transparent glimpses into an actual historical past, but rather, glimpses into the more nebulous realm of past sexual *fantasies* enacted through the indexical participation of flesh-and-blood performers. Although it is important not to automatically conflate political conservatism with nostalgia's privileging of an idealized past over a devalued present, we should remain cautiously attentive to the political connotations of such evaluative claims upon the past. Indeed, as McNair observes, the four decades since hard-core adult films first gained public visibility have actually coincided with declining incidences of sexual violence and the growing acceptance/equality of women, gays, and sexual minorities in those advanced capitalist societies where porn is least subject to censorship and most openly consumed. Despite the oft-apocalyptic rhetoric from antiporn groups with various ideological goals, "pornification" has accompanied—and, in some ways, even fueled—wider sexual liberalization, including feminism, gay liberation, and other progressive advances.[28]

Nevertheless, as Susanna Paasonen and Laura Saarenmaa note, popular historiography about early adult cinema still tends to reductively figure the relative "innocence" of earlier decades compared to present-day porn, focusing more on male pioneers' hedonistic rise and tragic fall, while relegating women and gay men's stories to secondary status. In films like *Bettie Page: Dark Angel* (2004) and *The Notorious Bettie Page* (2005), for example, Page is depicted as a naïve Southern girl who only becomes aware of her modeling's deeper implications (and consequently leaves the business) when photographer friend Irving Klaw is called to testify before a Senate investigation on pornography. Likewise, in *Boogie Nights* and both *Inside Deep Throat* (2005) and *Lovelace* (2013), fictional director Jack Horner (Burt Reynolds) and his real-life analogue Gerard Damiano are figured as wannabe artists whose ambitions were diluted by home video's unbridled profitability—despite the actual fact that earlier 35-mm porn films were no less economically motivated and that celluloid has proven no inherent guarantor of quality. (Although *Deep Throat* was itself little more than a crude sex comedy, as its director freely admitted, I would point out that Damiano's later, more self-consciously artistic films like *The Story of Joanna* [1975], *Odyssey: The Ultimate Trip* [1977], and *Skin-Flicks* [1978] are often overlooked in such historiographic accounts, since his more sophisticated films would complicate these latter-day portrayals of Damiano as an obliviously overreaching hack who merely *thought* himself an artist.) As Paasonen and Saarenmaa suggest, the supposed "quality" of 1970s hard-core narrative features has only retrospectively come into view with the shift to more episodic, shot-on-video productions, although the pre- and post-1970s history of pornographic films proves that 35-mm narrative features are more of a historical exception than a teleological peak in aesthetic progression[29]—as does the fact that even during the Golden Age of 35-mm hard-core narrative features, a large market for 8- and 16-mm loops continued to thrive (consisting of short vignettes or plotless numbers, and featuring many of the same performers as 35-mm features), retailed for home use, incrementally viewed in peep booths, or repurposed within a flimsy framing device to form feature-length "loop carrier" films.

This selective remembrance and revaluation of 35-mm narrative features is echoed in the retrospective discourse promulgated by 1970s–1980s adult film actors to justify their own historical value. These actors often assert that not only did performers have better material to work with in the pre-video/pre-Internet days, but that the smaller group of repeat performers in the early days was more talented, memorable, and rebellious before Viagra and home video cameras allowed any rank amateur to become a porn performer, and before legal precedents like *California v. Freeman* (1988) ruled that the shooting of hard-core films did not constitute illegal acts of pandering and prostitution.[30] "There was a certain amount of talent that would compel a consumer to want to sit there and watch something because there was no fast-forward back then," says one former actor. "Now you can't even think about porno without thinking about fast-forward, which is really a testimonial for why people didn't want to do videos."[31] Of course, such discourses downplay the many hundreds of anonymous, interchangeable performers during the Golden Age who did not become recognizable stars, much as they ignore the more diverse and interactive means that present-day porn stars use to actively build fan bases without the luxury of theatrical distribution for their work. These selective remembrances thereby find various ways to assert nostalgia for the past, despite the historical complexities that can—and, in many respects, *should*—nuance less critical (re)appraisals of adult cinema's past emergence.

As early erotic forms on the cusp of such changes, then, vintage porn represents the sleazy residue of cultural transition between a deeply conservative, prefeminist past and our more "enlightened" but virulently consumerist present, which is one reason why its renewed "chicness" has not wholly upended its stigmatization on both political and aesthetic grounds. As important as these cinematic representations may have been in visually figuring liberalized sexual attitudes, they still remain open to latter-day charges of regressive gender politics and artistic worthlessness, despite the various reclamation strategies that I will outline in the coming pages. Are these now-niche-interest films celebrated today as one-time exemplars of coming sexual liberalization or as a conservative past's "last hurrah" before the groundswell of second-wave feminism and gay liberation opened the traditionally hetero-male realm of pornography to the influence of much more diverse viewerships—or perhaps both? These are the questions the following chapters aim to address, particularly around the complex political uses of taste, historicity, gender, and sexuality.

This book is therefore a modest companion piece to my previous study, *Grindhouse Nostalgia*, which argued that nostalgia arises as a structure of feeling that both threatens and bolsters subculturally valued notions of exclusivity and connoisseurship when once-niche texts become more widely accessible on emergent video formats. Permitting both ironic and sincere revaluations of yesteryear's cheap and sleazy genre films, nostalgia echoes and fuels not only the tongue-in-cheek appreciation of a given film's humorous datedness, but also more earnest appreciation of its status as a historical object that can continue to successfully thrill viewers today. This emphasis on the visible historicity of such films is exemplified by fans' nostalgic fetishization of period-era marketing strategies and the material signs of filmic degradation which signal both the surviving text's past history of use and present cultural neglect.[32]

Much as I argued in that book that the contemporary taste politics of selective remembrance are persistently undergirded by class and gender inequalities, *Disposable Passions* explores the ideologies at play in the *eroticization* of nostalgia, especially among a fandom that has become more visible with the recent coalescence of a niche market for vintage adult films. Since this eroticization of a positively evaluated sense of pastness is entangled with subcultural discourses about the supposed authenticity and exclusivity of more obscure texts, the growing market for vintage porn can therefore be seen as a reaction against the apparent mainstreaming of adults-only materials during our second wave of porno chic—even as the easier cultural accessibility of such materials is also inseparable from the very modes of technological change and remediation (such as online discussion forums and streaming video) endemic to that second wave. Moreover, the temporal distance between our present moment and the historical origins of vintage adult films may lend them a retrospective air of quaintness that could seemingly soften their more politically problematic dimensions. Yet, they remain unlikely to be consumed through a wholly ironic lens that might simply render their potentially reactionary qualities progressive, instead retaining politically regressive implications through their more straight-faced reception as pornographically stimulating objects.

On one hand, the elements of heterosexual male fantasy in most vintage pornographic films may inspire ironic reactions to the silliness or datedness of their clichéd narrative cues—à la the ironic celebration of cinematic failure, famously described by Jeffrey Sconce as a common means of reading so-called "paracinema"[33]—while the bewildering effect of seeing documentary evidence of sexual acts performed in past time periods not often associated with sexual explicitness can evoke ironic distance as well. On the other hand, this same historical indexicality can still be read "straight" (pun intended) as autoerotically stimulating material even today, as can the bawdy narratives playing into hetero-male fantasies. As Susanna Paasonen notes, vintage porn may inspire camp's sense of ironic/aesthetic distance, but the visceral resonance of certain images upon the fan's body also bridges this distance, even as camp may problematically provide an ironic cover that "protects pornography from critical considerations in its insistence on the nonserious, the stylized, and the exaggerated."[34] Nathan Scott Epley, for example, argues that hip (sub)cultural preferences for retro-chic goods allow past sexist imagery like pin-ups to be consumed as ironically cool—not *despite* that imagery's politically regressive implications, but *because* of them (Figure I.2). A winking guise of knowing irony allows hetero-male consumers to enjoy unreconstructed erotic pleasures that have fallen out of cultural favor in feminism's wake, while simultaneously disavowing the conservative implications of such pleasures through a posture of elitist (or "reverse-elitist," as is typical of subcultural capital) distinction often rooted in a rejection of the supposedly "feminized" cultural mainstream.[35] Such reception possibilities remain central to this book's overall focus on the taste politics that subtend vintage pornography's fraught relationship with unequal histories of gender and sexuality.

Porn fandom and the vintage connoisseur

Even amid the rise of pornography studies, the question of porn *fandom*, as opposed to more casual or fleeting forms of porn consumption, remains a relatively neglected area of inquiry, and thus deserves a few prefatory words to better establish the stakes of this study. This lacuna can be partly explained by the fact that studies of porn fandom could seemingly play into outdated, negative stereotypes of media fans as lone obsessives, sexual deviants, or worse—all those stereotypes that the pioneering work of scholars like Henry Jenkins has helped counter.[36] Moreover, antipornography feminists have long rehearsed the unproven argument that repeated or prolonged exposure to pornography encourages sexual violence against women. Despite ethnographic research showing that porn use does not correlate with negative attitudes toward women (unlike, say, the far more telling correlation between religious belief and misogyny),[37] it is little wonder that fan studies have been reluctant to potentially play into such stereotypes by exploring how fans might actively incorporate porn consumption into their lived identities. On the flip side of this victimization argument, fears about porn addiction and other supposed media effects echo widespread "anxieties about the commodification of sex and technology,"[38] not unlike the erroneous suggestion that all devoted media fans are, on some level, passive victims of a mass-mediated culture, engaging in little more than masturbatory fantasies that attempt to "compensate for a lack of intimacy, community, and identity."[39]

Figure I.2 Cover of Scott Aaron Stine's short-lived adult film fanzine *Filthy Habits: Hardcore & Sexploitation Fare from the 1960s & 1970s* (2002–2003), which primarily espouses paracinematic discourses of "bad taste" and masculinist hipness. Courtesy of Scott Aaron Stine.

In this sense, the porn fan imagined as perpetually self-absent in an uncritical masturbatory haze—supposedly irrational, lacking restraint, and losing distinctions between fantasy and reality—is perhaps too close to other negative stereotypes of fandom in general to receive much detailed scholarly analysis, while also difficult to reconcile with more academically valorized images of the contemporary fan interactively using technology to share information and content (including his/her sexual preferences) through discussion boards, comment logs, and social networking platforms.[40] I would suggest that this reticence to address the porn consumer as fan also derives from an unresolved methodological struggle within pornography studies between, on the one hand, resisting antiporn activists' behaviorist arguments about supposed media effects and, on the other hand, analyzing media texts as ideologically interpellating the viewing subject. As Jane Gaines observes, for example, Michel Foucault's oft-cited concept of the "implantation of perversions" via socially constructed discourse about sexuality is very useful in describing pornography's ability to teach viewers what and how to desire, but despite its emphasis on the social construction of desires and bodies, this theory could be seen as implying that sexualized media inevitably manipulate viewers' bodies and minds, regardless of the vagaries of reception.[41] No wonder, then, that the resolutely antibehaviorist field of fan studies has been slow to differentiate porn fandom from more generalized forms of porn consumption.

To speak of an average porn user/viewer/spectator is one thing—but to speak specifically of a porn *fan* is a somewhat different matter, although these categories may overlap in practice. Whereas only a minority of porn consumers may purchase and/or consume large quantities of sexually explicit material on a regular basis, the porn fan in general need not fit this picture. Much as one can identify as a fan of a certain genre, text, or performer without necessarily consuming that material on a daily or even weekly basis, the porn fan may not regularly watch a statistically "excessive" amount of porn in comparison to the average porn user. Rather than identifying fans according to the *amount* consumed (although that quantitative measure may certainly be a factor), the *mode* of porn consumption is more important to consider here, since fandom often involves the qualitative exercise of discriminating tastes. Regardless of the degree to which vintage porn fans may still use these films for masturbation, these fans arguably differ from more casual porn users in their degree of investment with specific texts whose historicity can stimulate both body and mind. Unlike the stereotype of the insatiable porn addict, the porn fan—and especially the vintage porn connoisseur, given vintage texts' repute as "rare," "unique," or "endangered" documents—may collect specific types of materials from certain directors, performers, or time periods, often privileging these materials for their ability to stimulate one's own contingent erotic predilections, but not altogether reducing these materials to either masturbatory aids or sources of historically chauvinistic mockery.

Although a minority contingent of contemporary porn fans participate in traditionally subcultural activities such as attending adult entertainment conventions or live appearances by famous performers, porn fandom tends to be a far more diffuse and solitary form of fandom than subcultural models generally allow. Due to its lingering stigmatization and connotations of shamefulness, pornography is an area of popular media consumption where we find viewers especially reluctant to either self-identify as "fans" or to engage in reciprocal exchanges with fellow fans. It represents a salient example of how contemporary fandom can be rooted as much (if not more so) in the *intrapersonal* pleasures of individual consumption than *interpersonal* pleasures.[42] As Simon Lindgren's analysis of online discussion forums illustrates, for example, fan discourse about contemporary hard-core materials focuses predominantly on the (largely male) viewer's own pleasure, such as egocentric accounts of arousal and masturbation, secondarily followed by almost as many references to the homosocial viewing community as to the (female) performers on-screen. More traditional fan discourses devoted to collecting, reviewing, and ranking content are present, but—I would underline—are of far less prevalence in fandom of *contemporary* porn that lacks the historical distance of *vintage* texts.[43] Although I would not consider *Disposable Passions* to be a work of fan studies per se, then, the figure of the fan as viewer/collector nevertheless lingers in the background throughout this book, with his/her interpretive labor and market demand fueling this study's broader questions about the historical objects and narratives that emerge from the collectability of ephemeral niche-interest texts.

Hence, I opened this introduction with Tim Lucas's novel *Throat Sprockets* not only because it discusses adult films as something more earnestly redeemable than fodder for autoeroticism, but also because Lucas so vividly captures the cultism that, as I discuss in Chapter 1, blurs the lines between fandom and cinephilia in its focus on the sensuous materiality of the moving image. Investigating the provenance of the titular film—the age-reddened print lacking proper credits or even a copyright date—becomes an all-consuming passion that soon destroys the narrator's marriage, sending him into an underground subculture of bootleg video collectors. Although the novel thus plays into the stereotype of the fan as deviant obsessive, his narrator aptly describes how the visual degeneration of his bootleg VHS tape becomes a record of prior use by a wider imagined fan audience: "In essence what I had paid for was the evidence of the cassette's poor image resolution, which persuasively testified to the fact that I wasn't the only collector with an interest in this particular film." He finally realizes, with very mixed emotions, how "[t]he movie that I had always considered mine alone had never truly been mine alone."[44] Such comments about the uneasy relationship between intrapersonal and interpersonal pleasures gain autobiographical resonance from Lucas's own background as the founding editor/publisher of *Video Watchdog*, one of the most prominent fan magazines dedicated to serious appreciation of cult genre cinema, including adult films like 1960s–1970s sexploitation. Much as his fictional narrator laments the loss of subcultural exclusivity, even as he remains fascinated by the text's analog decay (whether evinced on celluloid or magnetic tape), Lucas's own video-fueled research demonstrates how the reevaluation of various forms of adult cinema has often fallen to fan cultures due to wider cultural neglect.

And yet, unlike Lucas's fan narrator, I cannot deny the carnal pleasures of studying these texts, since I am as subject to arousal, boredom, disgust, and all of pornography's other occurrent affective states as anyone who might view such material. Although feminist critics have sometimes accused heterosexual male academics of ulterior motives in studying pornography, it is important to heed Linda Williams's observation that if "pornography is not the monolithic expression of phallic misogyny that it has been stigmatized as being, then there is good reason even for heterosexual men to explore the pleasures of the genre without having to admit too many *mea culpas*."[45] When I first began writing an early version of what became this book's first chapter, early-twentieth-century stag films still struck me as almost surreally strange glimpses into a long-buried sexual past—fascinating as historical documents, but scarcely very erotic on a personal level. As the writing proceeded, however, Foucault's "implantation of perversions" seemed vindicated, for increased exposure to pornographic discourse that framed *how* I might find these surviving images erotic did heighten their visceral resonance with me—albeit without causing me to surrender my critical acumen or self-awareness that one's viewing pleasures are often more fluidly shifting than one's publicly claimed sexual identity. After all, as Paasonen argues, "a scholar studying porn who is never aroused by it is as anomalous and misplaced a creature as a researcher studying comedy who is never moved to laughter or a scholar working on horror who fails to jump or flinch."[46] Remaining somehow open to porn's affectivity thus remains important for scholars interested in combating those antiporn critics who either (a) have not seen a representative enough sample of pornographic material to account for its diverse audiences and uses; or (b) have seen enough porn to inadvertently disprove their own behaviorist arguments about its supposedly detrimental effects upon the viewer.

One might reasonably say, then, that heterosexual (but not heteronormative) men are among the best prepared to study forms of pornography historically targeted at a hetero-male viewership—provided they remain self-reflexively critical about the political implications of their potential pleasures—since they are most likely to avoid "misreading" the genre's intended effects. Of course, the wonderful world of reception studies demonstrates that differing readings are just as valid and useful practices to explore—particularly as we will see in the case of vintage porn imagery that has circulated beyond its originally intended viewership—and these divergent readings are not necessarily less stimulating than intended ones. But even if nonmale and queer audiences have taken up such films in ways that may be more politically recuperable today, the continuing resonance of vintage pornography's originally intended appeals for present-day hetero-male viewers remains a thornier question with important implications for these films' archival afterlives. For, as much as pornography's critics may want to ignore or bury these older texts (or at least downplay them in favor of more contemporary alternative pornographies), such cultural neglect merely spurs greater fetishization of these materials among their continuing viewership.

Whereas the film historian can safely crouch behind primary archival research to offer seemingly value-neutral, "just-the-facts" assessments of these films (though historical and archival practice remains a profoundly political activity, far from the ersatz neutrality after which some historians may style their findings), my focus on the distinctly *affective* uses of surviving ephemera allows me to be honest about my own ability as a researcher to be aroused (and bored, disgusted, etc.) by vintage pornographic materials, without surrendering the need to be self-reflexive about my interpellation as the demographically (if not historically) intended viewer of such films. Indeed, the fact that such images still have a viscerally affective impact upon viewers within and beyond the academy, and are not merely consumable as harmless kitsch, demonstrates the need to account for more than the routine historical data provided by primary materials alone. Rather, by using primary research into the historical reception contexts of adult cinema, combined with theories of affect and representation, I aim to explore what kinds of cultural histories about gender and sexuality these surviving materials can tell, and how the very telling of those histories can be a profoundly embodied experience. Accordingly, the bulk of my data derives from what were, at one time, publicly circulated forms of discourse, not sources that have wholly remained (as porn itself has so often been expected to remain) "behind closed doors."[47]

Although interested in issues of historiography, this book is not, strictly speaking, a historical study. Other scholars have addressed the history of various periods and modes of adult cinema now considered "vintage," and while I gratefully draw upon their contributions, I am more interested in exploring different manifestations of vintage heterosexual pornography's present-day appeal than exploring in great detail the historical contexts that originally gave rise to such films. Lurking beneath my chapter progression is a somewhat conventional historical chronology—from pre-1960s stag films, to 1960s theatrical sexploitation features, to the coming of home video, to finally the Internet era—but each chapter also jumps fluidly between sketching various films' original production/reception contexts and probing the latter-day uses that fans/historians/collectors can make of such archived or remediated artifacts. Each chapter is thus intended to explore a different facet of the vintage porn phenomenon by focusing on differently affective means of its contemporary consumption—all adding up to what surely cannot be called a *comprehensive* picture of such uses, but at least a modest survey of major threads in the renewed circulation of vintage adult films.

In Chapter 1, I examine the marketing discourses used in online and DVD remediation of early-twentieth-century stag films as both "art" and "porn" objects, arguing that retrospectively consuming these seemingly quaint and primitive hard-core shorts encourages reveries about the past that cannot be confined to any one aesthetic stratum or political position, despite their original function as lowbrow entertainment for an exclusively male audience. Using the metaphor of necrophilia, I locate a cinephiliac dimension in their fetishized textures of decayed celluloid and their moving-image depictions of historical periods typically made visible to us through the sexually staid worlds of classical Hollywood cinema. In teasing out these viscerally felt blurrings between cinematic fantasies and historical realities, I explore the underlying appeal of vintage pornography's eroticization of pastness, while also leveling cultural distinctions between high-toned cinephilia and porn fandom.

If my first chapter delves into the allure of ephemerality associated with latter-day spectatorship of decayed erotic films, Chapter 2 steps away from the remediated film itself and instead looks at the haptic allure of otherwise disposable paper paratexts like lobby cards, pressbooks, pulp paperbacks, and especially fan magazines surviving from the 1960s sexploitation era. Unlike then-illicit stag films, the adults-only film and publishing industries exploited a variety of nonexplicit sex movies as censorship restrictions gradually eroded over the decade prior to hard-core cinema's legal emergence in 1970. By examining discourse in several prominent fan magazines devoted to such films, I explore how sexploitation's generic tension between revelation and concealment figured a cultural shift from the earlier teasing of unfulfilled erotic fantasies in the 1960s to the lived sexual realities of American society in the increasingly permissive 1970s. Furthermore, I suggest that the ability for the historian and the fan-collector to palpably touch and preserve ostensibly ephemeral paratexts like sexploitation fan magazines reenacts the period reader's own fantasies about the tantalizing possibility of reaching out for elusive objects of desire.

By tracing the practical obstacles that inhibit the formal archivization of adult cinema, Chapter 3 expands on the similar fantasies that fans and historians share concerning lost films as catalysts for film historiography. Using my own rediscovery of one such previously "lost" film as a case study, I argue that film archives function as much as sites of cultural forgetting as of remembrance when the politics of porn are concerned. With so few archives and historians dedicated to preserving adult cinema, nearly a century's worth of cinematic sex remains in danger of turning to cultural dust, revealing vintage pornography's impending fate as a central structuring absence within the film preservation movement in general. Writing this book as a cinematologist instead of a preservationist, some in the preservation community may quibble (as they so often do) over an approach that is more academic than strictly technological, but I hope they will remove their anoraks long enough to engage the larger issues in their midst. The second half of the chapter then shifts from formal archival politics to cult video distributors' early efforts to fulfill the inevitably impossible task of rescuing and rereleasing such a large and unwieldy corpus to ardent fans during the same period that saw the mainstream porn industry performing its own acts of archival disavowal through the rights management and self-censorship of its more controversial Golden Age films.

Finally, Chapter 4 extends this discussion of adult cinema's home video distribution by examining the aesthetic and industrial strategies that several generations of video labels have taken in remediating 1970s–1980s hard-core films to present-day fans. Whereas earlier independent labels marked their subcultural differentiation from more "mainstream" porn studios by offering access to bootlegged or uncut versions of films whose content the adult video industry's veteran studios would no longer handle, a younger generation of video labels has eschewed these bootleg aesthetics for qualitatively superior editions on par with high-end DVD/Blu-ray reissues of classics from any other genre. If the questionable politics of representation in some early hard-core films were long mirrored in the unethical preservation practices of early video distributors, this newer generation of distributors has increasingly responded to fans' demands for respectfully restored reissues by directly invoking hard core's pre-video era of serious critical evaluation and lofty aspirations to more mainstream filmmaking standards. Yet, this ability for vintage hard-core films to belatedly take advantage of the benefits of DVD/Blu-ray has ironically occurred at a moment when the overall entertainment industry is shifting away from physical media altogether. Consequently, these "post-porn" attempts to preserve an older generation of adult cinema on home video in new ways have had to contend with an industry exploring how to reissue the early fruits of this quintessential body genre at a time when various forms of textual (and, by extension, spectatorial) physicality are in flux.

If, in Linda Williams's famous formulation, pornography is chiefly a genre about "speaking sex" through graphic depictions of bodies in erotic contact,[48] then this study suggests that vintage porn has become a subgenre about "speaking history" as well. As a pornographic niche in which the genre's larger cultural legacies are explored and reappraised, its vintage-ness raises important questions about who has been historically allowed to speak sex and what methods of textual/discursive circulation have been employed in such continuing enunciations. As contemporary video technologies allow us to revisit and juxtapose past cinematic representations of explicit sexuality with increased ease and perhaps even growing acceptability, we must remain attuned to the political implications of a historically bounded corpus that largely predated the diverse latter-day pornographies that move well beyond an intended straight male viewership. And yet, if vintage porn's nostalgic appeal is already fueled by its apparent wavering on the verge of historical obsolescence, then we gain nothing by continuing to unreasonably denigrate this important archive of twentieth-century sexual history and its continuing influence upon how our culture continues to *feel itself* both remembering and forgetting.

1

Eroticizing the Degraded Past: Stag Films, Cinephilia, and the Marketing of Necro-erotic Desire

One day you'll find out that crudity is in the eye of the beholder.
— *The Lickerish Quartet*

A wealthy couple (Frank Wolff and Erika Remberg) and their teenage son (Paolo Turco) watch a stag film together on the home film projector at their lavish Italian castle (Figure 1.1), becoming fixated upon the apparent authenticity of the silent sexual performance. Upon venturing to a local carnival, the couple watches a motorcycle stunt show whose female star (Silvana Venturelli) looks remarkably similar to a woman in the stag film. Imagining that she must have once been a prostitute lured into porn, they invite her back to the castle to sexually proposition her. Although the visitor denies being the stag actor, she successively seduces each member of the family as the plot unfolds, and they subsequently find themselves magically replacing the actors within the stag reel. As the narrative ends, the original quartet exists only within the stag film,

Figure 1.1 The enchanted stag footage, sporting a faux-aged veneer of prior use, unspools on a domestic projector screen in Radley Metzger's *The Lickerish Quartet* (1970).

transplanted into their cinematic fantasy, and are now being watched by a different quartet of wealthy viewers—the same four people initially seen in the stag film—who share the original family's verbatim reactions to the sleazy but mysterious images.

Released the same year that the first hard-core feature was nationally exhibited in US theaters, director-distributor Radley Metzger's sexploitation film *The Lickerish Quartet* (1970) lingers on the cusp of a decade that saw the explosion of both feature-length pornography and home video. Opening with an epigraph from Luigi Pirandello's absurdist meta-play *Six Characters in Search of an Author* (1921) over the sound of a film projector starting up, the film's convoluted narrative endlessly loops like the stag reel that it depicts, presenting us with a metacinematic commentary on the cinephiliac desire to intimately cathect with on-screen fantasies, as Metzger's diegetic viewers are effectively captured by their fetishization of the scratchy, degraded celluloid images. Not only does this sexploitation film take hard-core porn as its subject matter, but it does so in a sophisticated way that cannot be easily lumped into the supposed dregs of "low culture." Indeed, the narrative is interspersed with a series of monochromatic flashbacks and flash-forwards prefiguring how the various seduction scenes will end up blurring the boundaries between the family's fannish attempts to live out the pornographic stag fantasy in their own lives, and the subsequent literalization of this desire through their magical transformation into flickering monochrome images.

Stylistically echoing how a dirty movie is brought into the palatial setting as a signifier of sexual decadence, Metzger mixes taste appeals while offering one of the most incisive depictions of cinephilia ever filmed by showing how even a seemingly lowly object like a pornographic stag reel can become a powerful locus for different registers of desire and selective memories-cum-fantasies about the past, especially when that cinematic object enters domestic spaces. In its beautifully stylized depiction of viewers with a seemingly excessive drive to incorporate cinema into their lived experiences, *The Lickerish Quartet* presents cinephilia and fandom as complementary modes of reception, separated less in practice than by the respective connotations of high and low culture—although, as the film amply shows on the level of both form and content, these taste distinctions are themselves far from mutually exclusive. Metzger specialized in high-gloss, European-filmed sexploitation films like *Carmen, Baby* (1967) and *Camille 2000* (1969), before later bringing his heightened aesthetic sensibilities to the hard-core adult film with early genre classics (directed under the nom de porn Henry Paris) like *The Private Afternoons of Pamela Mann* (1974), *The Opening of Misty Beethoven* (1976), and *Barbara Broadcast* (1977). As a rare adult film auteur who cannot be easily shunted into cultural ghettoization, his work helps question historically constructed divisions between high and low culture, art and porn—much as Joan Hawkins argues that "high" art does not solely stimulate intellectual pleasures, whereas culturally "low" genres do not simply appeal to a viewer's bodily pleasures.[1]

As I suggested in my Introduction, adult films from across the soft/hard-core line may seem to operate upon the viewer's mind and body in different ways, but their cultural uses are not wholly hemmed in by largely arbitrary categories of taste or legality. Sexploitation films of the 1960s (see Chapter 2), for example, may still garner autoerotic responses today, much as they did at the time of their initial release, whereas fans who today collect 1970s "Golden Age" hard-core features may not necessarily use them exclusively for masturbation, instead heeding their historical significance or the quality of acting, writing, and direction within the budgetary and generic constraints of the form. In the uses of adult cinema, theatrical and home consumption have no respective claims on either aesthetic appreciation or autoeroticism. Indeed, home video formats have allowed these multiple uses of films to gradually sediment over time as films originally designed for (semi-)public exhibition have entered the domestic sphere, which has become the primary site of contemporary fandom and cinephilia alike.

To open up the conflicted taste politics surrounding such reception practices, this chapter examines the general viewing dynamics of vintage pornography through the example of hard-core stag films, which, because of their unsimulated and once-obscene content, more explicitly exemplify past and present notions of "the pornographic" compared to the evasive visual strategies of soft-core nudity and simulated sex in classical exploitation and sexploitation films made prior to 1970. As Russell Sheaffer has demonstrated, the very notion of a "stag film" had a vague, and not specifically *pornographic*, generic status before the 1930s, since references to "stag" films appeared in newspaper classified advertising as early as 1907, used interchangeably with other generic descriptors like "smut," "novelty," and "indecent." These advertised films might feature a variety of nonexplicit material, not just unsimulated sex, and were not exclusively exhibited at private, all-male events. It was only by the 1930s that short, hard-core pornographic films eventually accrued their more familiar generic connotations through reference to male-dominated "stag" settings—which, at the risk of following other scholars in historically telescoping the more diverse varieties of pre-1930s films once deemed "stag," is the shorthand definition at play in this chapter.[2]

In this regard, I am also admittedly guilty of reproducing what David Andrews calls the "hard-core-centricity" of porn studies, in which much scholarship on pornography tends to reproduce the hard-core adult industry's own strategies of cultural distinction by regarding hard-core imagery as "The One True Porn" compared to more "diluted" or "feminized" soft-core forms.[3] Since stags are commonly associated with a prelapsarian sexual past, however, they sometimes released today under the banner of "art" or "erotica," finding distributors not only within the porn industry but also with more "legitimate" niche distributors of art and cult films. Consequently, despite Andrews's useful observation, I still find it important to emphasize how the specifically hard-core quality of stags marks their continuing marketability *as porn*, despite some distributors' euphemistic turn to "softer" and more culturally validated descriptors.

Encompassing over a century's worth of photographed sex acts, vintage pornography is today most often compiled and marketed online as a distinct fetish category, either ensconced within niche-specific websites (such as Retro Porn Archive, Vintage Cuties, and Vintage Taboo) or listed as one of many subcategories on large porn metasites broken down by niche (e.g., specific body parts, performer types, sexual practices, and fetish objects). While the proliferation of such niches seemingly suggests user-oriented fantasies of sexual freedom and plenitude, Zabet Patterson argues that, "in reality, what cyberporn tends to offer—especially with a rapidly consolidating market—is an environment in which desire and subject position are produced as 'truths' of the self through a discourse of categorization and classification."[4] As I will elaborate, marketing discourses about the supposed allure of "vintage-ness" reveal how such desires are constructed around the wider (sub)cultural values of exclusivity, connoisseurship, and "authenticity"—all qualities also associated with high-cultural reading practices like cinephilia.

Websites for vintage pornography typically offer both photographs and video clips, each consisting of soft-core (glamour, burlesque, striptease, non-penetrative sex) and hard-core variants. Often serving as the centerpiece of vintage porn sites, stag films are traditionally (but not always) of the latter type, valued for the relative rarity and historically scandalous nature of the explicit hard-core acts they show. They were made well before the home video era, but are nevertheless reliant on those latter-day technologies for their continued marketability. That said, not all vintage porn websites span the same time periods; while some provide content stretching from the development of early photographic technology through the so-called Golden Age of porn in the 1970s and early 1980s, others delimit their product to a tighter range of years. (Even pornographic films as recent as several decades old can be considered "vintage" due to the relatively short careers of even their well-known performers, as I elaborate in Chapter 3.) The bulk of these websites, however, agree that the "vintage" era stretches until at least the mid-to-late 1960s—not coincidentally a period widely viewed as the beginning of a national loss of sexual innocence in the United States. Because this transformative period also marked the decline of the stag film once hard-core pornography began to increasingly surface from the shadows of obscenity into public visibility, this periodization suggests how central the stag film is to contemporary notions of what constitutes vintage-ness.

Unlike more porous, potentially overlapping niche categories (since "breasts," "close-ups," and "cum shots" commonly factor to some degree into the standard heterosexual hard-core scene, for instance), the existence of a niche market for vintage pornography suggests the discursive creation of a specific audience and set of viewing expectations built around the apparent age and appearance of these artifacts. Yet, what does it mean that pastness has become eroticized as a sexual fetish for today's viewers? How are archaic images of explicit sexual representation, originating at a historical remove from our supposedly "liberated" era, discursively framed for contemporary consumption? And how does cinema-infused memory animate desires for this particular kind of historical moving image?

While accounting for the variety and uses of vintage pornography as a whole is beyond the scope of this chapter, I will largely restrict my focus to the contemporary reception of stag films commercially available at the time of this writing, which, because of their privileged status as unsimulated moving images of hard-core sexual practices, powerfully embody many of the broader dynamics of vintage porn consumption. Although I will gesture at different uses that other demographics have made of these same films as they were revived on home video, I do not wish to foreclose how the eroticization of pastness may serve many different purposes for audiences less thoroughly accounted for than the heterosexual male audiences who predominantly constitute vintage porn fandom today. Indeed, the fact that stags were once made for a solely hetero-male audience, but have since found more diverse audiences on home video, is another important way that they crystallize vintage pornography's wider contemporary dynamics.

Furthermore, the vintage porn phenomenon invites a number of questions that I hope will not only point toward the workings of a particular proclivity, but also reveal larger implications for our understanding of cinephilia and fandom as kindred impulses united by turns toward nostalgia. I would argue that fans' aesthetically intimate engagements with past texts overlap with cinephilia's predominantly individualistic, high-cultural reading strategies, which are largely derived from many cinephiles' own nostalgia for a postwar public film culture supposedly "threatened" by home video. In this respect, high-minded cinephiles are not markedly different from vintage porn fans who may uphold cultural memories of other outmoded exhibition sites (such as the grind house or the storefront theater instead of the art house) while still routinely bowing to modern technology and consuming their chosen texts at home.

As I posit in this chapter, we can thus see cinephiliac potential in the stag film's remediation into the domestic sphere as both erotic art and pornographic fodder, representing a significant shift in historical viewing contexts that has engendered a range of pleasures which the contemporaneity of nonvintage hard-core films may less readily deliver. Much as vintage porn fandom is fed by nostalgias that inherently mediate between past and present periods, I argue that cinephilia's almost "masturbatory" pleasures in revelatory but fleeting filmic details similarly situate it as a species of fandom invested in contested territories of pastness, and therefore liable to be shaken from the lofty critical/academic pedestal such high-toned discourses have often claimed.

Although the private home has long been associated with feminine domesticity and the public realm with masculine mobility, this dichotomous gendering of spaces blurs in actual practice. Of course, it does so on a literal level with the social advances made by women into the workplace since the 1970s (and, to a lesser extent, the stay-at-home male partner), but also on a more symbolic level with imagined transitions to and from a sense of "home" that is not dependent on one's actual location. As Giuliana Bruno notes,

> A voyage deeply involves and questions one's sense of home, of belonging, and of cultural identity. At home, one may indeed travel. Home itself is made up of layers of passages that are voyages of habitation. It is not a static notion but a site of *transito*. More than simply a point of departure and return, it is a site of continual transformation.[5]

The home, for example, has often been figured in popular discourse as a conservative and even sacrosanct space in need of protection from invasion by pornographic imagery, with home porn viewing seeming to transgress these symbolic boundaries—but the relative privacy of the home has also been paradoxically figured as a privileged and even utopian site within pornographic fantasies themselves (especially those of the "amateur" variety).[6]

Porn consumption at home nevertheless internalizes a form of spectatorship that was once and remains implicitly "public" in its imagining of a wider shared viewership, not unlike the stag movie nights that historically occurred in all-male, homosocial spaces seemingly distanced from the "feminized" domestic sphere.[7] The one-time illicitness of stag viewing meant that such materials were originally screened to exclusively male audiences in quasi-public, members-only sites outside the home, such as union halls and fraternity houses, but these stag nights might also be advertised in local newspapers as open to members of such fraternal organizations—thus representing a strange mix of "public" and "private" consumption that has arguably descended to the present-day consumption of niche-interest adult texts with fan followings. Andrews, for instance, notes that the privatization of porn consumption may have encouraged the actual demographic of porn consumers to clearly expand beyond the stereotype of the pathetic, raincoat-clad male masturbator once associated with the theatrical exhibition of adult films—yet the very secrecy allowed by home viewing has allowed the stereotype of the déclassé deviant to survive.[8]

At the same time, however, home video's opening of vintage materials like stag films to wider and more diverse audiences than their original heterosexual male viewership means that the films can be more easily recoded for consumption by different cultural strata and gender/sexual demographics, calling the subcultural coherence of that imagined wider viewership into question. Indeed, the very name "stag film" recalls a specific historical viewing context that has changed significantly since the rise of home video killed off most public venues for screening adult cinema. Home consumption has engendered a heterosexual "couples' market" for porn, as diegetically reflected in some films by greater emphasis on narrative development and foreplay scenes that better reflect the rhythms of female sexual arousal. The growth of home video has additionally allowed women to have easier access to pornographic materials without needing to enter urban spaces coded as "masculine" and potentially dangerous.[9] This shift is further indicated by the transition from hard-core films with sexually suggestive titles that could have appeared on urban theater marquees, to direct-to-video releases with more descriptively crude titles for sale from adults-only retailers; after all, theatrical feature titles like *High Rise* (1973), *Expose Me, Lovely* (1976), *Maraschino Cherry* (1978), *Babylon Pink* (1979), and *Nothing to Hide* (1981) seem a world away from video titles like *Gang Bang Bitches 13* (1997), *Anal Openings and Face Soakings* (1997), and *Bang My White Tight Ass 17* (2004), to name only a few wall-to-wall porn videos directed by former Golden Age directors. In an adult entertainment marketplace in which such frankness has become commonplace, it is perhaps little surprise that vintage porn has developed as a niche market rooted in nostalgia for a time when pornographic material was not so easily visible and accessible to audiences at home.

To more fully explain the reasons for this use, we must first backtrack to what stag films are, and how they were initially used during their period of production. I will then return to their present-day consumption, which maps a conflicted sexual politics onto the past, all the while activating "necrophilic" desires rooted in cultural memories of cinema history. In finally circling back to cinephilia and fandom, I invoke necrophilia less as an examination of a powerfully taboo paraphilia than as a metaphor for complicating cinephilia's tendencies toward high-toned and elitist practices of cine-love. This fascination with the degraded image's ambivalent connection to death ultimately helps us account for aficionados' fetishization of celluloid decay and the other material markers of vintage-ness that are so central to the vintage porn phenomenon explored throughout this book.

This chapter thus focuses primarily on the marketing and consumption of vintage moving images themselves, whereas the next chapter opens out from the textual viewing experience to the erotic implications of tactile encounters with ephemeral adult film paratexts like posters, pressbooks, and fan magazines. By teasing what remains historically obscured vs. historically revealed, the allure of ephemerality is central to desires for vintage pornography, and the visually degraded state of once-illicit stag films exemplifies vintage texts' appeal as outmoded objects of (hetero-male) sexual expenditure. Demonstrating how such desires are not restricted to "lower" cultural strata thereby allows us to relate vintage porn's cultish appeal to the niche consumption of more "legitimate" cinematic forms, helping challenge the presumption that porn consumption is disreputably distant from the reception of less explicit films.

The form and historical function of stag films

Stags are commonly defined as silent, black-and-white hard-core films no more than one reel long (approximately twelve minutes or less). According to Joseph W. Slade, they probably first appeared around 1905–1906, several years after the introduction of longer film reels and the development of the close-up.[10] In their history of stags, Al Di Lauro and Gerald Rabkin note that most early titles existed as single prints produced and exhibited in a given locality, thus restricting their regional and global reach, although later films were successfully duplicated and imported/exported.[11] The films were usually untitled, with filmmakers and performers either uncredited or appearing under pseudonyms; while the male performers were typically amateurs, sometimes hiding their identities behind ridiculous fake mustaches and other disguises, the female performers were more likely professional prostitutes.[12] As implied by the name "stag," these films were quasi-publicly screened to exclusively male audiences, often in fraternal organizations and men's social clubs; the name "smoker" was also a common label for such films, derived from men's "smoking parties," as was the name "blue movies." An itinerant projectionist (often also the filmmaker) would be hired for an evening's entertainment, in which the men filled the silence with sexualized heckling, boasts, and jokes about the screened material. According to various period sources, a projectionist might be paid $25–100 for an evening's screening at a stag party.[13]

Many early stags were shot on 35 mm and center around a bawdy comic incident, usually involving sexual excitation "by visual means" (such as voyeurism), which swiftly culminates in heterosexual intercourse.[14] Later stags, dating from the years when 8- and 16-mm small-gauge cameras became more accessible to nonprofessionals, are typically more amateurish, consisting of mere copulation with little (if any) narrative pretense (Figure 1.2)—a shift prefiguring the eventual move from 1970s narrative-based porn

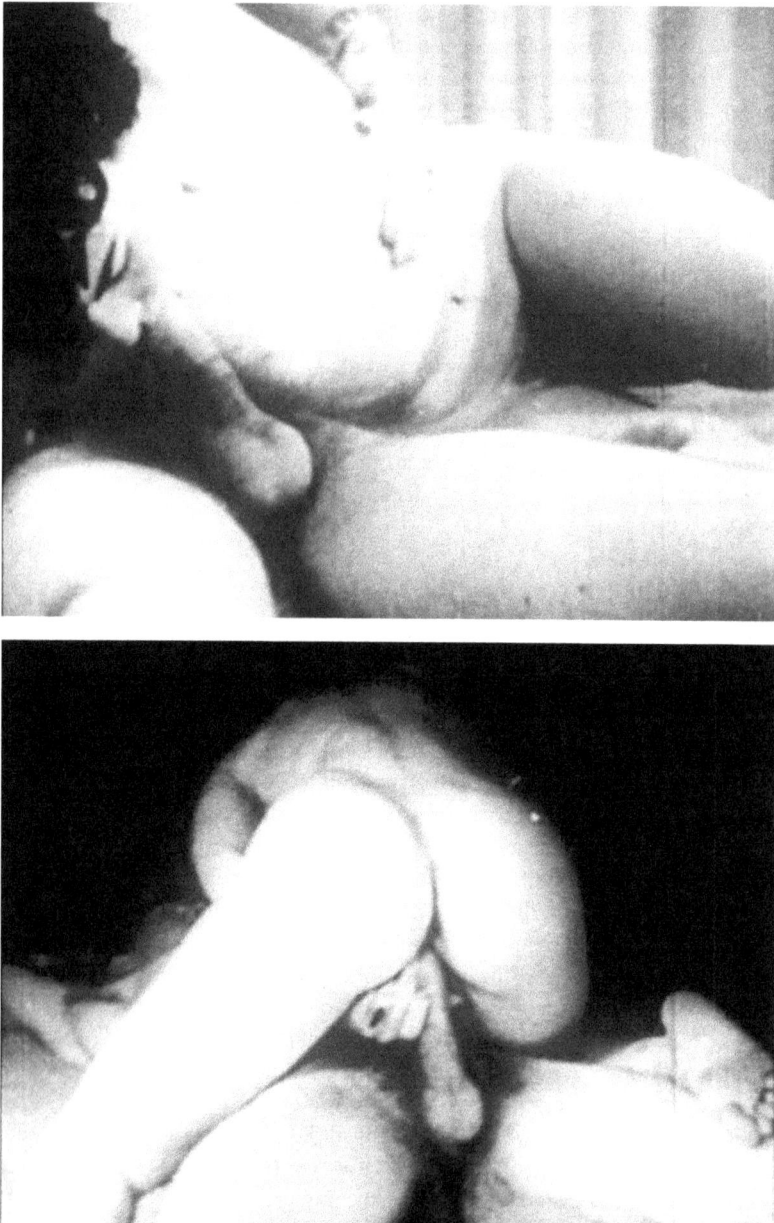

Figures 1.2 Hard-core images from the oft-circulated stag film *The Nun's Story* (ca. early 1950s), reproduced here in Alex de Renzy's documentary *A History of the Blue Movie* (1970). Note the degraded image quality and poor visibility of the performers.

to so-called "wall-to-wall" and "gonzo" porn, which occurred once video equipment became more affordable in the 1980s.

Displaying a "limited degree of [causal] narrative technique," the stag film's simple plot eventually falls apart into close-ups of genital penetration, which Linda Williams argues are addressed directly to the (male) viewer. With this footage displayed with a frontal presentationality as self-sufficient spectacle, the viewer is reminded of his place as a spectator, making difficult any identification with the on-screen male performer that could suture the viewer into the stag's diegetic space—precisely the obstacle that *The Lickerish Quartet* magically resolves for its characters in cinephiliac fashion.[15] Complicating the Mulveyan notion of visual pleasure in voyeuristic mastery of the objectified female, this performative aesthetic provides a pleasurable oscillation "between the impossible direct relation between a spectator and the exhibitionist object he watches in close-up, and the ideal voyeurism of a spectator who observes a sexual event in which a surrogate male acts for him." In other words, there is "the pleasure of the collective male group expressing its heterosexual desire for the bodies of women on display," alternating with "moving toward, but never fully achieving, identification with a male protagonist who performs sexual acts with the female body that shows itself to the viewer."[16]

Rather than identification-as-sameness per se, then, we are closer to Susanna Paasonen's useful concept of affective *resonance* as a means of explaining how some images—such as a particular shot in a film or image in a photo set—viscerally resonate with some viewers but not others, touching the viewer's body even in the absence of strong character identification or fully conscious choice on the viewer's part. Paasonen describes resonance as fleeting moments of arousal that bridge across the space between viewing subject and viewed object, not unlike André Bazin's discussion of the photograph as a metaphorical death mask of a passing historical moment or Roland Barthes's well-known concept of the *punctum* as a moment of recognition in photographic spectatorship that "pricks" the individual viewer in a way that seems to elude discursive explanation—two concepts that have proven influential in explaining what Christian Keathley deems the fleeting, revelatory moments in cinephilia as well. Importantly, these resonant moments are rooted in "somatic archives," or memories of past experiences that have accumulated and changed over time; that is, memories of how things carnally feel or how we imagine they might feel are activated as one views pornographic imagery, potentially triggering bodily responses in the viewing subject.[17] As I note below, these memories might also today be inspired by one's retrospective experiences with more "legitimate" forms of cinema, especially for contemporary viewers too young to have lived through the time periods captured on-screen in stags.

Because lacking the propensity for spectatorial identification with male on-screen surrogates that later, feature-length porn narratives would more likely provide, Williams and Slade both observe that stags retained this primitive aesthetic (recalling the "cinema of attractions" described by Tom Gunning) for decades, long after Hollywood narrative films had grown more technically sophisticated, because the awkward and amateurish qualities of the films and the performers therein served as apparent markers of "authenticity."[18] In addition to the results of economic constraints,

Slade goes on to speculate that stags' devotion to anachronistic primitivism and technical roughness may have enhanced their illicit appearance, their appeal to blue-collar tastes, and their role as a seemingly unchanging rite of passage for young men.[19]

Although Williams claims that "the primary pleasure [of stag viewing] seems to involve forming a gender-based bond with other male spectators," in which "the woman's body mediates the achievement of masculine identity,"[20] Tom Waugh observes that the homosociality of the all-male stag viewing also triggered anxiety and embarrassment for heterosexual men who tempered their arousal around other men by resorting to compulsory displays of aggressive masculinity and class-inflected misogyny.[21] Owing to this exhibition context, Williams observes that stags seem intended "to arouse and then precisely *not* to satisfy a spectator," making masturbation unto orgasm far less expected than for more solitary viewers of later, feature-length pornography that exhibited greater sexual numbers during the course of a narrative. In Europe, for example, stags were more often screened in brothels to turn on (male) customers while they waited to be serviced in the flesh. This viewing situation, she argues, is also why stags sometimes end with penetration shots themselves, not always the close-ups of external male ejaculation conventionalized in more modern hard-core films.[22]

If early stags, however primitive, seem more technically proficient and narrative driven than later stags, the prohibitive cost of filmmaking equipment kept the means of stag production out of most amateur pornographers' reach during the first several decades of the twentieth century. The price of 8- and 16-mm cameras and projectors made these technologies more accessible for home use by the 1950s, allowing stags to not only be more cheaply made, but also purchased for exhibition in the privacy of one's own home; as a result, quasi-public stag screenings became more rare, replaced by mail-order and under-the-counter sales of 8-mm stag reels.[23] In the late 1950s, a 50-foot 8-mm reel might cost three dollars and a 100-foot 16-mm reel cost double that amount, although prices also varied by locality (Figure 1.3). Moreover, for buyers without 8-mm projectors, mail-order stag ads from this period often promote the Melton Viewer, an inexpensive plastic viewfinder marketed as a user-friendly means to watch 50-foot 8-mm reels, whose hand-cranked apparatus also allowed easy rewinding and stop-motion capabilities (Figure 1.4).[24] The documentary *A History of the Blue*

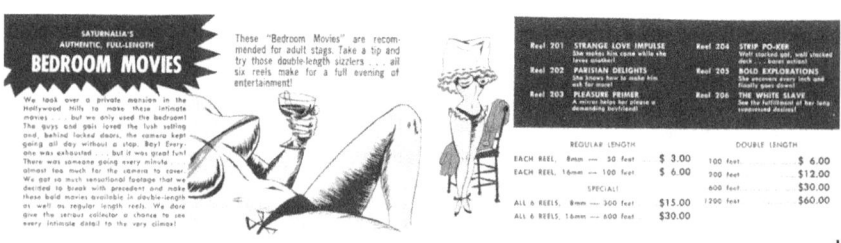

Figure 1.3 Stag films advertised in late 1950s catalogue for Saturnalia ("The Bachelor's Friend"), a small mail-order outfit [long defunct] specializing in stag films, slides, nude playing cards, and other "smoker and stag party merchandise" (author's collection).

Eroticizing the Degraded Past 33

Figure 1.4 Saturnalia catalogue ad for the 8-mm Melton Viewer, a device originally manufactured and sold as a personal film projector for children and families—hence this adults-only advertisement's assertion that it is "not a toy" but "a precision instrument" (author's collection).

Movie (1970) accurately observes that by the mid-1950s, a 400-foot 16-mm stag reel could be rented "under the counter at respectable camera stores … for five or ten dollars, or bought outright for twenty-five dollars or more (whatever the traffic would bear)," though the popularity of 8-mm equipment eventually supplanted that of 16 mm for the home market.

In previous decades, the class privilege of luxuries like home film equipment meant that stags "seldom would have fallen into the hands of children, minorities, or those of lesser economic means—the very groups around which American sexual anxieties usually flourished—and thus they attracted relatively little attention from censors and prosecutors during the 1930s and 1940s."[25] Meanwhile, the fraternal organizations at which stags were originally shown "started to fade from everyday life, sometime around the late 1960s,"[26] lessening men's opportunities to view stags in a social setting. Storefront peepshow arcades had already been playing risqué striptease and burlesque loops since the early days of the Kinetoscope, so when entrepreneurs like New York-based vending machine operator Martin J. Hodas and Cleveland-based adult magazine distributor Reuben Sturman launched an empire of peepshow machines in the mid-1960s, stags became a more explicit addition to a much longer tradition stretching across the twentieth century, quickly spreading to arcades and adult bookstores found in other urban centers. There, stags evolved into 8- and 16-mm single-reel hard-core loops, which often eschewed narrative altogether because shown in several-minute fragments on coin-operated machines, the film starting up where the last fragment left off. These machines were eventually placed in curtained booths to give viewers some small measure of privacy for solitary masturbation. (Of course, such arcade booths were never solely used for solitary sexual pursuits, often providing a location for homosexual encounters between customers.)[27]

This move from quasi-public, social viewing to the private, individualistic viewing of stags roughly coincided with decreasing legal restrictions on the public exhibition of other forms of sexually explicit adult films—and their subsequent introduction to the home on video. Eric Schaefer has traced the gradual industrial and technological progression from the illicit hard-core imagery of 8-mm stags and the licit soft-core narratives of 35-mm sexploitation features toward the open theatrical exhibition of hard-core feature films. He dates the end of the stag era at 1967, when advertisements first appeared for public showings of 16-mm "beaver films" (short, silent striptease reels focusing on female genitals), shortly followed by 16-mm "simulation films" (narrative films simulating intercourse but not showing penetration), and finally Bill Osco and Howard Ziehm's *Mona: The Virgin Nymph* (1970), often credited—erroneously or not—as the first hard-core narrative feature with nationwide theatrical distribution.[28]

Around this time, Di Lauro and Rabkin suggest, "classic" stags were pushed off the market by newer hard-core loops shot in color and sound, featuring higher production values, a wider array of sexual practices, and, with the swift rise of 1970s porno chic, the emergence of an alternative star system more appealing than anonymous stag performers. Writing in 1976, during the theatrical hard-core boom, they nostalgically lament how "the faded black-and-white images of the past are losing their erotic power," becoming "an endangered species."[29] Even as early as 1970, one adults-only paperback suggested that

> many who have seen the "smoker" movies of older vintage that are still making their illegal rounds today might, upon reflection, recall that the quality and mode of dress and undress were indicative of the period fifty years or more before. However with today's technically and erotically better product from Scandinavia, Britain, and the U.S., the old stag films are on their very last rounds.[30]

Yet, one of the earliest feature-length hard-core films to play theatrically was Alex de Renzy's aforementioned compilation documentary, *A History of the Blue Movie*, which contained both excerpts and full versions of stag films dating from as early as 1915. Like De Renzy's *Pornography in Denmark: A New Approach* (1970) from the same year, the documentary form provided a legitimating cover for depicting actual sex acts on-screen, paving the way for fictional porn features like *Deep Throat* (1972) and *Behind the Green Door* (1972).[31] Indeed, *A History of the Blue Movie* concludes with several examples of the color, sync-sound shorts filmed by De Renzy at The Screening Room, his storefront theater and studio space in San Francisco. In the final documentary scene, a hippie couple responding to a "modeling" ad in the *Berkeley Barb* meets the filmmaker and performs coitus for the camera. As they later exit the building, we glimpse their newly shot film being projected in The Screening Room's theater—a nice bit of product placement for De Renzy's operation, and documentary evidence of where the history of stag films had finally led. Di Lauro himself soon followed in De

Renzy's footsteps as the director of *Old, Borrowed, and Stag* (1973), another stag-based hard-core documentary, predating his coauthored study of such films.

The appeal of stag films as late as 1970 thus provided a major impetus for opening the door to the more "modern" forms of pornography that quickly displaced them, suggesting that the "erotic power" of stags had not diminished for all audiences, but was merely supplanted by the eroticism of newer products, increasing the apparent pastness of the former. Discussing De Renzy's documentary, Amos Vogel noted that "it somehow still remains surprising to see our forefathers (now dead) actually engaged in the same activities as we are."[32] Meanwhile, a handful of adults-only paperbacks continued to offer detailed reviews for prospective stag fans and collectors. Likewise, in the hard-core feature *Nostalgia Blue* (1976), a young couple inherit a chest full of old clothes and stag reels, commenting on the films with amusement from off-screen as they (and we) watch them in full; the film finally returns to this framing device as the couple, now sufficiently aroused and playing dress-up in the period attire, generates some pornographic imagery of their own. As these examples also suggest, the opening of stags to a mixed-gender market need not diminish the films' original erotic potential, but could rather reinstate the more instrumental function that stags had once served at European brothels.

Of course, this is not to say that stag films, or any other forms of pornography, are inherently erotic to any audience in any historical period, but merely that a continuity exists between hard core's earlier and later incarnations. Indeed, the appeal of pornography, like any filmic genre, cannot be divorced from its historicity—especially vis-à-vis the cultural discourses that mark it as licit or illicit in a given period. However, as I will now explain, the afterlife of stag films has proven far more complicated with their resurrection in the video and Internet age, making the historical distance represented by these films a source of eroticism in itself—and a site of potentially problematic sexual politics. Meanwhile, with the historical stag audience fracturing into more discrete segments befitting multiple consumption sites in the home video era, stag viewing has increasingly become subject to solitary pleasures undergirded by an awareness of the more interpersonal audience dynamics implied by the existence of a growing specialty market for such artifacts.

The contemporary marketing of stag films

Stag films were compiled on home video during the VHS porn explosion of the 1980s, spawning prolific compilation series like *Nostalgia Sex*, *Old-Time Blue*, and *Classic Stags*, along with video releases (Figure 1.5) of early theatrical compilations like *A History of the Blue Movie*, *Nostalgia Blue*, and *Old, Borrowed, and Stag*. These releases were already categorized as "specialty" films in the early video era—a label applied to many different fetish niches in adult video reviews of the time (as I elaborate further in Chapter 3).[33] Yet, due to the lower distribution costs allowed by digitization, the rise of the Internet has arguably created a more focused niche through the hypertextuality of metasites and search engines that categorize diverse sexual proclivities into easily

Figure 1.5 Box cover for *Nostalgia Blue* (1976), released on VHS in 1985 by Classix Video, a subsidiary of the prominent adult video label VCA Pictures (author's collection).

marketable commodities. Due to their short length and already substandard visual quality, stag films would seem particularly amenable to online use, even if the vintage porn niche may have become more fully developed by the time better connectivity and streaming video technologies improved the general visual quality of online video in the early 2000s. These technological factors aside, I am proceeding from the premise that erotic desire is, in large part, discursively constructed, so the ways these films are framed through promotion and advertising may tell us how fans' expectations about the films are shaped—and, in effect, how loyal viewers are taught *how to desire*. As Linda Williams reminds us, the physical effects (such as arousal) created by viewing body genres like pornography "may seem like reflexes, but they are all culturally mediated," produced through a historically constructed fetishization of the (female) body as a moving object about which knowledge (whether correct or not) is pleasurably gained by the (male) viewer.[34]

Unfortunately, fan discourses specifically surrounding stag films are difficult to find and even harder to interpret with much generalizability, especially because the untitled, anonymous status of many stags is not as conducive to the fan appreciation of specific performers or texts, at least compared with the fan activity surrounding more recent porn. When specific performers are mentioned, they tend to have been active in only the most recent decades to be considered "vintage" (the 1970s–1990s)—that is, years after the stag film had already largely given way to more contemporary forms of porn. On high-traffic websites like Vintage Erotica Forums and FreeOnes, there are discussion threads devoted to specific pin-up models and burlesque dancers, but very few of these women crossed over into working in stags—with a few notable exceptions, such as Candy Barr, a burlesque dancer who starred in *Smart Alec* (ca. 1951), one of the most widely distributed stags from the 1950s.

Instead, fan discourse tends to focus on the availability of stags, such as providing information about where to obtain them, or posting links to groups of films uploaded to file-sharing servers, which are often treated as largely undifferentiated clusters of content. Companies like Blue Vanities may list stag film titles (where available) and estimated dates of production on the backs of their compilation videos,[35] but the existence of the same uncredited film under multiple titles or in scattered fragments works against any clear sense of completism (also see Chapter 3). Still, even if individual stags are seldom catalogued in meticulous or accurate ways, the very collectability of, and knowledge about, these relatively rare objects can confer a sense of subcultural capital upon the collector, even without detailed information about each particular film. Furthermore, the shortage of known performers, filmmakers, or coherent narratives in most stags means that fans likely invest more in a given *time period* (such as the 1920s, the 1940s) than in particular people or characters—as also suggested by the various decade-specific compilations on the market. As such, the remarketing of stags better encapsulates the more general allure of vintage-ness than, say, the remediation of 1970s features containing recognizable performers who would rise to fame in hard core's nascent star system.

The discourses about stag films and vintage porn in general that are most visible and commonly available include the self-promotional discourses displayed prominently on the front pages of websites and on video box covers themselves, and also a considerable number of website reviews. Many of the latter are posted on review metasites like Porn Inspector and Vintage Porn Review, which profile numerous porn paysites as a service to prospective membership buyers. These review websites are sometimes affiliated with the websites they review—a fact enhanced by the sample photo galleries and video clips they offer viewers—so even if some of these oft-generous reviews are more mixed than others (at least outwardly suggesting the work of impartial critics), it is reasonable to treat them as an extension of the websites' self-promotion. In addition, the modifiers "classic," "retro," and "vintage" are not treated as mutually exclusive on vintage porn websites more generally, and there are no commonly accepted differences between the connotations of each (Figure 1.6).

To explore the marketing discourses around stag films and vintage porn through a few representative examples, we can first turn to one of the oldest and most notable vintage websites, RetroRaunch, which began operating in 1997 with the stated purpose of "bringing the tasty, nasty, wild, wacky, outrageous, shocking, beautiful, erotic and utterly special soft and hard-core porn from the past into the high-tech present of the internet."[36] This contrast between the past and the present is the most prominent discourse surrounding vintage porn, whether figured in terms of technology, performers' bodies, or cultural taste. For viewers who prefer more "natural" body types (e.g., curvier figures and unshaven pubic hair), for example, vintage porn may be a preferable niche, much as the desire to see "natural," unmodified women is also a major impetus behind the large market for so-called amateur porn.[37] Meanwhile, the temporal incongruence evoked by the signifiers of primitiveness in stag films feeds into a lingering awareness that possessing a taste for these thoroughly outdated artifacts is somewhat unconventional by today's standards.

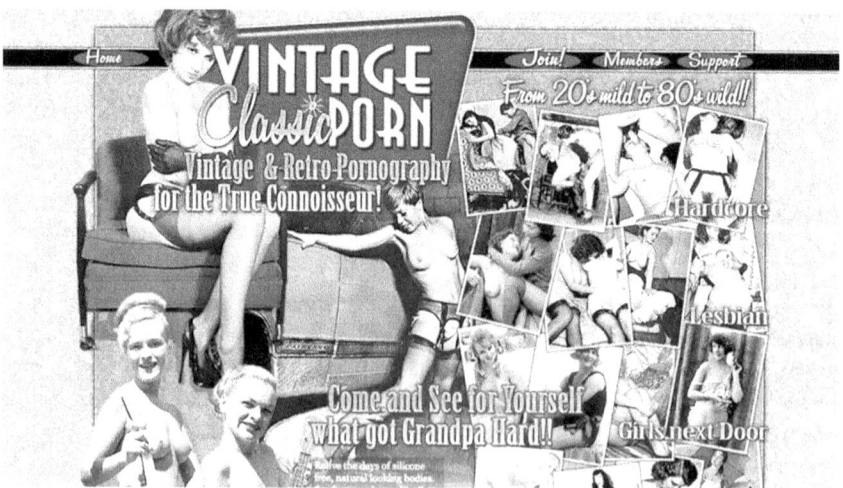

Figure 1.6 Website for Vintage Classic Porn, one of many niche paysites specializing in "Vintage & Retro Pornography for the True Connoisseur."

Weaving fantasies about a time with less complicated sexual politics, the past is nostalgically idealized as a lost sexual wonderland, more "authentic" and "natural" than the world of hard-core pornography today, but potentially no less explicit. From the perspective of the supposedly more sophisticated, sex-saturated present day of second-wave porno chic, this nostalgia for the then-newness (now-pastness) of explicit sexual representation rests upon imagining the pre-1960s past not as a wholly innocent time, but as a time in which sex was still illicit and obscene—or "*When Sex Was Dirty*," to cite the title of an early VHS stag compilation series. The notion of a sexually innocent or conservative past is mobilized only insofar as to charge these images with a lingering, retrospectively framed air of the taboo. To be more precise, this form of perceived innocence "lies in its obscurity, an obscurity not produced by modesty; for surely innocence is neither modest nor immodest. But it is obscure and can only be chanced upon," even in "some kinds of pornography."[38]

Whereas mainstream Hollywood films of the era sublimated their eroticism into kisses and implied-but-elided love scenes,[39] current marketing discourses imply that stags enacted the on-screen sexuality that less prudish viewers may have secretly wished to see, but were not adventurous enough to seek out—allowing today's fans to retrospectively occupy that exploratory role. For example, daring and originality are often credited to stag performers and filmmakers, as in fan-scholar Dave Thompson's comments that

> the girls who made cheap stag films in the 1920s were no less actresses than those who perform in the big-budget erotic movies today, and no less deserving of the viewer's admiration and respect. In fact, they may have even merited more, for today's stars are essentially rumpling sheets that have been rolled on for close to a century. The actresses of the 1910s and 1920s were looking at a freshly made bed.

Emphasizing their seemingly rebellious hedonism and low-budget primitivism, Thompson even compares stag filmmakers to early punk musicians.[40] Similarly, the rose-tinted documentary *American Stag* (2006) celebrates stag directors as the nation's first truly independent filmmakers, rebellious enough to risk arrest and prosecution for their pioneering work toward sexual freedom. At the same time that these appeals to "rebellion" may mirror the vintage porn fan's own assumed taste distinctions—since vintage porn's segregation into a niche market serves as a constant reminder of its "unusual" or "nonconformist" status—the act of watching a sexual act performed during the 1920s can nevertheless normatize heterosexual male desire as historically transcendent (especially given the rarity of homosexual acts in most early stags).

In the Frequently Asked Questions section of RetroRaunch, one of the questions asks if the site will ever run out of "fresh material," with the answer, "[S]omeday we certainly will[;] there's only so much in existence. But considering that there's an awful lot of it out there, RetroRaunch will be able to provide our members with thousands of fresh, never-before-seen-on-the-net ... images for well into the foreseeable future."[41] The past is thus figured as a period of historical plenitude, slowly revealing its lurid secrets for collectors to pour over, and yet, the limited quantity of these historical documents necessitates their archiving in modern digital formats like DVD and online video files—albeit more for profit than posterity (see Chapter 3). As another site says, "Of course vintage porn can't boast with [sic] millions of pics as the modern adult industry can but that's what makes our repro [sic] porn collection so unique. We did a really great job to collect these 40K vintage photos and 300+ videos. We really handpicked them sure that you deserve only the best."[42] However dubious such alleged curatorial acumen might be, webmasters for many vintage porn sites specifically include contact information so that newly discovered content from private collections can be sold or traded to the websites—though the process of acquiring and scanning/transferring vintage material from archaic photos or film prints to online databases presents a time- and cost-intensive challenge for websites specializing in this niche.[43] Nevertheless, according to RetroRaunch cofounder Hester Nash, "There have been a few instances of men sending us photos of their wives, taken long ago. The men always write sweet messages filled with love, longing, and wistful memories. [...] It's very touching to be offered these pictures, to know that they are willing to entrust us with their memories," suggesting a deeply earnest dimension to the nostalgia offered for sale on such sites.[44]

According to this quasi-preservationist logic, vintage pornography's transhistorically normatizing depiction of heterosexual male desire can serve an almost pedagogical function by revealing that the prelapsarian past was far less innocent than we supposedly think it today. These discourses are perhaps most clearly enunciated in the RetroRaunch site tour, in which each page contains a photo of a "prim and proper," 1950s-attired woman who gradually removes layers of clothing as one clicks through several pages of website description and sample photos. As this imaginary tour guide explains,

> Being a history teacher, it's perfectly natural for me to want to teach you about the history of sex and erotica. Of course, education is best accomplished with visual aides. People seem to think that nothing interesting happened in the world of sex until after the sexual revolution of the 1960s. Well, excuse me if I have a good giggle about that! Every single wild act, fetish, obsession, and nasty thought or deed that people indulge in today was indulged in by their parents and grandparents going all the way back.[45]

Because vintage porn celebrates sexual images temporally distant from us today, pornographic films made prior to the 1960s "sexual revolution" are privileged as novelties for showing a range of explicit sex acts not often associated with the prerevolution past, but which supposedly represent "a bridge between past and present porn, past and present attitudes."[46] As Eric Schaefer suggests, the 16-mm film gauge became associated with theatrical hard-core films around the time that the late 1960s counterculture adopted the gauge for underground and avant-garde films, thereby reinforcing "[t]he association among 16mm film, alternatives to mainstream practice, and freer sexual expression and cultural change."[47]

It is therefore the sex acts themselves that transcend the pre- and post-lapsarian eras, allowing 8- and 16-mm stag films to become exoticized artifacts of a seemingly ahistorical sexuality. Like the "itch vs. scratch" dynamic of concealment vs. revelation, the present-day viewer is teased by his/her historical distance from such alluring acts, while these films simultaneously exhibit far more sexually explicit imagery than one would otherwise associate with such bygone periods. Taking a similar marketing strategy as RetroRaunch, for example, a "male" tour guide (personified only through text, not photos, and thus retaining the same anonymity as male stag performers) at the website Good Old XXX describes his sexual adventures across periods of changing sexual mores, with each page of the tour devoted to a decade from the 1940s to 1970s—suggesting the fantasy of being an eternally youthful, eternally potent, male time traveler, with sex acts providing the historical continuity between each period.[48] "Don't be mistaken looking at old little ladies walking calmly with their respectable gentlemen—they know more about sex than you can imagine," says another website,[49] while a DVD box claims that, "You kids can wallow in all kinds of bathroom [sic] hijinks with guys and gals in masks doing things you can *still* get arrested for in some states."[50] Therefore, in so intently fetishizing the pastness of these historical documents, vintage porn discourses paradoxically *de-historicize* the actual sex acts portrayed, naturalizing these films' address to male heterosexual viewers. Following Michel Foucault, we can say that the perverse implantation of desire for vintage pornography rests upon the misleading assumption that the prelapsarian past was more sexually repressed.[51] In actual fact, however, our supposedly "liberated" contemporary era finds digital technologies of power proliferating the categorization of fetishes (as through pornographic niches), which, in the case of vintage pornography, reinforces the supposed historical transcendence of (male) heteronormative desire.

Ancestral connections are often cited as another means of temporal continuity between past and present. Stag films and vintage porn are frequently portrayed as discoveries from a father or grandfather's secret porn stash, things found hidden in attics and basements—an image suggesting that stags were originally meant for private, solitary viewing, not the quasi-public, social viewing context in which many of them were actually shown. The VHS compilation series *Grandpa's Hot Movies* promoted itself as "featur[ing] the films that got grandpa HOT," while one vintage website says, "Just imagine—your Dad or maybe even your Grandfather was crazy about these pin up girls and their 'next door' girlfriends."[52] Others even jokingly hint that one's own ancestors may be the performers in the films, constituting a recovered cinematic primal scene.[53] These Oedipal connotations of patriarchal lineage erroneously imply that sexual desires are congenitally inherited, not discursively constructed, but this paradoxically ahistorical universalization of male desire also extends to female stag performers. Explaining differences between modern and vintage porn, the RetroRaunch tour guide says,

> [I]n the old days the women looked like REAL women ... you know, the kind you can actually meet and get to know. The kind who never heard of silicone. The kind who knew what some really nice underthings could do for a gentleman's urges.

> The other difference is that the pictures weren't staged and fake looking. They were pictures of real people having a really good time, and it shows!⁵⁴

The apparent authenticity of "REAL women" accessible to the vintage porn aficionado is constituted through their difference from the stereotyped image of the heavily modified, heavily mediated, modern porn star—even as their anonymity translates into an alluringly mysterious quality, resonating with a sense of historical loss that still holds these once-"accessible" women at temporal arm's length. A Porn Inspector review of the website Vintage Cuties, for example, states that

> No photography tricks to highlight their hair, or an airbrush stroke to remove a scar, these ladies (and men) inhabit this content in their every day true form … […] And the best part of this site is it goes much further back in time, when rounded, ample bodied women were considered the epiphany [sic] of sexual desire. So what if their hips were a bit more full, that also meant their breasts were larger which made most nostalgic men lick their lips and ready to bed these beauties.⁵⁵

Yet, whatever small degree of body-positive sentiment is read into these seemingly archaic signifiers of "naturalness" is severely tempered by the essentialization of femininity as a historically transcendent ideal for women, to be consumed by men: "Elegant hats and silk stockings make these wonderful vintage ladies look so feminine and very much desired. No wonder men can hardly wait to probe their greedy holes!"⁵⁶ Even though stag films are sometimes praised for the diverse range of sexual practices they occasionally depict (lesbianism, bondage, group sex, and other behaviors that would later become more common in legalized hard-core films), those practices may not markedly complicate the essentialization of femininity because they remain primarily framed for the pleasure of their originally intended audience: heterosexual male viewers.⁵⁷ Thus, as Linda Williams cautions, "any nostalgia for these films must also partake of a nostalgia for an age when male spectators of pornography could take their pleasure in investigating the woman without having to worry much about *her* pleasure."⁵⁸

Vintage porn appropriations: (Post)feminist politics and subcultural tastes

This is not to say, however, that the vintage porn market is solely male- and heterosexual oriented today, for some of its iconography has also found admirers among women and gay men, and become adopted for a variety of desires as it has shifted away from its original exhibition sites during the home video era. Male-on-male sex is quite rare in stag films, owing to the need to avoid homoeroticism in the homosocial viewing contexts for which they were originally intended. Out of a sample of approximately 180 extant pre-World War II stags, for example, Tom Waugh cites about fifteen films with homoerotic moments of varying degrees, though some of these depict intermale or bisexual sexual contact as either a temporary source of humor or a prelude to heterosexual coitus. The slightly increased likelihood of intermale sex in European-made stags may have hinged upon their exhibition in brothels, where the private fulfillment of individual sexual predilections may have permitted greater sexual fluidity than the all-male American stag party. Likewise, the lack of an economically viable marketplace made exhibition to gay audiences in large urban areas unlikely until the 1960s. Although the stags themselves often frame intermale contact as "perverse" acts of freakery, stereotypically effeminate behavior to be homophobically mocked, or the unexpected result of transgender passing, Waugh argues that the films may have nevertheless functioned as inadvertent sources of queer pleasure for covert gay viewers by offering campy linguistic play in their intertitles or exhibiting a wider world of sexual behavior than these viewers had previously known. Given this potential, he notes that "stag films have a cultural ambivalence that certainly delighted gay spectators sixty years ago as much as they do modern-day gay audiences I have shown them to."[59]

Although usually drawing inspiration from materials of a higher cultural status than stags, the vintage realm has additionally proven a cultural site for women to locate retro-coded images of gender performativity that can complicate the hetero-male appeal of the original artifacts when re-appropriated in new contexts. For example, the apparent contradiction between historical plenitude and the limited quantity of surviving documents may be part of the impetus behind what Vintage Porn Review terms "modern re-creation" websites—including Martha's Girls and Vintage Queens—which largely feature nonexplicit images of contemporary models simulating vintage pastness through their dress, hairstyles, poses, props, and other elements of mise-en-scène. Some of these websites, such as Martha's Girls, even digitally manipulate the photos to more closely emulate the frayed edges, sepia tones, and hand-stenciled colors of surviving Victorian-era nude postcards, 1940s pin-up spreads, and so on. Similarly, the glossy soft-core nudes shot on period-era 35-mm cameras for *Jacques* magazine (founded in 2009; currently edited by cofounder Danielle Leder) are deliberately retro-styled after "classy" 1960s men's magazines like *Playboy*, pairing more "natural" bodies and settings with retro fashions and hairstyles befitting the magazine's hipster aesthetic.[60] Not unlike the tantalizing yet performative masquerade of femininity in Cindy Sherman's series of *Untitled Film Stills* (1977–1980) from B movies that never existed,[61] these strategies of simulating pastness are remarkably similar to the "retrosploitation" films I have explored elsewhere, particularly the soft-core imagery simulated in anachronistic sexploitation throwbacks like *Pervert!* (2005), *Viva* (2007), and *Climb It, Tarzan!* (2011).[62]

As Despina Kakoudaki notes, "Soft-core images such as the pinup have a wide range of cultural uses because of their ability to both 'pass' for mainstream images and to retain the excitement and explicit sexuality of their pornographic component."[63] This doubleness allows the discursive address of re-creation websites to generally be more gender-neutral, not solely presuming a male, heterosexual viewer. Indeed, Maria Elena Buszek observes that vintage erotic imagery has been previously appropriated for such diverse feminist purposes as (to name only a few examples) Kate Millett's 1970s faux-stereoscopic photos of female genitalia; Sherman's *Untitled Centerfolds* (1981) series of performative "self"-portraits; campy, pin-up-inspired imagery in the lesbian sex magazine *On Our Backs* (1984–2006); and fanzines in the 1990s "riot grrrl" movement. Members of the latter embraced recycled, mass-cultural "girlie" signifiers with a mix of criticism and affection endemic to third-wave feminism: "while recognizing the inadequacy of the pin-up to effectively represent women's complex experiences and vast potential, they also recognize and admit the appeal of the very sexualized imagery that they seek to upend."[64] That is, historical distance has allowed younger generations of women to reconcile nostalgic affection for quaintly stylized performances of gender with a critically and playfully ironic detachment from that very datedness, allowing such images to be repurposed without necessarily naturalizing one historical vision of femininity as an ideal.[65] Overall, then, the historical datedness implied by signifiers of "retro"-femininity can combine ironic distance and nostalgic earnestness to play up the role of gender as masquerade—particularly through references to time periods when femininity itself was allowed fewer but more idealized modes of expression.

A related, more problematically postfeminist sentiment can be found in the recent growth of "alt-porn" (or "alternative porn") websites like SuicideGirls and Burning Angel, which feature female models visually associated with rock music subcultures (punk, goth, emo, etc.) but sometimes drawing upon the iconography of vintage pin-up icons like Bettie Page.[66] Yet, while the pin-up-inspired, but primarily rock-modeled performers on alt-porn sites like Burning Angel may go hard core, modern re-creation websites seem reluctant to recreate the sort of hard-core imagery associated with stags, suggesting that even vintage hard core is too overcoded with patriarchal connotations for easy appropriation by ostensibly feminist or postfeminist media. Whereas nostalgically drawing upon different time periods can allow for certain kinds of progressive gender play, heterosexual hard-core acts may seem less performative by appearing to ground socially conventionalized expressions of (hetero-male) desire on an explicitly bodily level. Moreover, female users can more easily reconcile themselves to the erotic components of soft-core imagery because second-wave feminism valorized female masturbation as a key to sexual self-sufficiency, whereas the stigmas attached to autoeroticism were not similarly rehabilitated for heterosexual men—especially when hard-core pornography was concerned, given feminism's fraught history with the genre.[67] Although stags tend to depict male and female sexual pleasure as identical—which would seem conducive to postfeminism's depoliticization of collective female identity through a rejection of what is seen as a stereotypically (second-wave) "feminist" sense of political correctness—they also "represent the female body as a pure object of pleasure with no significant will or desire of its own."[68]

Consequently, while vintage pornography tends to essentialize femininity as a historically transcendent ideal that contemporary women might question with some ironic distance, hints of a gender-neutral address in vintage porn may actually encourage postfeminist female viewers of stag films to "distance themselves from the negative associations of femininity" by subculturally becoming "one of the boys."[69] Even if women now have access to stags through home video and the Internet (thus violating the male exclusivity of traditional stag viewing), I would argue that these films' remediation into the distinct "vintage" niche echoes stags' own move into more private viewing contexts since the 1970s. That is, we can see greater access in viewership compensated by the development of a niche category for erotic desires whose affective resonance seemingly reflects subcultural ideologies of authenticity and nonconformity. This move into the largely domestic sphere of fandom encourages stags' subcultural adoption by ostensibly distancing them from the cultural visibility loosely associated with the supposedly "feminizing" effects of populist or mass culture.[70]

In other words, even though hard-core pornography generally continues to be associated with heterosexual male audiences, the vintage porn niche casts the consumers of contemporary "mainstream" pornography as paradoxically "feminized" by passivity and a lack of (masculine) subcultural discernment, in distinction from the ostensibly discerning consumption of stags and other vintage items as historical artifacts. In this respect, Mark Jancovich observes that some consumers have implicitly privileged niche pornography over "ordinary" pornography, problematically reproducing a gendered and classed rejection of mass culture by celebrating specialty forms of pornography as a means of denigrating more "mainstream" tastes.[71] Indeed, when we see discourses celebrating vintage stags for offering the appearance of unmodified bodies, historical/pedagogical importance, and more "authentic" pleasures, it is hard not to be reminded of the appeals to subcultural distinction so often made by media fans of many stripes.

This presumed cultural distinction between the seemingly mundane aspects of mainstream porn and the more selective connotations of vintage porn can occur because stag films are today consumed not solely as culturally "low" pornography, but also as art and cult objects. Because they are fetishized as historical artifacts that must be collected and preserved, they are sometimes aestheticized as artistically pleasing for the connoisseur, despite the cheapness and crudity of their actual form. For example, many vintage websites and DVD box covers use art deco fonts and visual design, emphasize the international origins of some films (especially French stags), and proclaim (however misleadingly) that the films are restored and remastered to a higher quality.[72] The collectability of such mobile video archives thus recalls a general tendency in contemporary film collecting that "involves a complex interplay of nostalgia and presentism that glories in the past and its acquisition only if the past has been renovated through the newest technological standards."[73] Several vintage sites even include sections of erotic fine art; membership in Erotic Past, for example, includes online access to "Modern Art Galleries [that] feature some of the most prominent artists of the time including Klimt, Rodin, Picasso, Gauguin, and more."[74] Regardless of who actually acquires access to such material, these appeals to artworthiness and high technology imply a fan with higher cultural capital than the average porn consumer. For instance, RetroRaunch bills itself as "the thinking person's adult site,"[75] while Delta of Venus (named after Anaïs Nin's collection of erotica) prides itself as

> an alternative to the vast sea of unimaginative porn out there. Sex is a (the?) central focus of our lives, but I don't think endless photos of professional models getting screwed in every possible position really reflect what it's all about. Some people are happy with that, but this site is designed for folks who love sex, erotica, and obscenity but also want something literate & enlightening.[76]

This sense of a more active, "literate" viewership is paradoxically enhanced by how the poor-quality prints and amateurish filmmaking techniques of surviving stag films complicate the "maximum visibility" traditionally sought by hard-core pornography; that is, fans must literally pay closer attention and gaze harder to see all the naughty bits.[77] While these may be what Laura U. Marks deems *haptic images* due to their densely textured veneers of material degradation, they also invite a *haptic visuality* on the part of viewers who wish to engage such images with "a look that moves on the surface plane of the screen for some time before the viewer realizes what he or she is beholding," thus using vision like an intimate sense of touch instead of distanced perception.[78] One reviewer even compares vintage porn with spending hours watching unscrambled satellite TV channels for taboo bits of nudity: "That's the way I feel going through this site, these are the type of pictures and material that in no way were eyes suppose [sic] to really behold!"[79] This same dynamic also informs the haptic quality of more contemporary forms of amateur porn filmed using home video cameras, suggesting how the development of an "amateur" porn market is indebted to these more archaic forms of amateurism.[80] As Joan Hawkins says of bootleg exploitation videos, poor image quality becomes a mark of "outlaw status and a guarantor of its authenticity," spurring the high reader investment endemic to subcultural appreciation.[81] Perhaps it should be no surprise, then, that cult and exploitation film distributors have become a major source for stag films—as with Something Weird Video's *Grandpa Bucky's* series or the Cult Epics series of decade-specific *Vintage Erotica* DVDs.

Echoing stags' original exhibition sites, the imagined boundaries of cult film subcultures have thereby come to stand in as a quasi-public, homosocial viewing context, providing implicitly collective pleasures for solitary fans. Yet, as Emily Shelton argues, home porn consumption may allow hetero-male fans to "safely" indulge in autoerotic pleasures in private anonymity, but this very privacy allows their porn consumption to remain all the more haunted by the imagined interpersonal homosociality of shared affective response. In this sense, pornography generically "aspires to the closed structure of fantasy, demarcating a comfortable sphere in which the preferred scenario may unfold without interruption, intrusion, or outside interference," but this fantasy "always materializes in implicit reference to a structure of infinite variety: an imaginary, polyvalent sociality where any number of combinations are possible and the potential partners are anonymitically limitless." The hetero-male fan's anxious awareness of this lingering homosociality might be assuaged through laughter at bits of low comedy in a pornographic narrative, but Shelton allows that this ironically distanced but implicitly shared response can also be created by the "structural incompetence" of the films themselves.[82] In my estimation, this anxiety may be especially acute with stag films that were originally made for a homosocial reception context, since such archaic films may indeed be read as camp objects today, but even ironic readings cannot wholly dispel their continuing erotic resonance—thus preserving the sense of shame or anxiety that potentially lingers even in porn consumption behind closed doors. As Jane Gaines says, even solitary porn use can also be seen as "very mass and simultaneously shared, simultaneously personal and impersonal and even the public/private distinction is not so useful here since we are strangely open to the world as well as cut off from it in internet spatiality."[83]

While collecting may be "bound up not merely with acts of consumption but also with the powerful sense the collector has of being the source, the origin of the objects purchased and organized into a system,"[84] individualistic erotic pleasures are thus tempered in the cult context through the feeling of being part of a niche audience with shared, nonnormative tastes. For some hetero-male fans, this imagined shared response can bolster a desirable sense of subcultural community, while for others, it can represent a queerly open field of desire that spurs anxiety over who else might share such nonnormative tastes. In this sense, an imagined relation to a nostalgic but sexually enticing past can both unite and divide fans through cultural memories that mediate between personal erotic proclivities and more collectively held visions of rebelliously explicit sexuality—even in the absence of direct subcultural interaction. Like the scratchy images of the age-beaten texts themselves, then, the consumption of stags within domestic viewing contexts, haunted by an awareness of the outside world, allows these niche films' imagined audiences to move in and out of focus, echoing vintage pornography's metacinematic tension between titillating histories of revelation and concealment.

Whether consumed as art or cult objects or both, the application of high-cultural reading strategies raises stags from their lower socioeconomic roots, but this process can also gloss over their potentially misogynistic appeal—most commonly by associating them with middlebrow "erotica" over "pornography." This recoding would seemingly enhance their appeal to women, especially if we recall the argument advanced by many antipornography feminists that "erotica" is politically acceptable for women while "pornography" is not—an argument that, as David Andrews observes, is itself premised upon a gender essentialism that conflates higher class appeals with conservative notions of "genteel" femininity.[85] Unlike pornography, erotica supposedly "takes the viewer to the frontier of legitimate culture; it allows the viewer to be aroused but within the purified, contemplative mode of high culture."[86] Branding vintage material as erotica instead of just porn thus enables its wider marketability, while allowing a greater range of (soft-core) material to fall under that label (such as pin-up, bondage, burlesque, and striptease photos and films).

The banner of erotica encourages stags to be seen as cute curiosities, charmingly perverse anachronisms representing a "happier, more polymorphous era of sexual play"; for example, such remediated stags often have "tinkling piano accompaniment, as if the films were the equivalent of Harold Lloyd or Charlie Chaplin comedies, run[ning] the risk of a bogus nostalgia associated with mainstream silent films." Linda Williams identifies this approach in the French compilation documentary *The Good Old Naughty Days* (2002)—a more recent European reincarnation of *A History of the Blue Movie*'s sleazy alibi of educational sobriety—which enjoyed an art house release after playing at the 2002 Cannes Film Festival.[87] In a quaintly adolescent tone, for example, the intertitles between individual stags romanticize their role in initiating French boys into manhood, inviting us to occupy that viewing position: "Imagine the young men's astonishment while watching the secrets of a woman's body unveiled to them for the very first time, revealing at long last their box of tricks, their curlies, their butcher's window or even their little boy in the boat." The ironic distance potentially afforded by high-cultural reading strategies (and enhanced by stags' presentational aesthetic of attractions) thereby allows the apparent cuteness and innocence of stags as "erotica" to be held in tension with their depictions of acts as explicit as modern-day pornography. Although still primarily directed at male viewers today, this mode of address can also implicitly acknowledge a female audience who projects onto the historical past a more "feminine" desire for the sexual intimacy not often associated with most contemporary heterosexual porn—though it should not be assumed that women's responses to pornography are any more undifferentiated than men's, since different tastes and pleasures have no clear correspondence with gender.[88]

While stag viewing may have originally involved a snickering, "[a]dolescent male bonding at the expense of female difference," especially centered around the humor in seeing respectable women (who were "presumed to be more chaste than men") performing sex in the first place,[89] the potential humor in stag viewing today seems somewhat different, especially now that women are potential viewers. The quaintly adolescent humor of their bawdy narratives may continue to amuse (at least in the case of stags that do have narratives), but the once-novel existence of sexually adventurous women may now be campily obvious to both male and female viewers, even as explicit photographic evidence of them remains posited as a curiosity. Indeed, in her famed 1964 list of examples of the camp aesthetic, Susan Sontag notably includes "stag movies seen without lust."[90] Although I certainly would not discount what Waugh deems the queer erotic charge of viewing stags in the homosocial company of men, which could help facilitate a camp reading by gay viewers, I would argue that the private consumption of stags today more likely leads to the more depoliticized, mainstreamed readings of *straight camp*—which, following Williams, may be linked to our contemporary reactions to the apparent campiness of silent Hollywood films.

Nevertheless, the existence of a heterosexual-targeted *porn* market for stags, lucrative enough to enable the existence of a growing number of online paysites, suggests that the fetishization of these films is not simply reducible to the distanced contemplation of erotica or to camp's ironically affectionate ribbing, since those responses, while perhaps present, only capture part of the appeal. Contra Sontag, for some fans, stags are indeed still seen *with lust*, despite the almost prerequisite aesthetic distance entailed in their consumption. As an earnestly felt structure of feeling, nostalgia's dialectical highlighting of the loving gap between historical pastness and presentness enables this middle position between ironic distance and visceral resonance that I see as a common thread in the contemporary remediation of vintage adult films of many varieties. In this sense, a semi-distanced recognition of vintage pornography's datedness does not wholly subvert a nostalgic eroticization of its pastness, since both tendencies coexist in tension with each other in the reception process. This commingling of past and present pleasures may allow the conservatism of heteronormative desire to be problematically upheld for some present-day fans of stag films—albeit reframed so that a perverse cathexis upon pastness resituates the heteronormative impetus of stag films into the contemporary context of a subculturally inclined fetish niche.

Cinephilia and necro-erotic desire in and beyond stag fandom

Because stag films are categorized as objects that fetishize "normal" sex by virtue of their archaism, I finally turn to a fuller consideration of the viewing pleasures afforded by these films today, especially to fans who see themselves as collectors or connoisseurs of such artifacts. This is not to posit a universal spectator, nor to circumscribe all other possible forms of sexual pleasure provided by these films, but to hypothesize one major mode of cathexis: a broadly "necrophilic" eroticization of filmic decay. As a Porn Inspector review of the website Vintage Taboo says, in language rich with haptic connotations,

> You can almost smell the mildew type of aroma that will waft from yellowed pages in an old photo album, touching with great care so the film paper doesn't crackle and crumble under your touch. [...] Some of the material is so extremely aged on this site that it doesn't show with the clarity (far from it) that we are use [sic] to in today's digital age. But, in my opinion, *that's what enhances the erotic side of it.*[91]

As curious as this response might seem, I would argue that this erotic desire for decay notably overlaps with cinephilia in general, generating what we might term a *cinecrophilia* that allows stag films to activate viewing pleasures not often associated with contemporary hard-core pornography. Like cinephilia, there is a desire here to gently caress the decayed analog image with one's anxious vision, not to consume it brusquely or carelessly in a fit of masturbatory distraction. It seems to inspire an affectivity that may be difficult to put into words, offering fantasies of individual rediscovery that necrophilically blend arousal with mourning over moments forever slipping into the past. Once-orphaned texts are infused with nostalgia to defensively distance them from the more open (digital) access of the contemporary moment and thereby make them easier to contextualize when set within the broad realm of the historical past. The crude amateurism of stags ostensibly serves as a marker of authenticity, of a temporal anchoredness in a period seemingly distant from our own (hence the possible ironic responses they inspire), yet made recognizable to us today through the explicit acts they depict and even the mnemonic links they provide to contemporaneous Hollywood films from the same era. They are decayed vessels of cultural memory, salvaged by filling them with affect through an eroticization of their very pastness. No amount of remastering can make small-gauge stag prints look pristine and modern, so their scratches, grain, and outmoded mise-en-scènes are fetishized as material traces of prior use. As Amy Herzog notes, "The past (filmic and technological) is reanimated, while the [viewing] body remains rooted in the present,"[92] thus evoking nostalgia's seductive dialectic in the ultimately irreducible gap between past performers and present fans.

Given stag films' nonnarrative tendencies, it is no surprise that such erotically haptic and even cinephiliac responses are also invited and employed by avant-garde films like Carolee Schneemann's *Fuses* (1965), composed of hand-manipulated 16-mm sex footage shot by the artist herself; Bruce Conner's *Marilyn Times Five*

(1973), featuring stag footage erroneously purported to depict Marilyn Monroe; Peggy Ahwesh's *The Color of Love* (1994), consisting of repurposed and manipulated 8-mm stag footage; and other found-footage films like Gustav Deutsch's *Film Ist: A Girl and a Gun* (2009), which includes stag material culled from the Kinsey Institute for Research in Sex, Gender, and Reproduction.[93] As the narrator of *American Sexual Revolution* (1971) says, "The flickering forms augmented by the poor quality of a fifth-generation duped print dance across the screen in an almost hypnotic strobe effect. Little could the pornographer of the 1920s foresee his work as appearing to be an artistic and fascinating light show." Even if these films may evoke a certain degree of aesthetic distance as art objects, they remain infused with an unmistakable nostalgia inspired less by the lost clarity and transparency of these historical images than by the tantalizingly degraded, latter-day textures of dilapidated celluloid. Cinephilia and necrophilia share an acute attention to the historicity of culturally decrepit objects of desire, which can offer powerful erotic resonances undergirded by ambivalence over the awareness that one's decaying object of desire has also been loved by many others in the past. This awareness can complicate the primary pleasures of solitary possession, much as I noted that the stag film's domestic consumption today is secondarily contextualized by an anxious awareness of wider imagined communities, such as a specialty porn market or a cult film subculture replicating the elitist discourses of many high-minded cinephiles.[94]

Theoretical comparisons between cinephilia and necrophilia are certainly not without precedent. For Paul Willemen, cinephilia has "overtones of necrophilia, of relating to something that is dead, past, but alive in memory"[95]; while Susan Felleman observes that the process of mechanical reproduction overcomes death by "preserving dead objects of desire" in the cinematographic image, so that necrophilia serves as cinephilia's "mirror image."[96] Meanwhile, Thomas Elsaesser describes

> *the love that never lies* (cinephilia as the love of the original, of authenticity, of the indexicality of time, where each film performance is a unique event), [which] now competes with *the love that never dies*, where cinephilia feeds on nostalgia and repetition, is revived by fandom and cult classics, and demands the video copy and now the DVD or the download. [...] The new cinephilia is turning the unlimited archive of our media memory, including the unloved bits and pieces, the long forgotten films or programs into potentially desirable and much valued clips, extras, and bonuses, which proves that cinephilia is not only an anxious love, but can always turn itself into a happy perversion.[97]

This perverse "love that never dies" allows stag films to be reframed through the label "vintage," reviving these archaic, otherwise forgotten sex films for the high-tech era. Unlike old-school cinephilia's nostalgia for the fleeting revelatory moments noticed in the art house or repertory revival screening during the pre-video era, the new cinephilia feeds off a video-era intelligibility, wherein the viewer is potentially inundated with boundless access to former ephemera now accumulating in the home video marketplace.

Because cinema is "dead" in its response to our desires, unable to reciprocate, viewers can project their own memories (ego) onto it as an otherly container, much like the desire projected onto the necrophile's unresponsive partner. In this respect, cinephilia and necrophilia are both primarily narcissistic desires—which, in the case of stag films, translates into a disregard for female pleasure and explains why, according to Linda Williams, early porn narratives often involve the sexual coercion of women[98] (though necrophilia specifically involves a partner *unable* to consent). Lisa Downing theorizes necrophilia as "a radically narcissistic type of desire" that "mobilizes psychical energy in order to make a lost object return at will, but equally to enable a glimpse of self-loss in the perception of the other's death" by objectifying the corpse as a marker of "radical absence."[99] Necrophilia thus shares many parallels with Dennis Giles's psychoanalytic theory of heterosexual porn spectatorship, which is similarly based around the male spectator's intensely narcissistic projection of his ego's feminine aspects onto the empty, otherly space of the woman, allowing him to desire those parts of himself that he cannot openly acknowledge.[100] Like the corpse, then, the on-screen woman thereby serves as "not so much a female 'being' as a *lack* of being. [...] If the woman is nothing but a hole or series of holes, there is nothing and no one *there* to be loved."[101] Giles even posits the woman's transition from everyday subjectivity to this state of pornographic nonbeing as "a dying to the world"; symbolically speaking, "[i]nsofar as the woman is *dead*—to lie with her is an act of necrophilia."[102]

As culturally "lost objects," cinecrophilia can be more easily projected onto stag films than contemporary films in circulation today. Much as stags assumed that "viewer 'attraction' to these [on-screen] bodies will ultimately 'rebound' ... back toward the self because there is no [physically] *present* woman to touch,"[103] necrophilia and cinephilia are similarly invested in lost objects of desire that may have a visceral affect upon the beholder, but which are not *temporally present* in a reciprocal sense. The corpse/film may be present as a kind of material trace, but the selves that once animated those forms have been lost to death and the ravages of time, leaving the desire projected onto them narcissistically circulating back to the beholder's self. In this sense, the narcissistic self-projection involved in necrophilia and stag viewing alike also shares common ground with Cornel Sandvoss's theory of fandom as a narcissistic projection of identity onto texts that function as blank screens for reflecting the fan's self-image. The fan may flatter him/herself for having enough discerning taste to discover a niche-interest text that primarily serves *intrapersonal* affective pleasures absorbed into the self.[104] Yet, the more collective and *interpersonal* dimensions of (sub)cultural remembrance can undercut the extent of this narcissism by opening textual access to a far wider range of imagined viewers.

There is, then, a degree to which the haptic textures created by decades of age and use imply the films' prior passing before the hands and eyes of countless, furtively anonymous distributors, projectionists, and viewers who extend in time and space far beyond the narcissistic contemporary fan, testifying to the films' apparent historical value while also threatening narcissistic fantasies of possession. For films to which fans attend in close detail, "[h]aptic visuality implies a fundamental mourning of the absent object or the absent body," attempting to bring the desired image into close proximity while simultaneously acknowledging a lack of mastery over the inscrutable other.[105] In other words, this dynamic implies an eroticized desire for possession of the decayed object, while also evoking a haptic visuality that blurs the phenomenological boundaries between viewing subject and viewed object—particularly in the case of archaic films still used for autoerotic purposes that collapse the temporal and spatial divide between on-screen and offscreen touch.

Because this desire for signifiers of pastness resituates such antiquated material as objects of a specialized *fetish* instead of a purely present-day/heteronormative preference, the remediated stag film recalls what Elizabeth Freeman terms an "erotohistoriographic" encounter. The erotohistoriographic admits how contact with decaying historical materials can evoke a pleasurable bodily affectivity, queerly charged by different valences of historical time than otherwise endorsed by a heteronormative emphasis on futurity. As such, erotohistoriography "does not write the lost object into the present so much as encounter it already in the present, by treating the present itself as hybrid."[106] In this respect, the temporal disjuncture evoked by vintage pornography can open up queerly erotic relationships to historical time in multiple vectors, while also opening the potential for these materials to address a wider range of desires in their domestic consumption—particularly desires that might have been, like stag films themselves, culturally marginalized or confined to illegality before the 1960s "liberation era." Thus, as much as the remediation of vintage porn can reiterate the historical power of heteronormativity, temporal fissures in this edifice remain inevitable, admitting the possibility for "perversions" rooted in the multivalence of memory.

Moreover, if stag narratives often imply an optical visuality rooted in diegetic acts of voyeurism, then the shift toward a haptic visuality encouraged by the progression of celluloid decay might also open the door for more polymorphous erotics. That is, the material degradation of stag footage means that the pleasures of distanced vision are forced to give way to a wider range of tactile pleasures as aficionados pay closer attention to the seductively archaic surfaces of vintage material, thereby gaining a closer sense of proximity to the degraded image. Indeed, unlike the distance and mastery implied by optical visuality, haptic visuality implies an intersubjectivity that renders the viewer open and vulnerable to the image's power.[107] For Susanna Paasonen, porn viewership constantly oscillates between such haptic pleasures of contemplative proximity and the optical pleasures of observational distance, with affective resonance contingently filling the gaps in reference to memories of past physical experiences.[108] And yet, I would reiterate that vintage pornography's marketability as decayed and degraded material markedly veers toward the haptic in comparison with far less aged forms of adult cinema. This multiplicity of temporal contexts not only helps account for the somewhat uneasy appropriation of vintage erotic imagery by audiences other than heterosexual men, but, as I will elaborate in Chapter 3, can also tell us something about the pleasurable indeterminacy of identity in fandoms devoted to culturally vanishing and reappearing texts.

Returning now to our metaphor, Dany Nobus observes that breaking social taboos about the sacralization of death may be as important to the necrophile as the helplessness and unconsent of the dead partner.[109] In this respect, the fetishization of stag films projects desire onto female performers who are symbolically (and often quite literally) dead, but that projection excessively sexualizes a medium today most often regarded for memorializing Hollywood performers from the same era. As the chief producer of moving images during the stag period, classical Hollywood cinema serves as a mnemonic reservoir for temporal reference points seen in stags—including hairstyles, fashions, décor, etc.—that allow one to roughly estimate their decade of production (Figure 1.7). In this sense, vintage pornography's activation of "somatic archives" resonates with this other archive of pleasurable remembered experience that has accumulated over time for experienced viewers of Hollywood's cinematic past, commingling carnal and cinephiliac pleasures. Unlike the exteriors so often seen in newsreels, stock footage, and other pre-1950s documentary-style imagery, stags and classical Hollywood films offer extended representations of the domestic sphere's intimate details while also prefiguring their domestic consumption on home video.

This tendency points toward nostalgia's strong investment in mise-en-scène, particularly when retrospectively viewed as visible signifiers of historical excess. Elena Gorfinkel, for example, describes the cinematic lure of "dated sexuality" as rooted in a spectatorial attention to not only the eroticized bodies on-screen, but also the ephemeral products of mass-cultural consumption that appear within the frame of

Figure 1.7 Period mise-en-scène in a 1920s-era French stag film, reproduced in the compilation documentary *The Good Old Naughty Days* (2002).

outdated adult films, flattening bodies themselves into one more artifact of past eras with retrospectively fascinating aesthetic and political limitations.[110] Indeed, in an early article on porn spectatorship, Gertrud Koch argues along similar lines when discussing women's ambivalence about watching hard-core films, with female viewers potentially attending less to the "phallocentric generalization" of male pleasure's visible evidence than to "the details of a quivering world of objects" representing a multitude of polymorphous sources of pleasure.[111]

Due to the relatively high price of 8- and 16-mm filmmaking equipment during much of the classical Hollywood era and the shortage of distribution networks for nonprofessional material, amateur footage (such as home movies) from the pre-1950s period is far less familiar to us than 35-mm Hollywood films, allowing the latter to occupy the cultural imagination of movie buffs too young to have personally experienced that era. This imaginary perspective of history as seen through classical Hollywood allows stag films to gain a cinephiliac dimension uncommon in contemporary hard-core porn films—especially because vintage porn fans are perhaps more likely to have higher levels of cultural capital, and therefore have more potential knowledge of classical Hollywood, than other porn viewers today. Writing as a fan-scholar, for example, Dave Thompson says,

> There is an almost unmistakable ambience to the best stags of the 1930s, an almost surreal sense of glamour that was as tangible as that which pervades Hollywood's best-loved efforts of the same period. […] Hollywood portrayed life as a series of increasingly flamboyant fantasies. Stags reversed the equation, transforming fantasy into what was once (and, hopefully, would again become) real life.[112]

The apparent "authenticity" communicated by the amateurism of stags is thus complicated by the fantasy elements mnemonically associated with classical Hollywood, since both stags and classical Hollywood captured intimate details of the domestic sphere, albeit at very different levels of professionalization.[113]

When collected and archived in digital formats today, the stag's specific historical origins are abstracted into a broad notion of "the past" by the very presentness of modern technologies, allowing the "history"-via-Hollywood mnemonic to serve as a cinephiliac fantasy rooted less in the actual historical past than in an eroticized distance from that imagined past, as seen from the present day. This does not mean, however, that the temporal referents in stags become wholly irrelevant or free-floating signifiers of pastness, since they are often intensely focused on to place undated films within a certain decade—and thereby to eroticize them through the imagined juxtaposition with mainstream films from the same general span of years. Consequently, because classical Hollywood films are typically perceived as relatively wholesome testaments to their deceased stars, libidinally investing in stag films that provide numerous mnemonic links to old Hollywood product effectively violates the former's cultural sanctity in necrophilic ways, turning the nostalgia endemic to cinephilia into a means of "desecrating" the sacralized classical Hollywood fantasy. Indeed, today's stag fan is likely struck by the almost surreal sense of incongruity elicited by hard-core moving images taking place during the same time period as beloved Hollywood classics that seem all the more sexually staid by comparison.

Yet, such sexualized fantasies about stags and classical Hollywood were even reinforced during the classical era through rumors that certain stars began their careers as stag performers. There were persistent whispers about youthful on-screen indiscretions by actors like Greta Garbo, Joan Crawford, Marilyn Monroe, and even Ronald Reagan, though none of these rumors has been validated. Jean Harlow and Clark Gable, for example, were alleged to have filmed hard-core inserts for South American prints of *Red Dust* (1932) at the time they were already stars.[114] According to Joseph Slade, such rumors "reflect a cultural propensity to debunk and dethrone celebrities, but also a willingness to believe that stag films were commonly made in Hollywood."[115] A widely seen stag called *The Casting Couch* (ca. 1924), for example—in later years, rumored to feature Crawford—enhanced this suspicion, advancing the now-predictable premise of a movie producer propositioning a young starlet in exchange for a juicy part. Such desecrating fantasies about Hollywood celebrities also appeared in the pre-1950s "Tijuana bibles" (crude, pocket-sized comic books depicting sex between movie stars or other pop-culture icons) and also help explain the rise of scandal sheets like *Confidential* and its ilk.

The stag era even roughly paralleled the rise and fall of classical Hollywood, although it was a series of legal changes in obscenity standards that initially allowed hard-core pornography to emerge from the shadows, not legal challenges to the mainstream film industry itself. The stag market fell into decline around the time of the classical studio era's demise in the 1950s—yet this period also saw the rise of repertory theaters reviving classic films, which also spawned the cult film subculture that would rediscover exploitation films.[116] Among the imitators of *A History of the Blue Movie*, for example, *Hollywood Blue* (1970) claims to be an exposé of Hollywood stars' private lives, featuring excerpts from stags and other nude scenes attributed to classical Hollywood celebrities, while the doubly unauthorized quasi-documentary *Hollywood Babylon* (1972) mixes silent-era footage with soft-core reenactments of the more lurid scenes from Kenneth Anger's infamously sensationalized tome. As such, stags' fantasized desecration of Hollywood star images arguably set the stage for the emergent system of recognizably bankable adult film stars after 1970. This gradual transition from stags and classical Hollywood as contemporaneous entities to stags and classical Hollywood as retrospectively marketable commodities also primed niche audiences for the unearthing of stags as vintage porn in later years.

Of course, the mnemonic links between stags and Hollywood operate in the other direction as well, with modern Hollywood looking back to historically distant, vintage-era adult cinema as subject matter for imagining a more innocent, playful sexual past in films like *Inserts* (1974), *Boogie Nights* (1997), and *The Notorious Bettie Page* (2005)—a marked contrast from Hollywood's tendency to demonize contemporary porn as a source of contagion and addiction in films like *Hardcore* (1979) and *8MM* (1999). The ironic distance involved in viewing vintage pornography as historical documents implies that vintage material perhaps possesses an air of "safer" and less "debauched" consumption than the post-1960s hard core that may look too recognizably modern for ready reclamation as art or erotica. Unlike more contemporary forms of adult cinema, vintage porn is also historically distant enough to be posited as no longer in direct economic competition with present-day Hollywood, and thus open to a nonthreatening degree of romanticization by the latter. In recycling and memorializing past cinematic signifiers, films about vintage porn tend to "capitalize on the visibility of anachronism as a means of highlighting the pathos of historical difference." *Boogie Nights*, for example, "possesses an overwhelming fixation with the 'dated' status of 1970s porn; it is its very outmoded quality that imbues the film with bittersweet melancholia and wistful tragedy, as the obsolescence of porn on film becomes an allegory for various characters' mistakes, delusions, and frailties."[117]

These films may not depict a wholly innocent past, but as with the general appeal of vintage porn, the dark shadows cast by the mainstream film industry form part of the charm in such fictionalized chronicles. Even those darker biopics set during hard-core porn's Golden Age—such as *Rated X* (2000), *Auto Focus* (2002), and *Wonderland* (2003)—tend to move into their darkest phases when depicting the home video era's increased prominence, suggesting how the format change itself has engendered nostalgia for a brief period when hard-core features aspired to merge with Hollywood films. Such films also tend to depict pornography as becoming more dangerous to its creators with the move away from the institutionalized space of hard-core theaters, toward porn's entry into the alleged safety and sacredness of the domestic sphere—a spatial shift that actually allowed porn's proliferating niches to blossom far beyond a heterosexual male viewership. In this sense, even as these films may equate the encroaching home video era with death and degeneration, they neglect the sheer diversity of pornographic niches (e.g., feminist porn, queer porn, fetish porn) that nontheatrical markets enabled—thus implying that adult cinema's most valuable and significant years coincided with its most focused appeals to a hetero-male audience. That these more reputable films would capitalize on some of the more regressive sexual politics entailed in vintage porn discourses is perhaps of little surprise, but it points toward the marketability of a necro-erotic fascination that is, in its most explicit forms, confined to a pornographic niche, and yet is curiously attractive to wider audiences through the more common, seemingly innocuous workings of cinephilia.

Cinephilia was, after all, an almost perverse desire that had to be repressed—or, better yet, prolifically discussed under new names like "voyeurism, fetishism, and scopophilia"—in the development of film studies as an academic discipline.[118] If "cinephilia is itself symbolically masturbatory" in the "intellectual and emotional self-gratification" provided by "writing about the intense pleasures and ideas (importantly, *the pleasure of ideas*) that film affords us,"[119] then academic accounts of cinephilia tend to repress their own status as little more than a variant of scholar-fandom disguised by onanistically highfalutin discourse. Like the fan whose narcissistic pleasures seem threatened by the existence of a text's wider following, ardent cinephiles must hence distance themselves from their uncomfortably familiar others (e.g., fans and buffs). Adrian Martin, for example, suggests that "cinephilia severed from rigorous aesthetic investigation—scarcely distinguishable from the fandom celebrated by a certain strain of cultural studies—seems to me a bloodless pursuit, easily co-opted by mainstream capitalist interests."[120] Yet, this view leaves unquestioned academics' tendency to make moral judgments about which fan practices have more alleged political value than others, while also neglecting that the products of academic teaching and publishing typically remain deeply embedded in capitalist industries (even if ostensibly critical toward them).[121] As Jason Sperb wryly observes, "If one has any illusions of film as, if not necessarily a truly democratic medium then at least a more ambivalent one, then it is perhaps easier to *not* be a cinephile."[122]

Even if based in deeply affective and subjective moments of viewership, cinephilia seems much more invested in the use of elitist reading strategies than the cultural standing of the films that it takes as its objects. Paul Willemen, for instance, argues that even the most commercially motivated and formulaic cinema can be a hotbed of cinephiliac pleasures, since the fleeting moments of revelatory excess sought out by the cinephile can be especially pronounced there. He cites the exploitation films of Roger Corman, Jesús Franco, and José Mojica Marins as particular cases in point[123]—although most contemporary cinephile critics still focus on safely "tasteful" choices, ignoring exploitation and adult films in favor of waxing aphoristic over classical Hollywood, international art cinema, and experimental films. (Take, for instance, the antipopulist confluence of new cinephilia criticism and the "slow, or contemplative, cinema" trend since the 2000s, as it is no coincidence that many self-proclaimed cinephiles' embrace of deliberately languid films would privilege as "revelatory" those fleeting moments where *anything* notable distracts from the navel-gazing stupor of so many glacial long takes![124]) Whatever cinephilia's object choice, a sense of history infuses the image in these fragmentary moments where the profilmic real seems to unintentionally peek through.[125] Speaking of such chance encounters in a cinephiliac tenor, for example, Fred Chappell remarks that the bodies of female sexploitation performers are distinctively unique in their stripped-bare details, displayed on-screen in states of temporary indignity, but bearing corporeal traces of a lived profilmic history that confers a nobility which transcends the diegesis.[126] Like the pleasures of pornography or fandom in general, these subjectively experienced moments are less moments of textual excess than excessive viewing responses that remain primarily one's own, even when first encountered in a more social, theatrical exhibition context.[127]

In this respect, we can easily understand Jeffrey Sconce's concept of "paracinema" (a counter-aesthetic reading strategy rooted in the ironic celebration of "badness" in exploitation films and other cinematic detritus) as an ironically inflected species of broader cinephiliac practices, including what could be seen as their implicitly classist emphasis on the highly literate reader's own interpretive but culturally omnivorous acumen. The "double access" to high and low culture accommodating both ironic and earnest pleasures finds a parallel in the cinephile's bifurcated reading strategy of watching a film for sophisticated comprehension while also scanning for revelatory details that stand apart from the narrative as profilmic revelations. Cinephiles and paracinephiles alike collect and arrange these memories of outdated and seemingly meaningless image moments as souvenirs of experiences that inform their self-narratives.[128]

Sconce, however, associates these experiences with watching bootleg VHS tapes, whereas many scholars of cinephilia consider home video to have desecrated the "auratic" quality of the theatrical experience as a unique event. As James Morrison laments,

> The age of mechanical reproduction was supposed to have already robbed art of its aura, but it took these new avenues of access … to prove how much there had really been still to be stripped away. [...] It is clear in retrospect that the aura of movies was exactly what cinephiles had cherished, and though their love was certainly a form of fetishism, what they wanted was to possess the movies—not to own them.[129]

In this sense, we can track the history of cinephilia as a history of ongoing crises about the changing technologies of cultural memory. Periodically resurfacing around transitions in cinema's material sites, cinephilia's elitist rhetoric is often heavy with nostalgia since it takes as its object those fleeting moments that have "the quality of an involuntary memory—something that we seem to remember, even though we are seeing it for the first time."[130] But much as cinephilia itself is a primarily individualistic and even onanistic pleasure, format shifts do not mean that cinephilia has inherently become more solitary and degraded in the home video era. Like the imagined past and present audiences in the remediation of stag films whose degradation still foregrounds the fetishized "aura" of celluloid, cinephilia's secondarily communal dimensions have merely taken new forms to compensate for the specific opportunities and limitations of any format, much to the chagrin of some in the old guard.

If this is indeed the case, then we might question why cinephilia, pornography, and exploitation films have often seemed such unlikely bedfellows, despite their shared ability to generate earnestly fannish pleasures. Even Sconce seems to exclude hard-core pornography from the realm of paracinema, admitting soft-core films and other forms of exploitation cinema, but arguing that "hard-core pornography is not sleazy in that there is little subterfuge in terms of its production and reception." Paracinema is allegedly inflected with *sleaze* as "an ineffable quality" of "something 'improper' or 'untoward' about a given text." This involves not only "a circuit of inappropriate exchange involving suspect authorial intentions and/or displaced perversities in the audience," but also recalls the cinephiliac moment's tendency to evade or exceed discourse like the Barthean "third meaning" or *punctum*.[131] David Andrews likewise suggests that contemporary hard core's more obvious utility as a masturbatory aid makes it less recuperable by "oppositional" cult discourses, unless the "patina of age" attached to vintage texts adds a defensive degree of historic/ironic distance that seemingly mitigates the feminized or sexually deficient connotations of the masturbating (male) porn fan: "The lesson in this is that it is cool to cast oneself as a cultural other so long as that other is not wearing a semen-spotted raincoat."[132]

Similarly dancing around the erotic appeal of vintage texts, Jennifer Wicke claims that the graininess and archaic mise-en-scènes in vintage pornography "only have to be a shade off [contemporary expectations] to sunder any sexual response to the pictures and to instead open up a reverie on the *punctum* of any particular image, a *punctum* which is more mass-cultural than Barthes's rather ahistorical nostalgia for a past, frozen time."[133] Yet, while I agree that vintage porn imagery can evoke cinephilia's nostalgic search for a *punctum* that powerfully opens up (cultural) memories of particular time periods, I disagree that this datedness necessarily nullifies a sexual response to such images, as the growing specialty porn market for vintage material bears out. Despite the defensiveness of cult/cinephiliac discourses, there still is, after all, a thriving niche market for vintage material consumed *as pornographic*, not just recoded by historical distance for ironic consumption. Consequently, I would suggest that the minimization of hard-core pornography within some segments of exploitation film fandom is not primarily due to textual differences between exploitation films and those films socially constructed as "pornographic" at a given cultural moment. Rather, as I explain in later chapters, legal prohibitions that regulate the advertising and availability of pornographic materials to minors segregate some films as only for sale in specific places by specialist companies, and thereby play a larger role in shaping hard-core porn's uncomfortable proximity to exploitation films than the relative "sleaziness" of presumed authorial intent.

In the end, is there really so much difference between the profilmic glimpses visualized through, say, the mediocre acting and direction of a Herschell Gordon Lewis or Harry Novak sexploitation film and the moment when a fully nude and erect stag actor makes eye contact with the camera while preventing his fake mustache from falling off—particularly if this moment invites the solitary fan to imagine a homosocially shared chuckle? To find a nostalgic blend of ironic and earnest pleasures in the former but not the latter says less about the text itself than the text's perceived historicity. After all, stag films may seem all the more nostalgic today because they historically predate even the more recognizably modern forms of hard-core content that legally emerged in the 1970s. That is, they belong to an era when subterfuge was still a necessary component of adult cinema's production and circulation, when non-stag filmmakers still had to "sell the sizzle, not the steak," as sexploitation impresario David F. Friedman was so fond of saying in his resistance to the coming of hard core.[134] As the next chapter will show, that pre-1970s era of shifting and eroding subterfuge also saw the realm of *legal* adult films and their lurid paratexts becoming highly self-conscious about the degree of fantasy vs. reality that such films could deliver as sexual permissiveness gradually became more prevalent both on- and offscreen.

Perhaps too viscerally potent to be ironically mocked as "paracinema," yet boasting latter-day marketing and reception charged with intense longing for archaic and degraded cinema, the workings of cultural remembrance in our own latter-day era of stag film consumption nevertheless allow us to reunite early forms of hard-core pornography with the broader forms of adult film already found within exploitation cinema's retrospective domain (as discussed in the next chapter). If it has taken critics too long to recognize the correspondences between cinephilia, pornography, and exploitation film fandom, then we need only recall that the curiously erotic blend of high and low culture found in a sexploitation film like *The Lickerish Quartet* has already done their work for them. The contemporary remediation of archaic forms of adult cinema like stag films may uphold ideologically limiting fantasies about heterosexuality's historical continuity, but the same shifting distribution options and taste connotations that have allowed these once-illicit films to survive have also opened them to appropriation by more diverse audiences and reading strategies as well. Echoing the lure of cinephilia, haptic traces of ephemerality mark them as niche-interest fetish objects today, but such potential markers of erotic/cultural distinction have also made them retrospectively significant to others beyond their historically intended audience. Ultimately, selective remembrance frames stag films, and vintage pornography in general, as lurid artifacts made newly tantalizing because they linger from a bygone past—despite, or perhaps more precisely, *because* of efforts then and now to discard them from the historical record—but the many aesthetic/political/material wrinkles seen in their contemporary consumption have paradoxically prevented them from being irretrievably relegated to cultural obsolescence.

2

Ephemerality between Fantasy and Reality: Sexploitation, Fan Magazines, and the Adults-Only Film and Publishing Industries

As suggested in the previous chapter, the haptic and ephemeral qualities of vintage pornographic imagery remain one of its primary appeals to would-be consumers, encouraging erotic modes of viewing that gingerly caress the degraded image like a disintegrating picture in a photo album. In this chapter, I move further afield from filmic spectatorship itself, focusing instead on the more literally *tactile* pleasures of historicity associated with encountering paper documents and other material ephemera from an important period of cinematic transition between the era of the illicit stag reel and the legalized hard-core feature. The 1960s in particular saw the widespread phenomenon of sexploitation films, an adults-only mode of exploitation cinema that deliberately capitalized on the increasingly permissible spectacle of gratuitous nudity and simulated sex. While many of these films survive today on home video (as I discuss in the next chapter), the paratexts associated with sexploitation have spawned a thriving collector's market as well.

A specialty market for original sexploitation posters, pressbooks, lobby cards, fan magazines, movie-related pulp paperbacks, 35-mm production stills, and 8-mm excerpts appears through niche online retailers dedicated to vintage sleaze, and also through more generalist purveyors of used books and memorabilia like eBay. Indeed, like the collecting habits of many film historians, I myself have gathered a small personal trove of ephemera from such sources, which later spawned my wider research at more formal archives like the Kinsey Institute for Research in Sex, Gender, and Reproduction. In an era when so many of those erotic films that once would have been segregated into a peripheral market as adults-only texts are now widely available on DVD from major online retailers, it is no surprise that collecting the paper ephemera related to them has become more desirable, as if collector cultures are anachronistically replicating the limited market reach once occupied by the films themselves.

Amateur and professional alike, the historian "must always be an unintended reader," says Carolyn Steedman, "will always read that which was never intended for his or her eyes," and yet remains perpetually cognizant of the past reader over whose imaginary shoulder he/she voyeuristically peers.[1] Like the present-day stag viewer discussed in the previous chapter, then, a lingering awareness of one's own precarious position both inside and outside the erotic text's wider history of intended readership cannot be wholly avoided. As I will argue in this chapter, this tension between the unknown status of past uses and the physicality of the surviving artifact echoes a historical shift within the sexploitation films portrayed in extant paratexts like adults-only fan magazines and pulp paperbacks. That is, the very tactility of the cheap paper artifact whose past uses cannot be fully known echoes a film-historical tension between the erotic commingling of fantasy and reality, physically grounding the sexploitation genre's underlying tension between visual concealment and revelation in the unexpected afterlife of these collectible ephemera.

As Walter Kendrick observes, nineteenth-century bibliophiles were among the first collectors with an expensive hobby in collecting rare erotic books and manuscripts that "would today be called 'pornography.'"[2] Yet, the latter-day collecting of paper ephemera garners markedly different pleasures than, say, the classical bibliophile's collecting of hardback tomes designed to last. The grading of higher material quality (from mint condition all the way down the scale) may be commonly valued among collectors of older paperbacks, comics, magazines, newspapers, and so on.[3] But this value derives precisely from the fact that these "material objects that are, paradoxically, throwaways not thrown away"[4] were originally *meant* to be forgotten, often on taste-related grounds, yet have nevertheless stayed in relatively valuable condition *despite* their unexpected longevity. Unlike sturdy, library-bound volumes, for example, pulp paperbacks (Figure 2.1) were once seen as "disposable literature produced cheaply on disposable (almost instantly disintegrating) paper," with their ephemeral materiality thereby helping frame their cultural disrepute in similar ways as the magazines under consideration in this chapter.[5] Whereas "erotica," for instance, supposedly adheres in texts produced *above* the pulp line, "pornography" apparently falls below, into a realm where bodies (including the reader's own) are themselves treated as if undifferentiated pulp.[6] Furthermore, it is this sense of undifferentiated material from which the collector of erotic ephemera must seemingly "rescue" such artifacts—and, by extension, "rescue" him/herself as a discerning individual—through (sub)cultural reappraisal. Consequently, the delicate materiality of such items, including their ability to engage many different senses, can speak to the beholder in ways that even high-resolution digital scans of the same material cannot similarly deliver—especially if the beholder is also a collector who has personally adopted such materials for his/her beneficent protection.

I would argue that this retrospective valuation borne of historical devaluation is especially acute in the case of sexually explicit ephemera that now linger as "vintage" artifacts. Scans of 1950s–1980s men's magazines may be regularly posted on fan-oriented websites like Vintage Erotica Forums, for example, but ownership of the original artifact itself is all the more valued due to its scarcity. Speaking anecdotally, the ability to smell musty pages and handle delicate bindings is a profoundly different experience from the digitally mediated encounter, much as the experience of flipping through the content of an entire magazine is different than simply viewing digitized excerpts like nude photo spreads. As David Lowenthal says, "To see and touch palpably aged documents heightens the appeal of the past,"[7] which Elizabeth Edwards also describes in the tactile qualities that photos can accrue as relics in their own right,

Ephemerality between Fantasy and Reality   63

Figure 2.1 Ad for paperback pulp novels in adults-only catalogue (ca. 1970) for Baltimore-based mail-order company Central Sales, Ltd. [now defunct] (author's collection).

rather than as transparent windows into the past scenes indexically traced therein.[8] Because so many of these texts were directly aimed at an implicitly heterosexual male audience, it is no surprise that their intended quick journey to disposability should follow such a traditionally phallic economy of desire. That is, these texts were originally intended to be cast away by a sexually satiated (hetero-male) viewer, quickly reaching a personal/historical "climax" in the marketplace and thereby readying the viewer for whichever new text was on the way. There is, then, a sort of textual promiscuity implied by such materials—which makes them all the more retrospectively fascinating when they have nevertheless resisted cultural obsolescence and survived their respective periods of climax. Indeed, we should not forget that the rise of collecting such erotic ephemera has coincided with the partial recuperation and even celebration of some 1950s–1960s soft-core imagery (especially the pin-up) by broader audiences than heterosexual men: from feminist artists and performers, to high-class glamour models and make-up artists, to female and transgender participants in neo-burlesque shows and roller derby leagues—to name only a few examples of such imagery's restoration to physical presence and temporal presentness.

Moreover, unlike the digitized text, the materiality of erotic ephemera can encourage speculation about whose hands such artifacts have literally passed through over the decades, and what various activities those hands might have also been pursuing. If one feels a vague pang of unease about leafing through the same pages that might have once helped temporarily satisfy another reader's desire (as occasionally attested to by mysterious stains on select pages—a particularly corporeal form of marginalia), then tactile contact with the physical object of past (and retrospective) desires might even encourage one to speculate about the politically retrograde attitudes to which the vintage object may outwardly testify. Elena Gorfinkel, for instance, notes that the "shunted melancholia of obsolescence" experienced in watching 1960s sexploitation films today derives not only from their many temporal signifiers of datedness (e.g., period fashion, hairstyles, interiors), but also from their outdated ideological regressiveness as texts that champion "sexual liberation" but only on men's terms—and I posit that such tensions adhere in sexploitation's paper paratexts as well.[9] After all, if collectors desire a long relationship with ephemera that may have been promiscuously used and discarded, then it only makes sense that they should wonder about the provenance of such materials' prior circulation.

Amelie Hastie describes *collecting* and *recollecting* as profoundly interlinked processes, since the collector's stash of film-related ephemera can be read as a historical narrative suggestive of the very films associated with that collection. Much as writing about the past is a creative process blending historical evidence with informed speculation about what might have been, historians can use personal collections of ephemera in writing narratives about past films whose own fictional narratives also relied upon the one-time existence of a profilmic reality captured by the camera. The physical tangibility of the collection itself, then, might offer historiographical clues for understanding its film-related objects as uneasily positioned between fantasy and reality.[10] Indeed, cinema may position itself as a fantastic escape from everyday life, but collected ephemera bridge between such incredible experiences and the collector/viewer's quotidian pursuits, potentially allowing the historian a more immediate connection to the film's original moment of consumption.[11] As Vivian Sobchack notes, material objects can serve as traces of material events, including memories of experiencing the film itself, but possession can never satisfy the fan's desire. Touching the surviving object "may serve some [viewers] as a substitute for touching the *film* and inhabiting its dream," but the very inability for the object to ever wholly stand in for the beloved but elusive film can also engender a nostalgic "desire to desire itself."[12] Small wonder, then, that Jean Baudrillard famously compared the idiosyncrasies of collecting to the fragmentation and rearrangement of sexually objectified (female) body parts into "a perverse, autoerotic system," which (shades of my previous chapter's argument about necrophilia) is "less likely to occur within a true amorous relationship because of the partner's integrity as a *living being*."[13]

Following Sobchack, I would suggest that collected ephemera related to sexploitation films thus gain their powerful appeal as not only physical objects, fostering a sense of touch (including potentially autoerotic forms of touch) that imaginatively "literalizes" lurid cinematic fantasies through palpability, but also as paratexts replicating sexploitation's own generic strategies of the perpetually unfulfilled tease. As a surviving object about tantalizing sights from a bygone past, the sexploitation fan magazine exemplifies what Sobchack calls a "meta-object of desire,"[14] its unanticipated tangibility for latter-day collectors offering significant echoes of the lurid cinematic tales that it highlights. Furthermore, following Hastie's lead, we might say that collecting such ephemeral paratexts represents a fannish investment in the nascent history of sexploitation cinema that these publications were contemporaneously attempting to sketch—a history that was generally not covered (at least in such detail) by other periodicals, and which has only become retrospectively clearer with the accumulation of such magazines over time.[15] By collecting and perusing multiple copies, especially of the more critically substantive periodicals like *Adam Film Quarterly*, historical distance allows the present-day collector/historian to better track industrial and aesthetic changes within the adult film marketplace via an under-examined archive of discourse about a culturally shifting nexus of fantasy and reality that was once distinctly addressed to these films' intended historical audience, rather than to general readers of trade papers or the popular press. We can thus see how the 1960s sexploitation industry attempted to trace its own brief history—including the telling contradictions in its efforts to coherently do so—during the years of the so-called "sexual revolution."

The sexploitation film and self-reflexivity

Scholars have explored the fruitful synergies (and occasional conflicts) between American fan magazines and American movies as professional industries, most notably during the emergence and predominance of the classical Hollywood studio era. Much of this scholarship has focused on the role of early and so-called Golden Age movie fan magazines like *Photoplay*, *Modern Screen*, and *Motion Picture* in shaping the consumerist desires of their largely female readerships.[16] Far less attention, however, has been paid to the plethora of professionally published fan magazines that emerged during the post-studio era. Neither Golden Age movie magazines nor amateur fanzines, these publications nevertheless served as important incarnations of American cinema culture as the 1950s fall of vertical integration and 1960s crumbling of the Production Code Administration (PCA) heralded loosened restrictions on movie content and an increasingly fragmented viewing audience. During these transitional years, this fragmented viewership included the rise of "adults-only" films whose marketability was encouraged by the post-studio expansion of independent distribution channels and exhibition venues, such as urban grind houses and art theaters, alternately screening boundary-pushing foreign imports and other independently produced features. Many of these post-1950s adult films were sexploitation pictures largely aimed at a heterosexual male audience. Perhaps 1,000 sexploitation films (each budgeted between $20,000 and $40,000 on average, but also ranging from $3,000 to $100,000) were independently produced from 1959 to 1973, with US producers responsible for approximately 100–150 films annually during peak production years. These films would be regularly booked into roughly 600–700 US theaters by the mid-to-late 1960s, but they also expanded to other houses as well.[17]

Although sexual attitudes had been significantly shifting over previous decades, the 1960s was, in Bill Osgerby's words, less a "sudden, revolutionary change to prevailing social norms" than "the culmination of longer processes of transformative *evolution*."[18] Sexual liberalization (which, following Michel Foucault, is not synonymous with "liberation") gained its seemingly "revolutionary" thrust through the decade's media-fueled articulation of sexuality to postwar capitalism, engendering a sexualized lifestyle consumerism whose celebration of a distinctly American "good life" undercut traditional sources of moral authority.[19] Media coverage might frame such shifts as scandalous or harmful, but still perpetuated widespread public knowledge about sexual practices that were once far less visible. As one sexploitation publication noted of "wife swapping," for example, the popular media may have sensationalized the phenomenon as a product of suburban malaise, but "swapping is on an upswing, probably due in large part to the exposure in the mass media that soundly condemn such practices."[20] Arising in a climate in which the American film industry in general attempted to combat falling ticket sales with more "adult" content, sexploitation films were important ingredients of this liberalization. Of course, the explosion of media both comprising and fueling public curiosity about sexual liberalization included not only cinema's newfound sexual permissibility, but also the burst of adults-only magazines echoing and reporting on such changes—so the fruitful intertwining of the adult film and publishing industries must be taken into account in understanding how these films understood their own place in an important historical moment. By exploring how these magazines functioned as *publicity* for sexploitation films, we can better account for the era's increased *making public* of changing sexual attitudes.

Before proceeding further, however, we should note several of the sexploitation film's dominant features and varieties. Whereas earlier compilations of filmed burlesque performances, such as *Varietease* (1954) and *Teaserama* (1955), featured dancers stripped down to pasties and tassels, the sexploitation film's birth is often attributed to Russ Meyer's *The Immoral Mr. Teas* (1959), the first so-called "nudie cutie." Unlike the nudist camp documentaries screened to adults-only audiences at independently owned theaters since the 1930s,[21] the burst of nudie cuties following Meyer's lead had no explicit educational justification, often featuring a bumbling male voyeur gazing at unclothed women posed like men's magazine centerfolds come to life (Figure 2.2)—but his desire for physical contact is rarely anything but thwarted. As the name implies, nudie cuties are relatively innocuous comedies, free of any actual sexual contact between nude women (with no genital nudity shown) and male protagonists who, aside from their opportunities to leer, are often figured as far less than ideal on-screen surrogates for the presumed male viewer.

Ephemerality between Fantasy and Reality 67

Figure 2.2 Dopey men and topless women at a nudist camp in Herschell Gordon Lewis's formulaic nudie-cutie *Goldilocks and the Three Bares* (1963).

Later films like *Scum of the Earth* (1963), *Lorna* (1964), and *Body of a Female* (1964) marked a shift toward more complex, melodramatic narratives than the nudie cutie's parade of sun-kissed flesh. They also typically feature female protagonists whose sexual curiosity or entry into nondomestic spaces of sexual consumption results in peril. These films—variously dubbed "roughies" and "kinkies"—initially contained less nudity than nudie cuties, but compensated with scenes of violence as a narratively permissible form of bodily contact between the sexes. Like a psychosexual eruption of unsatisfied desires primed by the nudie cuties' perpetual tease, violence and sexual contact became misogynistically intertwined in these later films, with sexual violence (e.g., rape and coercion) or violent sexuality (e.g., bondage and sadomasochism) becoming framed as alternate forms of erotic spectacle. Sexploitation discourse in this prefeminist period often equated rape with sex (an *Adult Movies Illustrated* pictorial sports the screaming banner "Hottest Rape Scene Ever Filmed!"[22]), or casually described rape as more of a "fetish" for men and a nuisance for women than a pathological crime on par with murder, as second-wave feminists would soon redefine it.[23] Because this endemic rape culture already lurked beneath the era's much-vaunted "free love" rhetoric, women were under enhanced pressure to make themselves sexually available to men, and it is no surprise that cinema's more sexualized forms reflected such values. Some sexploitation films dating from the end of the decade, however, tempered such blatant misogyny and shock value in favor of extended soft-core sexual numbers that overwhelm the given film's narrative. With a greater emphasis on mutual, consensual sexual pleasure, this shift was a potential concession to not only women's liberation but also a growing couples' market.[24]

Overall, then, the sexploitation film's ideological ambivalence about the extent of 1960s sexual liberalization cannot be understood apart from the historical context that inspired not only its sociosexual dimensions, but also its industrial impetus as spectacles made newly possible by screen content's ability to go further than ever before (but not yet "all the way"). As Elena Gorfinkel summarizes, the sexploitation film in general "tempers ... sexual display with rhetorical and narrative strategies of denial in a logic of what I call 'guilty expenditure': sex can be bought and sold, but only at a particular cost. In the structured ideological economy of sexploitation—and counter to sexual liberationist discourses of the time—sex is never 'free.'"[25] Sexploitation films typically present sexual liberalization as a double-edged sword, paying lip service to the responsible adult's modest use of greater outlets for erotic desire, but more often dwelling on the unrestrained person's journey into moral corruption and degradation.

Echoing Gorfinkel, David Andrews, and others, this chapter rests upon the proposition that the sexploitation film's underlying erotic tensions between scenes evoking *titillation/freedom* and *punishment/limitation* mirror the metafilmic tension evoked between *the seen* and *the unseen* as the decade's censorship restrictions on sexual representation dissolved. The ratio between increasingly permissible spectacle and the alluring tease of forbidden fruit may have shifted over the decade as sexploitation filmmakers increasingly tested the limits of censorship. However, sexploitation's ideological ambivalence also echoes the industrial ambivalence at play as formerly taboo forms of erotic spectacle became more common in art films and major Hollywood films alike. Even as the independent creators of low-budget sexploitation might implicitly capitalize upon public interest in the lurid sexual content that increasingly found expression in films with higher cultural standing, this more widespread permissibility of screen content beyond the exploitation market also jeopardized the very prohibitions that had allowed sexploitation to survive.

Indeed, I would argue that sexploitation films and the fan magazines covering their development are remarkably self-conscious of these tensions—hence the many films and magazine articles that similarly narrativize the making of sexploitation films themselves. Posters, trailers, and other publicity materials repeatedly emphasize a given film's ability to show something not previously allowed on-screen in such graphic or "realistic" detail,[26] while the written commentary within sexploitation fan magazines likewise alludes to such legal changes. In fact, we might reasonably suggest that sexploitation's various paratexts were more acutely reflexive about the current shape of censorship constraints than any other similarly concentrated area of film publicity and criticism—a rhetorical commonplace that markedly differentiated sexploitation fan magazines from studio-era Hollywood fan magazines.

Back in 1934, coincident with the Hays Office's crackdown on Hollywood screen content, the Motion Picture Producers and Distributors of America (MPPDA) had begun requiring all fan magazine stories involving studio players to be submitted to the relevant studios for approval before publication, in an effort to manage unauthorized scandalmongering. The MPPDA also required all salaried and freelance writers for fan magazines to register for a "Hays Card" that would allow them studio access, a privilege that could be revoked at any time. By the late 1950s, however, the studios increasingly lacked control over the public images of their free-agent stars, opening the door for the scandal-based tabloid magazines that followed in the influential footsteps of *Confidential* (founded in 1952).[27] At the same time, the legal, economic, and social forces that threatened the major studios' control over the dissemination of publicity also fostered the rise of the sexploitation film and other "adults-only" pictures. These films, meanwhile, fostered the significant rise of movie fan magazines directly targeted at *male* readers during the same years that changing legal standards for the publishing and distribution of printed material allowed a new postwar boom in men's magazines, as epitomized by *Playboy* and its imitators.

As I will demonstrate, the emergence of sexploitation fan magazines sold at newsstands and adult bookstores was a crucial part of these films' popularity and survival during the 1960s. Gorfinkel describes sexploitation's textual content as already distinctively reflexive, because its "narratives were often *about* sex work and erotic labor. [...] The nude photographer's studio, the brothel, the escort agency, the vice dungeon—all become spaces for sexploitation to converse with itself about itself and thus to allegorize, through neighboring industrial models, its own production and consumption of sexual commodities."[28] Building upon this idea, I posit sexploitation's related magazines as an important *paratextual* component of this larger reflexivity, spurring readers' curiosity over the degree of fantasy vs. reality that sexploitation films provided. That is, as sexploitation's textual tropes of obfuscation vs. exposure both relied upon and teased 1960s cinema's larger legal relationship between the unseen and the seen, these texts and paratexts broached a related sociosexual tension between American society's *unfulfilled fantasies* and *lived realities* of sexual behavior during a highly mediated and increasingly permissive period of change. As one such magazine pondered, for example, regarding a film about the making of sex cinema,

> Since Gentlemen II Productions makes sexploitation pictures and *Casting Call* [1971] is one of them, they ought to know what goes on with the set and the company and the crew. But is this movie a Hollywood pipe dream or is it for real? Was it like turning the camera on a mirror for the "Gentlemen"? Or is this a big put-on for us local yokels?[29]

Such rhetorical questions spoke to readers' implied interest in the indexicality of bodies engaged in erotic performances that might somehow reflect what Linda Williams has called a larger shift from the culturally "obscene" to the "on/scene" within an underlying visual "dialectic between revelation and concealment"[30] that continues to resonate within the pleasures of collector cultures as well.

Although some of these magazines contained far more critical discourse than others, they collectively trace what I will describe as the sexploitation film's modularly rearrangeable attractions; its ideological incoherence about the desirability of a "sexual revolution" affecting all sectors of the film industry; and, perhaps most centrally, its shifting ambivalence between depicting (hetero-male) sexual fantasy and documenting what seemed an increasingly sexualized contemporary reality. While not the first magazine devoted to such films, *Adam Film Quarterly* (founded in 1966; renamed *Adam Film World* in 1969) was the most critically substantive of such fan magazines, representing a missing link between middlebrow men's magazines like *Esquire* and *Playboy* and the explicit hard-core visuality of later men's magazines like *Hustler* (founded in 1974).[31] Indeed, *Adam Film World* would become one of the most prominent chroniclers of the adult film industry during the 1970s emergence of theatrical hard-core cinema, although eventually overtaken by the trade journal *Adult Video News* (founded in 1983). Likewise, the magazine's stewardship under longtime contributing editor William Rotsler during the late 1960s and early 1970s is notable, since his career as an artist, filmmaker, and author treated the world of sexploitation cinema as both a prominent source of reportage and an outlet for pseudonymous creativity. His frequent contributions epitomize the tensions between sexual documentation and sexual fantasy endemic to these films, making him an exemplary figure in "fictioning" the era's changing sexual mores as a source of lurid curiosity and an outlet for personal desires—especially as the sexually suggestive fantasies of 1960s sexploitation gradually gave way to the practical realities of 1970s sexual permissiveness. With the luxury of retrospection after further decades down the path of sexual liberalization, we historically minded, latter-day readers of such magazines are thereby rendered "voyeurs" in a double sense—as observers of these lurid print images, and observers of an imagined past readership whose visual pleasures may have somewhat overlapped with our own—suggesting that the collector/historian's affectively charged search for sexual knowledge is not altogether different from that of the sexploitation publication's intended reader.

Men's magazines, industrial confluences, and the birth of *Adam Film Quarterly*

The postwar boom in men's magazines has often been discussed as a hypermasculine reaction to the expanding consumer economy for increasingly affluent, white, heterosexual men who had recently returned from wartime military service, but experienced a corresponding "crisis of masculinity" associated with the supposedly feminizing effects of domestic consumerism.[32] Upon its introduction in 1953, *Playboy* became the cultural standard-bearer by uniting *Esquire*'s urbane taste aspirations with "a greater emphasis on playful irreverence" befitting a younger demographic. Yet, as Carrie Pitzulo argues, whereas *Esquire* had initially tempered the potentially "feminizing" connotations of male glamour through "risqué illustrations of beautiful women and constant commentary on the pitfalls of modern femininity," *Playboy* premiered during a very different socioeconomic era. *Esquire*'s Depression-era roots (premiering in 1933) meant that its images of cosmopolitan male luxury remained an idealized fantasy for most readers, whereas *Playboy*'s postwar readers likely had greater access to modes of conspicuous consumption—and thus, *Playboy* fostered stylish-but-naughty lifestyle fantasies of swinging bachelorhood in distinction from "safe," middle-class, domestic responsibility.[33]

Hundreds of new men's magazines appeared between 1952 and 1961, and cultural commentators had roughly divided them into three categories as early as 1957. These categories included the many so-called "bachelor" magazines inspired by *Playboy* (many of which were actually consumed by married men), the true-crime and tabloid magazines inspired by *Police Gazette* and *Confidential*, and the manly adventure story magazines descended from older pulps like *Blue Book* and *Adventure*.[34] In the wake of the Supreme Court's landmark *Roth v. United States* (1957) decision defining "obscenity" as prurient and patently offensive material "utterly without redeeming social importance" (the qualifier "utterly" inadvertently opening the door to more and more content over the coming decades), a series of high-profile court rulings over the publication of controversial novels like *Naked Lunch* (1959) and *Tropic of Cancer* (1934) further redefined the legal boundaries for literary works. The titles of early adult film magazines like *Banned*, *Barred*, and *Daring Films & Books* reflect such legal conflicts, while, of course, claiming to heavily illustrate what was formerly taboo.

While serious literary works more easily escaped obscenity statutes on taste-related grounds by displaying "redeeming social importance," the more suspect taste connotations of culturally "lower" forms like films and magazines still faced legal threats, especially when those latter forms highlighted images over words. Even a champion of middlebrow taste like *Playboy*'s Hugh Hefner was brought up on obscenity charges in 1963 over publishing a Jayne Mansfield nude pictorial, the same year that the magazine *Barred* reported on the recent legalized publication of so-called "pornographic" books like *Lady Chatterley's Lover* (1928), *Fanny Hill* (1748), and the *Kama Sutra*; and the legal existence of physique magazines for gay men and specialist magazines for transvestites.[35] Although Hefner would argue that his signature brand of sexually suggestive photos were not obscene, even if they did not constitute "art,"[36] the names of sexploitation magazines like *Adult Art Films* and *Art Films Review* reflect more defensively euphemistic strategies. Consequently, the terms "art films" and "art theaters" often appear in 1960s sexploitation fan magazines, interchangeably used in reference to the films and exhibition contexts that commingled both low-budget sexploitation products and censor-baiting foreign imports from canonical art-film directors.

Like the creators of the films their magazines covered, many of these adults-only publishers functioned under multiple pseudonyms, intermittently changing the names and addresses of their business operations to avoid legal harassment. Also, like the films they covered, it might seem charitable to consider some of these magazines "professionally" made, since certain titles are qualitatively shoddy creations with no authorial credits or even correct pagination—but they were still primarily made as commercial endeavors. And, much like sexploitation film companies, some of these magazine publishers were fly-by-night operations that did not survive beyond several issues, whereas several companies established more significant market longevity. In their 1970 findings, the President's Commission on Obscenity and

Pornography estimated approximately eighty to 100 adults-only book and magazine publishers operating in the United States, with only twenty to thirty companies of real significance.[37] The latter included Classic Publications, Cine-Arts, Sari Publishing, Orbit Publications, New Link Publications, Knight Publishing, Dominion Publishing, and Seven Seventy Publishers, while Golden State News was a major distributor for multiple publishers.

Sexploitation movie magazines generally consist of multiple pictorials, with caption text (typically a brief plot synopsis adapted from a film's pressbook, plus several fleeting critical comments) far outweighed by lurid production stills. Still photographers directly supplied many of the photos used in such magazines, turning these ancillary publications into extensions of the industry's publicity apparatus in ways not dissimilar to the classical Hollywood fan magazine. Since prolific photographers like William Rotsler, Marv Lincoln, and Titus Moody depended on producers for steady access to film sets and production stills, it is little surprise that negative criticism of the films themselves is kept to a minimum in their magazines. Pictorials are often framed as previews of upcoming films, reviews of existing films, or thematic compilations of images from multiple films. On-set reports about the making of adult films are also a recurrent feature in some of the more prominent sexploitation magazines. Likewise, camera equipment and crew in action are occasionally all-too-visible in preview pictorials (Figure 2.3), further framing the profilmic setting as, for readers, a fascinating nexus for the era's on-screen and offscreen eroticism. Since these slicks were typically purchased for similar purposes as other skin magazines of the era, it would be inaccurate to describe them as trade publications, for they clearly address outsiders to the industry, curious about the process of sexploitation's creation, but far more invested in photos of nude bodies than in-depth coverage of distribution or exhibition practices.

Specific information about where these films theatrically screened is rarely presented, so as much as these publications served as cross-promotional tools between the adults-only film and publishing industries, the images themselves—modular elements of attraction that, like the cinematic scenes they captured, could be flexibly shifted and recombined—would apparently suffice for many readers. The final page of one publication, for example, lists several theaters in major cities that screened the films discussed in its pages, and readers might be occasionally invited to write editors for details about theatrical playdates, but these sources of timely or practical information about theatrical bookings were fairly exceptional.[38] This also suggests the magazines' wider distribution at newsstands beyond the urban areas where sexploitation films regularly played—although the mail-order sale of 8-mm excerpts of sexploitation features would have somewhat mitigated this limited theatrical distribution. One adults-only paperback does, however, suggest that "Often, scenes in the magazines are the 'rough' edited version of the movie, and many fans have been known to complain of this to the theater managers"—although the veracity of this comment is doubtful, given the many fabrications elsewhere in the book.[39]

Ephemerality between Fantasy and Reality   73

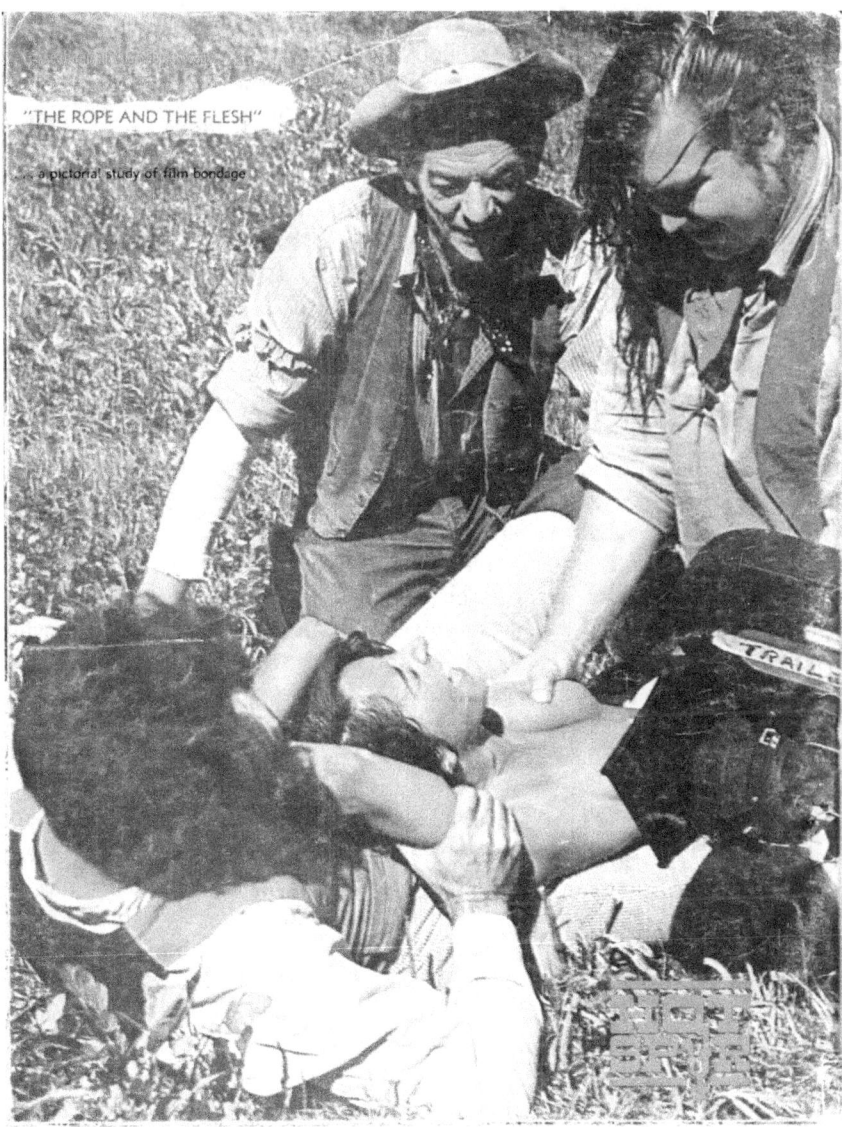

Figure 2.3 Production still taken while filming the trailer for the western-themed roughie *Hot Spur* (1968), as reproduced on the back cover of *Adult Movies Illustrated* 3, no. 1 (1969) (author's collection), published by Orbit Publications [now defunct]. Note the 35-mm camera marked "Trailer" visible at lower right.

Advertisements in the backs of sexploitation magazines tout mail-order products like 8-mm nudist, stag, and bondage films; artificial aids for sexual stimulation and masturbation; prints of photo sets catering to various fetishes and body types; nude photos and personalized letters supposedly written by attractive single women; other adults-only books and magazines; and so on. In other words, these magazines primarily catered to the sexual fantasies of a male market that may or may not have regularly consumed sexploitation films, but was still assumed somewhat familiar with the existence of such films as readers. A film like *Mail Order Confidential* (1968), for example, could promote itself as "The story behind the ADS in THOSE MAGAZINES," presuming the would-be consumer's familiarity between sexploitation's cinematic and periodical forms. Indeed, for period readers, these magazines' mail-order ads operated in similar ways as sexploitation's own rearrangeable generic attractions, with fly-by-night pleasure purveyors promising both erotic fantasies and the tantalizing (if unlikely) hints that one could live out those fantasies in one's own life. And even for latter-day readers like the historian/collector, these strange ads for virtually untraceable businesses can powerfully fascinate as signifiers of a mysterious but once-booming shadow economy in sexual goods driven by the force of the 1960s male cultural imagination. Like my previous chapter's discussion of the stag film's cinephiliac potential, then, these ephemeral details catch one's imagination (not unlike Barthes's photographic *punctum*), opening up reveries about exciting-but-obscure pleasures of the sexual past. Revealing less than they conceal, such traces of the era's expanding sexual economy seem to offer glimpses into the decade's heavily gendered cultural unconscious in no less remarkable ways than the feature films also operating within that economy.

Despite the frequent mention of "art theaters" in these magazines, then, access to sexploitation content was often more explicitly associated with home consumption than theatrical viewing. A *Knight* article on *The Aqua-Nudes* (1964), for example, features an "Editor's Note: We don't know how soon the AQUA-NUDES will screen at your local theatre—but we have been advised that some of the livelier sequences from the film are available in 8mm and 16mm for home projection from ELGIN FILMS, P.O. Box ..."[40] Ads for Diamond Films offered 100-foot 8-mm selections and 35-mm slide sets from the early nudies *Daughter of the Sun* (1962) and *Bell, Bare, and Beautiful* (1963). Similarly, ads for photo sets from *The Defilers* (1965) teased themed images (e.g., "beach scene," "whipping & spanking," "rape," "love in a car," "behind the scenes") supposedly deemed "too hot" for inclusion in the seminal roughie, while 8-mm excerpts from the kinkie *The Girls on F Street* (1966) were regularly advertised in *Adam*. Another ad states, "We started out to make a feature film, but ... well, it was just too 'unusual' ... so we felt it would be better if we sold it directly to the home" in 200-foot excerpts (Figure 2.4). As this ad hints, the interplay between theatrical and home-viewing opportunities even played upon the illicit repute of then-illegal 8-mm hard-core stags, much as publicity for *The Sexploiters* (1965) misleadingly claimed that the 35-mm film contained footage originally shot in 8 mm. Indeed, David F. Friedman produced the early roughie *Scum of the Earth* in shadowy black and white to deliberately evoke the "dirty" look of an underground stag reel, setting a visual standard for the subgenre in distinction from the full-color nudies.[41]

Ephemerality between Fantasy and Reality 75

Figure 2.4 Full-page advertisement for 8-mm loops and 35-mm slides from a sexploitation film billed as "too 'unusual' ... so we felt it would be better if we sold it directly to the home!" From *Adult Movies Illustrated* 3, no. 1 (1969) (author's collection).

In any case, the sale of small-gauge sexploitation excerpts and photos helped accentuate the form's underlying tease by deferring the viewer's desire to see more of the feature-length film in question, particularly if access to theatrical feature versions was limited in some locales. Like the nudie cutie's male protagonist, then, the sexploitation magazine reader might want to experience something that had become erotically visible on public screens for the first time, but these advertised/exposed pleasures could only remain tantalizing given the "immense—but not *too* immense—disparity and desire between spectator/reader and star/text" endemic to fan magazines in general[42]—including a disparity between the ostensible shortcomings of domestic viewing in relation to theatrical consumption. Thus, for many period readers, feature-length sexploitation films might also constitute the unseen object teased as a locus of unfulfilled sexual fantasy if the full theatrical experience itself was locally unavailable—another reason that such magazines can affectively resonate with the latter-day fan/collector as "meta-objects of desire."

These magazines might additionally encourage multiple purchases by serializing coverage of a significant new film across multiple publications: *Adult Movies Illustrated*, for example, called *Hot Spur* (1968) "quite possibly the best film ever made in the sexploitation field. WILDEST FILMS and its companion movie magazines have shown segments from 'Hot Spur' in recent months, but in this exclusive [pictorial] sequence the motive for revenge is finally revealed."[43] Letter columns also suggested that readers purchased multiple magazine titles from the same publisher. After *Adult Movies Illustrated* printed a pictorial on the application of body makeup to nude female actors, for example, a reader's letter in the following quarterly issue of *Art Films Review* remarked, "Who do you guys think you're putting on[?] I saw your feature in one of your other magazines about the body makeup. I know that they have girls that do that, not guys." The editor replied that, unlike major Hollywood productions, men were allowed to perform this task on small, nonunion films—and as evidence, printed several on-set photos of hairy forearms daubing makeup on exposed breasts between takes.[44] Rewarding readers' requests for more photos of a specific actor, film, or theme was a common means of encouraging active fan participation in these publications, and thereby gauging interest in what might prove profitable in future films/issues.

Home consumption of adults-only material was also encouraged through the use of sexploitation production stills as illustrations in paperback novels, the latter of which could typically describe more explicit sexual content via written text than was permitted in images. Larger adults-only publishers produced both sexploitation magazines and paperback novels, so cross-promotion was common. This cross-promotion might include novelizations of sexploitation films (such as the heavily illustrated Olympic Foto-Reader series published by B. B. Sales Co.) or adaptations of existing paperback novels into sexploitation films that were then previewed in the magazines (Figure 2.5). By the same token, paperback "novelizations" were sometimes credited as based on films that did not actually exist.[45] Such examples illustrate how sexploitation's film and publishing outlets fed off each other for inspiration and profits, even if one side of the equation might (like sexploitation's sensationalized content) be based more in fantasy than reality.

Flimsy pornographic fictions and fabricated sexological studies coexisted in paperback form alongside fan magazines about their on-screen counterparts. On movie screens, for example, a mid-1960s cycle of documentary-style exposés facetiously posed as either on-location chronicles of sexual practices or faithful recreations of psychiatric case files; examples include *Chained Girls* (1965), *Mondo Freudo* (1966), *The Lusting*

Figure 2.5 Cover of *For Love or Money*, a 1968 Olympic Foto-Reader novelization (featuring extensive production stills by Bill New) of Don Davis's sexploitation film *For Love and Money* (1968). Davis's film was itself adapted from the Edward D. Wood novel *The Sexecutives*, so Wood's novel was subsequently recycled as the film's novelization, published by B.B. Sales Company [now defunct] (author's collection).

Hours (1967), *The Hookers* (1967), and *Sex by Advertisement* (1968). A documentary-style framing device proved an ideal strategy for quickly joining disparate segments of sexual attraction, much as what one pulp paperback author called "modules," or prefabricated sex scenes ("a basic seduction scene, a copulation scene, a voyeurism scene, a rape scene, a Lesbian scene"), might be recycled and recombined from one novel to another.[46] Meanwhile, a late 1960s cycle of colorful and often comedic costume pictures offered "adult" versions of classic stories already securely in the public domain; examples included *The Notorious Daughter of Fanny Hill* (1966), *The Secret Sex Lives of Romeo and Juliet* (1969), and *The Adult Version of Jekyll & Hide* (1972). Overlapping with this latter cycle, Calga Publishers released a series of "*Adult Version of…*" novels, liberally adapting Jules Verne, Victor Hugo, Robert Louis Stevenson, and other classics, "written as [they] might have been if the author had today's literary freedom" (as the cover copy boasted). Likewise, Paul J. Gillette's numerous paperbacks for Holloway House included not only ersatz Kinsey-style studies of deviant sexual behavior, but also dubious "translations" of the Marquis de Sade, *Satyricon*, and the *Memoirs of Casanova*—all of which were apparently cribbed from preexisting translations and drastically rewritten by Gillette to add more explicit sexual content.[47] Excerpts from Gillette's "translated" classics were also published serially in the pages of *Adam* and *Knight*, several adults-only bachelor magazines released by Holloway House's sibling company, Knight Publishing.

Subtitled "The Man's Home Companion," *Adam* (launched in 1956) was Knight Publishing's major monthly periodical, although the company also published bachelor magazines of lesser renown like *Knight*, *Cad*, and *Mankind*. *Adam* was less conspicuously preoccupied with high fashion or cosmopolitan aspirations than *Playboy* or even *Penthouse*, and thus presented somewhat "lower" class/taste appeals— including coverage of culturally "lower" sexploitation films. As a 1965 letter to the editor complimented, *Adam* eschewed shock value for the sake of shock, unlike less reputable "magazines of your type today [in which] one sees so many absurd and distasteful extremes: the ones that still show Nazis torturing naked women are a pet peeve of mine."[48] Meanwhile, a 1966 *Adam* article on "Fifteen of the Worst Films Ever" rejects mainstream Hollywood offerings like *The Searchers* (1956), *Cinderfella* (1960), *King of Kings* (1961), and *Cleopatra* (1963), implicitly associating them with feminized tastes or compromised masculinity. A subsequent letter to the editor, however, says *Adam* has no business criticizing Jerry Lewis or *Cleopatra* because not only is the magazine nowhere nearly as profitable as those films, but "[y]ou also had the audacity, while talking about bad movies, to try and sell, not ten pages away, such trash as: Nudist Movies, Drenched Photos, Stag Movies, Unusual Films, and various other filth."[49] Positioned precariously between middle-class and lowbrow tastes, *Adam* thus strove for the contemporary bachelor magazine's measure of semi-respectable masculinist rebellion, but was not above advertising far more blatantly sexual materials to its readers as well.

Like many of the more significant bachelor magazines of the time, *Adam*'s contents typically combined short pieces of fiction and nonfiction (by noted writers like Harlan Ellison, Ray Bradbury, and Robert Bloch), nude pictorials, humor pieces, and advice columns. From 1964 to 1966, for instance, it ran a monthly "Ask Althea" column, in which Hollywood-area stripper and occasional sexploitation actor Althea Currier

(Figure 2.6) dispensed with sex and dating advice straight from a member of the "Go-Go Generation." *Adam* also included serious opinion pieces when there was a sex-related hook, such as a 1965 essay by Mamie Van Doren advocating the legalization of abortion.[50] Interviews with female actors associated with sex appeal—such as Van Doren, June Wilkinson, Carroll Baker, Ann-Margret, and Claudia Cardinale—were other common features, as were pictorials featuring actors and models who would prominently appear in West Coast sexploitation films, including Marsha Jordan, Kathy Williams, and Vincene Wallace.

Whereas the studio-era Hollywood fan magazines "retained some element of independence from the Hollywood studios" because their editorial offices were located in New York or Chicago instead of Los Angeles,[51] most sexploitation magazines were based in the Los Angeles area. Since American sexploitation films were primarily produced in either New York or Los Angeles, this meant the magazines' on-set pictorials and profiles of female actors were heavily biased toward coverage of the Los Angeles industry hub—although this did not mean neglecting the inclusion of more generic photo spreads for films produced in New York, Europe, Japan, and elsewhere. In addition to movie coverage, *Adam* offered pictorials on other entertainments that offered glimpses of partial nudity, such as popular go-go clubs, annual Artists and Models Balls, and showgirl revues. For my purposes, however, one feature that set *Adam* apart from other men's magazines of the time was its inauguration of a

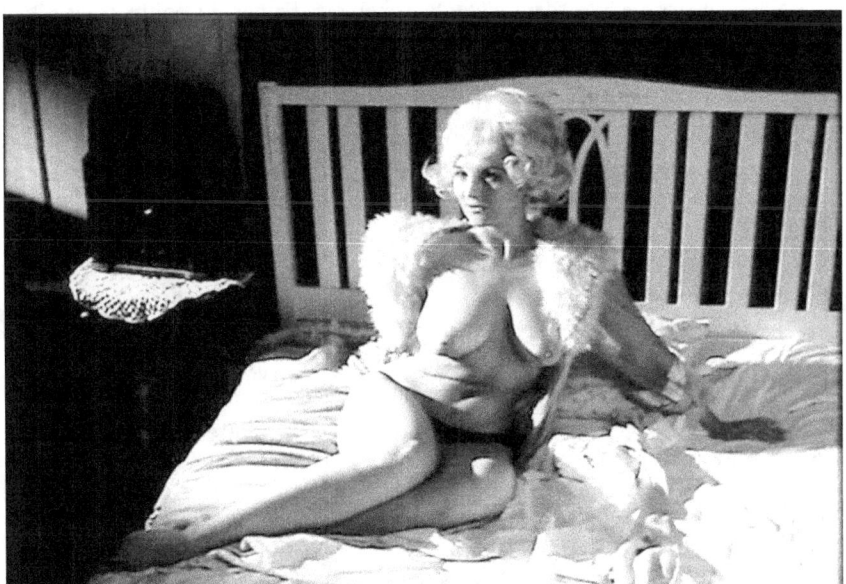

Figure 2.6 Los Angeles-based stripper and sexploitation actor Althea Currier in the 1920s-set kinkie *The Girls on F Street* (1966), a.k.a. *The Maidens of Fetish Street*, a film prominently advertised in *Adam*. From 1964 to 1966, Currier also dispensed advice (and rebuffed many marriage proposals) in *Adam*'s "Ask Althea" column.

regular sibling publication devoted specifically to cinema. Features on censorship and sexploitation movies were regular offerings in *Adam*'s pages by the early 1960s and did not substantially decrease until after *Adam Film Quarterly* premiered in 1966.

Adam Film Quarterly was the brainchild of William Rotsler, a prolific California-based abstract sculptor, cartoonist, and industrial filmmaker who had developed an interest in nude photography around 1958. He soon became one of the most active on-set still photographers in Los Angeles' burgeoning sexploitation market. As Rotsler later explained to *Knight*, a sex film photographer was crucial in creating publicity spreads for men's magazines, especially when some newspapers would not carry ads for low-budget adult films.[52] He had already photographed multiple nudes for *Adam* by the early 1960s, but Knight Publishing heads Bentley Morriss and Ralph Weinstock thought highly enough of his photo portfolio for *The Notorious Daughter of Fanny Hill* (in which Rotsler also acted) to publish it separately as the first issue of *Adam Film Quarterly*. Although several short-lived sexploitation magazines had appeared since 1963, the success of competitor New Link Publications' *Wildest Films* (begun in 1965) had encouraged former entertainment agents Morriss and Weinstock to follow suit. Unlike its competitors, however, *Adam Film Quarterly* built upon *Adam*'s existing reputation for fiction and articles by featuring a far more substantial amount of film criticism—much of it penned by Rotsler and a handful of other contributors—alongside its pictorials, with the amount of written text going well beyond the facile regurgitation of pressbook synopses found in qualitatively lesser magazines. Eventually outselling the magazine that spawned it, *Adam Film Quarterly/World* differed from its competitors because Knight Publishing and Holloway House shared the same in-house distribution company, All America Distributors Corporation, which Morriss and Weinstock formed to handle their own product. By cutting out the middleman, they could increase their profits and thereby invest in commissioning more original, detailed content.[53]

Beyond his magazine work for *Adam Film Quarterly*, Rotsler himself became a sexploitation writer/director/editor and occasional actor, making approximately twenty-six feature films (and innumerable 8-mm mail-order shorts), many of them for Boxoffice International Pictures producer/distributor Harry Novak. Several of his notable directorial efforts include *Agony of Love* (1966), *The Girl with the Hungry Eyes* (1967), *Mantis in Lace* (1968), and *Street of a Thousand Pleasures* (1972). Encouraged by Harlan Ellison, Rotsler also moved into writing science fiction in 1969, particularly after becoming disillusioned with stingy film producers. He had been a contributor of cartoons to amateur science-fiction fanzines since 1944 and would eventually win five Hugo Awards for his fan art before his 1997 death.[54] Although his reputation as a satirist requires that his reportage about the sexploitation world be taken with a large grain of salt with regard to its veracity, this very potential for unreliability is indicative of the lurid films and magazines he produced. Consequently, as I will explain below, his creative endeavors in sexploitation filmmaking and reportage were not so different from the fantasies spun in his subsequent career in fiction writing.

The years 1965 and 1966 had seen the sexploitation film markedly diversifying beyond the nudie cutie, which, in combination with the success of spicier European imports like *I, a Woman* (1965), *Blow-Up* (1966), and *Persona* (1966), accelerated reader interest in an adults-only cinematic marketplace previously glutted with nudies. The Supreme Court's 1964 decision in *Jacobellis v. Ohio* had established "community standards" for obscenity at the national level, which gave far more legal freedom to producers and distributors to launch nationwide releases of sexually oriented films (with, at first, the notable exception of "hard-core" pornography)—at least until 1973's *Miller v. California* decision returned community standards to the local level.[55] By placing the burden upon local censor boards to prove why a given film should be considered obscene, distributors were less often forced to defend themselves in court—a shift aided by the Motion Picture Association of America's (MPAA) 1966 loosening of restrictions on many of the Production Code's original taboos.[56] Accordingly, after the premiere issue, *Adam Film Quarterly* was devoted to multiple varieties of films, including not just sexploitation but also (to a secondary degree) imported art films, major-studio productions featuring nudity or simulated sex, and even underground cinema.

The (film) world according to *Adam*

As fellow travelers in the sexploitation industry, the partisan commentary found in fan magazines like *Adam Film Quarterly* and its heavily illustrated competitors might gently point out the flaws in these films, but they more often tend to ascribe culpability to general tendencies in the field than to particular filmmakers. In ignoring or finding excuses for aesthetic shortcomings, they recall the puff pieces found in studio-era Hollywood fan magazines—yet, unlike promotional coverage of technically polished Hollywood products, they also reveal a somewhat more reflexive dissatisfaction with the sexploitation film's endemic deficiencies as erotic content became more widespread on 1960s movie screens.

Approximately 150 nudie cuties had been produced in the three years between Russ Meyer's *The Immoral Mr. Teas* and the premiere of the first sexploitation fan magazines.[57] These films joined the wave of imported European art and genre films—such as *Young Sinners* (1959), *Rocco and His Brothers* (1960), *The Virgin Spring* (1960), *Two Women* (1960), and *Seven Daring Girls* (1960)—whose scenes of sex and violence were profiled in the first issue of *Banned*. This magazine, like several of the other early sexploitation publications, featured pictorials of "Scenes You'll Never See" and side-by-side comparisons of "hot" and "cool" versions made to satisfy censor boards in different localities.[58] By teasing footage that could not have appeared on American screens, readers were made acutely aware of how US and international censorship standards differed, with denial priming readers' demand for future relaxations. In other cases, American distributors might insert "hotter" scenes to capitalize on European art cinema's reputation for sexuality, as openly acknowledged by these magazines: "In the sex-exploitation tradition, this is an European import with some wild sex scenes added for our lusty American market!"[59]

Consequently, no matter whether US or international versions of a given film were deemed sexier, the most important factor for readers was the implication that more on-screen sexuality was on the way. A 1962 *Adam* article on the history of the Production

Code, for example, concludes by mentioning Meyer's *Mr. Teas* and *Eve and the Handyman* (1961) as new cinematic developments that "spoof sex even though they are jammed with it." Although the author ascribes changing restrictions to the end of the family audience and increased competition from television—even predicting the age-based ratings system that would be instituted six years later—he (incorrectly) foresees definite limits to this liberalization: "American taste is changing, but it will never change to such an extent that it will be possible for the average Bostonian or Philadelphian to buy a ticket, walk into a comfortable theatre, and witness hard-core pornography on the screen, as any tourist can—or could—do in Havana, Barcelona, or Hamburg. Nor should it."[60] Greater freedoms might eventually exist on movie screens elsewhere in the world, but rhetorically distancing and thus defending early 1960s adult films from the then-obscenity of hardcore pornography meant preserving sexploitation's profitable tease of the as-yet-unseen—although the taint of hard core would grow less reprehensible as the decade went on.

A convergence of films from different taste strata can be seen in *Adam Film Quarterly*'s sheer coverage of films once it became a freestanding publication. Early issues include features on sexploitation films by Meyer, Stephen C. Apostolof, and Barry Mahon; Dean Martin's Matt Helm spy movies; Japanese pink films; European art films from Luchino Visconti, Luis Buñuel, and Roger Vadim; counterculture-themed teenpics like *The Love-Ins* (1967) and *The Trip* (1967); and major-studio prestige productions promoted for their adult content, like *Reflections in a Golden Eye* (1967), *Bonnie and Clyde* (1968), and even Franco Zeffirelli's *Romeo and Juliet* (1968). The inclusion of implied nudity or simulated sex—particularly as captured in publishable production stills—remained the key factor uniting virtually all of these films. For example, a caption notes that Warner Bros.' Norman Mailer adaptation *An American Dream* (1966) "has exactly four things going for it: nude scenes by Janet Leigh, Eleanor Parker and Susan Denberg and a fantastic performance by Miss Parker that very well may earn her an Oscar for best supporting actress."[61] Stills of Denberg in various states of undress constitute the pictorial's primary images, while a full-length feature article on *Cool Hand Luke* (1967) devotes nearly as much description to bit player Joy Harmon (featured in "the sexiest car wash ever filmed") as to Paul Newman's starring performance.[62]

Overall, then, the commonality of nudity in the magazine's production stills collapsed cultural hierarchies within the same pictorial layouts. In subsequent years, this same logic found *Adam Film Quarterly* pondering "[w]hether Ingmar Bergman is a true artist or merely a crass pornographer capitalizing on sex and sadism for his own profit"; while the same issue championed the underground cinema movement for creating "sexy and beautiful" films that "*say* … important things" as a visible part of broader social changes in sexual mores, "along with the teeny-boppers, the Pill, dirty words in books and comments about whether there *are* any 'dirty' words or not."[63] Yet, however much the euphemism "art film" may have been applied to early sexploitation films, adults-only magazines still implied that most American nudie cuties were qualitatively inferior to European or Japanese imports. "Perhaps the day will come when American film-makers will make a more substantial use of the 'Nudie-Cutie' form," read *Adam*'s review of José Bénazéraf's *Notte Erotique* (1963). "The French, the Italians, the Japanese and the Germans have already proven their grasp of the medium."[64]

As *Adam* noted in 1963, about thirty nudie cuties were currently in production, of which all the American offerings were comedies. This was a generic strategy that, as Eric Schaefer argues, may have helped defensively displace their eroticism away from censorable limits, but at the risk of relegating the films as "juvenile, if not downright infantile, in their approach to both humor and sexuality."[65] A contributor to *Banned* denounced these "phony nudist movies" for misrepresenting and thereby incurring a moralistic backlash against the ostensibly healthy, asexual nudist lifestyle. "Some slob who is obviously a degenerate and pretty close to being a moron, who drools over naked females," was not an image that actual nudists apparently endorsed.[66] *Adam*, however, countered that, whereas "plotted" nudies at least offered the "hilarity of the contrasting social lives of nudists vs. non-nudists," the earlier generation of nudist camp films offered little more than "that 'natural habitat' documentary technique with which Walt Disney might reveal lemmings on their annual march to the sea."[67] In this regard, if 1960s nudie cuties did not aspire to the (ersatz) educational sobriety of earlier nudist films, then delivering comic nudity with no pedagogical pretense meant they could at least aspire to social value as timely exemplars of contemporary sexual liberalization. Indeed, *Wildest Films* even ran a recurring "Camp Cinema" feature devoted to publishing and mocking stills from 1930s and 1940s classical exploitation films, further emphasizing the generational difference between older cinematic provocations and the hip, new screen freedoms signaled by sexploitation.

Many precedents for the PCA's 1960s erosion came from court decisions around major-studio films or imported art films, since many low-budget US sexploitation films either did not seek or were not granted a seal of approval—but nudie-cutie apologists still touted their content as notable cultural advances from which even the cinematic mainstream might benefit. When a 1963 issue of *Adam* presented a list of the best recent nudie films, for example, among them was *Surftide 77* (1962), which combined typical nudie-cutie laffs with a more complex detective story (à la namesake *Surfside 6* [1960–1962]) to become a "prototype of the kind of picture that turns the current flesh film fad into serious entertainment—opening the door, that is, to legitimate nude sequences in big-studio dramatic productions."[68] Premiering two years before Sidney Lumet's Holocaust-themed drama *The Pawnbroker* (1964) became the first major US film containing topless female nudity to be granted a PCA seal of approval, *Surftide 77* could thus be championed by adult film aficionados as a precursor of (hopefully) better things to come. Indeed, as *The Pawnbroker* would prove, nudity in the service of a serious dramatic narrative could seem increasingly permissible for adult audiences, even if that narrative dealt extensively with themes of degradation and brutality.

David Andrews argues that 1960s sexploitation had a "tendency to displace its abjection" by differentiating itself from even lower cultural forms like hard-core stag films,[69] but I would reiterate that even the more violent sexploitation variants could point toward outside inspiration as sources of aesthetic aspiration. The roughies' shocking violence against women, for instance, could still be associated with a certain aspirational quality through their greater degree of narrative justification and an ethos of "realism" associated with the art films with which they were euphemistically linked, similarly advertised, and sometimes screened alongside (Figure 2.7).[70] The stateside

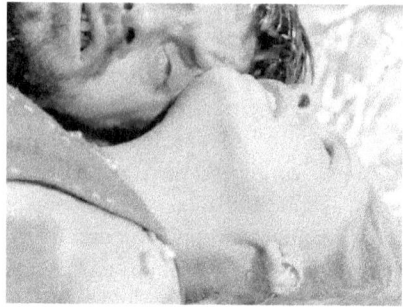 

Figure 2.7 Starkly monochromatic, tightly framed rape scenes from (left) Ingmar Bergman's European art film *The Virgin Spring* (1960) and (right) Lee Frost's American roughie *The Defilers* (1965)—both covered in the pages of *Adam Film Quarterly* for their sexual content.

release of films like *The Virgin Spring* and *Two Women* had recently introduced audiences to more realistic depictions of rape and degradation than generally associated with Hollywood productions, so scenes of sexual violence became a (temporary) marker of cultural distinction from the cinematic mainstream. Still, when narratives about the breaking of former sexual constraints often result in dire consequences for roughie/kinkie protagonists, it is difficult not to see these consequences as echoes of the metatextual opportunities and constraints facing filmmakers and audiences within the decade's expanding sexual economy. That is, like the films' protagonists, sexploitation's filmmakers and fans were caught between wanting to see/do more on-screen and trying to avoid moral/legal punishment for transgressing socially accepted boundaries—particularly during a period when the expansion of adult content in major-studio films like *The Pawnbroker* or the aforementioned art films sent mixed signals about how far movies would be allowed to go without incurring the wrath of local censor boards.

By the late 1960s, comments in sexploitation magazines specifically referred to nudie cuties as relics of an earlier time, though they still intermittently appeared as second features in some theaters. *Art Films Review*, for example, noted in 1968 that several revived nudies "cannot be classed along with the general run of Adult Movies presently playing. They are a throwback to the old 'Nudi-Cuties' … […] If you like heavy sex and violence we do not suggest you catch this double billing."[71] By comparison, monochromatic palettes and handheld cinematography accentuated the roughies/kinkies' far darker tone and scenes of brutality, since the outdated use of monochrome cinematography after the 1950s could alternately connote "Hollywood or Europe, glamour or seediness, realism or aestheticism, poverty or affectation, archival evidence or clever stylization."[72] This combination of traits made them seem a different species of adult-oriented film than the mainstream Hollywood drama and nudie cutie alike, yet one whose narrative impetus crept closer to the major-studio picture than the threadbare nudie-cutie plot. As Rotsler noted in the 1966 premiere issue of *Adam*

Film Quarterly, these "sex 'n' violence pictures have a little less nudity and a *hellava* lot more sex. Rape is an almost certain event in any of these. Whipping, spanking, and/or torture of some sort is a must." Yet, despite these tropes, he optimistically predicted sexploitation and major-studio films eventually converging: nudies needed to provide viewers with actual Hollywood-style stories and empathetically developed characters, not just skin; while major Hollywood films needed more exploitable elements than color and widescreen to successfully compete with television.[73]

In the pages of *Adam Film Quarterly*, "Hollywood" more accurately serves as a literal geographical location than a metonym for the major studios, stretching the term to include the Los Angeles-based sexploitation industry in the magazine's own backyard. "[T]he same Hollywood producers who did the nudies are now churning out the exploitation films," notes one article, going on to stress the influence of foreign films upon sexploitation's newfound desire to "start out with a good erotic script" instead of merely "a camera and a couple of girls with well-developed breast-work."[74] Much as sexploitation's lurid content confused the boundaries between imported art films and their own independent status, then, sexploitation films could seemingly aspire to greater cultural standing by similarly blurring the boundaries between themselves and major-studio films geographically produced in the Hollywood area, generating discursive associations with a longer history of "serious" filmmaking. Sexploitation specialists Entertainment Ventures, Inc., for example, even portrayed themselves as one of the major Hollywood studios in their self-reflexive comedy *Starlet!* (1969), which was shot on the old Monogram studio lot.

Yet, this indirect aspirational association was primarily possible once mid-to-late 1960s major-studio films began prominently incorporating the nude scenes and implied sexuality that constituted *Adam Film Quarterly*'s *raison d'être*—and thus began simultaneously endangering the sexploitation film's once-profitable distinctions from the cinematic mainstream. As the Commission on Obscenity and Pornography observed in 1970, "Today, perhaps the chief distinction between at least some sexually oriented general release films and exploitation films is that the latter (a) are much less expensive to produce (which is usually obvious to the viewer) and (b) are ordinarily exhibited in far fewer theaters."[75] Therefore, despite the hints of inspiration/aspiration that mainstream Hollywood's gradual move toward more "adult" content might indirectly provide for low-budget independents, sexploitation filmmakers still needed to push the boundaries of permissibility to differentiate themselves and thereby remain viable. Consequently, even as a potential convergence of subject matter across different sectors of the film industry might signal opportunities for wider audience interest, mid-1960s sexploitation producers made their films more violent or kinky to avoid becoming unable to compete with the majors' gradual encroachment on lurid sexual spectacle.

Comparisons with Hollywood were also evoked by *Adam Film Quarterly*'s lengthy and often well-researched articles devoted to the US film industry, with a particular focus on censorship, classic movie stars, and the history of popular genres that intersected with the sexploitation film. Consonant with the magazine's implied readership, the classic genres and stars profiled in such articles tend to endorse a predominantly masculinist ethos. Cliffhanger serials, westerns, war movies, crime films, and horror films received articles in early issues, each of which had provided generic tropes more recently reworked within the sexploitation film. The September 1969 issue, for instance, contains back-to-back pictorials on *The Wild Bunch* (1968) and the sexploitation western *Linda and Abilene* (1969).[76] Like these articles on popular genres, lengthy articles on the fraught history of cinematic sexual representation also attempt to trace a historical continuity between past and present imagery, with speculations on future changes always teased. These articles, for instance, detail the Production Code's evolution, contemporary films challenging censorship, the rise of homosexuality as cinematic subject matter, the increase of nude scenes in major Hollywood films, and the first X-rated films.[77]

Male stars such as Rudolph Valentino and Clark Gable also received feature articles, with the more bisexual or androgynous aspects of their star texts downplayed or omitted. An article on Errol Flynn, for example, recounts his dramatic rise and fall against the backdrop of his scandalously oversexed personal life—including the later years when Flynn's agent (and future sexploitation mainstay) Barry Mahon directed the actor's final film, *Cuban Rebel Girls* (1959).[78] Meanwhile, Gable is described as resisting or manhandling "elegantly emancipated women" like Jean Harlow, Joan Crawford, and Norma Shearer. "For the feminine audience to whom the female stars represented all the possibilities of their sex's liberation, he was the ultimate reassurance," the author opines. "Even if women became equal with men, they need lose nothing by surrendering their traditional femininity. There would still be a super male, muscular, bare chested and brutal, able to see through their pretensions, to reassert the historical relation of the sexes."[79] It is not difficult to imagine how male readers on the cusp of a burgeoning second-wave feminist movement could have appreciated the reactionary allure of this retrospective construction of Gable. Women's increased entry into nondomestic spaces as working women was necessitating a drastic recoding of that common roughie trope, male-perpetrated sexual brutality, as a serious criminal act, so regressive ideas of 1930s women voluntarily acquiescing to male strength and effectively "enjoying" their domination echoed sexploitation's generalized backlash against women's contemporary social advances. However, these retrospective articles linking Hollywood's own history to the more recent sexploitation crop would largely vanish around 1970, when the sexploitation market was already well established and the gauntlet of legalized hard-core imagery was finally thrown down, removing some of the last vestiges of the unseen.

Modular attractions and critical appeals

If fan magazine pictorials effectively taught consumers what to desire from these specialized films by reflexively foregrounding sexploitation's common themes and visual tropes, "it was only because this mode of discourse proved economically effective for the [sexploitation] industry as a whole."[80] This was especially true of pictorials compiling photos from multiple films under specific themes or cyclical variations (e.g., costumes and party scenes). This is not to say, however, that these recontextualizations of particular images under a given theme always represented the cited films accurately, particularly if many readers might have far more exposure to adults-only films through a magazine's pages than in theaters. Indeed, the editors of less polished sexploitation magazines like *Art Films Review* even admitted to rarely seeing the films under review: "We cannot speak for those of you who see the pictures. We can only speak from the background of seeing hundreds of stills crossing our desks extolling the sexuality of this picture or that one."[81] *Adult Movies Illustrated*'s 1969 bondage-themed compilation pictorial "The Rope and the Flesh," for instance, features a photo of a woman allegedly pouring "blood" onto the head of a bound man in *The Girls on F Street*, but despite this caption, the actual film's narrator identifies the liquid as the far less macabre molasses. This same pictorial features films from across the roughie/kinkie years, but also includes "[p]roof that bondage scenes aren't limited to sexploitation films" by including a photo of a bound woman tied to a moving lumber saw in the innocuous teenpic *Beach Blanket Bingo* (1965).[82] These inclusions suggest that male readers' (and editors') erotic imaginations could be readily spurred toward particular flights of fancy, especially in the absence of countervailing evidence that might emerge from seeing the films themselves. Furthermore, they suggest how these publications about fictional narratives could perpetuate their own fictional narratives about the genre itself, thereby affecting their latter-day veracity as archival evidence of an otherwise neglected slice of film history.

Golden Age movie digest magazines like *Screen Stories* operated through a similar "concatenation of stills, other photos, and text, brought together under the primary relay text of the motion picture, that perhaps creates a space, literally and figuratively, in which third meanings can be added to films through compensatory or retroactive viewings as well as readings." However, since sexploitation films may have been less theatrically available than the classical Hollywood narratives covered in movie digest magazines, the disproportionate ratio of images to written text in sexploitation magazines could all the more enable readers' enflamed imaginations to make creative significations well beyond a given film's actual plot.[83] An *Adult Movies Illustrated* pictorial for *My Brother's Wife* (1966) exemplifies this unpredictable concatenation, as the written plot synopsis is no more than several hundred words overall, spread across every other page. A collage of uncaptioned production stills dominates each page, with the scant amount of plot synopsis leaving readers to discern what might be happening in each image. The subservience of plot to images is reinforced by the fact that the final two pages are printed out of order—thus rendering the plot synopsis incoherent by describing the protagonist killing herself on one page but still alive on the final page.[84] These types of ambiguity—purposeful or not—played upon sexploitation's central tension between exposure and obfuscation, providing space for erotic flights of fantasy even as they proffered some indexical evidence of performed sexual behavior. (Likewise, for today's retrospective reader, the printed appearance of color stills from black-and-white films spurs imaginative possibilities for how these films could have turned out differently under other aesthetic and budgetary circumstances.) Whether in their pictorials or ads, then, sexploitation magazines became flexible realms of fantasy whose slipshod construction echoed that of the very films they covered, with images and attractions drifting free from narrative anchoring and recombining in tantalizing ways.

With roughies and kinkies introducing greater narrative dimension and more diverse sexual practices to the sexploitation film, their common modular attractions might be easily rearranged in episodic fashion from one film to the next, regularizing a variety of sexual tastes of potential interest to various (hetero-male) viewers. As cinematographer/director C. Davis Smith recalls, a film's budget determined how many segments should be written devoted to different situations or kinks; a 65–70 minute feature might thus be divided into roughly five 12-minute sequences, each shot in a day.[85] These strategies are implicitly acknowledged in sexploitation magazines, as when one notes that a film ending in a series of simulated sex scenes could hypothetically continue indefinitely with new combinations: "For example, what happens if the guys suddenly split from the girls or vice versa. There is always enough room for another motion picture to be written around the whole next episode, which might not be a bad idea."[86] Like the aforementioned ads for mail-order photo sets organized around *The Defilers*' particular scenes, sexploitation magazine pictorials emphasized this modular quality, as when the 1965 premiere issue of *Wildest Films* invited readers to write in with nominees for a recurring "Wildest Scenes of the Month" pictorial, with each selected scene themed around categories like "spanking," "rape," "dope," and "strip."

Even as sex scenes grew lengthier and less violent in late 1960s soft-core films, *Adam Film Quarterly* noted that, "In sex-exploitation films of this type, the main story line won't hold interest for the voyeur-filmgoer who patronizes them. So the quick-thinking producers added subplots that result in blunt sexual encounters of mothers, daughters and boyfriends."[87] William Rotsler delineated the sex film's common modular elements as "the Obligatory Orgy, the Mandatory Swinging Scene, the Inevitable Lesbian Scene, the Optional Rape, the busty and the petite, the chase and the orgasm. Mix together and jump back! Another film is on the way!"[88] Yet, as much as such elements may have uneasily drawn inspiration from the censorial boundaries pushed by more culturally reputable pictures, the persistently imbalanced ratio between sexploitation's limited narratives and modular attractions remained a point of critical contention over how these films were to be valued. That is, if combining violence and sexuality could no longer differentiate sexploitation from art films or major-studio films (and might also alienate a growing mixed-gender market), then drastically upping the proportion of sexual numbers to nonsexual narrative scenes might prove a means of market differentiation—even at the risk of complicating the films' aspirational aesthetic connotations.

According to these magazines, narrative justification, originality, and emotional nuance were important aspirational qualities for generating eroticism from moments of spectacle, even if many independent sex films fell short of such achievements (a sentiment still espoused by many present-day fans of 1970s–1980s hard-core films, as discussed in Chapter 4). Discussing *Motel Confidential* (1968), for example, one reviewer says, "We found the scene, though quite candid, to be an interesting one, primarily from the shading of emotions given by the director [...] Unfortunately this quality is lacking in too many pictures in the adult market today."[89] Likewise, *Adam Film Quarterly* complains that the clichéd dialogue in Barry Mahon's *Hot Skin and Cold Cash* (1965) spoils the picture's erotic mood and detracts from a decent story: "In all honesty," it "would be a better film had it been made as a silent screen effort back in the Twenties."[90] Nevertheless, reviewers themselves might espouse ambivalence over the ratio of spectacle to narrative, well aware of the primary reason these films had an audience: "We personally feel that rather than a mish-mash of sex, thrown wherever it might logically fit into the story, the average person would like to see his sex with a bit more originality to it," says one reviewer, who then immediately privileges modular attractions by deeming a "good story" to be less about plausible or distinctive storytelling than the necessity "that every girl who appears in the picture must have her turn in the sack at least once."[91]

Critical appeals to timeliness, realism, and education might also help excuse apparent aesthetic deficits, as when Mahon's *The Warm, Warm Bed* (1968) is praised for telling the "truth" about the wife-swapping and suburban prostitution that readers would have already encountered in contemporary newspaper reports. "In a frank analysis of the picture one could spend much time commenting on the production values and acting that is [sic] lost in limbo," the reviewer says. "But to criticize such points, points apparent in most of the pictures currently available on the adult market, would be taking the easy way out." Rather, "the Barry Mahon name" makes the film worth seeing because of his supposed knack for exposing the harsh truths of a changing society.[92] Likewise, *Adam Film Quarterly* calls *The Game People Play* (1967)

> not just another nudie film that emphasizes the showing of naked bodies for the sake of sex alone. [...] [Director Sande N.] Johnsen shows through the series of events that if one is content sexually[,] other problems will work themselves out. This is a picture that combines the visual with the emotional, and answers problems everyone is bound to face sooner or later.[93]

A film's shortcomings could thereby be excused if containing a potentially informative message—much as Rotsler claimed that adult films, by depicting diverse sexual practices and contemporary liberalized attitudes, could not help being educational in spite of themselves.[94] Yet, these magazines also acknowledge that the films can be ideologically incoherent in their attitudes toward sexual liberalization. As a review of *The Swingers* (1968) concludes, with tongue firmly in cheek,

> It might be interesting to speculate just what the moral of this morality story is: Could it be that honeymoons in Hollywood are out for the boondock dwellers? Or is it that if you make out with strangers you should first check their credentials to see if they are wearing underwear underneath the furs? What about the fact that a marriage on the rocks after a few drinks on the rocks wasn't made to last anyway? These new films are hard to puzzle out![95]

This ideological ambivalence was heightened by the magazines' subordination of critical commentary to lurid photographic layouts of the main attractions. Scandal magazines of the era, such as *Confidential*, already constructed what Mary Desjardins calls "composite-fact stories" by proximally arranging disparate photos and captions in their layouts, and allowing readers to imaginatively fill in the blanks. In my estimation, sexploitation magazines encouraged readers to perform a similar labor. Readers could mentally stitch selected filmic images to wider media coverage of changing sexual practices, and thereby discern a supposed "ring of truth" in the timely or scandalous subject matter depicted.[96] These magazines thus reinforced the disproportionate emphasis on sexual spectacle that intentionally separated the low-budget sexploitation film from the mainstream Hollywood product to which it so often qualitatively paled, and from which it would increasingly face competition by late 1960s. *Art Films Review* aptly captured this conundrum:

> Certainly, as in practically all pictures on the adult theatre market today, there are production shortcoming[s], some bad lighting, etc. Nor can we get over enthused about the acting abilities of some of the girls and guys who appear. These shortcomings, though, are becoming a standard thing in this business. The budget will only stretch so far and until the number of theatres showing the product enables the producers to up their budgets, we will be faced with such problems.[97]

Sex films would only become more artistic once audiences demanded higher quality product, Rotsler likewise predicted, but the artistic cream could only rise in conjunction with market expansion to more theaters and larger potential profits. Yet, demanding better quality paradoxically meant that viewers must not simply criticize sex films for their obvious budgetary shortfalls or scant narratives, since standing critically "above" the films would merely defuse their underlying erotic appeals (for him, the true measure of a sex film's quality).[98] In foregrounding the sex film's modular attractions, sexploitation magazine layouts (including Rotsler's own) gladly supplied such appeals, often at the expense of detailed, rigorous criticism. Indeed, it was tellingly defensive for the most substantial film criticism in *Adam Film Quarterly/World* to be focused on the history of Hollywood stars and genres, censorship standards, or on-set profiles about the making of adult films—with far less detailed criticism devoted to the respective aesthetic qualities of finished sexploitation films themselves.

Although nearly all sexploitation-related publications were professionally produced extensions of the industry itself, and therefore understandably partisan in their commentary, one notable exception was *ARTISEX*, a typewritten fanzine newsletter published (first biweekly, then monthly) between January 1968 and September 1971. Based out of Arlington, Virginia (and later Tallahassee, Florida), the newsletter, subtitled "Honest Reviews & Previews of the SEXploitation Films," promoted itself as an antidote to the sexploitation industry's false promises: "HELLO SUCKER! Have you been *gypped* at the box office? Are you fed up with shelling out $4.00 for … A 1964 rerun? A 1966 nudie? No plot? Lousy acting?

Bland sex?" Some of the reviews—many of them far more negative than found in the professional sexploitation magazines—were based on films seen at the Penn Theatre in nearby Washington, DC, or recalled from screenings seen elsewhere. In addition to updates on relevant legal changes in censorship standards, letters to editor "R. T. Sechs" agreed that sexploitation publicity was too often misleading and better films needed to be demanded. To aid such discernment, the newsletter's main feature was a digest of ratings, with films scored according to the following criteria, for a potential total of 100 points: "Direction (10), Technical (15), Interest (20), Looks (10), Nudity (10), Sexiness (30)." In case the reviewer's expertise was in doubt, *ARTISEX* assured readers that "Direction and Acting for the Digest are judged by a Master of Fine Arts in Dramatic Art." By the late 1960s, *ARTISEX* advertised subscriptions in publications like *Sexual Freedom: The Journal of the Sexual Freedom League*, one of several periodicals from a nationwide "free love" organization whose platform included a staunch anticensorship stance. By fall of 1971, however, the newsletter went on permanent hiatus, with Sechs stating: "The hardest core stag films are now being shown commercially in almost every major metropolitan area. [...] The time has come for a high quality, slick bi-weekly review to take the place of ARTISEX."[99]

By the end of the 1960s, screen censorship had eroded to the extent that scenes of fairly explicit simulated sex could dominate sexploitation narratives, making the legal boundary of soft-core vs. hard-core content one of the only remaining lines separating sexploitation from its cultural others. As Eric Schaefer explains, producers of 35-mm sexploitation films formed the Adult Film Association of America (AFAA) as a trade group for combating censorship restrictions, but largely as a last-ditch means of legally differentiating themselves from the increasing number of 16-mm hard-core producers emerging after the release of *Mona: The Virgin Nymph* (1970). Meanwhile, the MPAA bristled at public confusion between X-rated films produced by major studios and sex films with self-applied X ratings, especially after many major newspapers responded to the controversy by banning ads for all X-rated pictures in 1969. Although sexploitation magazines served as an additional source of publicity in spite of the newspaper ban, their far smaller, predominantly male readership meant the ban could still detrimentally affect the profitability of not only sexploitation's growing couples' market, but also Hollywood's move into "quality" X-rated films like *Midnight Cowboy* (1969) and *A Clockwork Orange* (1971). While the MPAA had no difficulty denouncing hard-core producers for misappropriating the non-copyrighted X rating as a signifier of smut, Schaefer observes that the AFAA found itself in the more difficult situation of advocating against screen censorship but still trying to maintain a denigration of the cheaper 16-mm films encroaching on their business.[100]

As might be expected, such changes were reflected in the pages of sexploitation magazines like *Adam Film Quarterly/World*. By decade's end, Lee Frost's roughie *The Animal* (1968) could be described as "tak[ing] magnificent advantage of the new freedom won in the courts" by "explor[ing] the nudity of the girls with almost as much fervor as that shown by the tortured [male] protagonist—all in a very unnerving experience." Yet, despite this implied identification between the reader/viewer and a sadistic voyeur, the magazine ruminated on future implications in less-than-alarmist terms. It was

> only one of many [films] moving toward that ultimate day when there will be no restrictions of any kind imposed by censorship. The only restrictions will be those of the story and plot. If there are any doubts on the matter, all one needs to do is look back at the last twenty years or so of nudie films to realize that we have been moving ever closer to free expression. And we venture to say that it won't spell the end of morality; probably nothing more catastrophic will happen than members of the audience leaving the theatre at the end of the film and heading for a nearby bar for a beer. The exploitation filmmakers will have the troubles then, because they [will] seem to have reached the end of the line separating erotica from pornography.[101]

Indeed, AFAA president David Friedman had long argued against the coming of hard core, since it would allegedly destroy sexploitation's tension between the seen and the unseen, rendering tantalizing erotic fantasies into the boring, clinically documented realities of human anatomy. Conversely, hard-core actor Mary Rexroth criticized sexploitation's bait-and-switch tactics as less "moral" than hard core's open display of the bodily "truth" that patrons had paid to glimpse.[102] Although sexploitation's alternating scenes of titillation/freedom and punishment/limitation once offered a moralistic echo of the metafilmic tension between cinema's on/scene and obscene, the formerly "obscene" realm of hard-core cinema could increasingly reverse this moralism once filmmakers and viewers were no longer destined for legal punishment for crossing the hard-core line.

Coverage of transitional, proto-hard-core forms began appearing in sexploitation magazines around 1969, starting to cast aspersions on contemporary soft-core pictures as becoming little more than updated nudie cuties in comparison with what was on the way. A lengthy article on "beaver films" (short 16-mm loops featuring close-ups of female genitals, first theatrically exhibited in 1967), for example, conflates sexploitation features ("the semi-legitimate film with naked characters plus a shabby plot") and 10–15 minute striptease loops as "pitiful things indeed. There were two types [of sex films] and only two," whereas the newer crop of beaver films is hailed as a cinematic epiphany.[103] Meanwhile, luridly illustrated paperbacks from adults-only publishers had led the way for their cinematic equivalents in "marriage manual" films like *Man & Wife* (1969) and *Sexual Freedom in Marriage* (1970). These so-called "white coater" films were pseudo-documentary features showing hard-core footage under the guise of educating married couples on "healthy" sexual behavior.[104] Much of the February 1971 issue of *Adam Film World* was dedicated to the white-coater *101 Acts of Love* (1971), wherein the director claims "it's classified as a 'sexploitation' film. But they say it's closer to real life and more artistic, so that, I think, separates it from films it happens to sit beside simply because they also show the sex act."[105] More "real" than fictional sexploitation features but also more technically proficient than 16-mm features,

35-mm white coaters could thereby mark their distinction from older sexploitation forms in several different ways.

Yet, despite such emergent forms, *Adam Film World* continued devoting prominent attention to soft-core sexploitation films into the early 1970s. The newspaper advertising ban may have meant that "[p]roducers either worked to cut their films back to a solid R-rating or pushed headlong into the increasingly ghettoized production of hard core,"[106] but if the magazine was largely an extension of the sexploitation industry's publicity apparatus, it is no surprise that its prior enthusiasm about relaxing censorship standards had grown more mixed with the rise of legalized hard core. The prolific market for 8- and 16-mm loops soon begat a large supply of low-budget 16-mm narrative features—the so-called "one-day wonders" (or "three-day wonders," as Steven Ziplow more accurately terms them in his 1977 guide to making low-budget hard-core features)—which remained a hard-core staple of adult theaters until the mid-1970s, when "there was a sufficient backlog of older 'A' releases in reduction prints, which could then be slotted into double bills with newer films."[107] As one producer-distributor explained in 1971, there was not enough 35-mm sexploitation product to fill exhibitor demand once 16-mm storefront theaters began profitably specializing in more explicit product. Consequently, some older theaters found converting to 16-mm projection more efficient than blowing up 16-mm prints to 35 mm, thus signaling a marked turn away from the earlier sexploitation forms that had also fueled the ancillary magazine market. Meanwhile, other independent companies found ways to develop mild sexploitation content within R-rated standards, such as the early 1970s teen-oriented output from New World Pictures and Crown International Pictures like *The Student Nurses* (1970) and *Cindy and Donna* (1970).[108]

Eventually, fewer films overall were reviewed in each issue, and more pages devoted to William Rotsler's pseudonymous reports on his personal experiences in the adult film industry. It was not until the June 1974 issue that *Adam Film World* belatedly featured articles specifically on *Mona* and Linda Lovelace, despite the *Deep Throat* (1972) star's monumental rise to fame two years earlier.[109] Like the larger adult film industry, then, magazines once specializing in sexploitation had to either begin specializing in R-rated films or jump into the hard-core market. In starting to cover the hard-core feature film in far more detail than simply generic terms, *Adam Film World* followed the latter course, bridging the gap between an earlier generation of adults-only movie magazines and the images of hard-core film stars appearing in later magazines like *High Society*, *Cinema-X*, and *Velvet's Erotic Film Guide*. Meanwhile, by the early 1970s, its publisher was increasingly taking a bifurcated strategy: Knight Publishing's men's magazines would continue to target a primarily white, middle-class readership (with the exception of its black-themed magazine, *Players*), while Holloway House's paperback line began specializing in black pulp writers like Iceberg Slim and Donald Goines, whose blaxploitation-style novels became enormously popular with a young, black, urban readership during Black Power's boom years.[110] The film and publishing markets were rapidly changing, and periodicals like *Adam Film World* would have to quickly adapt for survival.

"Fictioning" the sexual revolution

In effect, the 1970s R-rated sexploitation teenpic was still more sexually explicit than early nudie cuties had been, but that content also seemed increasingly defanged in comparison with its hard-core cousins. The 1960s sexploitation film had thrived upon an evolving tension between sexual fantasy and sexual documentation, with the force of unfulfilled, hyperbolic fantasies arguably the more important factor in priming viewer demand for what was yet to come as censorship eroded. By the 1970s, however, this equation had reversed, and adult viewers' ability to easily see the supposed "truths" of unsimulated sexuality—the logical endpoint just beyond the sexploitation film's asymptotic tease—meant the veil of fantasy seemed increasingly flimsy. From now on, the screened reality of bodies penetrating each other carried greater persuasive force than soft core's inherently unfulfilled intimations. By the same token, the relative mildness of R-rated sexploitation seemed to cast it into a register of fantasy which, because largely targeted to a youth audience, could seem all the more naïve and insufficiently erotic compared to adults-only hard core. Small wonder, then, that, despite the plethora of R-rated sexploitation films released in the 1970s,[111] so few of them would be profiled in *Adam Film World*, despite the shortage of more explicit soft-core films.

Furthermore, uncensored sexual reality outweighed the force of fantasy, both onscreen and offscreen, during a decade that saw far more promiscuous sexual practices than in the 1960s, as confirmed by a burst of research on the rise of swinging and other alternative lifestyles.[112] Although it had been a lurid sexploitation theme since the mid-1960s, swinging as a real-life practice became more common in the 1970s, as indicated when bachelor magazines like *Adam* and *Knight* began printing their "Club Adam" and "Knight Club" directories of swinger personal ads in the mid-1970s. Rotsler was at the forefront of these changes—whether writing a regular sex advice column in *Knight*, or prominently pictured in a subscription ad for sibling magazine *Swingers World* (Figure 2.8)—since his experience within the sexploitation industry made him a prominent commentator on the screen's explicit sexual realism. This is not to presume, of course, that more readers of such magazines were necessarily now engaging in more permissive sexual practices that had earlier seemed more likely confined to the realm of fantasy, but that the increased avenues for sexual expression previously teased in 1960s sexploitation films were hypothetically becoming more openly accessible in real life.

Already one of the earliest and most frequent contributors to *Adam Film Quarterly*, Rotsler had parlayed his films *Suburban Pagans* (1968), *Like It Is* (1968), and *House of Pain and Pleasure* (1969) into prominent pictorials in several Knight Publishing magazines by the time he effectively became *Adam Film World*'s uncredited managing editor in 1972. By that time, the publication increasingly showed signs of becoming his one-man show—a situation not uncommon with the company's smaller periodicals. Rotsler's name and his many pseudonyms (e.g., "Shannon Carse," "Cord Heller," "Clay McCord," and "Philip Dakota") began dominating each issue's contents, as revealed when many of his articles and interviews about the adult film industry were reprinted under his own name in his 1973 Penthouse/Ballantine book *Contemporary Erotic Cinema*, one of the first mass-market paperbacks about sex films that was not specifically designed for sale at adults-only bookstores. Given his experience in many aspects of the industry, Rotsler knowledgably published (self-)interviews with these pseudonymous crew members, alongside interviews with other adult film personnel; casting himself as both subject and chronicler of this important transitional stage in film history, he was in an especially privileged position to document this nexus of erotic fantasies and real-life industrial practices. By 1975, however, Edward S. Sullivan was credited as *Adam Film World*'s editor, with Rotsler still onboard as a contributing editor amid a raft of new contributors and a new subscription policy, suggesting the latter's tenure as head writer/editor was over.

Yet, despite Rotsler's extensive use of pseudonyms to populate a sort of imaginary world of contributors within the pages of *Adam Film World*, his articles also strip away much of the fantasy to expose the profilmic reality of labor within the adult film industry. When, for instance, he notes in his 1972 article "Are Sex Film Stars Really Swingers?" that adult film actors are no more or less swingers than anyone else (including the magazine's own readers), this sentiment distinctly echoes *Adam*'s 1957 article "Are Our Sexpots for Real?" which asserted that sex symbols like Marilyn Monroe were far more the product of hype than real-life sexual dynamos.[113] Furthermore, Rotsler repeatedly declared that adult films were far more likely reflections of male producers/viewers' fantasies about sexual liberalization than accurate depictions of lived reality:

> The sexual myths these films promote are easy sex, sex without strings, sensuality abounding, free sex, orgies galore, beautiful nude girls who will do anything, crazy laides [sic] who will couple with anyone. And so on. There are elements of truth in all these "fantasies" but by depicting the extremes or the unusual as the "norm" they are promoting a sexual myth. I've done it myself in over two dozen features.[114]
>
> Whether the films are "simulation" or hard-core porno, they depict a world that bears only a superficial resemblance to life. [...] But the image they put forth of women—the raving sex lover, the seducer of men, the rape-victim-that-becomes-aroused, the live-it-up whoopee girls—is a fantasy image that many men have of women. Thankfully, women are more complex than that, for they would quickly bore us if they were so simplistic.[115]

For Rotsler, then, the excessive fantasies these films constructed and catered to were still rooted in the alleged psychic lives of actual male readers/viewers, but some small kernels of "truth" might persist behind these lascivious images—as evidenced by his own swinging lifestyle. That is, he might reassure readers that adult films were largely fictional, but his own sexually privileged place as a significant player within that industry was a first-person reminder to readers that real life had indeed become less censored by the promiscuous 1970s. He testified, for example, that actual "balling" often occurred during the shooting of simulated sex scenes, but was later trimmed out in the editing room; that girl–girl scenes allowed curious women to sexually experiment under the guise of acting; and that the younger countercultural generation did not regularly attend sex films because they were already living the "liberated" lifestyle obliquely reflected on-screen.[116] Whether or not these details were actually true, Rotsler's overall testimony—whether due to his actual insider information or a credit to his writing skills in both fiction and nonfiction—still contains far more in-depth content and less prurient sensationalism than the average adults-only paperback exposé of the adult film market.

Not unlike the classical Hollywood fan magazines analyzed by Marsha Orgeron, sexploitation fan magazines thus "urged readers to think themselves worthy of participating" in that sexually liberalized culture, "[e]ven when playing on their reader's insecurities, often by evoking the disparity between readers' ordinary lives and celebrities' extraordinary lives."[117] Yet, unlike Hollywood's glamorous celebrities, Elena Gorfinkel notes that "the ordinariness of sexploitation's amateur female actors without question provided a more vérité object of male sexual fantasy, literally proffering the girl next door, the office girl, or the shop girl."[118] A disparity might indeed exist between the fantastically exaggerated sexual exploits in these films and the likelihood of enacting such scenes in one's own life, but obstacles to participation in the adult film world were not wholly insurmountable. In addition to articles about how to make sex films, for instance, Rotsler also published practical advice about "How to Become a Porn Star," including how to find an agent and producers (e.g., contact information for the Mitchell Brothers in San Francisco); what to expect for a pay scale and working conditions; and what types of intercourse would be expected and how to perform them for the camera.[119] For readers then and now, "the tangibility of the advice and knowledge contained therein might match the tangibility of the [magazines] as objects," affectively uniting fantasy and reality for those in possession of such ephemeral publications.[120] In effect, the potential accessibility of breaking into adult film work became a new element of fantasy fueled by these magazines, but one rooted less in the earlier decade's thick veneer of impossible fulfillment than the tantalizing (if still remote) possibility of real-life attainability.

Indeed, Rotsler's life behind and before the camera bespoke a blurring of fantasy and reality that might seem increasingly within reach for 1970s readers already invested in the alternative sexual lifestyles evidenced by these magazines' directories of personal ads. Many of the same authorial pseudonyms from his articles were found in the credits of his films and would even become the names of his filmic characters—as when he played a sex film director named Shannon Carse in *Shannon's Women* (1969). "99% of the credits were pseudonyms. On the 'lesser' productions, I'd direct as Shannon Carse and if I acted, I'd be Barney Boone. If I acted in a Rotsler-directed film, I'd be Shannon Carse," he recalled.[121] "*The House of Pain and Pleasure* was shot by director William Rotsler for Bolo [P]roductions in his own 'kinky' home," reported an *Adam Film Quarterly* pictorial, while 16-mm footage originally shot during nude photo sessions in his backyard "harem tent" was eventually cobbled together with linking scenes to form *Street of a Thousand Pleasures*.[122] As he explained to an interviewer, "I love to create fantasies[;] that's my whole trip, to make a fantasy. My house is a fantasy. I am heavy into science fiction but it's not an escape from reality[;] it's more like an enhancement of reality."[123] Thus, whereas 1960s sexploitation films invoked lurid fantasies themselves for their *raison d'être*, fantasy could serve as an

Figure 2.8 William Rotsler and an unidentified model in an August 1974 *Knight* magazine advertisement for sibling publication *Swingers World*. Courtesy of Knight Publishing Corp.

"enhancement of reality" upon the rise of a 1970s swinging subculture that seemingly transcended the once-less-surmountable divide between adult cinema's spectator and spectacle.

Although Rotsler would describe his men's magazine reportage as little more than a fun form of "creative typing" instead of the true *writing* represented by his science-fiction novels like *Patron of the Arts* (1974) and *To the Land of the Electric Angel* (1976), I would argue that his later fiction career is suggestive of his earlier work for the sexploitation fan magazines. Whether writing his original novels and short stories, or work-for-hire like paperback spin-off novels of existing media properties (such as *Star Trek* and *Planet of the Apes*), he sought to locate multiple texts within the boundaries of specific intertextual universes.[124] In a like manner, we can see Rotsler's many pseudonyms and intertwined roles within the adults-only film and publishing industries as constituting a sort of intertextual universe which, through the pages of his largely single-authored *Adam Film World* issues, reflected wider sociosexual changes but was also very much a product of his creative design. He thereby asserted his role as *author* in multiple ways: not only as a creator of written fictions, but as a sexploitation actor/filmmaker and as an authority on that industry. That is, as much as he reported on actual people, films, and industrial shifts, adult cinema's inextricability from at least some degree of erotic fantasy—particularly around the on-set production context as an ambiguous nexus point for indexical images of bodies performing erotic desire—meant that he was helping effectively "fiction" the sexual revolution's contours through the extent of his magazine work. As someone who would also develop a set of subculturally heralded "Rotsler's Rules" for fan convention cosplay (e.g., "Don't go to bed with anyone crazier than yourself"), it is little surprise that his life and work so deftly performed the part of the swinging sexploitation character made flesh (Figure 2.9).

There had already been precedents for this creative slippage in sexploitation fan magazines. Much as the same film might be advertised years apart under different titles, it was common for production stills from actual films to be recycled and recombined alongside a synopsis for a nonexistent film. Because sexploitation's modular attractions easily drifted free of their corresponding narratives, opening their imaginative potential for further repurposing, ersatz film pictorials might be assembled from photo sessions taken independently of any existing film production—thus providing another example of how sexploitation magazines' potential allure and profitability were not dependent upon the theatrical booking of actual films. The magazines *Unreleased Dynamic Films* and *Unreleased Blazing Films*, for instance, almost entirely consist of photos purportedly shot for nonexistent films, while their cinematic cousins like *Censored* (1965), *Banned* (1966), and *Mondo Oscenità* (1966) misleadingly claim to be compilations of sexploitation footage already deemed "obscene" by censors, but actually consist entirely of fragments either shot specifically for these films or compiled from other films.

Sexploitation fan magazines, then, already had a tradition of playing upon the imaginative potential of such modular attractions by the time Rotsler's cast of pseudonymous characters crowded into *Adam Film World* during the 1972–1975

Ephemerality between Fantasy and Reality 99

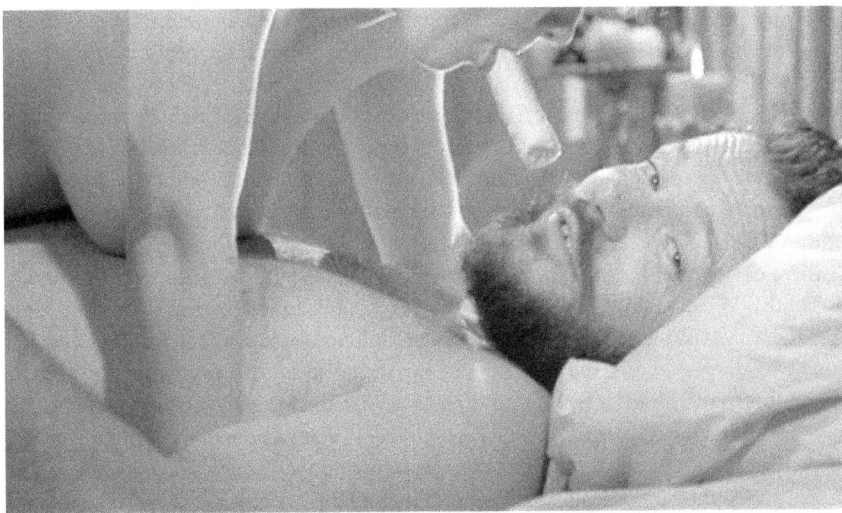

Figure 2.9 Rotsler (a.k.a. "Shannon Carse") hams it up as the Prince of Verona (opposite Dee Lockwood as Juliet) in Peter Perry's *The Secret Sex Lives of Romeo and Juliet* (1969), a bawdy comedy whose stagey, dress-up qualities prefigure Rotsler's emerging interests in fan-cultural cosplay.

span of his primary authorship. His sense of humor and interest in science fiction are easily discerned in an uncredited 1968 pictorial for the nonexistent film *Astral Trip*, the supposed story of drug-addled, "nude college students … shot into a love-out in space!" Unlike its cheaper and less critically inclined competitors, *Adam Film Quarterly/World* rarely tried to pass off fake films as the real deal, which makes it all the more notable that *Astral Trip* is a short, illustrated humor piece disguised as an actual film preview.[125] However, whereas *Astral Trip* is a self-reflexive jab at the silliness of some sexploitation narratives (such as Byron Mabe's *Space Thing* [1968], which premiered several months later), Rotsler would intersperse more serious bits of short erotic fiction into his later magazine coverage. His 1972 piece "Pornographer's Diary," for example, is written as a series of journal entries about a director becoming sexually involved with a masochistic woman whom he auditions during the production of a hard-core BDSM film. Illustrated with repurposed stills from the roughie *Linda and Abilene*, the article is not explicitly signaled as a piece of fiction, especially given its resemblance to the practically recounted details of adult filmmaking provided elsewhere in Rotsler's reportage.[126] In effect, his role as both a sexploitation creator and fan *par excellence* allowed the magazine to become a personal outlet for a sort of sexploitation fan fiction. While most of his magazine contributions were factual accounts of films or filmmaking, we can thus see how sexploitation's underlying tension between fantasy and reality nevertheless created space for one author to fictionally expand the contours of an intertextual universe, even during a period when the realities of sexual liberalization may have seemed all the more within the average reader's reach.

By the mid-1970s, hard-core adult cinema had become an established part of the cultural landscape and even achieved some crossover critical appeal beyond adults-only publications, so the earlier ability for magazines to pass off photo sets as legally "banned" or "obscene" films of their own invention was increasingly difficult. Unlike the fabrication of fake films that only existed in the realm of fantasy, Rotsler encouraged fans to actively participate in shaping an emerging adult film canon (a task that would protractedly continue on into later decades, as my next two chapters observe), even without getting in front of a camera. His capsule reviews and evaluative ratings of "All-time Favorite Porno Film Hits" appeared in *Adam Film World* in 1975, becoming a monthly "Erotic Film Checklist" column in which he urged readers to become more qualitatively critical, and thereby increase demand for better product. Readers were not only encouraged to clip and save the column, but also to help overcome the vagaries of adult film distribution by writing directly to Rotsler with titles, production credits, and critical remarks on films they had seen playing somewhere in the United States.[127]

Unlike the 1960s sexploitation magazines' indifference about whether readers could actually view their profiled films in theaters, inviting this active fan participation not only demonstrated how the 1970s had become a time when the reality of access to liberalized sexuality now seemed to outweigh fantasy, but it was also a "making real" of select films through their canonization as notable or important works. These canonization processes were further extended in 1976, when *Adam Film World* began annually awarding its "X-Caliber Awards" according to readers' votes. By this point, the magazine had begun reporting on the rise of home video as a revolutionary means of overcoming the dearth of hard-core features released to the 8- and 16-mm home market.[128] "The Videosex Scene" began as a recurring feature in the May 1980 issue, the first column tellingly titled "Shooting Your Own," detailing how to use camcorders for shooting one's own homemade pornography.[129] Heralding the impending end of a market for theatrically released sex films that stretched back to the distant nudie cutie, the loop between erotic fantasy and lived reality had, for some readers, finally been closed.

In our own period, these surviving magazines remind us that the 1960s sexploitation film has again become the domain of domestic viewing—albeit in feature-length form on VHS and DVD instead of short excerpts on small-gauge celluloid. These magazines may have once teased the reader's difficulty in accessing the films in question—but despite the sheer number of sexploitation texts released on home video in recent decades, the loss of many others continues to serve that tantalizing function today. When seeing multiple magazine pictorials about, say, a distinctly gimmicky but currently lost sexploitation entry like *You* (1968)—"the world's first 'Feel-a-Vision' film," shot entirely from a first-person perspective, à la *Lady in the Lake* (1947)[130]—the collector/historian cannot help being reminded of what curiosities still lie beyond his/her grasp, even in the home video era. Indeed, if ephemera allow one to feel/imagine more immediate access to a film's original moment of consumption, then possession of such tangible but rare paratexts can reactivate similar pleasures over the concealment and revelation of actual films that—as I elaborate in the next chapter—have since become no more practically accessible than entirely nonexistent titles like "*Astral Trip*" and the like (Figure 2.10). Understanding how sexploitation magazines rhetorically operated

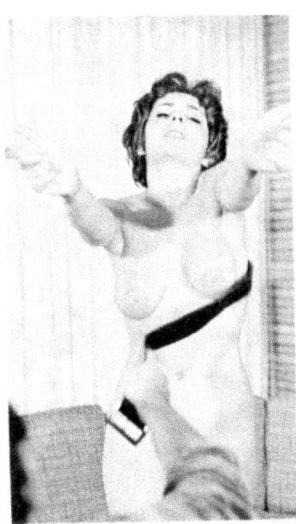

Figure 2.10 Photo (left) from the uncredited "*Astral Trip*" pictorial (likely attributable to Rotsler), depicting a supposed scene from the entirely nonexistent science-fiction sexploitation comedy; and (right) photo of veteran sexploitation actor Maria Lease in a whipping scene from Olympic International Pictures' no-longer-extant sexploitation film *You* (1968); both published in *Adam Film Quarterly* (in the April 1968 and February 1969 issues, respectively). Courtesy of Knight Publishing Corp.

in their initial period of circulation thus tells us something about the imaginative-cum-palpable pleasures they can still deliver for readers and viewers today. They may have been one of the few publishing outlets attempting to cover cinematic texts that exemplified, in both form and content, a historical period of national-sexual change already recognized (and entrepreneurially flogged) as socially significant. And yet, their continued circulation as desired collectibles also offers insight into the affectively charged histories of sexual representation that they can continue to tell.

3

"Whatever Happened to Gigi Darlene?" Object Lessons for a Disappearing and Reappearing Corpus

> [N]othing starts in the Archive, nothing, ever at all, though things certainly end up there. You find nothing in the Archive but stories caught half way through: the middle of things; discontinuities.
>
> —Carolyn Steedman, *Dust*[1]

A man relieves himself in the urinal of a grungy strip-club restroom, meanwhile glancing around at the crude graffiti scrawled on the wall. Amid the usual mixture of dirty jokes, insults, and other inked ephemera, the production credits of a film are also scribbled there, with pseudonyms like "A. Dick Feeler" easily blending into the surrounding nonsense. Credited to "Julian Marsh" and "Anna Riva," a.k.a. Michael and Roberta Findlay, a New York-based husband-and-wife team responsible for some of the strangest and most misogynistic sexploitation films of the mid-to-late 1960s, *The Curse of Her Flesh* (1968) is the second film in a macabre trilogy about murderer Richard Jennings (Michael Findlay) and his crazed torturing and destruction of all women who remind him of his unfaithful ex-wife. With its restroom wall credits appearing over the sound of a long, heavy piss, this brief sequence blatantly acknowledges the film's execrable taste appeals—especially when Jennings quickly and bloodily dispatches the urinating man, his ex-wife's lover from the trilogy's first film *The Touch of Her Flesh* (1967). As the authors of the fanzine *Sleazoid Express* recall,

> An intense study in S&M cinema as it veered toward hardcore, the *Flesh* series defined a sleazoid aesthetic for a generation of moviegoers. By the late 1970s, prints had been unavailable for years, although production stills and posters would surface in fetish-oriented outlets like Manhattan's Movie Star News. If you were too young to have seen the films, but had a distant memory of their lurid newspaper ads and posters, you had to rely on the words of elder sleazemongers, who only emphasized the severity.[2]

The Findlays' surviving films have, however, since been uncovered and released on VHS and DVD by Something Weird Video (SWV), allowing the *Flesh* trilogy

104   *Disposable Passions*

and other adult films to be taken up by a new audience, as I will discuss in more detail later in this chapter.

One particularly interesting detail, though, is a graffito (Figure 3.1) sharing Roberta Findlay's cinematography credit on the aforementioned restroom wall, reading, "Whatever happened to Gigi Darlene?"—an oblique reference to a curvy blond actor who had appeared in many New York sexploitation productions since the early 1960s, from bit parts in various Barry Mahon films to a starring role in Doris Wishman's *Bad Girls Go to Hell* (1965). While some female sexploitation performers came from an acting or dancing background, others like Darlene, June Roberts, and Darlene Bennett came into the field through figure modeling. Like their other jobs posing nude for art classes or camera clubs, no real acting talent was required of these latter performers, and all of the major New York sexploitation producers had their contact information on file in case a nude body was needed on short notice (Figure 3.2).[3] Depending on the film's budget, one such minor actor might make $50–85 per day, or be hired for $200–300 per week.[4] William Rotsler even estimated that 98 percent of female sexploitation actors were also figure models for still photographers—an exaggerated figure, no doubt, but still indicative of this important source of on-screen talent.[5] Yet, despite being one of the most recognizable faces/bodies available to the small network of New York sexploitation filmmakers, Gigi Darlene (real name Heli Weinreich, though her

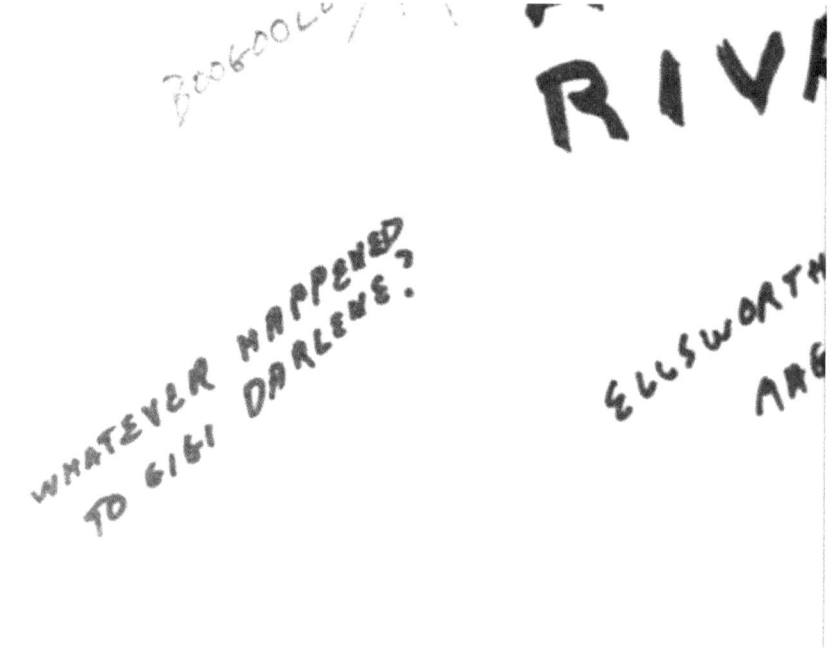

Figure 3.1 "Whatever happened to Gigi Darlene?" graffito scrawled on opening credits of Michael and Roberta Findlay's *The Curse of Her Flesh* (1968).

"Whatever Happened to Gigi Darlene?"

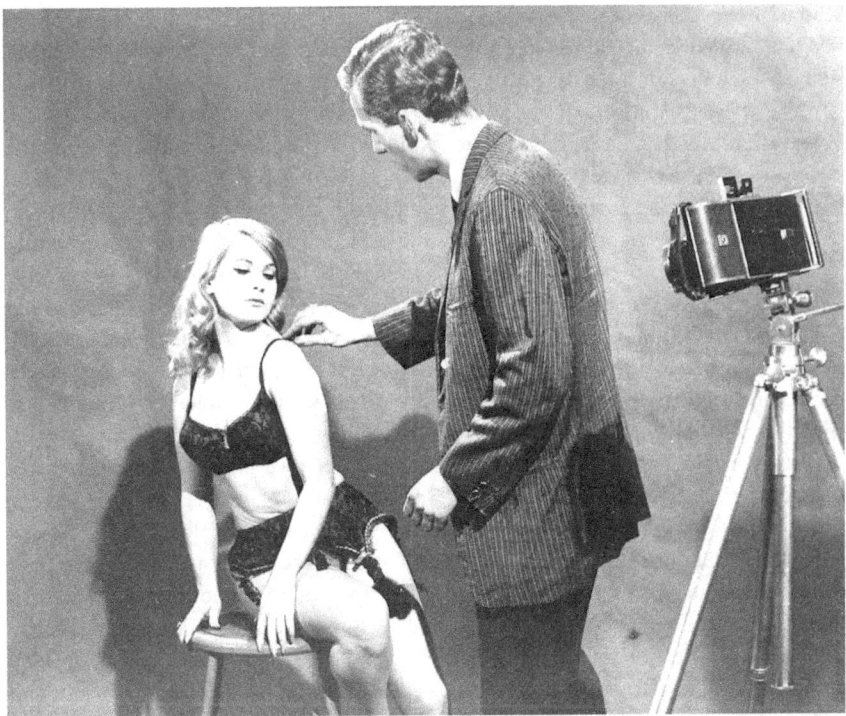

Figure 3.2 On-set photo of Gigi Darlene being posed by sexploitation filmmaker Lem Amero, a friend and colleague of the Findlays, in the mid-1960s (collection of Michael J. Bowen).

thick accent as a German immigrant was typically concealed by the extensive use of post-synchronized sound) apparently appeared in no more films after 1967—hence, the rhetorical question fleetingly posed the following year in *Curse*'s credits. Only absent from the scene for about a year by the time of *Curse*'s release, she was, it seems, already missed by those in the know.

Beyond the relatively small cadre of New York sexploiteers, it is unclear whether the average audience member would have similarly noticed Gigi Darlene's absence from the screen. The retrospective cult fame of recurrent minor actors like Darlene, Roberts, and others is, after all, primarily a product of such texts' remediation during the home video era—such as the ability to access and watch multiple titles from different years at will, to say nothing of pausing or replaying a film to single out fleeting appearances that were often little more than stand-ins or extra roles—although there were some signs of potential for sexploitation stardom during the 1960s. An *Adam Film Quarterly* preview of *The Acid Eaters* (1968), for example, remarked that "Though the pseudonyms flashed on the screen as cast credits are new, the nudie fan will recognize many of the faces—probably a good thing, because some of the girls are beginning to read a line so it is almost believable."[6] As Kenneth Turan and Stephen Zito note, the few female actors who gained some small measure of recognition had already made a name as strippers or nude magazine models before moving into these films, while an "unusual physical gift" like "larger-than-life breasts" might also do the trick.[7] David F. Friedman recalled that he and his fellow sexploitation producers had missed a lucrative opportunity in not actively promoting a sexploitation star system, since they (much like early Hollywood producers in the 1910s) had feared that low-budget filmmakers would be at the mercy of stars' demands, and reasoned that audiences instead wanted a constant stream of new faces/bodies[8]—although the 1970s hard-core market would be far less reticent to promote its bigger names. However, for lesser performers like Gigi Darlene, the one-time possibility to become something more than just a familiar face was never actualized during sexploitation's boom years, making her recurrent but ostensibly anonymous appearances in so many remediated sexploitation pictures all the more infused with the historical pathos of lost potential.

Although she had never appeared in the Findlays' own films, Darlene's cinematic disappearance also came on the cusp of a larger exodus of personnel from the adult film business, triggered by the coming of hard core. Many sexploitation actors and filmmakers did not make the jump into hard-core territory (although some, including the Findlays themselves, made the leap with few qualms, to say nothing of the viewing audience as well), so this apparent generational turnover has merely heightened the sense of loss or obsolescence infusing the latter-day reception of vintage adult films from before and after hard core's arrival. Furthermore, as the authors of *Sleazoid Express* observe, many of the Findlays' own films would become "lost" bodies subject to vivid recollection in the ensuing decades, vanishing like Darlene herself. Films and actors alike, then, these cinematic bodies once populated the adult film corpus during a particularly fruitful period of soft-core filmmaking later supplanted by the hard-core boom—but, of course, the 1970s hard-core era also produced its fair share of now-lost films and performers, so a sense of contemporary nostalgia for the historically vanished cannot be confined to sexploitation alone. Indeed, as I have been arguing throughout this book, adult cinema's underlying dialectic between concealment and revelation involves not only the bodies exhibited within the films, but also extends—in the mode of "vintage" appreciation—to the concealment and revelation of the films themselves as they gradually disappear from and reemerge into the marketplace on home video and other popular means of archivization. In this respect, the very process of appraising someone or something as a "vintage" body relies upon recognizing its uneasy proximity to the potential for historical openness or loss—a mode of retrospection that, as I noted in the previous chapter, has important implications for the narratives that surviving artifacts can tell.

Preservationist Paolo Cherchi Usai suggests that the very writing of film history is contingent upon the fact that films and their historical viewing contexts inevitably disintegrate and become lost over time. After all, if films never physically deteriorated through duplication and circulation, then there would be no need to write histories of historical change ascertained from filmic texts themselves. Although we might push back against his claims by arguing the need for histories written based on changes in film circulation and reception, he usefully posits that the potential "Model Image," which theoretically exists in a pristine state prior to the processes of degradation that give birth to film history, is merely an impossible ideal, never something that can actually be preserved or reconstructed.[9] In this sense, he intriguingly sees the Model Image's counterpart in the pornographic image:

> The lack of recognized artistic value ... and the fact that such imagery is intended to flaunt the moral codes generally accepted in public life, make its destruction an occurrence not merely inevitable, but one that is quite taken for granted. While the Model Image is the abstract of unachieved possibility, its opposite is one that should have never seen the light in the first place.[10]

The pornographic moving image, then, is arguably one of the most central to the very notion of film history as a mode of discourse, due to the genre's highly ephemeral and often endangered nature. Much as films themselves are creative acts of storytelling, so too does the film historian imaginatively narrate the processes of decay and destruction leading from the hypothetical Model Image to the various "traces left by each viewing on the relics of an entity recognized as being no longer extant."[11]

As a shadowy and denigrated entity to begin with, however, the vintage porn film is a privileged example of a text bearing witness to the destructive-cum-creative forces of history in both material and discursive ways. It is physically scratched, dilapidated, and torn to shreds until its thick veneer of wear-and-tear renews its erotic charm; while its elusive, poorly documented, and condemned cultural status can spawn tantalizing reveries about what unknown bodies still lie in dusty storerooms, warehouses, and abandoned film labs—all potential sources of pleasure whose lingering eroticism now remains inextricable from adult cinema's larger ties to the shadows of historical obscurity. And yet, if a previously "lost" film is rediscovered in the vaults and brought before the desiring minds and bodies of potential consumers, the filling-in of such gaps in the historical record (note the potentially phallic undertones of this attempted mastery of the corpus) becomes all the more illustrative of how the affective thrills of anticipation, surprise, arousal, satisfaction, and so on associated with watching adult films can also apply to the very processes of archival and distribution practice as well.

Take, for instance, the supposition that Gigi Darlene did not end her sexploitation career in 1967, but rather continued on with a recently discovered final film, *Lust of the Eyes* (1968), found in a New Jersey film-processing lab in 2014. An apparent one-off production by Perfect Vision Films, the crew credits contain no names familiar to other New York sexploitation efforts of the same era. Credited to director Andrew Kapp (a likely pseudonym), the black-and-white film concerns Suzy (Susan Fuller), a young model who becomes drawn into a web of vice after her dancer friend Barbara (Darlene) agrees to perform at a fancy stag party thrown by a rich businessman (Lou Sands). Shot primarily in and around small apartments in the Hell's Kitchen neighborhood, the film's settings hardly look upscale enough to match its premise, but these locales at least provide the director with the excuse for nocturnal excursions to the adjacent Times Square area. Through voice-over narration, Suzy introduces the two women to us as they careen past various 42nd Street theaters and adult bookstores en route to the party, stopping along the way for a dinner date with their boyfriends. Less concerned about their partners' evening plans than with making it to a nearby show in time, the boyfriends soon depart and the women continue on to the party.

Not surprisingly, Suzy and Barbara arrive at the cramped apartment to find a bacchanal in progress, with successive scenes focusing on the men partnering up with various hired women. Barbara soon takes her place amid the revelers as a striptease showpiece, while Suzy's voice-over registers her shock and gradual acquiescence to the scene. Meanwhile, the businessman skirts around the edges of the party before excusing himself to the next room to watch an 8-mm bondage film (his stock-in-trade, we are led to assume) featuring a woman being whipped. Suspecting that she is being sized-up as an uninvited interloper, Suzy begins following Barbara's lead, her overwrought narration commenting on the unexpected draw of Barbara's nude body: "As she danced, I felt myself swell with excitement, moving in time with her once-mysterious contours." Becoming both subject and object at once, Suzy imagines how these men must lust after Barbara, which also reminds her of her own guilty feelings about a secret crush on Barbara's boyfriend.

Ironically, the only extant print of *Lust of the Eyes* is missing its third reel, so between the first two reels and the concluding one, Barbara abruptly vanishes and is never again mentioned in Suzy's voice-over—a disorienting elision echoing Gigi Darlene's own abrupt disappearance from the sexual economy depicted within this film. The narrative concludes with Suzy fighting off the businessman as he ominously advances upon her with 8-mm camera rolling, shown through a leering, handheld point-of-view (POV) shot not unlike something from a horror film. After bashing him over the head with a nearby lamp shaped like a nude woman, she flees into the street and escapes, her narration explaining that she will never delve into such questionable places again. As the biblical allusion in the film's title suggests, a moralistic lesson has been learned—but the forces of sexual corruption are still out there, as suggested by a reappearance of the earlier shot of Suzy from the camera/businessman's POV, looping over and over as the end title card comes up.

And I should now reveal that, despite the preceding paragraphs, the film *Lust of the Eyes* does not actually exist any more than "*Astral Trip*" or any of the other fake titles, illustrated with photos from nonexistent productions, which filled out the pages of some 1960s sexploitation fan magazines. The preceding synopsis is entirely of my own invention—but, because the adult film corpus is so full of undocumented "orphans" and its history has been so loosely sketched, most readers would not doubt the existence of "*Lust of the Eyes*" or something reasonably like it, had I kept the truth concealed. Much as I already discussed in the preceding chapter how William Rotsler "fictioned" the nexus of erotic fantasies and realities through his mix of reportage and creative writing in *Adam Film World*, so do the historians and conservators of moving images have a certain degree of creative leeway in narrating a history of films that has too often been suppressed or left untold.[12] The premise of my little thought experiment about a nonexistent Gigi Darlene film would be highly improbable had it involved a historical corpus that receives meticulous attempts at research and preservation—even in, say, the case of a corpus that already involves a considerable number of lost films, such as the nitrate films that captured so much of the American film preservation movement's attention for decades.

Although film preservationists once touted 90 percent of American silent-era feature films as presently lost (a figure more accurately placed at 70–78 percent, according to various estimates),[13] we might ask whether the loss of many films from far more recent decades like the 1960s–1970s is any less egregious and deserving of archival attention. In the case of adult films, however, finding a degraded print of a previously unknown rarity would scarcely merit mention among most historians, scholars, and even preservationists, due to the low cultural standing of such films. Indeed, as historian Michael J. Bowen notes, even when an eminent resource like the *American Film Institute Catalog of Motion Pictures* transitioned from print editions to an online ProQuest database, this shift resulted in ProQuest's intentional omission of over 200 titles previously categorized in its print editions as "sex films"—as this designation might reflect poorly on the catalogue's marketability to educational institutions—while adult films given other genre labels like "comedy," "melodrama," and even "exploitation" were retained.[14] As one means of selectively—and quite arbitrarily—constituting the "acceptable" objects of a history of American cinema, such blatant omissions from commonly consulted records pose significant obstacles for a public wishing to know which films existed in the first place, to say nothing of which ones are today considered "lost." According to collector and preservationist Joe Rubin, essentially "complete" versions of approximately 40 percent of all heterosexual soft-core and hard-core adult features are currently missing or lost, and original camera elements are lost for about 65–70 percent of such films. For all-male adult films, closer to 75 percent of complete versions are now lost, given the smaller number of prints struck and kept.[15]

One of the other major reasons that adult films have received short shrift in most existing film histories is that, until relatively recently, the films themselves were rarely available in any accessible form after passing out of theatrical circulation, since archives and repertory circuits generally wanted little to do with them. When scholars like Eric Schaefer, for example, began researching the independently produced exploitation films marketed to adults-only audiences until the mid-twentieth century, most of the classical exploitation corpus had not yet been brought to home video. Although it would take until film studies' mid-1980s turn toward "new cinema history" to begin seriously contemplating what it might mean to "do" film history without textual access to the films themselves, these same years also saw the rediscovery of early adult films as nostalgic fodder for home video catalogues and the fan cultures developing in conjunction with them. Even today, the finding of a previously obscure adult film would likely garner far more excitement from fans and home video distributors as a newly recovered source of erotic potential than serious historical attention from scholars—despite, or perhaps precisely *because*, the rediscovery of already-neglected adult films from the 1950s to 1970s is more common than the rediscovery of, say, a silent-era nitrate film. Hence, the material signifiers of historical use/neglect—those "love marks" which, as I have argued in earlier chapters, can generate these films' erotic and subcultural value among vintage porn aficionados—are also difficult to separate from the imaginative possibilities opened by a rediscovered film's apparent ability to rewrite film history by adding a missing piece to the already ill-defined corpus.

James Kendrick usefully notes that in a home video age in which so many cult and niche-interest films are now being remediated, opened to far easier access by wider potential audiences, film lovers can be lulled into forgetting just how many thousands of films remain beyond our hungry grasp. Unlike *orphan films*, which, "while rare and often neglected and forgotten, are nevertheless accessible to those who seek them out," Kendrick terms *phantom films* those that "cannot be viewed, either because they are inaccessible or because they do not physically exist, yet they have left an impression on the cinema." Furthermore, "they remain beyond our reach and must instead be reconstructed imaginatively."[16] Likewise, Darragh O'Donoghue suggests that the cinephiliac allure of the lost film resides in not only the pathos of historical neglect, but also the productive potential such unseen artifacts unleash in the cinephile's imagination:

> There is, perhaps, a sense that the cinema shows too much, places the viewer in too passive a position; the lost film, the fragment, the butchered stump, so tragic a loss of an original vision, nevertheless liberates the viewer, activates his or her imagination, to take what remains, and, unbounded by human or historical probability, send it in directions the filmmaker may never have intended.[17]

For these critics, the lost or phantom film's attraction resides in its potential to revise film history if found—even a seemingly trivial and insignificant bit of film history, like the date of Gigi Darlene's exit from the sexploitation business. As mentioned, her abrupt exit predated the coming of hard core by several years—hence the imaginative speculation that a further entry in her filmography might stir. Ultimately, it was not until a mid-2014 blog entry on fan-historian Ashley West's well-researched website *The Rialto Report* that fans learned much more about "whatever happened to Gigi Darlene" than Michael and Roberta Findlay did in 1968—she left the sexploitation world after marrying hypnotist Charles Lamont and became a part of his stage act until his death in 1980; she herself died at age 58 in 2002[18]—but the crucial point is that a hypothetically "lost" film's very *inaccessibility* may bestow as much affective value upon the phantom text as the potential for eventually rediscovering and writing it back into history.

In this chapter, then, I focus on issues of archival practice and home video distribution to explore how the erotic allure of the vintage adult film's historicity can reside in its potential—or lack of potential—to be *recapitalized* upon by archives and entrepreneurs alike, decades after its initial emergence into the marketplace. The patient reader will hopefully permit me a somewhat circuitous route through these issues and case studies, befitting the strange contingencies of disappearance and rediscovery addressed across this chapter. Through several object lessons in the unexpectedly long afterlives of vintage adult films—from my rediscovery of an actual "phantom" sexploitation film to the archival detective work of adult video distributors—I sketch some of the practical realities shaping the fantastic potential of "lost" erotic cinema as artifacts lurking in and beyond the historical archive. Rather than a reservoir of stable cultural meanings, then, I explore the archive, in both its physical and symbolic forms, as an affectively charged site for generating (subcultural) pleasures from the same forces of historical flux and discontinuity that help shape fan identities.

In using a flexible notion of "archives," my discussion therefore includes not only formal nonprofit archives but also the commercial repositories and personal collections (such as fan-collectors' private troves of ephemera noted in the previous chapter) that many scholars would not consider *proper* archives because they are not dedicated to cataloguing, publicizing, and preserving their holdings for open perusal by outside researchers. Yet, by figuring the discursive concept of the archive, in its both official and unofficial forms, as a site of open and shifting possibilities for change, I explore how affective value and historical value can uneasily comingle in the processes by which adult cinema's "lost" bodies are brought to light. I will thereby trace the affective resonance—animated throughout by a constant tension between cultural remembrance and cultural forgetting—that these shadowy bodies can have upon such intertwined, archive-dependent figures as the fan, the collector, and the historian.

Whatever happened to *The Orgy at Lil's Place*?

As Walter Kendrick argues, the archival life of aged pornographic artifacts has always been fraught with conflicting value judgments. Dating all the way back to the ancient frescos unearthed at Pompeii in the eighteenth century, many pornographic antiquities have not been automatically destroyed upon their discovery, in large part because of their very historicity. Ambivalence over their aesthetic and historical value has instead meant that archaic forms of pornography were long archived in "secret museums" open only to learned gentlemen—and carefully segregated from the sight of supposedly "impressionable" populations like women, children, and the poor—a dynamic somewhat recalled in the adults-only back rooms of video stores centuries later. Indeed, the very fact that such materials might otherwise be condemned to destruction by crusading moralists often meant that they were all the more eligible for preservation by those with the knowledge to "properly" appreciate them.[19] In our own era, however, the secret museum is itself very much a thing of the past, for once-"pornographic" antiquities seemingly pale in comparison with our more modern, explicit, and viscerally stimulating forms of pornography like hard-core adult cinema. Small wonder, then, that the older forms of our more recognizably modern pornographies, such as twentieth-century moving images, occupy a liminal space in the archive. By virtue of their relatively recent vintage, they are far less recuperable to normative standards of aesthetic/historical value than long-established relics consigned to the art world—and yet, their "vintage-ness" relative to other forms of erotic moving images still inspires ambivalence over the possible importance of preserving such artifacts, especially when these cinematic objects (whether celluloid prints, analog/digital video transfers, etc.) already exist as copies of an oft-obscure "original" form.

Eric Schaefer describes adult films as "perhaps the loneliest orphans," since "[m]any of the films have fallen out of copyright, and an even larger number were never even registered." Although these films should thus be a priority for preservation, various cultural, political, and practical obstacles have made such reassessment difficult. These include (among others) the low cultural standing of adult films to begin with, the under-the-radar status of surviving records kept by producers and distributors, and the fact that a very limited number of prints of each film often circulated for long periods, with re-cutting, re-titling, or releasing separate "hot" and "cool" versions making it difficult to discern which extant prints are worth preserving. As Schaefer warns, however, "preserving only 'complete' prints, when censored or incomplete prints also exist, may [additionally] do a disservice to scholars by robbing them of the opportunity to see the varying ways in which audiences experienced a film."[20]

Anthony Slide suggests that the Library of Congress initially hesitated accepting hard-core films because they could not guarantee against governmental seizure and destruction of prints when obscenity statutes were up in the air during the early 1970s. By the same token, some hard-core producers did not formally file their materials with the U.S. Copyright Office, due to fears of federal prosecution—especially when organized crime funded much of hard-core pornography (especially the loops) in the 1970s.[21] (Library of Congress librarian Ralph Whittington did, however, take it upon himself to collect the pornographic materials that his federal employer did not, which led to three decades amassing and cataloguing a huge private collection that would later be donated to New York's Museum of Sex in 2002.[22]) This meant that any text made prior to 1978 without a complete copyright notice in its on-screen credits would not be covered under the Copyright Act of 1976 and would therefore immediately pass into the public domain unless a new copyright notice was filed.[23] Furthermore, the 1976 act no longer required copies of texts to be deposited in the Library of Congress as a prerequisite for US copyright protection—but such a deposit had to be made in order to legally claim copyright *infringement*—thus relegating the preservation of culturally marginalized and unregistered texts to private citizens.[24] After 1976, then, a *formally deposited* film would receive more assured copyright protection than an unregistered film whose copyright claim rested primarily in its on-screen credits, but many adult filmmakers only took the latter route to protect their work. Without firm copyright assurances from the government, therefore, the debatable rights to adult films have frequently been tracked through chain of title, with multiple owners and distributors often making claims upon the same film over the years.

Historian Casey Scott, who has extensively researched the provenance of adult films at the U.S. Copyright Office, observes that, contrary to popular belief, most 1970s adult films are not actually in the public domain today. Yet, chain of title over multiple decades is often so convoluted to establish that many companies presume that public domain applies, not doing due diligence in documenting their efforts to track down current rights owners. Complicating matters is the fact that some companies continue to hold original contracts for theatrical distribution rights to a given film while others own the contracts for home video distribution—but when these contracts have expired over the years, each side can make spurious claims to home video rights as a result.[25]

In the late 1980s, for example, Arrow Film and Video (originally run by the Peraino crime family) sued a minor distributor who claimed that *Deep Throat* (1972) was never copyrighted and had thus passed into the public domain. Although Arrow threatened litigation until the smaller distributor conceded, the former could not actually provide positive proof of copyright.[26] Such issues would reemerge in 2009, when Arrow sued VCX for distributing *Deep Throat*, while VCX countersued over Arrow's distribution of *Debbie Does Dallas* (1978). With neither party able to definitively prove the copyright provenance of either "classic" film, Arrow and VCX finally agreed that both companies would retain the full rights to one movie each.[27]

Since the years prior to 1978 constitute much of the era of so-called "vintage" pornography, many vintage adult films (especially hard-core ones) now exist in a state of legal limbo, which has made some archives more hesitant to include them in their holdings. Although archives are legally allowed to collect prints without first obtaining copyright permission from rights holders, any public exhibition still requires copyright clearance—so even when obscure films exist in archives, they generally remain for internal use only—and even those nonprofit archives that have preserved a film at great expense are unlikely to acquire copyright control over the results of their preservational handiwork.[28]

This is a considerably different state of affairs than films made by major studios, since the major studios' libraries contain vast copyright holdings that are key to their annual corporate cash flows, whereas independent companies lacking such accumulated capital have had to historically proceed in a more piecemeal manner with the production and circulation of each title.[29] Since the 1988 passage of the National Film Preservation Act, the US government has regarded profit-making entities as responsible for preserving their own product, whereas public monies are instead reserved for the preservation of orphan films lacking clear copyright protection. As Karen Gracy notes, however, whether commercial films are considered "orphaned" is still left largely to the whims of original copyright owners, who may not immediately reassert their rights or may refrain from doing so until residual market demand for an older title materializes (as a result of preservation or video distribution efforts, for example). With its overwhelming focus on the nontheatrical and/or noncommercial, the concept of "orphan films" thus downplays the many copyrighted films that rights owners may nevertheless see as not profitable enough to preserve—a category that Gracy terms "films in stasis."[30]

Although the 2005 Preservation of Orphan Works Act extended legal protections to libraries and archives, allowing them to more easily preserve and make orphan films available for scholarly and educational purposes, commercially made adult films' disrepute has dissuaded many archives and libraries from either collecting or at least cataloging them for such uses. Whereas a handful of film archives have major institutional funding (especially if affiliated with a research university), many other archives already face difficulties gaining funding to preserve more innocuous forms of orphan films (such as industrial, educational, and home movies), so pornographic films face far more challenges in justifying to funding sources their very need for preservation. Furthermore, since films are often considered culturally "lower" objects than other types of art, largely due to their dominant associations with commercialism, film archives may attempt to defend their own value as cultural institutions by deliberately neglecting films from culturally suspect genres like pornography in the first place.[31]

There are notable exceptions, however, particularly in the case of those few specialist archives devoted to collecting and providing access to historical materials about sexuality, such as the Kinsey Institute for Research in Sex, Gender, and Reproduction at Indiana University, Bloomington. A research institute affiliated with the university, its archives remain under the legal guardianship of a nonprofit corporation independent from the university itself, which has allowed the Institute to continue operating in a largely conservative geographical region since 1947. In addition to being the source of many research materials examined for this book, the Kinsey Institute was also the source of my own modest involvement with an effort to conserve a number of 35-mm adult and exploitation films—including at least one formerly "lost" sexploitation film found amid an incoming collection of anonymously donated prints. Unlike my *"Lust of the Eyes"* fabrication above, the following case study is wholly true, and it represents a notable example of archival practices devoted to otherwise orphaned adult films. Although every archive is different and generalizations based on limited examples can only be considered provisional, the Kinsey Institute's status as one of the few nonprofit archives to actively collect a large number of adult films as part of its specialist mission sets it apart as a particularly relevant case.

While writing my doctoral dissertation on exploitation cinema at Indiana University in 2011–2012, I was invited to assist with the accession of approximately 1,200 35-mm film prints donated to the Kinsey Institute, which were temporarily housed in a university warehouse for sorting, en route to stable storage at an auxiliary library facility that also houses the Indiana University Libraries Film Archive. Along with several other scholars who work on exploitation and adult films, I was asked to select several dozen significant titles from the shipping manifest, which would then be prioritized for later cataloguing and patron access—although the criteria for my selections would be left to my own judgment. Old shipping labels on the heavy metal shipping containers testified to a network of grind houses across the United States where these films, mostly produced during the 1970s–1980s, regularly played. Upon opening these containers for inspection of contents and testing for acetate film decay ("vinegar syndrome"), one could find old newspapers inserted to prevent the reels from shifting during transit, flyers promoting certain people for leadership in the projectionists' union, and projectionists' scrawled observations about a print's physical deterioration ("Bad film") or visceral impact ("Shot my load to reel 3"). Not surprisingly, the collection itself contained films from many of the major distribution companies who provided grind houses with a steady stream of sensationalized cinema, including Aquarius Releasing, Howard Mahler Films, Monarch Releasing Corporation, Silverstein Films, plus hard-core-centric distributors like Big Apple Releasing, Leisure Time Booking, and New York Releasing. Generically, films in the collection ran the gamut from art films and independent dramas to action, horror, sexploitation, martial arts, and hard-core porn features. Most titles had already been released on home video in some format, although several had not—making them prime candidates for selection. In addition to questions of historical significance and existing availability, my experience as an exploitation film fan also factored in potential "entertainment value"—a criterion that even nonprofit archives often assess as a means of boosting "positive attention" for themselves[32]—knowing that some of the selected titles might eventually be publicly screened at the Indiana University Cinema.

Due to the Kinsey Institute's donor confidentiality policies, the original provenance of this print collection could not be disclosed, but it was clear from the grimy, rusted, and beaten-up condition of the shipping containers that the films had not been used for many years. Further obscuring matters, the piles of shipping containers were seldom matched, turning the hunt for "complete" prints of a given title into a giant matching game—and also a physically demanding process, providing a powerfully embodied experience very different from that of watching the films themselves. Much as I suggested in the previous chapter that owning and protecting ephemeral documents offers markedly different pleasures than simply gleaning data from a clean digital scan, Carolyn Steedman writes of the dust that historians encounter when working with archival materials—in this particular case, many hours spent lugging around fifty-pound film cans, leaving my back aching and my hands covered with a thick layer of black grime—and how that sensory encounter of the researcher physically *"having been there"* is a key source of his/her authority to tell an artifact's story.[33] To wit, this search also uncovered many surprising titles that had not been accounted for on the original shipping manifest, meaning that we would have to record their unexpected presence.

Archivist Sean Smalley (who also worked with me on the print accession) observes that primarily film-centered archives are inclined to preserve not only a wide range of film prints, but also paper material, photos, and other related ephemera. Special collection archives that do not specialize in film, however, are typically devoted to collecting a certain type of content (such as the Kinsey Institute's focus on sex, gender, and reproduction), usually have fewer staff and resources, and thus treat film prints as just one of many possible priorities for cataloguing and preservation.[34] Describing more logistical difficulties that film archives often face, Janna Jones notes that shortage of personnel and storage space means that large donations are often backlogged for extended periods while awaiting cataloguing, especially if gifted to avoid prohibitive storage costs elsewhere. These backlogged materials can suggest archival wealth and abundance, but also excess and the potential for loss—especially in the case of independently produced films about which less contextual information is available for even "low-level cataloguing" purposes. That is, a given film may be physically saved within an archive, but its presence can remain otherwise "invisible" until historians (who typically have more inclination to investigate individual films than archivists themselves do) come along to speak for the film.[35] Moreover, we might emphasize that these archive-dependent people often *feel* for particular films as well, since, like pornography itself, the archive "suggests a fundamental fantasy vision of the world in which every desire—documentary, historiographic, or sexual—can be satisfied."[36]

Such was the case with one unaccounted-for film stumbled across while sorting this collection: *The Orgy at Lil's Place* (1963), an early, highly profitable sexploitation feature produced by distributor William Mishkin, whose offices were based amid the grind houses of New York's 42nd Street. Having distributed a mix of exploitation and B-grade genre films through his eponymous company since the 1950s, Mishkin moved into low-budget production as the writer/producer of *Violated* (1953), a thriller about a sex killer, and would later produce many of Andy Milligan's horror and sexploitation films—several of which we also found in the same Kinsey Institute collection. Following market trends, Mishkin distributed nudie cuties, roughies, white coaters, horror films, and various imported pictures[37] until handing the company over to his son Lewis in the late 1970s. *The Orgy at Lil's Place*, however, was one of his most profitable hits and one of the earliest roughies made in New York, premiering the same year as the other first extant roughie, *Scum of the Earth* (1963), and before films like *White Slaves of Chinatown* (1964) and the still-lost *Body of a Female* (1964). According to a full-page *Variety* ad in January 1964, the film broke records at prerelease engagements, and would go into general release on March 28 of that year. "The film can be advertised with emphasis on either 'The Orgy' or emphasis on 'At Lil's Place,'" the ad continues, suggesting ways to downplay the provocative title in different locales, despite the film itself being "passed without any cuts whatsoever by the Censor Board of the State of New York" due to "the good taste of its presentation."[38] Indeed, Mishkin successfully submitted the film for an R rating in 1972, suggesting its relatively mild content ("Total nudity: a few female bare backs, a brief shot of a man's behind") and long shelf life.[39] As the sexploitation fanzine *ARTISEX* declared in its negative review (a score of 35 out of 100) of the film, "If you think you are going to see an orgy, forget it. This release predates the relaxation of censorship in New York, where it appears to have been made, and the short orgy sequence 'at Lil's Place' could now be shown on TV."[40] Nevertheless, the film posted significant box-office returns through the late 1960s—totaling over $300,000 in gross profits on an initial $35,000 investment—and was still advertised among Mishkin's available product into the late 1970s.[41] Small wonder, then, that *Orgy* was rediscovered on a wooden shipping pallet with a handful of other Mishkin-distributed films, though none dating nearly as far back.

Produced and directed by Jerald Intrator (under his frequent pseudonym "J. Nehemiah"), who had previously made the burlesque film *Striporama* (1953) and the noirish sexploitation picture *Satan in High Heels* (1962), *Orgy* was long considered a lost film, its modular attractions only discernable from lurid clues (Figure 3.3) on surviving posters ("SEE Beautiful Girls Wrestling! SEE The Attempted Assault! SEE The 'ART' Class! SEE The Whipping Scene," etc.). Mishkin allegedly "saw no further commercial potential in his earlier films and, tired of paying storage fees, destroyed all prints and negatives" in the 1970s.[42] (The film's title card claims Mishkin himself as the copyright holder.) While the unknown provenance of the Kinsey Institute-owned *Orgy* print[43] prevents us from ascertaining how it survived prior to its donation—though we might speculate that it was once held by one of Mishkin's various subdistributors—its hazy path to preservation has nevertheless received wider attention than most rediscovered adult films, since the print came to the attention of the conveners of

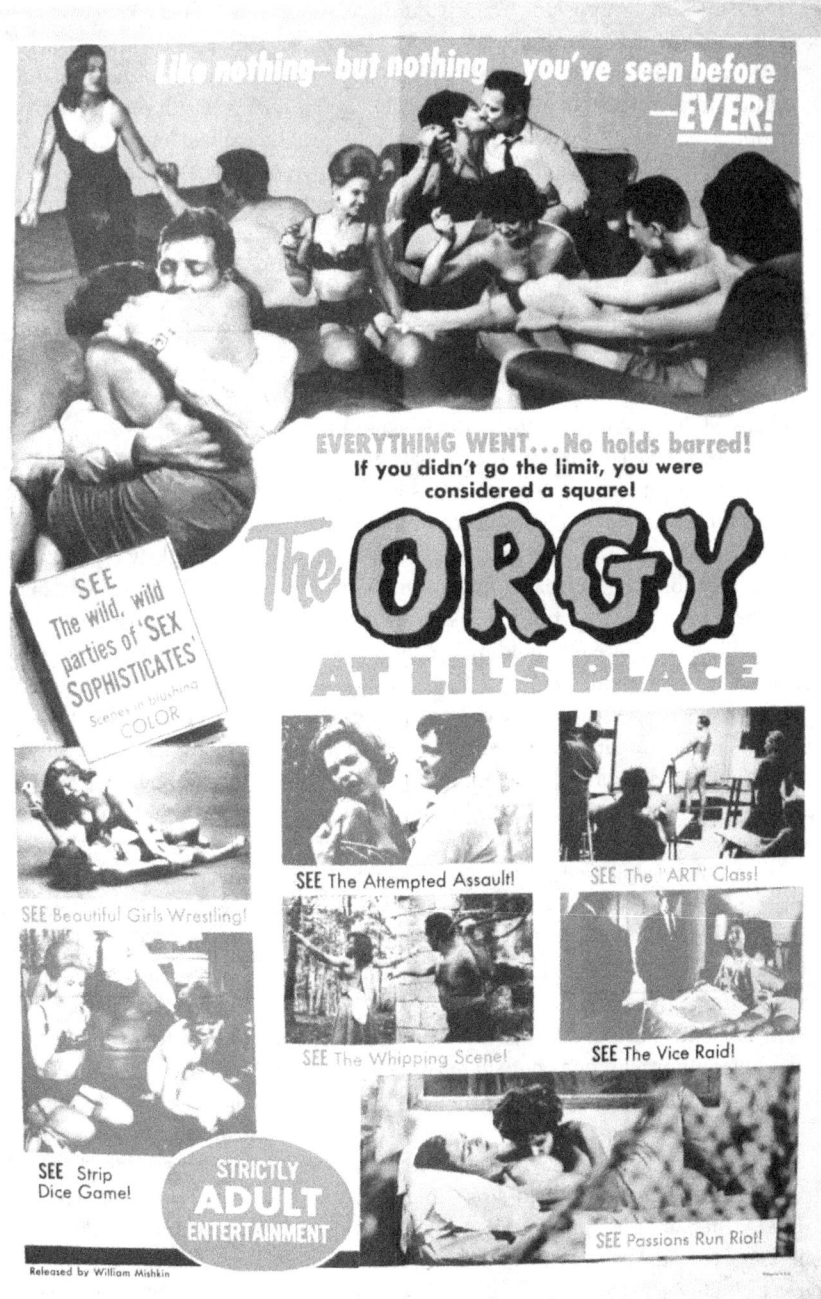

Figure 3.3 Theatrical poster for *The Orgy at Lil's Place* (1963), one of the few extant clues to the film's contents prior to its latter-day rediscovery and preservation.

the Orphan Film Symposium, then planning a summit at Indiana University with participation by the Kinsey Institute.

The orphan film movement is, after all, as deeply dependent upon the prerequisite of cultural forgetting as its own heroically self-aggrandizing acts of preservation and remembrance. Like the vintage porn aficionado, the so-called "orphanista" shares a fetishization of loss, dilapidation, and decay as preconditions for the pleasures of rediscovering such otherwise pathetic artifacts and their paratexts—pleasures that cannot be confined to intellectual pursuits alone.[44] Although the orphan film movement does not often focus its attention on adult films, it is nevertheless undergirded by similar impulses to not just investigate but also bring niche-interest films back to the screen for its cultish cadre of historically minded viewers. A 2K digital scan of the 35-mm print was subsequently produced by Mike Mashon at the Library of Congress, and the resulting Digital Cinema Package, introduced by Eric Schaefer, was screened at "Orphans Midwest: Materiality and the Moving Image" (September 26–28, 2013) and later made available for Kinsey Institute patrons. "If a film was not publicly recognized as significant before its preservation," says Janna Jones, "it is likely that it will be after its preservation, due in part to its increased exposure."[45] However, the Kinsey Institute's noncirculation policies dictate that the 35-mm print of *Orgy* will likely remain under lock and key for the foreseeable future, while a video copy will only be available to researchers by appointment in the Institute's reading room. As is the case with many other archives with rare film holdings, rediscovery of a given text does not necessarily mean that access becomes widely available, which—unlike more common paratextual artifacts or even remediated video objects belonging to one's own personal collection—impacts its ability to affectively stimulate the beholder through fantasies of individual ownership or possession.[46] The film may now be known to still exist, but it nevertheless remains "out there" in a closed archive, beyond the appropriative grasp of individual fan–collectors.

Carried by the voice-over narration of its main protagonist, *The Orgy at Lil's Place* depicts aspiring actor Ann Carson's (Kari Knudsen) wide-eyed journey from small-town America to live with her sister Sally (June Ashley) in New York City. Like Sally's job posing nude at her boyfriend Bob's (John Lyon) art classes, Ann has difficulty finding work in the big city, so she becomes a cheesecake model to pay the bills. Meanwhile, she starts a relationship with Bob's best friend Charlie (Bob Curtis), a struggling author who does not share Ann's desire to settle down and start a family. An unscrupulous agent eventually invites Ann to the titular gathering (as Ann later clarifies, "It wasn't a party—it was a full-scale orgy!") at sophisticated socialite Lil Duncan's (Terry Powers) apartment. After the agent forces herself on Ann, who drunkenly imagines herself kissing Charlie (since she "didn't want to act like a square"), she flees this "pit of human forms, mauling and squirming," and returns to Sally's apartment. After Bob receives a large commission for his paintings, he and Sally agree to finally get married, and the following day, Charlie (his book now accepted) proposes to Ann as well, apparently past his hesitance to put down roots. As soon as he proposes, Ann begins flashing back (in a seven-minute Eastmancolor sequence) to preceding scenes from her urban travails, and quickly consents. "It was Charlie who would make fantasy come true," she says over a remembered image of herself posing in a bridal gown during a modeling session. Unlike many later roughies, neither sister is narratively "punished" for her sexual forays, but both sacrifice their independence to marriage once their boyfriends become stable providers.

Like the same year's *Scum of the Earth* (also about a young woman drawn into nude modeling), *Orgy* is exceedingly tame, tentatively posed as a transitional film between the happy-go-lucky nudie cuties and the darker, more narrative-driven roughies. Unlike the foreboding and jazzy library tracks recurrently used on the soundtracks of later New York roughies/kinkies, Intrator uses chirpy, upbeat production music throughout, reinforcing a benign travelogue quality in the many scenes of Ann being shown the city's landmarks and new buildings. Glimpses of female nudity are fleeting and indirect, often framed through a morally unassuming context. When Sally poses nude for Bob's paintings (Figure 3.4), for example, Ann's narration reminds us that he is a serious artist honing his craft (not just a leering pervert) within their healthy heterosexual relationship, since nothing "improper" occurs during such sessions. When Sally and Bob later have sex, it is only after they have just agreed to get married, and the camera predictably pans away to a melting candle, creating a temporal elision

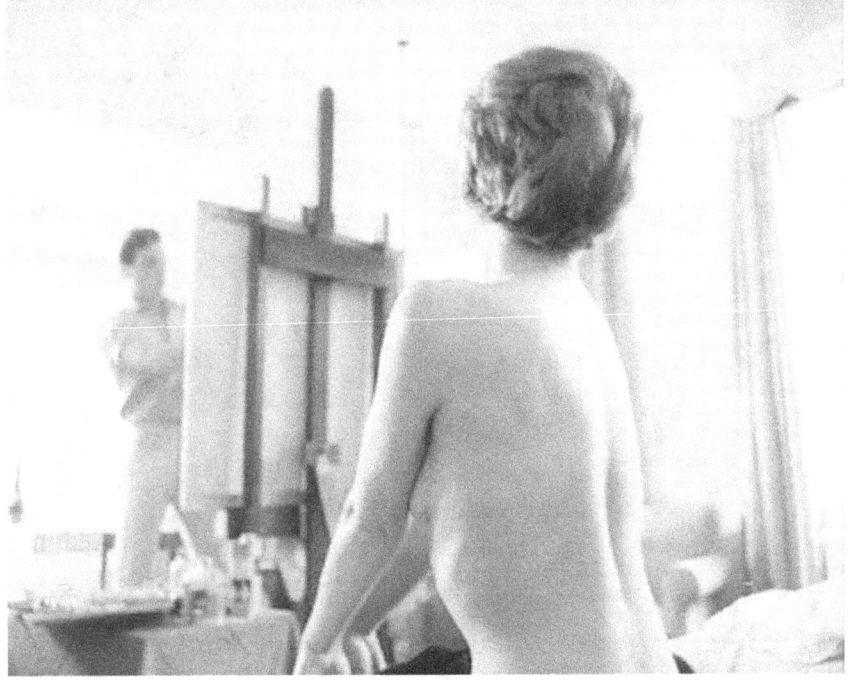

Figure 3.4 Brief flashes of nudity—but nothing "improper"—as Sally poses for future husband Bob's paintings in *The Orgy at Lil's Place*. Courtesy of The Kinsey Institute for Research in Sex, Gender, and Reproduction.

that removes the scene of coupling altogether. Even when the Eastmancolor sequence finally appears, the affective impact that a sudden switch to color might have during more sexualized scenes is muted by the fact that we only see a montage of earlier moments. Likewise, the most lurid scenes teased on the film's poster ("Beautiful girls wrestling," "the attempted assault," "the whipping scene," and "the vice raid") all involve Ann acting out staged scenarios for a photographer. For instance, she is hired to shoot photos illustrating scenes from a paperback pulp novel about suburban wife-swapping and reiterates to us that she and the other models were "treated with respect" during the shoot. When she is shown being bound and whipped by a bare-chested man—a scene foreshadowing later kinkies—she explains how the supposed scourges on her back were just lipstick streaks (Figure 3.5).

By thus diegetically foregrounding the very process by which *Orgy*'s own misleadingly vivid publicity materials were created, the film consistently undercuts its own illusionism in an effort to defensively defuse its erotic potential. Similar plotlines would be taken up in later New York sexploitation films like *The Sexploiters* (1965), *One Naked Night* (1965), and *Rent-a-Girl* (1965), but would tend toward more corrupt

Figure 3.5 Holding a makeup kit, the photographer applies lipstick "scourges" to Ann's bare back while chatting with her supposed tormentor during a break in the photo session. From *The Orgy at Lil's Place*; courtesy of The Kinsey Institute for Research in Sex, Gender, and Reproduction.

and perverse characterizations of models' employers. As a gentle precursor to the more explicit texts that followed, watching the film today does confirm its long-rumored historical value as a groundbreaking roughie, even if it may more closely resemble a staid urban travelogue than a tantalizing descent into depravity. Of course, the considerable disjuncture between an actual film and the lurid promises in its publicity materials is endemic to exploitation cinema in general, but this disjuncture between the prospective affect generated by publicity and the far less stimulating experience of seeing the film itself is all the more striking when the temporal gap teasing these coming attractions lasts *decades* instead of weeks or months.

In my estimation, *Orgy* has had far more affective potential as a "lost" text than a found one, since its prior afterlife as nothing more than a surviving poster arguably had greater power to stir latter-day sexploitation aficionados' imaginations in the absence of any "countervailing textuality on offer from the film ... itself to challenge the paratextual frames" of meaning.[47] Up until its recent rediscovery, then, fans and historians have been in little better position to gauge *Orgy*'s erotic/historical potential to thrill than the film's original intended audience, retroactively spurring corporeal feelings of anticipation over what the film might contain if found. In this sense, it was precisely the *loss of access* to any extant prints of *Orgy* that had previously allowed contemporary fans to pleasurably place themselves in the speculative mind-set of the film's original, paratext-primed, previewing audience, whereas the recovered film itself reveals those paratextual teases to be as phony and erotically underwhelming as the truth behind Ann's staged paperback photos.

This potential for disappointment might beg the question of why we should worry about rediscovering these obscure films in the first place if their original power to tease is better replicated by letting them remain unfound. I would argue, however, that the alluring pathos of historical loss that undergirds so much vintage porn consumption must uneasily coexist with the historical and economic benefits of rediscovery. One's imagination alone benefits from these films remaining lost, whereas archives and video distributors have a more vested stake—whether that be cultural or economic capital or both—in bringing them back to light. As adult cinema's underlying dialectic between the seen and the unseen is resurrected in the form of archival discoveries and omissions, the affective value of the tease may have to be sacrificed for the historical value of better understanding how generic pioneers like *The Orgy at Lil's Place* contribute to our broader understanding of adult film history. As a nexus point for the imaginative potential of what remains fascinatingly out of grasp vs. what is rendered routinely accessible, the archive's own mediating role between historical fantasy and reality can thereby mediate between the culturally neglected/misplaced text's ability to both heighten and threaten the fan/historian's affective thrill in attempting to encounter an inherently unknowable past. Since the affectivity of watching a given film will depend on the individual viewer him/herself, we cannot simply predict that the film's status as either a lost or found body will correspond with more or less affective potential for the present-day beholder, but it remains important to understand that the forces of cultural forgetting (however partial they may invariably be) can be as productive of erotic/archival thrills as the practicalities of cultural remembrance.

Thus, returning to the question of the archive as a site of both imagined plentitude and potential loss, Giovanna Fossati notes that, due to copyright restrictions and other legal concerns, most archives do not offer online catalogues of their complete holdings, which can prevent certain archival films from being known about or seen.[48] Moreover, such cataloguing omissions have traditionally been endemic when pornography is concerned, as Jennifer Burns Bright and Ronan Crowley have described in their history of pornography's shifting visibility in libraries.[49] In fact, my very discussion of working with the Kinsey Institute's donated collection is restricted to only mentioning titles that have been formally catalogued in the Indiana University Library Catalog, which means excluding specific mention of most titles in the donated collection (even if otherwise widely available on home video) and focusing only on those deemed of higher priority for preservation. Ironically, as one of the scholars invited to draw such distinctions in the first place, I consequently set unintended boundaries for my own research.

Several adult film historians have noted the Kinsey Institute's zealous—some would say paranoid—degree of control over its collection of vintage pornography (for which, again, it does not own the copyright—if one ever existed—only the artifacts themselves), including legal threats against scholars publishing images from the archive's gay erotic photography and the archive's own reticence to release an academically curated compilation DVD of stag films—all allegedly due to fears over potential legal liability in the unlikely event that a descendent come across some indiscrete photos of his/her progenitors.[50] Indeed, the cynic might argue that such restrictions over its closed stacks (as opposed to an *open archive* where researchers can freely browse materials) contradict the Institute's stated mission of "providing ... scholars from a wide variety of fields access to Institute collections" and "creating and disseminating knowledge and understanding"[51]—effectively reenacting in a new guise the "secret museum" only open to learned scholars. For my purposes, however, it remains enough to say that the same archival confidentiality rules preventing me from ascertaining more knowledge about the provenance of the Kinsey Institute's collection inadvertently reproduce the tantalizing tension between concealment and revelation that is so vital to the continuing allure of vintage pornography. As much as the Kinsey Institute may paint itself as a neutral repository for whatever sexually explicit materials are donated, its own collection policies aid in reactivating the affectively stimulating tease of those very materials by virtue of tightly controlling access to knowledge that might be gained from material encounters with its holdings. David Squires, for instance, suggests that any archive's access policies and taxonomic logic might outwardly seem antithetical to pornography's affective appeal, forming a "dead" space compared to the "liveness" of the sex circulating outside its walls, but the archive's inevitable status as a place of openness, disorder, and unpredictability can allow pornographic materials to retain their affectivity during the archival encounter.[52]

Had these films remained in their backlogged state, the print of *Orgy* would not have been found so soon, much as my chance encounter with the previously unacknowledged print allowed the film to eventually be brought to renewed (albeit limited) public attention instead of slipping back into the proverbial pile to be passed over as just another undocumented title. We might say, then, that the forces of cultural forgetting that have long been the bane of an accurate adult film historiography can sometimes come perilously close to the mode of *passive* cultural remembrance exemplified by the archive. It was, after all, a winnowing of the archive's backlog—a process that, in less judicious hands than the Kinsey Institute's, might have resulted in the casual destruction of unwanted or low-priority prints—that led to the rediscovery of *Orgy* at all. Furthermore, without the occasion of the approaching Orphans Midwest event, it is unclear whether the Kinsey Institute, which lacks the funding for an ongoing film preservation program or a dedicated film archivist,[53] would have made *Orgy* a priority for digitization, in which case the 35-mm print would have still been physically saved in stasis but likely remained unavailable to researchers—and therefore effectively been little better than simply remaining "lost." The present-day film archive "is in a constant state of unfinishedness," Janna Jones reminds us. "Its relentless destabilization, incomplete films, always decaying matter, filmic materials stacked to roof tops, and partial (at best) documentation" underline the contingencies and discontinuities of history itself, the unstable meanings that cultural objects garner when they move into such inherently fluctuating spaces.[54] Had whatever anonymous donor to the Kinsey Institute been as thorough as Mishkin himself—even if said donor may well have had similar motivations for dispossessing such a large number of prints (e.g., a lack of capitalization, making storage fees unjustifiable)—we might never have found a surviving copy of an extremely rare film, but by the same token, it was the very disposing of such an excessive body of prints that allowed a hidden gem to be eventually unearthed.

As Steedman suggests, an archive may be a bounded physical place where things are stored, but through the cultural work of historians, it can become "one of the few realms of the modern imagination where a hard-won and carefully constructed place, can return to [the] boundless, limitless space," where imagination and memory intersect in the telling of historical narratives.[55] In this particular case, a series of archival contingencies allowed a print of *The Orgy at Lil's Place* to be discovered and added back into its significant place in the historical narrative of 1960s sexploitation cinema—and yet, although I proudly thought I had found the only extant version of the film, I was later informed by Eric Schaefer that a Dutch film archive (EYE) already had a subtitled 35-mm print in its nonpublic holdings.[56] And in late 2014, another 35-mm print of *Orgy* was discovered in a mislabeled film can at the American Genre Film Archive in Austin, Texas. Thus, even the supposedly "lost" film wasn't as lost as I had originally thought, calling into question my own fannishly egotistical fantasies of rediscovery and shepherdship (a common symptom within the archival community)—though the print's digital preservation by the Kinsey Institute and Library of Congress was no less important in the end. After all, as Jacqueline Stewart suggests, the common rhetorical slippage between assertions of a rediscovered print's material rarity and its publicly promoted value as a cultural "treasure" may be undercut by the lesser-known existence of other extant prints—and yet, multiple prints, each bearing traces of a given text's circulation histories (e.g., international distribution and translation), are likely to yield far more significant historiographical information than a lone surviving rarity.[57]

In the case of orphaned/lost films that are found, the passage from planned obsolescence to disappearance to rediscovery is a common narrative that can confer value upon the conservators themselves,[58] but not one that always teleologically leads from forgetting/obscurity/openness to remembrance/accessibility/closure in actual practice. Even as the process of rediscovery may seem to "defeat history" by retrospectively rewriting the past, archival demands are as likely to undercut such triumphalist narratives as to undercut one's perceived sense of subcultural capital as a rare text's benefactor, thereby potentially restoring an eroticized longing for the historiographically obscure film as an ungraspable body. As the rest of this chapter will elaborate through the example of for-profit enterprises, even when barriers to archival access are less onerous, such unreliable narratives about gaining mastery over history can also affect the wider community of home video collectors whose fan identities may resonate with the very historical openness of vintage pornography's loss-infused corpus.

The "Silver Age of Porn" and the rise of "classics" on home video

In the opening credits of the aptly titled 1965 film *The Sexploiters*, the main cast members are divided into two columns—"The Buyers" and "The Sellers"—reflecting their characters' respective relationships to erotic labor within the narrative. In like manner, we can think of adult films themselves as bodies made available for sale within particular markets when private companies and even individual collectors may have far more expansive holdings than most nonprofit archives. Since the 1970s, the private sector has been held increasingly responsible for archiving and preserving 35-mm print elements, which ironically privileged celluloid at a time when other delivery media, such as home video, became fresh sources of revenue for past films.[59] Indeed, the responsibility for preserving and providing access to adult films has more often fallen to for-profit enterprises due to the reluctance of most nonprofit archives to engage with them. This is, however, a mixed blessing, as Schaefer observes, since these companies do open ready forms of access to many otherwise obscure films, but the resulting videos may sometimes be recut, re-titled, or transferred from qualitatively inferior elements—to say nothing of the films' future provenance if these companies were to go bankrupt.[60] In this section, I will explore these issues through a brief history of the adult video industry's consolidation and its attempts to remediate film-born adult movies as "classics," despite the industrial and legal constraints upon its desired recovery of increasingly outdated cinematic bodies.

In terms of historiographic accounting and assessment, hard-core adult films have generally fared even worse than sexploitation features. Again, aesthetic and political valuations play an obvious role here, but the semi-licit nature of the hard-core market has also left it more prone to the piracy of prints (and later, videotapes) throughout its commercial history. Without simply conflating the two time periods, we might draw useful comparisons between the emergence of a legal hard-core market and the early days of cinema in general. As Jane Gaines observes, unauthorized copying—whether through piracy or the wholesale imitation of others' ideas—was rampant in the years before approximately 1909, allowing film producers and distributors to quickly and economically compete with each other in the absence of more formalized corporate strategies for seeking remuneration over copyright infringement. Rather than viewing such derivative practices as symptoms of creative bankruptcy, Gaines suggests we might instead view them as highly productive means of satisfying increased market demand and retaliating against competitors during the nascent industry's "outlaw" period. And yet, because duplicates of competitors' films filled distributors' catalogues, it has become far more difficult to historiographically account for an "original" version of a given film.[61]

In my estimation, a similar state of market chaos and rampant duplication reigned when hard-core pornography emerged as a widespread legal entertainment in high demand after approximately 1970. Exhibitors, subdistributors, and film-processing labs were all possible culprits, since even temporary possession of a release print meant that a duplicate could be quickly struck and diverted to one's own informal entrepreneurial purposes. Furthermore, because they sought to avoid a paper trail that might later legally incriminate them, hard-core distributors were more likely to sell release prints outright to exhibitors than to rent prints out, as sexploitation distributors typically did. Because already dealing in legally questionable material, most producers and distributors had little recourse to seek indictments or remuneration for piracy through official legal channels. In the years when organized crime funded much of pornography's so-called "Golden Age," threats or violence might be used to punish known pirates, but such actions were generally not pursued in a systematic way. Indeed, in his indispensable history of the adult video industry, Peter Alilunas argues that the threat of economic competition from pirates (such as those selling film-to-video transfers of hard-core porn to sex-oriented adult motels) actually spurred porn producers to officially release their films on home video in the early 1970s, long before the rise of the 1980s video rental market.[62]

Yet, this situation later became all the more common once an expanding home video market allowed material to be surreptitiously copied by telecine operators, wholesale tape duplicators, retailers, and video rental stores—although some producers might also simply sign contracts with multiple video distributors at once, hoping that short-term profits would outweigh the possible costs of any future litigation. (There were notable exceptions, however, such as celebrated adult filmmaker Cecil Howard, who has zealously protected the rights to his high-gloss hard-core films like *Neon Nights* [1981] and *Firestorm* [1984], largely by only releasing them through his own distribution company, Command Video.) The word "dupe" became only too appropriate as low-quality duplicates of duplicates proliferated, with little attention paid to sourcing better-quality transfers from fresh print elements or early-generation video masters. Early hard-core video distributors' catalogues were rife with competitors' titles and only the larger and more "connected" companies could afford trying to staunch the widespread duplication.[63] As the back cover (Figure 3.6) of a 1979 TVX sales catalogue states,

THE FINEST QUALITY ADULT FILM VIDEO CASSETTES

FEATURES Because of their immense popularity, TVX tapes are pirated. Why buy from these bootleggers? Why get ripped off by fly-by-night pirates who sell you 3rd, 4th and 5th generation copies of TVX tapes?

Deal only with authorized dealers and/or distributors, or direct with Cinema Video Sales. Only Cinema Video Sales is licensed to produce TVX titles. Anyone telling you otherwise is directly subject to legal action. Dealers ... you are equally liable under the law if you retail TVX titles obtained from any source but Cinema Video and/or licensed Cinema Video distributors. If in doubt, call us.

THE BEST OF X ON TVX

New Releases for 1979 · Exclusive

**FIONA ON FIRE • SWEET SAVAGE
SENSUAL ENCOUNTERS OF EVERY KIND
EXPENSIVE TASTE • CHOPSTIX**

TVX Distributors Division of

1643 N. CHEROKEE AVE., HOLLYWOOD, CA 90028 (213) 462-6018
From outside California call toll free 1-(800) 421-4133

X-RATED MOTION PICTURES ON VIDEO TAPE The *largest* and *finest* assortment of x-rated films licensed exclusively by TVX for the home.

Figure 3.6 Back cover of TVX [now defunct] sales catalogue from 1979, warning videotape dealers to avoid buying or selling bootlegs of TVX-licensed films (collection of Peter Alilunas).

Because of their immense popularity, TVX tapes are pirated. Why buy from these bootleggers? Why get ripped off by fly-by-night pirates who sell you 3rd, 4th and 5th generation copies of TVX tapes? [...] Dealers ... you are equally liable under the law if you retail TVX titles obtained from any source but Cinema Video and/ or licensed Cinema Video distributors. If in doubt, call us.[64]

Like nonprofit archives such as the Kinsey Institute, then, early video companies may have acquired copies of many films to which they had no formal ownership or distribution rights—but unlike reputable archives, these companies had few qualms about attempting to profit off their surreptitiously acquired libraries.

Beyond the outright selling of prints and, later, video cassettes, hard-core producers' own practices of compiling and recycling existing material exacerbated their piracy problems. As Roberta Findlay recalls, directors might shoot two or three films simultaneously, using the same assembled actors and locations but different scripts—which actors might resent when they realized they were only being paid for work on one film.[65] In creating slipshod, modular texts to begin with, hard-core narrative features could thus be easily fragmented and reassembled by many different parties, with or without permission. Whereas unscrupulous minor distributors might simply place a new title or box on a preexisting film and sell it as a new product, it was already common for older loops, outtakes, and other material to be endlessly recycled by a film's original producers and distributors for as long as market demand would bear. Once actors signed a model release form for their per diem performances, they had no say over how their images could be exploited in future releases, since the payment of residuals would not only be impractical for all parties involved but would also contribute to an incriminating paper trail between filmmakers and performers who, until the late 1980s, were considered the legal equivalent of pimps and prostitutes, respectively.[66]

These circulation practices have, of course, continued to some extent to this day, even as the production and distribution of hard core pornography has developed into a more "legitimate" corporate operation. Compilation videos are now far more common releases than narrative features, whereas the legion of "pirates" may now include uploaders to torrent and tube websites who informally compile and recirculate hard-core material less for profit than for the pleasures of access (see Chapter 4). As such, while the hard-core industry has moved toward aboveground corporatization since the late 1980s and has since increasingly asserted copyright control over its (more recent) holdings, strong echoes of the industry's older shadow economies continue to linger. As Ramon Lobato observes, films circulated through informal distribution practices, such as piracy, are more likely to exhibit textual additions and subtractions that fragment the idea of a single, stable text—whether those be visible signs of material degradation and unauthorized duplication or the fragmentation and recombination of constituent parts.[67]

On the one hand, then, piracy has long spread "illegitimate" copies of adult films far and wide, which would seem to increase their continuing accessibility—and yet, the history of adult video also shows distributors gradually reasserting proprietary control over their films, variously recutting, withdrawing, and reissuing specific titles as the wildly uncontrolled early days of home video eventually gave way to corporate consolidation and a re-staking of legal ownership over these unstable texts. In the case of vintage pornography, these qualities can be especially seen in the remediation of film-born texts onto home video platforms, since increased demand for access to past films does not mean that these texts have always reappeared in historically stable forms; due to the vagaries of their production and distribution histories, fragmented, degraded, and inferior iterations are as likely to resurface on home video as complete, pristine versions of a given text. Much as performers themselves sacrificed the residual value of their labor when making these films, there is a distinct instability to the residual value of older adult films when they have garnered renewed demand for their "vintage" pastness but still exhibit destructive traces of their long and sometimes unauthorized histories of circulation.

As numerous historians have observed, pornography was a key driver of home video's widespread adoption during the early to mid-1980s, since video allowed sexually explicit material to be more easily consumed in private homes instead of the public movie theaters that were increasingly subject to harsh zoning restrictions against adults-only businesses. As I remarked at the end of the previous chapter, home video technologies had already been promoted to adult film aficionados in publications like *Adam Film World* since the mid-1970s. The privacy and convenience of home consumption remained video's chief virtues for many viewers, as indicated by the early success of prerecorded videos that "viewers would probably want to watch either privately (pornography) or repeatedly (workout routines)."[68] Along with children's videos, early best-selling VHS cassettes were typically associated with activities occurring within the domestic sphere (e.g., childrearing, exercise, and sex) and were thus segregated into marginal spaces within rental stores (such as back rooms or alcoves), reserving store space for the theatrical genres that better reflected the VCR's changing cultural role: from its initial function as a technology for time-shifting TV broadcasts to its later reputation as a dedicated player of prerecorded movies on video. In 1982, Paul Fishbein and I. L. Slifkin, employees of Philadelphia-based home video distributor Movies Unlimited, began publishing *Adult Video News* (*AVN*) as a newsletter offering recommendations for adult video retailers and customers. Growing into an ever-expanding magazine, *AVN* soon became the adult video industry's most respected trade publication and remains an invaluable resource for primary information about the industry's travails from the early 1980s to today.[69]

In 1980, the lowest priced adult videotapes included pirated feature films and legitimately released compilations of old 8- and 16-mm loops. Caballero Control Corporation, for instance, began repackaging small-gauge sound loops as their *Swedish Erotica* and *Collection Series* video lines, which sold for $20–30 per tape. Remarking on the low quality of many loops, *AVN* described these tapes as not only appealing because they offered an inexpensive means to begin building a video collection at a time when legitimate copies of popular features still sold for $80–100 per tape, but also because these compilations showed now-popular stars in early, less glamorous roles, unencumbered by the higher budgeted hard-core feature's attempts at narrative justification. These videos "reincarnating the 8mm loops of the past" present "a potpourri of sexual styles, not all of which will please. But with patience comes rewards," says one *AVN* reviewer, remarking that *Swedish Erotica* tapes track a history of changes from "the men in black masks [i.e., stag actors] of my youth to the artful lovemaking of the present, for the interested viewer with a specific need."[70] Even this early review, then, notes the allure of remediated film-born artifacts as fascinating historical documents for discerning tastes.

In this same 1983 issue, *AVN* also offered a feature article informing the reader that, contrary to popular belief, hard-core films did not begin with *Deep Throat*, but rather extended back through the history of early stags—as several recent video releases could testify. The magazine's "Recommendations of Nostalgia Sex on Videocassette" followed, highlighting theatrically screened compilations like *Old, Borrowed, and Stag* (1973) and *Nostalgia Blue* (1976), plus compilations first appearing on home video like *Nudie Classics* and *Famous Smokers of the Past, Vol. 1 and 2*.[71] Yet, as much as stags and loops might be prized for their historic and collectible value, their technical crudeness ("Those with special interests in no-frills sex should take note while those wanting to choose something new and slick should stay away"[72]) also highlighted a sense of pastness that might inspire both ironic distance ("You cannot help but laugh at some of the sexual attitudes presented here"[73]) and carnal resonance ("These poorly shot films can rival most of the adult films made today"[74]). We can thus see the roots of vintage pornography's renewed marketability in the reception of these early stag/loop videotapes, although it would take several more years for early examples of more technically sophisticated hard-core films to acquire enough pastness for similar nostalgization as "classics."

By 1983, 35-mm hard-core features cost approximately $40,000–150,000 to produce, with around 120 released annually to theaters—although some of those might have been pieced together from outtakes from earlier productions.[75] By 1985, however, it was five times less expensive to produce a video-born pornographic feature than even a 16-mm feature film. Tapes could be quickly and easily duplicated, and sold to distributors or subdistributors for a 100 percent profit due to the above-average retail prices that porn tapes garnered compared to other prerecorded tapes.[76] A shot-on-video production, filmed over two days, might only cost $8,000–40,000 to produce, and perhaps 200 new video titles (a figure including both shot-on-video and remediated shot-on-film features) were released per month by the mid-1980s. Shot-on-video releases constituted half of all new tapes by 1985, and that year began being reviewed in separate sections of *AVN* from film-born pictures. With the theatrical market in sharp decline (a drop from approximately 950 theaters to less than 200 theaters over the 1980s) as a result of the home video boom, some producers and distributors spoke of an increasing nostalgia for celluloid—especially since the remaining adult theaters had generally shifted to video projection. Meanwhile, proponents of shot-on-video releases defended their newer product, claiming that theaters would not be missed because they consistently ripped off distributors through the reporting of falsified receipts, and that a high-quality video-born feature would be indistinguishable from its film-born counterpart.[77]

Yet, among many adult filmmakers, critics, and performers, there was still a sense that shot-on-video features had far less permanence than celluloid, since films from the 1970s "Golden Age" were fondly looked back upon as boasting higher budgets and better quality, in addition to more compelling narratives than the stag-like skits constituting many video-born productions of the home video bubble that Laurence O'Toole, Jennifer C. Nash, and others have called the "Silver Age of Porn" (beginning around 1983).[78] Critic Jim Holliday complained that "Shot on video (or dare I call it shit on video) is simply a historical return to loops—most video features are an elaborate series of sex scenes disguised as a complete entity. Loops are fine as long as they are recognized as such."[79] Indeed, one of the major reasons that the ratio of narrative to sexual numbers became increasingly lopsided in Silver Age videos was the presumption that, unlike the theatrically released Golden Age film, the home video viewer could fast-forward through these extended sex scenes if so desired. As a reviewer of *Sexual Freedom in Denmark* (1970) commented upon its 1986 video release, "This movie is the kind you would like to keep on your shelves as a sort of an historical piece. […] What makes this movie somewhat of a classic is that sex is portrayed as something positive and healthy. Something that has been sorely missing in the current trend of shot-on-video."[80] Video-born pornography's sense of disposability was so great that "the production of the cover photo and the printing of the box literally cost more than the movie itself," recalls Superior Video founder David Jennings.[81]

Until the mid-1980s, notes Chuck Kleinhans, major video producer-distributors like VCX, Essex, Cal Vista, and TVX might have advanced $40,000–60,000 in production costs as a guarantee for the home video rights to a theatrically released film, but such offers dried up when those studios realized that the same amount could pay for the distribution rights to four shot-on-video features. With overall budgets falling, individual titles selling fewer copies in an increasingly glutted market, and increased competition over would-be renters as Hollywood studios eventually embraced the prerecorded video market, the retail price of tapes dropped sharply by the late 1980s, although a corresponding increase in market diversity meant that demand for so-called "specialty" and alternative tapes devoted to niche sexual tastes could still garner higher prices.[82] *AVN*'s monthly sales and rental charts consistently showed newly produced videos as top performers, which led to concerns that, despite the instant name recognition of "classic" theatrical features like *Deep Throat*, *Debbie Does Dallas*, or *Insatiable* (1980), the glut of new releases was pushing these older, consistently profitable standards off store shelves. Meanwhile, *AVN* found fifty-nine out of 100 surveyed stores carrying tapes of pre-1970s stags and loops in 1986, but only 3 percent of consumers declaring such videos as their "favorite sub-genre" (a figure comparable to those who identified instructional sex tapes, fat-themed tapes, and undubbed foreign tapes as their favorite subgenre).[83]

On the one hand, then, new releases threatened to displace the historic and economic value of established genre classics and other older material, but a contravening tendency was consumers' increased willingness to look for tapes with specific content, not necessarily just selecting tapes with the newest or flashiest box art. *AVN* thus recommended that distributors' catalogues and rental stores' shelves increasingly divide films by categories and subgenres to aid more selective viewers.[84] Overall, oversaturation of the marketplace had finally caused the porn industry's video bubble to burst by 1986, encouraging both established and newly formed studios to shift toward niche-based product differentiation. Meanwhile, future industry leader Vivid Entertainment began distinguishing itself from its increasingly fetish-driven competitors and the early pioneers of low-fi "gonzo" porn through glossy production values and a strict adherence to kink-free sexual acts, mainstreaming a particularly conservative correlation between "quality" and straightness.[85]

In a move that *AVN* would later consider one of the industry's most significant decisions, New York-based studio Distribpix Inc. dropped the per-unit price of its entire Video-X-Pix catalogue to $39.95 in October 1984, much as Hollywood was then experimenting with the potential of a sell-through market for popular film-born titles that would be aimed at bypassing rental stores and directly reaching individual video collectors. As in the non-adult video industry, this experiment proved that priced-to-own popular titles could sell in large volumes, while less popular or more specialty tapes aimed at rental outlets continued to garner higher prices.[86] Over the next three years, several of the other largest video distributors—including Essex, Caballero, VCA, and Arrow—would follow suit, all marketing their discounted bestsellers as "classics" lines that might be purchased for as little as $15 each. In its July 1986 issue, *AVN* also began a new recurring section called "The Classics," with each installment featuring a different subgenre, director, or star of note. By this time, even Caballero's popular loop compilations had subdivided into a line of *Classic Swedish Erotica* tapes, in distinction from the ongoing series' more recent strings of shot-on-video scenes.

As was true of the non-adult video industry, the eventual rise of sell-through tapes as the industry standard helped overcome declining profits during the mid-to-late 1980s product glut; by the time DVD was introduced in 1997 as a home video technology specifically intended for sell-through units, adult distributors (as usual) quickly adopted the new format and released their older "classics" as some of the first available titles. Even though a product glut still existed, with 5,775 new releases in 1995 alone (including compilations and reissues), sell-through pricing had helped the industry's falling profits recover, while decreased political and legal pressure from antiporn activists and federal investigators also allowed adult video to spread with fewer obstacles by the mid-to-late 1990s.[87]

In my estimation, then, the growth of an alternative market for "vintage" pornography emerged from these shifting economic factors: older film-born material originally intended for theaters might have once comprised the pornographic "mainstream" in the years before the video boom—and might have thereby been destined to garnering lower home video revenues when marketed as disposably "average" product once tape prices for conventional hard-core films fell and some porn companies began going out of business. Yet, even if sell-through videotape prices for these "classics" lines dropped, their increased repackaging as historically significant texts hedged against too much devaluation because their pastness became associated with more niche, connoisseurial tastes compared to the newer wave of shot-on-video porn—and thus potentially garnered significant sales from genre buffs already willing to pay a premium for specialty/alternative videos. As Jennings says, "Consumers finally rebelled against the garbage videos flooding the market. A new generation of porn fans discovered—to their delight—the high quality of the 35[mm feature]s from porn's 1970s 'Golden Age.'" As more companies went bankrupt during the industry crisis, two long-standing studios—Caballero and VCA—bought out many of their competitors' libraries of older films and emerged as industry titans.[88] Whereas earlier video companies had illicitly amassed huge quantities of their competitors' titles, the Caballero and VCA libraries eventually ballooned through more legitimate means (including copyright control) as the adult film industry in general made moves toward its increasingly corporatized mainstreaming that would spawn the post-1990s second wave of "porno chic."

The 1980s shift to video-based production and distribution may have thus engendered nostalgia for adult cinema's celluloid past, but this nostalgia also fueled the potential profits to be made from videos that remediated earlier film-born texts as important genre classics and/or a distinct sexual preference. With so many porn videos pouring onto video store shelves—and now onto streaming video websites in our own period—Linda Williams warns that the "possible sociological or historical impact" of any one text

> recedes into the background. This apparent timelessness, though, is only the illusion of a group of texts that the parent culture would prefer to disown; part of the challenge of reading them is to put them back into time, to note the historical demarcations in the seeming monolith, the way they are as much about change as about repetition.[89]

With the consumption of "vintage" pornography in particular, however, the historicity of these texts is already highlighted in a more acute way through their marketing as an alternative niche, since their original period of production is foregrounded for latter-day viewers in the very process of simultaneously receding into the historical distance. Indeed, as I suggested in my first chapter, vintage pornography's retrospective allure resides in not only signifiers of historical change, but also the documentation of sexual acts that have seemingly remained timeless. With virtually all pre-1990s film-born pornography now distant enough to obtain a sense of "vintage-ness," déclassé stags/loops and best-selling Golden Age classics have come to similarly share the allure of a perceived historical difference from the more contemporary look and nonnarrative tendencies of much video-born pornography. Even in early 1970s-era, 8- and 16-mm loops with little (if any) narrative basis, for example, their very age, primitivism, and celluloid materiality have come to connote a larger historical narrative of generic change that now subtends the more fragmentary individual text. In the final sections of this chapter, I will now note several examples of how historical change has been highlighted in the disappearance and reappearance of certain archival porn texts over others, and how the destabilizing effects of these shifts in distribution can have affective implications for the fan identities of historically minded adult film aficionados.

Industry self-censorship and the birth of the "Alternative Adult" market

Prosecutions of theater owners for obscenity increased after the U.S. Supreme Court's 1973 *Miller v. California* decision returned responsibility for obscenity definitions to the judgment of local community standards, meaning that "smaller hard-core theaters suffered through a lack of product and a suddenly more discerning hard-core audience."[90] One of the major implications of this legal precedent was a deliberate toning down of ostensibly aberrant or "taboo" content in many post-1973 hard-core films. In the early 1970s, 8- and 16-mm hard-core loops depicting urolagnia (a.k.a. "watersports"), bondage and sadomasochism (BDSM), fisting and other "foreign insertions," and even actual, unsimulated acts of bestiality and child pornography might be sold under the counter at adult bookstores or screened in peepshow arcades, but were not meant for theatrical screening. Since loops were so inexpensive to produce and small enough to circulate in limited editions, loop filmmakers could take greater chances with illicit content than theatrical filmmakers, since legal interception of their product would not mean huge financial losses and would be harder to trace back to the source. Although bestiality and the use of actual underage performers were already strictly prohibited by law across the board, both then and now, those other aforementioned practices were more often subject to the vagaries of local sodomy laws and other obscenity statutes, and thus still ran the risk of arousing the wrong kind of attention. As such, these loops became more and more rare as underground commodities, and some of them (such as the ones depicting unquestionably illegal acts) understandably never made the leap to remediation on home video.[91]

In the theatrical pornographic feature, meanwhile, illicit acts seldom appeared to begin with, but even a handful of 35-mm genre "classics"—such as *The Story of Joanna* (1975), *Femmes de Sade* (1976), *Barbara Broadcast* (1977), *Pretty Peaches* (1978), *Candy Stripers* (1978), and *800 Fantasy Lane* (1979)—suffered trims of select scenes when later appearing on video. In most existing VHS and DVD versions of *Barbara Broadcast* distributed by VCA, for example, a scene featuring Jamie Gillis fucking Constance Money while the latter is bound in BDSM-submissive chains and leather cuffs (Figure 3.7) blatantly trims all shots of visible genital penetration, effectively rendering the scene closer to soft core than its original theatrical version.[92] As David Jennings recalls of the Los Angeles filmmaking scene, "In the wake of the crackdown on kink in the mid-'70s, L.A.'s police and pornographers had forged a truce: the LAPD wouldn't bust porn manufacturers if they'd refrain from urination, defecation, bestiality, child sex, fist or foot insertions, flagellation with penetration, bondage with penetration, and shooting in L.A. county."[93] In some cases, then, directors intentionally omitted such content to begin with, while in other cases, distributors made hasty trims to preexisting films. Though not exclusive to heterosexual pornography, hard-core features fictionally depicting incest, rape, or other forms of nonconsensual sex—a thread stretching back through the sexploitation roughies—became less far common over the 1970s (though exceptions like the incest-themed hit *Taboo* [1980] remained), and such scenes were often cut out of later video reissues where possible—a selective rewriting of adult film history that Laurence O'Toole compares with the Soviet doctoring of photographs to erase the existence of purged officials.[94]

In the wake of feminist activism against pornography and especially the 1986 Meese Commission's neoconservative crackdown on obscenity, the combination of unsimulated, penetrative sex acts with fictional depictions of force or restraint only seemed to play into antiporn crusaders' worst fears, so reasserting hard core's legal

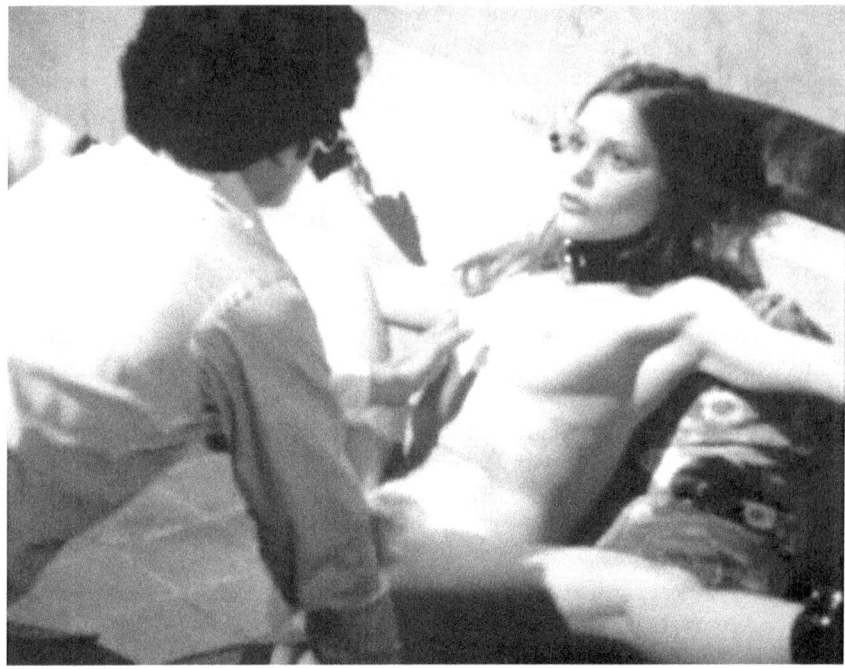

Figure 3.7 Constance Money is restrained in BDSM-submissive gear while Jamie Gillis approaches, in VCA's self-censored DVD edition of *Barbara Broadcast* (1977). Cuts made in the wake of VCA head Russ Hampshire's 1988 obscenity conviction eliminated all clear shots of genital penetration in the scene.

legitimacy necessitated the industry's move toward self-censorship. In his 1986 guide to the best adult films, Jim Holliday complained,

> Antiporn idiots who speak from the heart rather than the head have claimed that porn has become more violent, more explicit and more demeaning to women in recent years. As a porn historian, my response is exactly the opposite. Any fool could notice that fisters, pissers, excessive violence, rape and young girl themes have been heavily self-censored by the adult industry themselves.[95]

Arrow, for example, released the rape-heavy hard-core roughie *A Dirty Western* (1975) on VHS in 1987 as part of their sell-through "classics" line, but by 1996, Holliday noted in *AVN* that it, along with dozens of other so-called "Lost Classics," had since been voluntarily withdrawn from circulation.[96] After VCA founder Russ Hampshire's release from prison on a 1988 obscenity conviction, for example, he tasked several editors with censoring potentially offending material from the company's 3,000-title accumulated library, although one of these editors recalls that at least fifty films (such as *Femmes de Sade*) suffered so many cuts that they were taken out of print altogether.[97]

Moreover, these cut versions have remained the iterations predominantly available today, since most so-called "classics studios" have merely imported their older video transfers to DVD and not bothered to reinstate previously trimmed footage. The misleadingly sensational title of the high-gloss comedy *Desires within Young Girls* (1977), for example, initially caused legal trouble in some locales, even though this frothy story of a social-climbing woman (Georgina Spelvin) trying to profitably marry off her two high-school-age daughters (Annette Haven and Clair Dia) only features legally adult actors. As Holliday complained, this legal trouble was "A real travesty ... It's a classic for crying out loud. What is next? YOUNG DILLINGER [1965]?"[98] Today, a number of torrent websites describe it as "A true vintage romp, it's difficult to tell which parts of this are kinky, and which are just 1970s,"[99] although different scenes in Caballero's various video editions (e.g., an expository scene of the two daughters leaving private school wearing their schoolgirl uniforms) have been cut out to downplay the connotations of underage sex.[100] In video editions of other films, specific lines of dialogue were clumsily dubbed over if originally containing passing reference to sex with women any younger than 18.

As this suggests, then, the late 1980s adult video industry may have been experiencing a glut of new product, but the contested circulation and ownership of many hard-core features in their various iterations meant that some older films had quickly slipped back into obscurity or at least been rendered less controversial. This also suggests how, unlike the uncontrolled duplication rampant during the industry's "outlaw" early years, the very notion of hard-core genre "classics" became increasingly contingent upon several prominent porn studios increasingly asserting copyright control over their libraries, and thereby helping restore value to texts that once might have circulated in disreputably fragmentary and unauthorized forms—though some notable bootlegging of these out-of-print versions has remained active (as discussed in the next chapter).

The mainstream heterosexual porn industry's selective forgetting of its "rougher" or more "taboo" past when certain texts reappeared on home video can thus be seen as an understandable concession to more contemporary forms of political correctness—especially as the video market increasingly targeted heterosexual couples instead of lone men—but it can also reproduce a particularly vanilla vision of sex by erasing from its visual register various practices like bisexuality, BDSM, urolagnia, fisting, and various fetishes that originally appeared in select scenes of even major theatrical hits—such as the fellatio scene (Figure 3.8), cut from some video versions, between a male sadist (Jamie Gillis) and his manservant (Zebedy Colt) in *The Story of Joanna*, a film otherwise focused on female masochism; or *The Opening of Misty Beethoven*'s (1976) titular character (Constance Money) "pegging" a wealthy businessman (Ras Kean) during a threesome with another woman (Gloria Leonard). Moreover, unlike the occasional occurrence of kinkier sexual acts in early stag films, which unsurprisingly (given their once-exclusively male audience) framed fleeting instances of sexual diversity as sources of hetero-male pleasure, the appearance of kink in longer, feature-length narratives could open mixed-gender viewers to more fluid identificatory positions than simply "phallus" and "hole."[101]

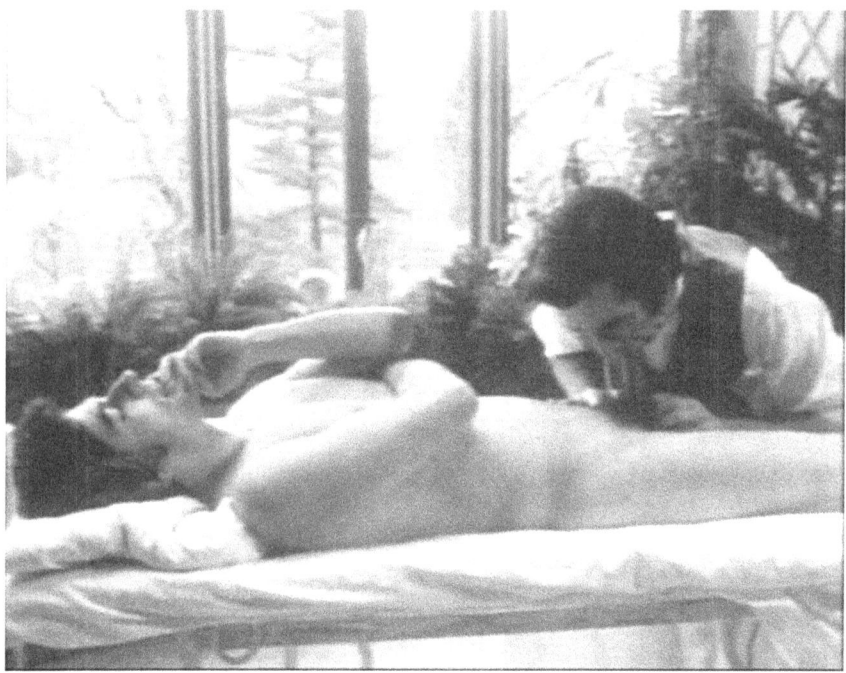

Figure 3.8 A homosexual fellatio scene between Jamie Gillis and Zebedy Colt in Gerard Damiano's BDSM "classic" *The Story of Joanna* (1975), cut from many video editions in order to render the film less "threatening" for heteronormative male viewers.

Indeed, Linda Williams notes that the industry's post-1973 efforts to both avoid obscenity prosecutions and raise its cultural repute were gradually achieved less through a separation of non-explicit from explicit representations than a separation of "normal" from "perverse" sexualities.[102] As the porn industry took steps toward mainstream corporate legitimacy over the 1980s and 1990s, for instance, the latter practices became increasingly segregated into *AVN*'s separate category of "specialty" adult tapes (largely made by much smaller companies), implicitly setting boundaries for how the presence or absence of particular sexual practices within pornographic features could shift from being seen as historical signifiers of a less "tasteful" past to generic signifiers of sexual marginality.

Consequently, even as the larger industry players self-censored the content of older films when it was presumed to be potentially "shocking" to local community standards, such content could still be split off and capitalized upon as "specialties," but at the risk of whitewashing the diversity of acts—however troubling some of them might be for certain viewers—that were once more permissible for inclusion in 1970s hard-core features. When Jim Holliday, for instance, presents his "Memorable Missing Moments: The Famous Forbidden Fist Chart" in his 1986 book *Only the Best*, this list of fisting scenes since trimmed from 1970s heterosexual hard-core films cannot help but remind us of fisting's valorization within queer theory as a "new" sexual practice originally developed by twentieth-century queers.[103] One of the limitations, then, of denouncing the "rougher" strain of behavior within some 1970s hard-core films as the "bad old days" of a more conservatively masculinist past—which some vintage porn fans may indeed regressively nostalgize (e.g., the cult repute of Shaun Costello's notorious roughies *Forced Entry* [1973] and *Waterpower* [1977]), much as fans of proximate genres like horror and other exploitation-ready texts similarly nostalgize the 1970s as a "grittier" and less homogenized past—is the corresponding danger of denigrating queerer forms of sexuality through an ultimately conservative conflation of 1970s-era "political incorrectness" with "bad sex." Hence the need for accessing multiple versions of films and carefully analyzing individual texts on their own terms, rather than merely relying on broad generic generalizations that fail to account for the sexual complexity found even within films ostensibly aimed at a heterosexual theatrical market.

And yet, if the informal distribution (such as piracy) of hard-core features in theaters and on video has meant that stable and unchanging iterations of particular films were once difficult to standardize within the marketplace, then the vagaries of circulation mean that retrospectively exploring the world of vintage pornography— such as collecting old VHS and Beta tapes, both cut and uncut DVDs of films that were censored on VHS, or compilations of clips excised from preexisting films—can uncover unpredictable records of fragmentary and seemingly "excessive" varieties of sexual expression. The adult video industry may have attempted to standardize its available product to avoid certain legal and political pitfalls, but the fantasy of stumbling across the suppressed pieces of a text's history retains as much of vintage pornography's retrospective appeal as the more common reality of encountering a mutilated text. Much as horror film fans seek out uncut versions of particularly gory films, for example, some vintage porn collectors will compare and recommend different video editions for mere seconds of missing footage (as also discussed in the next chapter). Yet, as much as collectors may often want to see a given film as it was originally meant to be seen, the crude trims and alternate versions seen in remediated editions can also remind viewers of what has since passed back into the realm of the cinematic unseen.

Contradicting common assumptions that hard-core pornography has teleologically moved toward greater and greater explicitness since coming aboveground in 1970, the continued circulation of these censored iterations bespeaks a tantalizingly uneven history of sexual visibility. Each absence, then, is a signifier of loss, but however much one might reject such censorial efforts, these absences also remind the historian and fan of the alluring temporal gap between then and now, the historical distance encouraging an eroticized longing for the past. As these outmoded and sometimes deleted forms of sexual representation have become temporal signifiers in their own right, the adult film industry's for-profit strategies of selective forgetting have thereby comingled with its selective remembrance of more esteemed genre "classics," ultimately forming a variegated corpus perpetually open to contested sexual/cultural tastes and fantasies of historical rediscovery.

Going back further than the aforementioned shifts from film-born to video-born movies and from the diversity within 1970s features to the segregation of specialty tapes, this sense of historical change between then and now also obviously resided in the earlier shift from soft-core to hard-core visuality. As I suggested in earlier chapters, the legalized proliferation of hard-core cinema after 1970, first in theaters and later on home video, colonized popular perceptions of what constitutes the bounds of "pornography" proper—especially in comparison with the simulated sex in sexploitation films from before the 1970s theatrical hard-core boom and also the soft-core features later flooding into the 1980s–1990s late-night cable television and direct-to-video markets. Indeed, with various forms of soft-core adult cinema continuing on into the 1970s–1980s, and thriving through nontheatrical distribution into the present day,[104] we should keep in mind that hard-core pornography did not wholly replace sexploitation in a clear teleological sense, even after the monumental success of landmark films like *Deep Throat*. Rather, there were particular historical precedents for the continued coexistence of soft-core and hard-core forms in the marketplace, with each playing off the other through mutual acts of legal and cultural distinction. As already suggested, soft-core and hard-core iterations of vintage pornography can be difficult for some latter-day fans to reconcile, since it may seem easier to nostalgize less explicit forms than hard-core films, despite a textual proximity that might only be separated by the legal demarcation of either showing or eliding genital penetration. However, even the hard-core adult industry attempted to draw such distinctions from their side of the hard-core line, increasingly segregating soft-core forms as an "other" or "alternative" market as historical forms like sexploitation became remediated as vintage products on home video.

Because local obscenity standards were often more restrictive and arbitrary after 1973 than national standards had been, some film (and later, video) distributors avoided sending their product to more conservative parts of the country altogether, such as Utah and the Deep South, and theater owners (and later, video stores) faced increased harassment from local authorities—including, for instance, the bigoted targeting of theaters and other adult businesses frequented by gay men.[105] This shift also meant that many nervous film producers who had shot their sex films in both soft- and hard-core versions only opted to release the former, seeking to avoid potential exhibitor hesitation and costly legal wrangling. Drive-in theaters and indoor theaters in nonurban areas were especially prone to screen soft versions over hard ones. *Deep Throat Part II* (1974), for example, was filmed soft enough to earn an R rating, while *Variety* noted in 1976 that "a toned-down, soft X version" of *The Story of Joanna* earned the first "class" booking for "a heretofore hardcore pic," playing a metropolitan showcase of eighteen New York theaters following the hard-core version's twenty-two-week run in less prestigious houses.[106] If not delivered films with alternate "soft" angles, some distributors simply cut hard-core sex scenes short, just before the appearance of any potentially offending footage, and hoped for the best with the truncated prints. *Variety* later ranked the trimmed-down, soft-core version of the X-rated musical *Alice in Wonderland* (1976) as one of the highest grossing films of the year, representing the challenge that the hard-core industry still faced from "the proliferation of quasi-respectable soft-core sex films" with higher production values than many of the era's cheaper hard-core features.[107] As filmmaker Steven Ziplow noted in his 1977 how-to guide to pornography, a seventy-five-minute 35-mm hard-core film made for under $40,000 would still likely turn a profit, even though the novelty of hard-core theater attendance that had drawn crossover crowds several years earlier had since subsided. In an adult film market left with a larger number of theaters and circulating pictures in the wake of the initial period of porno chic, he consequently recommended shooting both hard and soft versions to reach the broadest possible audience.[108]

Hence, the chicness and related controversy of legally available hard-core features may have increasingly (but not entirely) dominated public attention in the more permissive 1970s theatrical marketplace, but once home video use became widespread in the mid-1980s, various types of soft-core films ironically saw a gradual resurgence of interest—despite the increased conflation of terms like "X-rated," "adult," and "pornography" with hard-core films alone. Whereas earlier guidebooks to adult cinema, such as William Rotsler's *Contemporary Erotic Cinema* (1973) and Jim Holliday's *How to Build Your X-Rated Video Library* (1980), included a variety of sexploitation films from the 1960s and 1970s, the glut of hard-core content released onto video was the predominant focus of later consumer guides, as if responding to a suddenly more pressing need to critically evaluate tapes for an adult film audience that had gradually become more discerning but simultaneously faced a massive explosion of buying/renting options. In later guides like *The X-Rated Videotape Guide* (1984) and *Adam Film World*'s *X-Rated Video Directory* (1985), Radley Metzger, Russ Meyer, and Just Jaeckin soft-core titles might make the cut for inclusion, but other sexploitation specialists like Doris Wishman, Bethel Buckalew, Lee Frost, and Barry Mahon had vanished.[109] Writing in 1980, Holliday remarked that only five hard-core features—*Deep Throat*, *Behind the Green Door* (1972), *The Devil in Miss Jones* (1973), *Wet Rainbow* (1974), and *The Opening of Misty Beethoven*—could be legitimately considered genre "classics," but his 1986 book *Only the Best*—still perhaps the most substantial critical attempt to construct a hard-core canon, not just provide a comprehensive consumer guide—had expanded to lists of "Top 40 Best Adult Films," with passing reference to stags, loops, and sexploitation segregated onto a few separate pages.[110] By the late 1990s, each new 800-page volume in Robert H. Rimmer and Patrick Riley's series of *X-Rated Videotape Guides* published by Prometheus Books had only enough room for capsule reviews of the previous two or three years' video releases. Small wonder, then, that as the larger and increasingly "mainstream" porn studios more often construed the ranks of adult cinema aficionados as hard-core video consumers, a niche demand for early and pre-hard-core forms of adult cinema grew among cult film fandom as a means of redressing this growing neglect of earlier texts.

AVN's small section devoted to soft-core films—variously named "Softcore Corner," "Soft Focus," and "The OtheR Side" (emphasis on the "R," as in the MPAA rating) over the years—covered the belated release of various 1970s exploitation films featuring gratuitous nudity, such as the work of Meyer, Tinto Brass, Jess Franco, Jack Hill, and genres like the women-in-prison film. Meyer's RM Films continued to take out full-page ads in *AVN* until the mid-1980s, while *AVN*'s *1986–87 Video Buyer's Guide* offered a "Top Softcore Picks" section stretching all the way back to *...And God Created Woman* (1956) and *The Immoral Mr. Teas* (1959). During the adult video industry's mid-1980s downturn, however, hard-core producers and distributors began reviving the older practice of "hot" and "cool" cuts, diversifying into soft-core versions that could be sold to cable television and to video stores in socially conservative areas. "Essex Video Announces Cable Version: The Profitable Alternative" read one 1986 ad, while *AVN* elsewhere reported that adult video manufacturers were turning to exploitation films, children's films, and other "general release" genres as more bankable product lines.[111] Indeed, when pornography was under fire from the Meese Commission, sales for soft-core films, including Meyer's work, saw significant gains as viewers and retailers who still wanted sex films began shying away from hard-core videos.[112] And yet, while the major hard-core video distributors were busy releasing their own sell-through lines of "classics" to weather the video bubble's burst, the late 1980s and early 1990s also saw *AVN* beginning to review video reissues of striptease and burlesque films, sexploitation features and trailer compilations, and other pre-hard-core films released by minor distributors like SWV, Filmfare Video Labs (a.k.a. Blue Vanities), Global Media International (a.k.a. Historic Erotica), Elite Visuals, Rhino Video, Sunset Software, and Video Dimensions.

AVN's coverage of both vintage and contemporary soft-core forms was increasingly folded into the catchall category of "Alternative Adult" releases. As editor Gene Ross remarked, the term "softcore" carried higher taste connotations than "hardcore" and was therefore to be avoided in a trade magazine primarily promoting hard-core products, although the publication still retained "hardcore" to avoid using the overdetermined term "pornography."[113] In this sense, much as some cult film fans today hesitate to include hard-core films under the retrospectively constructed umbrella of "exploitation cinema," the hard-core industry itself was somewhat uncomfortable including soft-core forms within the term "adult" without some qualifiers. Although terms like "softcore" and "alternative" gradually became synonymous in *AVN*'s pages to differentiate hard core from its cultural others, Ross speculated that *vintage* soft-core forms garnered an unexpected renewal of interest due to a niche audience's rejection of the more contemporary soft-core forms then being made for nontheatrical distribution: "whatever is prompting it—the ongoing wave of nostalgia or the sad look of much of the current softcore film market—sexploitation films are enjoying a revival." In his estimation, the sheer rarity of 1960s sexploitation films compared to hard-core product—with perhaps 1,000 sexploitation titles made over the entire 1960s vs. 1700 hard-core titles released in 1987 alone—combined with the lack of available titles then released on home video was a significant part of their attraction.[114] Although that situation has certainly changed in the intervening years, I would argue that *AVN*'s one-time investment in the rediscovery of "lost" vintage films speaks to not only the economic allure of an untapped market, but also an intertwining of historical value and erotic potential undergirding the subcultural fandom of vintage pornography in general. The hard-core adult industry did not just take notice because vintage soft-core videos were becoming a growing market segment, but also because these seemingly archaic films could "put a glow on any collector's cheek" by appealing to an older generation's erotic fantasies.[115]

As increasingly "vintage" forms of adult cinema became relegated to historical and industrial marginality, cult film fanzines and bootleg tape sellers/traders took them up as objects of subcultural interest and mail-order circulation. For retailers hoping to break into this potential market, *AVN* even recommended reading cult film magazines like *Psychotronic Video* and *Film Threat* to find fresh product in cult video sellers' mail-order ads, since these publications would be more promising sources of information about recent rediscoveries than hard-core-centric trade magazines.[116] After all, the legally indeterminate status of surviving prints and video sources, both then and now, has allowed some fan–collectors to become niche-market entrepreneurs in their own right, especially when longtime collectors of prints move toward opening their personal archives and profitably recirculating texts. Such outfits have subsequently developed into prominent labels among adult film aficionados, devoted to locating and transferring "new" material for video distribution, especially when the increasingly corporatized, "mainstream" hard-core studios have generally been more concerned with capitalizing on their more recent catalogues than uncovering the vast wealth of decades past.

Today, most home video distributors focus on either side of the hard-core line, since that line tends to separate where they can advertise and which retailers will carry their product. Films with extensive hard-core content are generally more difficult to find through major retailers and are more likely acquired directly from companies that specialize in hard-core pornography. Larger vintage labels like Historic Erotica, Blue Vanities, and Alpha Blue Archives, for example, specialize in many-volume compilations of hard-core content while largely omitting soft-core films, but may bolster the revenues made off their in-house releases by also selling 1970s–1980s hard-core DVDs from classics studios like Arrow, TVX, VCX, and Distribpix. There are, however, several notable labels that currently distribute considerable quantities of both soft-core and hard-core vintage films: Something Weird Video, Alternative Cinema, and Vinegar Syndrome. Although I will discuss several of these labels' DVD/Blu-ray and streaming video releases in more detail in the following chapter, SWV pioneered the home video reemergence of vintage pornography as an "alternative" market, and thus serves as a prime example of turning neglected archives of adult films into a for-profit venture—albeit a venture whose fantasies of newfound access to the past can powerfully impact fans' identities as historically minded connoisseurs.

When *AVN* editor Gene Ross began championing the growing wave of "nudie nostalgia" in 1987, he noted that most pre-1970s sexploitation films, such as *Teaserama* (1955), *Blaze Starr Goes Nudist* (1962), *Surftide 77* (1962), and *The Defilers* (1965), were still considered lost and therefore all the more tantalizing as potential rediscoveries. Apart from the hazy memories of those old enough to have originally seen the films in theaters, surviving trailers and other advertising paratexts still constituted the primary means of knowing what these films might contain.[117] However, Ross would soon credit Seattle-based outfit Something Weird as "leading the pack in uncovering some of these long lost treasures, and then bringing them back to the market in attractive, nostalgic packaging,"[118] since many of these films previously thought lost were among SWV's first releases.

The brainchild of Mike Vraney, a comic book and memorabilia collector who had worked as a projectionist in Seattle's storefront porn theaters in the 1970s–1980s, SWV began as a mail-order business around 1990 for Vraney to sell bootleg transfers of the disused prints he collected from his theater connections. With only about 100 sexploitation titles then released on video, it was a vastly untapped nostalgia market. Once he began advertising in fanzines as a commercial enterprise instead of just a grey-market trader, however, he had to begin seeking legally legitimate arrangements in cases where rights owners survived. When producer David F. Friedman first contacted him with a cease-and-desist warning over one such pirated film, Vraney convinced the irrepressible showman to officially license several of his films to SWV on a trial basis. When that arrangement proved a success, Friedman convinced other producer-distributors to license their films to Vraney. Over the next few years, Vraney began officially licensing sexploitation films from original producer-distributors like Friedman, Harry Novak, Dan Sonney, Louis Sher, and Arthur Morowitz; video distributors like Jimmy Maslon (owner of the Doris Wishman and Herschell Gordon Lewis film libraries); and collections of disused prints discovered by cult director Frank Henenlotter, including the once-lost Michael and Roberta Findlay films with which I opened this chapter. As the company's reputation spread, other print collectors began selling their private archives to SWV or offering tips on where to find disused prints in film labs and warehouses, such as a massive haul of prints from Movielab in New York City.[119] In some cases, SWV tracked down original rights owners, often managing to license films in perpetuity because the original owners saw little ability in further capitalizing on them. In other cases, they distributed orphaned films that were unlikely to spawn cease-and-desist letters from current rights holders (especially family members who might be embarrassed by relatives' past experiences in adult filmmaking).[120]

It is important to note that Vraney and Henenlotter initially resisted including hard-core films in SWV's catalogue, out of fears that associating older sexploitation films with less questionably "pornographic" content might jeopardize a new generation's ability to legally access softer forms of archaic adult cinema.[121] By the same token, *AVN* initially recommended that "alternative adult" titles be placed in separate sections in proximity to each other within stores, but without indiscriminately mixing X-rated and R-rated product together, since hard-core and soft-core audiences might not profitably overlap.[122] Yet, Vraney would later credit *AVN*'s reviews of his soft-core videos with allowing him to branch beyond mail-order sales to larger volume distribution in video stores—especially once hard-core films were added to the mix. In return, Ross credited SWV's prolific number of new releases with allowing video stores to start stocking "nostalgic XXX" subsections.[123] By 1994, SWV was prominently advertising to would-be retailers in the pages of *AVN*:

> A mere 4 years ago, the skeptics all said we were crazy to offer vintage sexploitation flicks to the video-buying public. With the abundance of hardcore films on tape, who'd care about the kinder, gentler, grindhouse movies of yesteryear? Well ... Today business is TREMENDOUS, and we want to pass on this good news by inviting you, the retailer, to jump aboard the SOMETHING WEIRD VIDEO bandwagon![124]

By 1997, Vraney's earlier fears over a "mixed marriage of sexploitation and XXX" had been assuaged by the profits to be made by creating "a completist phenomenon that similarly drives the collectibles market." He henceforth moved into distributing hard-core features, following his prior success with a line of *Bucky Beaver's Triple XXX Stags, Loops, & Peeps* compilations, and the acquisition of over 300 hard-core films from a Tennessee storefront theater chain, which became his line of *Bucky Beaver's Dragon Art Theatre Double Feature* tapes. A separate catalogue, the SWV *Blue Book*, appeared in 1997—by convenient coincidence, just around the time of *Boogie Nights*' 1997 release—to foreground the company's hard-core offerings. This "document for fandom," as Vraney called it,[125] may have still segregated SWV's hard-core films into a separate catalogue, but as much as the hard-core industry and SWV initially wanted to differentiate themselves from each other, both eventually found it profitable to capitalize off one another by crossing the line separating soft-core from hard-core material.

As SWV's catalogue expanded with fresh rediscoveries over the years, fewer "lost" adult films have continued to exist—although the company's periodic catalogue supplements have highlighted newly uncovered titles (which, given its orphaned status, would likely include *The Orgy at Lil's Place* if the company were to obtain a print), continuing to tease fans/historians over what remains left to find. Nevertheless, Caroline Frick's observation holds true that most "new" discoveries of past films derive from distribution prints that may be mutilated, re-titled, or in other states of historical disrepair—not pristine prints preserved for posterity in official archives. As such, keeping more and more reproduced copies of a given film (such as pirated prints and bootleg transfers) in circulation may better ensure a film's existence than simply waiting for archive-ready original negatives or camera elements to be uncovered.[126]

Despite many adult video distributors' claims to offer "remastered" transfers of older texts, detailed restoration work is relatively rare, particularly in the case of culturally marginalized films (although, as I note in the following chapter, that is starting to change). Consequently, as much as companies like SWV may resurrect cultish desires for what it might have been like to watch an older generation of adult films, the versions continuing to circulate are inevitably partial and open to historical flux. As Giovanna Fossati explains, the fact that multiple, oft-different copies of a given film once circulated may seem to deterritorialize the "aura" of originality associated with a single extant print, but when that print becomes part of an archive (no matter whether nonprofit or commercial), it can also reacquire a sense of auratic value as a surviving artifact. Indeed, the idea of an authentic "original" version can mean different things to different parties: the "original" version as the filmmaker initially intended it to be seen, for instance, or the version of a print in the artifactual state "originally" obtained by an archive.[127]

Such contingencies in assigning archival value mean that even when companies like SWV recirculate vintage texts as residual products, aficionados may be as reminded of the alluring gaps that remain in the adult film corpus as the gaps filled in by cult video distributors' archival detective work. As with the *Orgy at Lil's Place* example discussed earlier, even a significant find can merely tease viewers over what remains in the shadows of historical obscurity, and not just close down curiosity about what is still out there. Furthermore, much like the paper ephemera collecting discussed in the previous chapter, the remediation of film-born texts on home video does not wholly replace collectors' desires for the materiality of earlier formats. As one fanzine author notes, SWV's release of many stags and loops on video "squelches some of the demand for the film itself, [although] there are still numerous collectors who wish to obtain them simply for the box art, if they boast such luxuries."[128] Indeed, websites like the Adult Loop Database, with its scans of surviving boxes and catalogues from pre-video 8-mm loops made in the United States and Western Europe (some of which are still sold in the adults-only section of eBay), demonstrate the lingering value of celluloid forms as all the more collectible artifacts, given their increased ephemerality in the home video age—although, for legal reasons, the Adult Loop Database generally omits information about the early 1970s Color Climax loops from Denmark that featured underage performers or bestiality, to give another example of deliberately selective remembrance.

At the same time, even home video companies that may be outwardly devoted to keeping vintage films indefinitely available must sometimes come up against the practicalities of their own limitations as for-profit archives—such as when their licenses to distribute certain films have expired (SWV's eventual relinquishment of distribution rights to the film libraries of producers Harry Novak and Manuel Conde, for instance), casting once-accessible films out of print and back into shadow economies. Much as vintage adult films teased their original audiences by pushing the boundaries of what could be seen, today's exciting rediscoveries of past films can quickly transform back into tomorrow's obscurities as collectors quickly snap up out-of-print editions, and most nonprofit archives continue to neglect such material.

Cyclical fandom and found films as *memento mori*

Mary Desjardins argues that thriving marketplaces for collectibles, such as eBay, foster not only fleeting instances of commodity exchange, but also an "eroticization" of the display and exchange of objects related to one's self-identity as a fan. In their affectively charged desires for the objects reemerging for sale, collectors expand the afterlives of their chosen objects, much as the serialized process of collecting can only end with the collector's own death.[129] In my estimation, this notion of the collecting process as an eroticized attempt at acquiring an inevitably fleeting past corresponds to the historian's attempts to search the past "for something (someone, some group, some series of events) that confirms the searcher in his or her sense of self, confirms them as they want to be, and feel in some measure that they already are."[130] Geoff Nicholson also suggests that the collecting of specifically erotic ephemera amplifies this dimension, since sex "implies a certain vitality, a profound separation from mortality and death. And yet these old photographs, of people probably now dead, remind us that the separation isn't so profound after all."[131]

Already layered with material signifiers of dilapidation and decay, historically neglected films like vintage pornography might move from uncertain archival status to a place in one's own personal archive, but these reminders of their contingent path through history may serve the collector less as ego-bolstering fantasies of conquering history through acquiring its once-lost treasures than as *memento mori* over the impossibility of truly achieving that goal. This final section, then, speaks to a broader affective phenomenon within longtime film fandom than one limited to the cult repute of vintage adult cinema alone. Yet, recalling Paolo Cherchi Usai's comments about our culture's taken-for-granted annihilation of the pornographic image as a corollary to the inevitable contingencies of material destruction that make film historiography possible, we might say that vintage pornography bespeaks an especially privileged example of a fandom circling around the counter-historical potential of discontinuity.

Much as adult film completists encouraged SWV's eventual move into opening up a "whole new world" by distributing vintage hard-core films, Matt Hills speaks of *cyclical fandom* as an experience that "combines a self-reported level of affective 'intensity' and activity with cyclical shifts away from discarded fan objects and toward newly compelling objects." In this way, "fan identity ... is open to multiple revision and rewriting without prior fan objects necessarily being viewed as embarrassing, inauthentic, or deficient. This leads to the emergence of patterns of (routinized) surprise in iterated media consumption and fandom." The fan may not self-consciously seek out "new" objects based on those objects' preexisting fan following, but rather for far more individually gratifying uses (including, say, autoeroticism) that are not necessarily rooted in direct interaction with other fans of the same object—although some lingering awareness of other fans is inevitable through the fact that this object has resisted obsolescence due to its continuing marketability to others.[132]

Becoming habituated to certain types of vintage adult films and then moving on to newly explorable cycles or variants (e.g., stags, roughies, kinkies, white coaters) is thus a prime example of cyclical fandom at work, with the many subcategories in sales catalogues from retailers like SWV and its kin bespeaking how acquiring more subcultural capital as a fan by developing a deeper engagement with the corpus typically requires moving further afield than the historically and textually limited range of a single cycle. The "new" object's affect is gradually "absorbed into a sense of self" as the fan digests it through the acquisition of knowledge about the text, then moves onto fresh discoveries without necessarily jettisoning the prior fan object's importance to his/her sense of self. This desire, however, is not rooted in the idea of a stable and unchanging self, but rather a self that maintains its supposed authenticity and individuality through perpetual openness to surprising discoveries that continually expand the self outward in search of new personal pleasures. Importantly, then, cyclical fandom is about "preserving the open self," rather than becoming fixed on one object, and may thus shift across various life phases, with the discovery of fresh fan objects accumulating into a sort of mnemonic map of one's life experiences.[133] Additionally, affective responses are particularly variable with longtime fans and/or fans with high levels of potential subcultural capital, since these fans are particularly "aware that age and desensitization means they are not always affected in ways intended by filmmakers,"[134] encouraging the tendency toward ironic distance that coexists with more earnestly affective and appreciative responses in vintage porn consumption.

Because the sheer diversity of adult cinema fuels the potential subcultural competencies that one can acquire over time to justify one's interest in this broad corpus, the fan may also try to interpret its history as a linear generic narrative so that it resonates with his/her own linear conception of self-identity. Indeed, "long term fans' *existence* is gradually transformed into *texistence*—the self unfolds over time in ongoing dialogue with the media object that helps define and sustain it," helping structure the fan's changing life narrative.[135] In other words, feeling our remembered personal histories structured by the retrospectively constructed corpus that we have encountered over our lifetimes, we can attempt to justify those personal histories by projecting them back onto the history of the adult film corpus itself, and thereby hoping to find discernable sources of (personal) continuity and value across these myriad texts. Hence, the fan's ever-threatened desire to make chronological and categorical sense of an unruly corpus based on valued concepts like "authenticity" and "originality" that one would like to see oneself performing as an individual, fan, or scholar. Despite their often imitative nature as cyclical products, championing the supposed authenticity and originality of vintage adult films becomes a means of mutually justifying those qualities in one's own perceived sense of self, especially as a sort of connoisseurial defense over holding an interest in culturally devalued movies. Since the adult film corpus and adult film audience are similarly denigrated in normative society, a defense of one often implies a defense of the other.

This is especially the case in cyclical fandoms that echo the cyclical nature of the adult film industry itself, less offering clear-cut lines of generic descent than a fragmented picture that reflects the fan's perpetually open self. As I mentioned earlier, for instance, sexploitation's various cycles were not wholly supplanted by hard core in the 1970s, nor are more recent hard-core features necessarily more sexually explicit and diverse than those from that transitional decade. Stitching together a linear sense of continuity between the individual texts and clusters of films that comprise adult cinema's cyclicality recalls classical Hollywood cinema's attempts to conceal the unavoidable "seams" and potentially estranging moments that would otherwise threaten the monolithic unity typically sought by its narratives. In unifying the point system of memory into a linear sense of narrative continuity, individual memory thus serves similarly territorializing functions that attempt to minimize memory's inevitable gaps, slippages, and disjunctures.[136] Conversely, if we consider that adult cinema more likely offers a menu of items, attractions, and intensities—modular elements visually splashed across a film's lurid promotional paratexts and endlessly recycled into various new forms—threatening to drift free of classical narrative norms in moments of sensational spectacle that are cyclically reiterated, then our conception of the unwieldy adult cinema corpus can magnify the fractures and slippages between disparate historical moments that create unexpected generic tangents and hybrids. These film-historical bits of spectacle will ideally fix in viewers' own memories—especially since memories are powerfully embedded through affective appeals to the viewing body—and thereby promote seemingly endless imaginative potential within appreciative viewers themselves.[137]

In this way, the spurts of difference-in-repetition that mark the regeneration of film cycles can indicate temporal ruptures opening toward a multiplicity of generic and reception possibilities. These deterritorializing moments of difference will inevitably be subject to memory's reterritorializing functions as one tries to make sense of adult cinema's intersecting cycles and influences, but they at least fleetingly point toward less linear, more contingent understandings of film history and personal history alike. That is, delving wider and deeper into the adult cinema corpus over the years may not simply result in an ego-boosting sense of mastery over this overlooked area of film history, but can also unearth a dizzying variety of cyclical products that only seems to grow more countless and uncontainable by the fan's ego the further he/she descends down this film-historical rabbit hole. Much as my initial egotism and potential marshaling of subcultural capital over finding a surviving print of *The Orgy at Lil's Place*, for example, was undercut by the unexpected fact that a copy already existed in a Dutch archive, the apparent rarity of any find is always subject to contestation when copies of a given film may reside uncatalogued in proper archives or in collectors' basements. Although a rare film like *Orgy* resists mastery because it remains sequestered in a closed archive and cannot currently be owned on video by individual collectors, even the video editions of readily available films in one's own personal collection are likely to bear marks of their unstable routes through history.

Subcultural capital and nostalgia may work in tandem to establish an imagined degree of continuity between the fan's sense of self and a filmic past over which he/she gradually gains knowledge—but the fact that adult cinema's past has been largely forgotten, its more obscure texts vanished into dusty basements and warehouses, means that it is impossible to exhaust the myriad and contingent paths of textual discovery that one can pursue within the imagined spatiotemporal realm of a bygone cultural past. Battered 35-mm franchise prints of once-lost adult films are continually being found, transferred to video, and brought to open availability through companies like SWV and its successors. This openness of film history, albeit most often technologically delivered to consumers for economic gain, thus allows for a perpetual accumulation of subcultural capital over the fan's lifetime. And yet, as I noted earlier, with perhaps 40 percent of adult films missing or extant only in incomplete forms, desires for wholeness and unity must be endlessly deferred when considering not only a particular cinematic corpus but also the fan self with longtime investments in that corpus. Each release into the home video marketplace serves as a nagging reminder of how many countless cyclical products are still waiting for rediscovery and potential incorporation into a shifting sense of self whose ragged contours belie the thought of a closed and coherent fan identity.

Consequently, the reciprocal openness of both the fan's sense of self and his/her grasp of adult film history can allow the experiences of cyclical fandom to become "life strategies" for suspending the logical but inevitable end of one's own self-narrative: death. Milly Buonanno describes these life strategies in the interrupted and prolonged pleasure of television serials and series that, respectively, delay narrative closure indefinitely or cyclically suspend time's flow through "the eternal return to the present." These affective appeals become strategies for working against time's incessant forward march, thus disavowing or assuaging the inevitability of one's own demise.[138] Adapting this argument, I believe that by nostalgically immersing oneself in a filmic past that is constantly unfolding and exposing its cyclical riches, even as one retains a foothold in the lived present by recognizing the vintage datedness of such films, the longtime fan's own life experience develops a cyclical dimension that acknowledges the threat of fatal futurity (especially since past adult films are increasingly inhabited by the now-deceased), even as it attempts to hold the future at bay through the present force of cyclical rediscoveries. "Although film cycles appear to die or disappear after a few years," notes Amanda Ann Klein, "in practice their themes and images continue to circulate, even if in a highly diluted or altered form, decades after the original cycle has disappeared."[139] In like manner, I would argue that the personal obsolescence represented by the fan–collector's own death is disavowed or at least assuaged by the reciprocal awareness of filmic cycles' ever-delayed "death," a knowledge that is continuously reiterated as subcultural capital is garnered through idiosyncratic strings of indefinite cyclical discoveries across one's lifetime. "I've figured out what exists, what is and isn't out there, what's left to find, who made it, why it's lost, [and] how many prints were made," Mike Vraney boasted in 2005[140]—but even this confidence over his knowledge of the corpus seems, in light of his January 2014 death from lung cancer at age fifty-six, a somewhat defensive admission that much remains inevitably unreachable within even the most devoted fan's lifetime.

Recognizing one's own embeddedness in such self-narratives, however, need not erase the compulsive desire to construct them. Rather, in gaining a self-reflexive awareness of the cyclical patterns that one represents to (and about) oneself in reference to one's diverse range of chosen texts, the cyclical fan might pleasurably mutate his/her self-conceptions by embracing the fluidity of the numerous film-historical moments, cycles, and periods through which one's perpetually open self is constantly reformed. While one cannot step wholly outside the discursive frameworks that shape these cultural memories, one might privilege less habitual experiences of pastness by amplifying the moments of difference within and between these viscerally powerful texts: those cyclically productive moments of sensationally exploitable attraction that can force cracks in historical or narratological coherence and radiate potentiality in nonlinear directions across and against time. If cyclical fandom involves explorations of the past media landscape for self-sustaining sources of "originality" and "authenticity" (which, from an empirical standpoint, remain dubious claims at best), then accepting the openness of self-identity is perhaps the most fitting means of likewise incorporating the rhizomatic map of adult cinema into one's own ongoing aesthetic-mnemonic project of piecing together those multiplicitous fragments of remembered experience that make fans, collectors, and historians who they are.[141]

In this respect, I am inspired by Carolyn Steedman's discussion of archival "dust" as that historical material which, despite outward appearances, refuses to go away: "It is not about rubbish, nor about the discarded; it is not about a surplus, left over from something else: *it is not about Waste*. Indeed, Dust is the opposite thing to Waste, or at least, the opposite principle to Waste. It is about circularity, the impossibility of things disappearing, or going away, or being gone."[142] For Steedman, the historian too often takes cultural disappearance and erasure as a given, since this logic also conveniently fuels the narratives that historians tell: someone or something once existed but does no longer, and the historian's narrativizing work seemingly performs a restorative magic upon such ostensibly "lost" objects of desire. Yet, the material traces or "dust" that remain bespeak how, much as historians can never resurrect the past as it actually was, they can only narrate *endings* amid history's constantly moving flow toward an unnarrativizable *end* that the historian him/herself will never see.[143]

Like the incompleteness of the archive itself, then, the texts found there are full of insurmountable narrative discontinuities—as the visible traces of historical contingency seen in the damage and decay of surviving vintage adult films testify only too well. When their on-screen images of sexual pleasure viscerally resonate with our own viewing bodies, affectively connecting us to the cinematic bodies of performers who may themselves now be deceased and texts that are now likely decayed, I find it difficult not to reflect on how we will all one day similarly join the scrapheap of history—a feeling consistent with the Bataillean twinge of melancholy that so often accompanies *la petite mort*, for even our greatest ecstasies are as inevitably fleeting as these preceding generations' documented pleasures in the face of *la grande mort*. Although I thus cannot claim to relinquish the seductive idea of cultural disappearance in my own analysis—especially when discussing films that have so often been marginalized from traditional histories and left uncollected by most archives—Steedman's theory should at least remind us that cultural forgetting and cultural remembrance are inextricable from each other, giving rise to not only historiographical labor (including my own) but also the affective potential of (imagined) contact with the past. If the physical impact of experiencing material traces of age in once-ephemeral pornographic materials can form affective bridges across the times and spaces separating past and present reception contexts, then we can better explore how the visceral and political resonance of such texts shapes their continuing potential for wider cultural recollection.

4

Preservational Ethics, Cultural Distinctions, and Vintage Pornoisseurship in the Internet Age

We could wait 20 years until we turn up a 35mm vault negative of [A] Climax of Blue Power [1974], *or we can put out a watchable but unimpressive version now. Trust me*[;] *we would love a stellar version on DVD, but we need to serve fans and collectors in the now and not try to become the Criterion Collection of 70s porn.*
—Jacy Catlin, Alpha Blue Archives[1]

We're pornographers, if you will. We're not even [pornographers]. We're more historians, but the people in the business are pornographers.
—Steven Morowitz, Distribpix Inc.[2]

"You can't censor memories," reads the motto on the box for *The Original Classic Stags*, an 8-mm series of pre-1960s hard-core shorts sold for home consumption in the 1970s. And yet, as we have seen in the previous chapter, attempts at self-censorship have been present in the mainstream porn industry since at least 1973, becoming especially noteworthy with the industry's moves toward corporatization and legitimization since the 1980s. "I'm sure that there will always be missing/edited footage here & there," admitted the creative director of TVX in 2005,

> which sadly is the game most classic companies play when releasing sevearl versons [sic] of the same title—which is better, which has the better cover, etc. […] Also, even though these films are (some) well over 25 years old—none of us ever know if we will fall under the hammer of the government's microscope at any time—thus the reason for the editing & the accurate records we keep.

Certain "taboo" or non-normative sexual practices (in this TVX executive's words, "pee, very rough rape enactment, certain foreign object insertion[s], etc.") have been selectively rendered out of Golden Age films in their remediated video versions.[3] Whereas veteran adult studios like VCA, VCX, and Caballero may promote these sanitized "classics" plucked from their compiled film libraries, a handful of smaller video labels have been working to flesh out the historical record by providing access to a far more diverse, and sometimes more "politically incorrect," range of vintage pornography.

This question of access is a crucial one, since the meaning of surviving films is not ultimately shaped by the state of pristine prints or original camera elements safely locked away in archives, but rather by the practices that reproduce and circulate vintage films in the marketplace.[4] Indeed, Caroline Frick argues that the film preservation community overwhelmingly fetishizes high-quality "original" materials secured within archives, since these materials can be upheld as safely stable containers of cultural heritage—a claim that would help legitimize film archives as cultural institutions. Conversely, she says, the process of offering consumers continual, active use of mass-reproduced copies (such as through home video distribution instead of just formal archivization) more appropriately evokes cinematic texts' dynamic *legacies* among successive generations of viewers, belying the more conservative notion of a passively inherited *heritage*.[5] With so many official archives reluctant to collect or preserve adult films—to say nothing of their relative rarity as "acceptable" programming for repertory theaters and other public venues for cinema's commemoration—the legacies of such films have more often fallen to the whims of for-profit video distributors and their unofficial archival repositories. Meanwhile, the shadowy mafia connections behind so much Golden Age pornography have been replaced by the cutthroat competition for rare prints among a small band of film collectors turned independent entrepreneurs aiming to recapitalize on neglected adult films. But even among these present-day adult video distributors, there are marked differences—often falling along generational lines—between the ethics of film preservation practiced by these companies.

Nonprofit film archives and many for-profit archives follow preservational "codes of ethics," as prescribed by organizations like the International Federation of Film Archives (FIAF) and the Association of Moving Image Archivists (AMIA). Such guidelines include, for example, restoring and preserving filmic artifacts without changing the original materials; respecting creators' original choices and existing rights holders' claims; nonjudgmentally protecting material endangered by legal and political shifts; and prioritizing long-term preservation over short-term economic exploitation.[6] In the case of adult films, however, which largely lack formal archival homes, such preservational ethics far more rarely adhere in actual practice. Since many FIAF archivists view film-to-film transfers as the only means of ethically preserving master copies,[7] for instance, this fetishization of celluloid as a medium for both storage and projection means that adult films—which typically circulate today as low-resolution video copies and are seldom preserved, restored, or screened on celluloid—are doubly damned by dominant archival practices. Likewise, despite ethical guidelines to neutrally prioritize preservation and restoration based more on the provenance/condition of surviving elements than on filmic content, archives typically bump to the top of the list those films apt to generate more positive publicity for the archive (such as films linked to notable directors, stars, or historical events) while de-prioritizing more marginal or disreputable content.

Although Karen Gracy offers the useful distinction between film *conservation* (archival storage), film *preservation* (physical copying, whether through photochemical or digital means), and film *restoration* (reconstruction of a lost "original" version), she observes that many archival players define even basic terms like "preservation" very differently.[8] If anything, the rise of digital formats like DVD and Blu-ray has only served to further blur such distinctions, since common marketing terms like "remastered" can easily become confused with the far less common process of restoring films from meticulously reconstructed original elements. Moreover, "[e]thical issues have become more urgent" with the advent of digital technology, says Giovanna Fossati, "since film restorers can alter the aspect of the film more easily and more profoundly," such as the much-criticized use of digital noise reduction that can remove the celluloid image grain from Blu-ray transfers of film-born movies. Her research demonstrates how the ethical principles that might be widely endorsed as abstract ideals still remain hotly debated in actual cases of preservation and restoration, since the idea of an authentic "original" version can mean many things to many interested parties.[9] But when potentially "prurient interest" (the legal yardstick for defining obscenity, as per *Miller v. California*) enters the fray, vintage pornography's (sub)cultural value as sexually provocative surviving artifacts becomes an issue fraught with more radioactive political connotations than perhaps any other genre.

I noted in the previous chapter that Something Weird Video's (SWV) initial library of vintage soft-core releases gained attention in the hard-core-centric trade magazine *Adult Video News* because of those films' appeals to the nostalgia of both a demographically older generation and a culturally hip, younger generation of adult film fans, each seeking something different from the flood of more recent, shot-on-video pornography. In this chapter, I suggest that when independent labels like Something Weird and Alpha Blue Archives (ABA) branched into the collectors' market for vintage hard-core cinema in the mid-1990s, they constituted an important early generation of video distributors devoted to recirculating older films that were either neglected or mutilated by adult video's larger and more established studios like VCA and Caballero. Much as I said in Chapter 1, vintage pornography's cult repute is often established through its perceived subcultural difference from the pornographic "mainstream"—a distinction that upstarts like Something Weird and Alpha Blue wisely exploited by carrying on the adult video industry's earlier bootlegging practices to provide access to "uncut" or otherwise unavailable films whose age and historicity increasingly rendered them niche-interest titles once newer, video-born pornography began dominating the marketplace.

Yet, if this early generation of vintage hard-core reclaimants was first and foremost concerned with providing *access* to rare films and versions, a more recent generation of independent distributors like Vinegar Syndrome has emerged, staking their reputation upon not only cultish rarity but also the superior audiovisual preservation of their remediated products. Whereas earlier chapters have focused on the haptic and degraded qualities of such films as appealing signifiers of past use and present neglect, these more restorative developments in vintage pornography's recirculation thus mark an important step in a different direction, necessitating other attributions of retrospective value.[10] This generational shift from a sense of connoisseurship based on *access* itself to one based on *quality* may rely on more traditionally recuperative standards of cinematic artworthiness, but it can also imply a more ethical approach to reclaiming a historically important genre that has long been in danger of turning to cultural dust. Although most of the independent companies discussed in this chapter currently release both soft-core and hard-core films, I will primarily focus on their hard-core offerings because these have historically been the most difficult varieties of adult cinema to politically and aesthetically salvage—and thus the most notable examples of attempted cultural reclamation. They have also been the most forthcoming companies in participating directly with fans on discussion forums devoted to vintage adult cinema, whether by plugging upcoming releases, answering complaints about DVD quality and censorship, or intervening in fans' frequent discussions over who owns the rights to various films.

Vintage hard-core features and recuperative fan discourse

Much as I noted in the previous chapter that the historical value of rediscovered films may outweigh the affective value of the previously "lost" film as an imagined entity, I suggest here that the ethical necessity to preserve adult cinema outweighs the sometimes dubious representational ethics within the texts themselves. Because anti-porn discourses have so often denigrated hard-core adult films as "immoral" or politically "harmful" in their unsimulated representations of sexuality (particularly in the case of older films fictionally depicting acts of sexual aberrance like rape, incest, or sex-murder, which have since fallen out of favor within most mainstream pornographic representations), these films have been subject to far less ethical preservation practices by most video labels as well. However, because the research of porn studies scholars has roundly rejected misguided behaviorist arguments about the supposedly detrimental effects of viewing violent or explicit films from culturally "low" genres, it has become more tenable to approach the vagaries of hard-core cinema's past representational ethics and contemporary preservational ethics on shared ground.

Fans, for instance, frequently imply that classics studios which edit rape or incest scenes from Golden Age narrative features inadvertently condemn the films' value in a circular way: by editing certain scenes to avoid potential obscenity issues, these alterations destroy the very character motivations and authorial intent that would otherwise help defend the text against legal accusations that a given film lacks redeeming social/artistic merit.[11] Moreover, by removing or subsequently avoiding such content, mainstream porn companies have implicitly played into antiporn activists' spurious media-effects arguments by undercutting their own defensive (if one-sided) claims that fictional films depicting unsimulated sex should merely be seen as harmless fantasies.

This question also brings us back to the figure of the porn fan broached at the beginning of this study, and the fan-cultural discourses that Jacques Boyreau calls the "post-porn rise of the pornoisseur."[12] Much as previous chapters have shuttled between the historical contexts which gave rise to vintage pornography's artifacts and latter-day collectors' uses of those material traces, this final chapter loops back to how vintage hard core's fans have resisted censorial efforts while revaluing a genre whose post-1970 legal availability has paradoxically tainted its Golden Age corpus with a sense of contemporaneity that has proven more difficult to aesthetically recuperate than the archaic quaintness of once-illicit, pre-1970 stags. Whereas the previous chapter explored how vintage films from Something Weird were discussed in the hard-core trade press, in this chapter I draw upon fan discourses and the words of vintage porn distributors themselves to explore the connoisseurial strategies that newer generations of technologies have encouraged among an emerging generation of vintage porn aficionados expecting more from their favored genre than access alone.

Valuing the aesthetic vision of the uncut text, these "post-porn" discourses appreciating the genre as a variegated corpus in its own right—rather than simply the interchangeable masturbatory aids that these fans more often associate with present-day pornography—have become a means of distancing older hard-core material from its cultural demonization while still recognizing the genre's unique status as one of the most hotly contested cinematic forms. As one fan says:

> I personally think they're two different animals—for me[,] something like a Something Weird Bucky Beaver DVD serves an entirely different purpose than a volume of ASS PARADE. A CD by Pink Floyd is not the same as a language learning CD just because they're both sound recordings issued on the same format. The XXX stuff that I leave out for guests to see are ones that I put in the "movie" category. […] Mainly stuff from the 70's that has a plot and acting. I don't *use* those DVD's, I sit down and watch them. […] The stuff that I hide is the "porno" and I look at that in the same way I do fitness DVDs—they're interactive "motivation" tools.[13]

As the above quote implies, the relationship between narrative and sexual numbers is a recurrent discussion topic within vintage porn fandom, with most fans claiming that "serious" Golden Age filmmakers used shorter and more narratively justified sex scenes—in addition to sex scenes not solely or primarily intended for triggering masturbatory climax—unlike the tendencies of later, Silver Age films and beyond. For these fans, then, many younger viewers simply do not know how to approach older hard-core narratives—like older examples of any filmic genre—with the "proper" expectations:

> I constantly recommend young folk quality (i.e., older) XXX and even if they (usually begrudgingly) admit that it was much better than they expected, they can rarely get over how "campy" or "dated" they perceive it to be, which, [in my opinion], is a total bullshit/copout excuse for not being able to appreciate anything older than they are (young folk often exhibit similar reactions to any older Hollywood films as well).[14]

> They see a low budget film, often with some sub-par acting that, inexplicably (to them) has a story, dialogue, characters, sex scenes which develop the characters and enhance the narrative, and they get confused. They think "why is all this time being wasted on plot when there could be more fucking?" So, as people so often do when they don't understand things, they dismiss them, or try to look for any other shortcoming so that they don't need to think about what they don't

understand. What's more, is that if they find the sex unarounsing [sic], strange or even repugnant, they immediately write off the film as "bad" because it seemingly clashes with what [they think] porn is supposed to do: turn you on.[15]

Not only do people I talk to assume porn shows women enjoying rape, but they often think porn depicts women in pain and suffering for male spectatorial pleasure. I think the "rape" movies are best to watch after you've realised that porn isn't just about jacking off.[16]

By downplaying the potential for arousal, such discourses are an obvious defensive formation against a history of antiporn feminists and moralists who politicized *all* hard-core pornography as supposedly "pro-rape." Moreover, David Andrews notes that the recent wave of hard-core art films like *Romance* (1999), *Intimacy* (2000), and *Nymphomaniac* (2013) tends to differentiate itself from hard-core pornography by "habitual use of realistic, often downbeat materials," such as rape, violence, incest, emotional cruelty, and existential angst—that is, subject matter that connotes "serious" artistic intent and gives a critical "free pass" to art cinema's viewers of such content (a strategy recalling the overlaps between 1960s soft-core roughies and European art cinema, as mentioned in Chapter 2).[17] As the above quotes suggest, porn fans can make related aspirational claims for Golden Age features by asserting that many of these narratives deal with more challenging or intellectually stimulating subject matter than the "pornotopian" pleasures of consequence-free, narrative-free copulation—but with these films likely lacking the aegis of art cinema's accepted modes of circulation and critical reception, convincing wider audiences of this recuperable value can be an uphill battle.

Much as seasoned horror movie fans often assert that (unlike more "naïve" non-fans) they are no longer scared by a body genre that may have frightened them as children,[18] fans of Golden Age pornographic features are similarly concerned with finding more nuanced sources of pleasure than mere autoerotic affect, less out of being "densensitized" (a still-popular term among antiporn moralists for connoting moral and political apathy) than *habituated* to the genre's narrative conventions, as long-time fans of any genre eventually are. On the other hand, as Martin Barker has shown, such disavowals of the potential for arousal in fictional rape scenes displace the fact that sensory arousal and intellectual reflection often coexist when viewing cinematic representations of sexual violence, precisely because most viewers reflect upon the aesthetic justification of such "politically incorrect" but viscerally impactful scenes through their prior knowledge of generic codes[19]—codes which, as these vintage porn aficionados worry, may well be lost on a younger generation of viewers, particularly given the self-censoring practices of some video companies. This is not, then, simply a case of hetero-male viewers enjoying unreconstructed pleasures under the cover of a knowing sense of irony that would disavow the anti-feminist stakes of such "bad taste" preferences.[20] Rather, an awareness of the genre's historical codes, including its narratively justifiable use of imagery that might be verboten today, can encourage fans to critically reflect upon their own historical distance from or proximity to the Golden Age viewership for whom these films were originally made.

For my purposes, however, this presumed generational shift in how to appreciate vintage hard-core features is all the more significant as a technological shift as well. Take this representative quote:

> [H]ow could you figure that people watch these classics for their smut value when they contain but a fraction of spankable material in comparison to what is being made today. [...] Fans of these films watch them equally if not primarily for their cinematic qualities in addition (or as opposed) to their ability to arouse. Shit ... If one just wants to blow their load, they've got internet porn for that![21]

The circulation of such fan discourses is, of course, encouraged by the very same online technologies that have (re)popularized more fragmentary, non-narrative varieties of contemporary pornography—thus reinforcing hard-core cinema's predominant consumption (at least since the 1980s video boom) as a furtive and largely anonymous practice behind closed doors. Although many of the same arguments could just as easily be made about an earlier generation's privatization of porn use through VHS tapes, online viewing practices (such as the streaming of free, low-resolution clips from tube sites) have become increasingly equated with relatively quick and undiscerning masturbatory utility, whereas the feature-length narrative forms originally made for theatrical consumption have become comparatively nostalgized as texts offering more diverse aesthetic and cultural uses. As feminist porn blogger The Gore-Gore Girl astutely notes, "Consider, how would the state of things be different if we felt comfortable openly watching adult films? In my opinion, the privacy and anonymity of video, [the] internet, and then illegal downloading have a lot to do with the [evaluative] problems outlined above."[22]

Beyond the shift from pornography's theatrical to home video consumption, then, ongoing technological shifts in textual circulation play a notable role here in framing the qualitative connotations (or lack thereof) championed by different generations of fans. The adult video industry has typically been an influential early adopter of new technologies like home video and the Internet, but much more in terms of convenient access than qualitative superiority. As industry veteran David Jennings recalls, "In the early days of home video, the big question customers asked was, 'How's the quality?' For good reason: some manufacturers dubbed from Beta and VHS masters instead of the ¾-inch professional standard. Some sold 6th-generation knockoffs. The respected Caballero still transferred off a movie screen with a single-tube industrial video camera."[23] When newer formats like DVD and Blu-ray were later introduced to the wider video marketplace (in 1997 and 2006, respectively), they tended to be associated with high-cultural or cinephiliac appeals to auteurism (interviews and filmmaker commentary tracks), nostalgic access to the past (trailers, photo galleries, and featurettes), and audiovisual excellence—all connotations previously pioneered by laser disc.[24]

In the case of hard-core adult cinema, however, the shift from magnetic videocassettes to digital discs was not accompanied by a corresponding qualitative shift, since even well-established classics studios like VCA, TVX, VCX, and Caballero often merely imported their existing VHS/Beta transfers of older films to DVD.[25]

Their DVD reissues of Golden Age 35-mm films are notorious for being presented in the wrong aspect ratio, with murky audiovisual quality, and including few (if any) relevant bonus features. Many claims on DVD packaging about "remastering" are either wholly disingenuous or misleadingly refer only to a return to the S-VHS or Beta video masters, not the original source prints. Since these DVDs are presumed to have little crossover appeal beyond the legally segregated world of adults-only retailers, these studios do not find it cost-effective to strike new transfers from the original print elements (if available) or to commission extensive bonus features in the way that more widely retailed, non-hard-core cult labels like Blue Underground can afford.[26] Furthermore, the lingering copyright vagaries surrounding older films means that few studios surviving from the adult video industry's early years are willing to invest the considerable expense in restoring films whose legal provenance is still potentially in question.[27] As one fan comments, "It acutally suprises [sic] me how much effort some [younger] companies put into new releases these days. Too bad companies like WICKED and EVIL ANGEL aren't as old as VCX and the like. I'm sure you'd see some good releases if they had classic material to put out."[28]

This obvious disjuncture between the mainstream porn industry's patterns of early technological adoption and the low-quality remediation of its once-profitable older texts has proven a particular source of anger and frustration for vintage porn fans. Although fan-produced discourse about adult films is far from a recent phenomenon (as seen in the example of the *ARTISEX* fanzine discussed in Chapter 2), the explosion of cult movie fanzines in the 1980s–1990s and online newsgroups, forums, and blogs since the 1990s has allowed fan discourse about vintage pornography to rapidly proliferate, particularly when it can be exchanged anonymously. Text-only newsgroups like rec.arts.movies.erotica (later housed at rame.net) spawned exhaustive databases like the Internet Adult Film Database, while later discussion forums such as Vintage Erotica Forums, Adult DVD Talk, AV Maniacs, FreeOnes, and Rock! Shock! Pop! have facilitated far more interpersonal discourse between fans. These forums have also allowed adult filmmakers and performers to discover that their decades-old films have a continuing following, giving them an outlet to come out of the proverbial woodwork and openly interact with fans and even participate in reissues. Whereas a pre-Internet generation of porn fans might have had to rely on industry-friendly magazines like *Video-X*, *Velvet's Erotic Film Guide*, *Adult Video News*, and *Adam Film World* for practical information about home video releases, online fan discourse has undeniably allowed such information—including plenty of vitriol over what they perceive as video companies' ill treatment of vintage films—to become far more widely accessible for participation. "[W]hen has any classic been given the full treatment it deserves?" asked one Adult DVD Talk forum participant in 2003, with another chiming in,

> I have thought about boycotting companies like VCX (they're not the only ones guilty of this but are probably the worst offenders) but they have released some genuine classics and, in the absence of competing releases from other territories, therefore hold "all the aces." Perhaps if enough people make their feelings known on boards like this we can shame these companies into producing higher quality disks.[29]

As another fan likewise remarked in 2005, "There's really not one true special edition of any pre-[19]85 porno that I can think of off the top of my head. Most of them are shoddy vhs to DVD transfers with no extras at all."[30]

Since the late 1990s, the adult video industry's technological neglect toward upgrading the treatment of so many of its older hard-core films has thus coincided with the rise of online networks allowing fans to roundly criticize such practices, helping further construct vintage porn fandom's ethos of opposition to the forms of mainstream corporate power from which subcultural capital distinguishes itself. If it was common until the late 2000s for vintage hard-core DVDs to reproduce outdated transfers in all their audiovisual degradation, suggesting that these historically significant films had since been qualitatively forgotten by their one-time owners, recent years have seen a turn toward home video editions that finally reveal the "full treatment" expected for classics of any cinematic genre.

As such, I argue that the resurgence of vintage porn fandom has been spurred this very tension between, on the one hand, a substantial number of Golden Age narrative films remediated in limited quality or incomplete form and sold as simply "porn"; and, on the other hand, a smaller handful of adult films qualitatively restored and sold as a legitimate genre. Furthermore, these "post-porn" attempts at recuperating Golden Age adult films have been shaped by not only different preservational practices but also different distribution strategies—including some that are, like the films themselves, similarly returning from the past in recently revalued forms. As much as the allure of vintage pornography derives from the textual interplay of concealment and revelation, then, this ongoing allure is all the more encouraged by the interplay between residual and emergent efforts to monetize past content through older and newer technologies of film and video distribution. In other words, despite decades of intervening change, echoes of the porn industry's past business strategies—including piracy/bootlegging, pay-per-view video, and even theatrical exhibition—continue to resonate in present-day efforts to revitalize the vintage porn market in the Internet age, helping shape fans' desires for culturally residual films that are reclaimable as both viscerally stimulating and aesthetically appealing.

An ethics of access: Something Weird Video and Alpha Blue Archives

Although Mike Vraney began SWV as an extension of his desire to collect "every goddamn movie that had naked people that wasn't porno," his label's belated move into offering transfers of 35- and 16-mm hard-core feature films through its *Bucky Goes to the Movies* and *Bucky Beaver's Dragon Art Theatre Double Features* VHS series (both inaugurated in the mid-1990s, albeit sold through the separate *Blue Book* catalogue) allowed him to commercially recirculate hundreds of vintage hard-core titles (Figure 4.1) that larger and more established adult video companies generally did not carry. In keeping with the label's focus on "weird" films, most of these 1970s hard-core titles contain themes and content less easily recuperable to the Golden Age adult

Figure 4.1 Front cover for one of Something Weird Video's many *Bucky Beaver's Dragon Art Theatre Triple XXX-Rated Double Feature* DVDs, sourced from battered 16-mm prints recovered from a Tennessee storefront theater. Courtesy of Something Weird Video.

industry's gradual focus on a more "aspirational" couples' market.[31] The majority of these films do not have subculturally heralded directors and date from the early-to-mid 1970s, before fictional depictions of nonconsensual sex, underage sex, incest, BDSM, and so on became increasingly verboten. Likewise, most of SWV's hard-core titles are technically incompetent "one-day wonders," made in 16 mm with few of the aesthetic aspirations seen in the first-wave "porno chic" productions that attempted to cross over to middle-class neighborhood theaters. Indeed, although the *Blue Book* contains an article by David F. Friedman on California's relatively upscale Pussycat Theater chain (which, through Vince Miranda's ownership, epitomized attempts to establish porn theaters as clean, well-lighted places open to couples), the catalogue primarily emphasizes these films' evocation of "going to a genuine Seventies storefront theatre in your own home!" By privileging the small, cheap, and dirty storefront theaters that, as noted in Eric Schaefer's *Blue Book* article on these venues, exploded in skid row districts after the legalization of hard-core cinema, SWV thus frames the cheapness and sleaziness of its hard-core offerings as not only historically appropriate for their era, but also qualitatively distinguished from the slicker product that hard core's larger industry players would produce by the late 1970s (and would quickly remediate onto home video in the early 1980s).[32]

By largely focusing on earlier, "weirder" films made by small, fly-by-night companies far more likely to have orphaned these films, SWV could not only avoid potentially costly copyright negotiations, but also offer a substantial amount of stock that was previously unavailable on home video. In its early years, SWV frequently released 50–70 new titles per year, effectively flooding the market with newly rediscovered product as a means of firmly establishing the label's bona fides as a major player in the cult film world. As soon as new prints were located and acquired, telecine transfers were made and new tapes made available for mail order, with relatively little restoration work performed in the process. In a few cases, films were even re-titled or transferred with the reels in the wrong order. Most of Vraney's rare hard-core offerings derived from especially battered 16-mm release prints, full of splices and other material dilapidation, allowing the evoked image of the storefront theater to also serve as a convenient justification for the shoddy source materials and questionable transfers.[33]

Although Vraney would eventually become interested in acquiring original camera negatives instead of just battered release prints—a long-term advantage once higher-definition transfers were required for the company's line of special-edition DVDs, pressed and distributed for retail sale by Image Entertainment since 1999—the majority of his catalogue, including his hard-core offerings, appeared through a clear logic of speed and proliferation over quality and curation. Because Image refused to sell hard-core adult films but had no qualms about distributing soft-core material (including numerous sexually violent roughies), SWV has not re-transferred much of its back catalogue to match the higher audiovisual standards of post-VHS video formats. The films distributed by Image—which garnered significant crossover visibility for vintage soft-core texts in mainstream retail outlets like Tower Records—may have received new transfers for DVD,[34] but SWV still generally uses its original film-to-VHS transfers for the mail-order DVD-R and download-to-own titles offered through its website.

In a wide-ranging 2012 interview, Vraney explained how his background as a comic book collector and 16-mm print collector since the 1970s inspired his business strategies. Much as comics collectors seldom seek out individual titles in their own right and instead prefer to amass large runs of multiple series, Vraney banked on fellow fans' completism, rejecting criticism of his sometimes subpar source materials and transfers (often bearing a SWV watermark) or of the label's titles that might eventually go out of print. "We [collectors] have it. I don't care if it's crystal-clear or not," he says, "That's just like this snobby game going on."[35] For Vraney, access superseded arguments about quality—an understandable argument from one of the pioneers of bringing significant numbers of vintage adult films to home video in the first place, before the rise of DVD effectively mainstreamed cinephiliac demands for uncut versions, correct aspect ratios, and pristine transfers. As I noted at the end of the previous chapter, however, a fan's desire for completism over the shadowy adult film corpus can only ever remain partial, threatened by the many titles that still remain lost or inaccessible. Even Vraney seemed to implicitly cede this point in the years prior to his 2014 death, with SWV losing more of its accumulated catalogue through expired licensing deals than announcing newly uncovered titles.

In some respects, this plateau is unsurprising, as not only had SWV amassed a vast library of material over the years (including over 300 tons of film prints), but the overall DVD market dropped precipitously in 2008, spurred less by the global economic recession than the market saturation of popularly demanded titles already released on the increasingly aging format. With home video sales comprising the bulk of industry profits, it has not boded well that the average consumer has already purchased nearly all the older library titles for his/her household that might generate widespread DVD profits from a mass-distributed release. Even before his illness, Vraney had become disillusioned with the changing video industry and, eager to spend time on his other passions, sought new ownership for SWV—although the sheer size of the company's material assets posed both financial and logistical obstacles for most potential buyers.

Meanwhile, the format transition to Blu-ray has not yet gained a comparable foothold in either machines sold or titles available for sale at the time of this writing. Whereas the DVD player was the most rapidly adopted household electronic technology in US history,[36] Blu-ray represents less of the qualitative and extratextual paradigm shift seen in the VHS-to-DVD transition than a modest update of what everyday consumers already own. Moreover, the oft-subpar condition of surviving adult films has made their Blu-ray release less appealing for some video distributors. Vraney, for instance, allowed his fifty-film licensing deal with Harry Novak to lapse in the late 2000s because Novak's existing film elements were too dilapidated (due to poor storage conditions) to justify re-transferring onto Blu-ray—a format that, compared with DVD, would far more prominently display such flaws. As long as Blu-ray players remain reverse-compatible with DVDs, many examples of vintage adult cinema may thus remain stranded on this earlier generation of digital videodiscs, their source elements too degraded to justify the leap to Blu-ray's high-definition capabilities.

It is no surprise, then, that the late-2000s decline in DVD sales saw even the major Hollywood studios begin mining their extensive libraries for niche-interest titles that might generate additional revenue from sales of physical discs to collectors, cultists, and other assorted cinephiles, but without the high overhead cost of mass-pressing lots of discs. Spearheaded by the Warner Archive series, the burgeoning manufactured-on-demand (MOD) market is notable for selling DVD-Rs of semi-obscure library titles at premium prices with little investment in detailed restoration or curatorial bonus features.[37] Although coming from more culturally "legitimate" genres and companies than adult films, these rediscovered Hollywood pictures still evince qualitative doubts when their un-remastered, barebones MOD reissues are compared with the elaborate DVD/Blu-ray reissues of well-known Hollywood classics. Chris Anderson's influential concept of "long tail" distribution is an operative strategy here, whereby the deep catalogues of online operations allow the combined profits from numerous small sales of niche-interest goods to far outweigh the profits from mainstream products with a broader cultural demand but also greater overhead costs.[38] The resulting convergence of cultural tastes seen when niche films from many different strata commingle in online catalogues is thus paralleled by a convergence of industrial strategies, since the major studios' MOD branches have begun adopting the model of mail-order DVD-R sales pioneered by independent cult distributors like SWV. Although mainstream Hollywood studios may have a distinct economic advantage in their turn toward revenue from niche titles, these "new" corporate strategies are old news among taste cultures valuing obscure films with far less cachet than one of Hollywood's own "deep cuts." Small wonder, then, that Vraney cited the Warner Archive as a "genius" idea and the most exciting thing to happen in the film-collecting world over the last decade.

Tellingly, Vraney admitted that he thought most of his label's movies were "terrible," and had a hard time watching any movie more than two or three times. Much as he resisted ostensibly elitist criticism of his products' quality, he rejected attempts to analyze these profit-motivated films too deeply, finding them fascinating time capsules but instead hoping that fans would collect and champion personal favorite films and filmmakers for their sheer eccentricity. Vraney's love of these films, then, was that of the paracinephile described by Jeffrey Sconce, who ironically celebrates low-budget oddities for their badness or weirdness, but who may not find more serious value in them, except as historical documents of filmmaking desperation.[39] Although sometimes semi-ironically compared with high-cultural video labels due to its focus on films from a particular taste strata,[40] SWV markedly differs from labels like the Criterion Collection, whose self-described roster of "important classic and contemporary films" is not only bolstered by releasing titles whose existing cultural value is rarely in question, but also by selectively releasing relatively few new titles per year.[41] Although it may include avant-garde and art cinemas under its banner, Criterion's reinforcement of existing film canons is ultimately quite conservative from the standpoint of taste politics. Whereas Criterion releases are renowned for their superior transfers, ample bonus features, critical essays, and stylish packaging—all intended to reinforce the elitist perception of particular films as rewatchable art objects—SWV's plethora of candy-colored DVD releases, crammed with random or indirectly related ephemera (e.g., trailers, shorts, and educational films), beg not to be taken too seriously. By downplaying the cultural or aesthetic value of the films themselves, Vraney could thereby better justify his own profit-motivated inclination to provide quick access to many titles instead of qualitatively recuperating a select few titles through carefully curated DVD and Blu-ray editions.

Due to the preexisting high-cultural connotations of its reissued films, Criterion adheres more closely to the preservational ethics of nonprofit film archives with regard to digitally preserving texts in as close to their originally intended condition as possible, its liner notes often containing information on the source elements and restoration/scanning equipment. (Throughout his interviews, Vraney repeatedly conflates "restoration" and "preservation," although SWV only significantly practices the latter, by producing copies of its acquired prints.) Yet, as easy as it would be to write off Vraney's efforts as simply trying to capitalize on films originally made for crassly commercial purposes—sexploitation impresario David F. Friedman once proudly dubbed Vraney "the Forty-First Thief," in reference to the roving pack of exploitation film businessmen who peddled sex films across mid-century America[42]—SWV's initial resurrection of so many otherwise neglected films still constitutes a preservational ethics based in cultural access, since the label's recirculation of films that might seem good for little more than ironic humor has not circumscribed more serious modes of aesthetic appreciation.

Indeed, I would argue that, from a historiographic perspective, SWV is one of the most important video labels—far more so than Criterion—by making available an extensive catalogue of not just adult and exploitation films, but also African American race films, 1930–1940s American B films, 1960s–1970s European and East Asian genre films; and all manner of ephemeral and nontheatrical short subjects, including striptease loops, soundies, educational/propaganda/industrial films, and other forms of so-called "useful" cinema.[43] Though SWV is more of a business enterprise than an archival project and thus may have motives that would fall afoul of many preservational codes of ethics, following Caroline Frick's aforementioned argument about mass-produced copies better evoking the notion of ongoing cinematic legacies, Vraney's completist drive to indefinitely extend the afterlives of so many ostensibly ephemeral films through mass video reproduction at least represents an ethical contribution to cinema history that few other labels can claim.

Yet, one of SWV's major contemporaries, Alpha Blue Archives, distinguished itself as "essentially the all-hard-core equivalent of Something Weird Video," "[d]edicated to preserving out of print or never-available [on video] adult films from the Golden era."[44] Founded by print collector David Naylor in 1992, the company took its name from *The Satisfiers of Alpha Blue* (1980), a Gerard Damiano hard-core science-fiction film whose official video releases have notably excised the theatrical version's scenes of urolagnia and fisting—an example of the industry self-censorship practices that Naylor's company deliberately flouts. Like SWV, ABA began by offering vintage loop compilations and soft-core features on VHS before later branching into hard-core feature films; unlike SWV, though, ABA later phased out its soft-core releases after it became better known for its hard-core offerings.

"When I first started working at ABA I expected their clientele would be mostly fans of exploitation films who crossed over into XXX. 20–30 somethings who collected weird movies like myself," says long-time employee Jacy Catlin. But he soon discovered that ABA's customers were largely "[o]ld timers who saw these films/stars back in the day, or at least heard about them."[45] Like SWV's early celebration by Gene Ross in *Adult Video News*, then, there is an element of generational nostalgia at work here, not just subcultural taste, and Catlin admits that fandom of particular films/directors/stars (especially when their work is contained within a feature-length narrative) tends to outweigh predilections for particularly censorable sexual acts that can be more easily accessed through contemporary fetish videos: "You can easily get extreme fisting videos nowadays, uncensored, but with the classic stuff, since the fisting scenes were often cut for video release, it becomes a big point to collectors to get the uncut version. It's not that they are big fans of fisting, just that they want the complete versions of the movies they are fans of."

Compared with SWV's primary reputation for selling non-hard-core films, ABA's current catalogue more closely resembles that of other hard-core video companies, offering double- and triple-feature releases themed around either particular Golden Age porn stars or particular adult filmmakers (such as Damiano, Alex de Renzy, Roberta Findlay, Doris Wishman, Shaun Costello, and Anthony Spinelli) through its *Cult 70s Porno Directors* DVD series. Unlike SWV, more of ABA's feature films originated as higher-budgeted productions, shot on 35 mm and intended for crossover theatrical audiences. Also unlike SWV, ABA supplements its own in-house product by distributing vintage porn DVDs from other classics studios, including Arrow, Cal Vista, TVX, and VCX—many of which better exemplify the adult film industry's aesthetically and politically aspirational moves during the 1970s–1980s. ABA's sale of these in-print DVDs from other studios may also help dissuade competitors from taking legal action against ABA over its in-house releases that the larger companies also distribute in cut versions, says Catlin:

> AB makes money for Arrow and TVX selling their titles. Online vendors make money selling AB DVDs. Those vendors may be owned by the same folks that own other video labels. There is no love lost when it comes to AB and a few other video companies/individuals, but for purely business reasons sometimes causing legal trouble for each other is not the best idea.

Like these competitor studios, ABA also offers many of its in-house releases through video-on-demand (VOD) websites like AEBN, Hot Movies, and Gamelink, from which films can be streamed in whole or on a scene-by-scene basis (with options to pay per minute, per day, or to purchase in perpetuity)—a notable access option to which I will later return.

ABA is, however, even more blatant than SWV in its willingness to sell vintage hard-core films containing "taboo" content under its own label, which have become the company's best sellers. Its *Taboo Triples* series, for example, contains feature films themed around fictional depictions of underage sex or incest (often involving teenagers), while its *Sadistic Seventies* line includes BDSM-themed hard-core films. Its self-explanatory series of *History of Rape* and *History of Incest* DVDs move into even more extreme territory, including 8-mm loops themed around fictional depictions of sexualized torture and murder. Much as SWV's hard-core catalogue emphasizes storefront theaters, ABA similarly invokes Chelly Wilson's Avon chain of 42nd Street storefront theaters through its series of *Avon Dynasty* box sets (Figure 4.2). Bill Landis and Michelle Clifford's article on the Avon theaters, published in the "Porn History" section of the ABA website, contextualizes the chain's penchant for 16-mm rape- and BDSM-themed hard-core roughies (bankrolled by Wilson for play in her own theaters and a later, short-lived Avon Video label) beginning in 1975, after such content had already become less common in the wider theatrical porn market.[46] "History," then, becomes a major operative term in ABA's product listings, teasing prospective buyers that these films offer spectacle that has become far less permissible today, but which might be legally excusable as historical documents of a bygone (and thus safely contained) past. By bolstering its bottom line with more "tasteful" (often self-censored) DVDs from other studios, ABA's overall catalogue thus includes hard-core feature films representing the industry's moves toward aboveground legitimacy, while its in-house releases simultaneously focus on the taboo content that was gradually marginalized from the post-1973 industry. "The only case of us 'self censoring' was the fogging of a foot fucking scene" in one compilation DVD, says Catlin. "That one scene is the only example in 200+ DVD releases of purely commercial censorship."[47]

This commingling of taste appeals in ABA's catalogue is exemplified by the label's release of not just transfers from Naylor's personal collection of 16- and 35-mm prints,[48] but also, when celluloid prints are unavailable, films copied from S-VHS masters or out-of-print VHS/Beta tapes released decades ago by now-defunct video companies. "I often 'operate' on tapes," says Catlin, "take the guts out and put them into brand new cases to try to get them to track better. I run all tape masters through some hardware that is specifically for digitally cleaning up old tapes." Some of the label's in-house releases even assemble "uncut" versions using composite transfers from both celluloid and video sources, since many early home video editions featured less self-censorship than later ones. As reviewer Casey Scott observes, for example, ABA's release of Roberta Findlay's *Anyone But My Husband* (1975) was sourced "from a beautiful 35mm print and a faded video version, resulting in some obvious quality jumps. Heck, there are even tracking rolls which appear during some of the more controversial footage" (e.g., whipping, fisting, and vaginal insertion of a champagne bottle).[49] ABA's deliberate marketing of the "bad taste" of politically retrograde or verboten content thus becomes mirrored in the very audiovisual inferiority of its product—and yet, paradoxically, some film restorers would argue that attempting *not* to disguise the disparity between these different sources is actually a more ethical choice because it more obviously testifies to a film's "disparate provenance."[50] In a

Figure 4.2 Alpha Blue Archives' *The Avon Dynasty: 1980s* DVD box set, featuring cheap and kinky hard-core films made and theatrically screened in New York, well after hard-core roughie content had been increasingly phased out by larger porn producers in favor of couples-friendly films. Courtesy of Alpha Blue Archives.

sense, ABA is emulating the older, analog bootlegging practices once endemic within the early, pre-corporatized years of the adult video industry—albeit now with the no less profit-motivated goal of capitalizing on otherwise unavailable uncut versions. However, since many of the larger and more "legitimate" classics studios surviving since the early 1980s still continue to merely import their own subpar, heavily edited video transfers to DVD, failing to take qualitative advantage of newer formats, ABA can better disguise its own grey-market practices as quasi-legitimate.

Like SWV, then, ABA's in-house releases largely consist of orphaned or in-stasis works, but Naylor's label also draws materials from more recent sources than SWV, including orphaned videotapes, even at the risk of bootlegging films to which other studios may currently make (questionable) proprietary claims. In this respect, ABA's quasi-legal reproduction practices complicate a historical teleology that would posit the adult video industry as simply moving from early widespread piracy to later corporatization. The label can be said to participate in an ethics of access by reproducing and selling films that would otherwise be unavailable or censored, but it does so by engaging with what Lucas Hilderbrand calls video's sense of "inherent vice." Hilderbrand notes that analog videotape began as a blank format for the illicit copying and timeshifting of television broadcasts, before it became a medium associated with prerecorded content. The defining aesthetic features of videotape become visible through the audiovisual degeneration that occurs through "repeated duplication, wear, and technical failure"—in other words, the various fuzzed-out colors, horizontal tracking lines, and murky soundtracks that, until only recently, had been endemic to viewing hard-core pornography on home video (sometimes with a degree of difficulty that, as I noted in Chapter 1, can actually heighten the vintage moving image's appeal). Catlin, for example, alleges that ABA receives the majority of its customer complaints over transfers from dilapidated film prints, not its watermarked transfers from old VHS tapes: "The average video viewer is much more accustomed to the soft look and pale color of VHS than they are a scratchy film. [...] So while it is our personal preference to use a film print, it is actually NOT preferred by our typical customer, assuming there is even minor damage."

If, as Hilderbrand suggests, such tantalizing qualities mark videotape's history of illicit uses as one associated with an erotics of access,[51] then ABA's poor-quality, multiple-generation transfers from out-of-print videotapes still importantly signal the historicity of vintage hard-core films by reminding viewers of an ephemerality that pornography and analog video have historically shared. Much as classics studios like VCA, TVX, and Caballero may today rely more on the nostalgic value of their longstanding company names (their websites and catalogues frequently trumpeting their ties to porn's "Golden Age") than the anachronistic audiovisual quality of their remediated product, the no-frills DVD reissue imported from earlier video transfers also nostalgically evokes the early, "outlaw" days of adult video, when one might see something taboo that was subsequently censored.[52] Although older studios may have the benefit of longevity and name recognition, industry watchers warn that many of their websites make it difficult to find a studio's best-regarded classic films, and may only offer outdated or low-quality file formats, inadvertently doing more damage to themselves than potential copyright infringers like free tube sites.[53] Much like SWV's Mike Vraney, then, it is no surprise that ABA's Jacy Catlin similarly rejects complaints about audiovisual quality over access, valuing the content of the text itself over its means of presentation: "I'm not saying it's not preferred to have something look nice when possible, but if people want to bitch about our quality I hope they also are bitching at companies who put out nice looking DVDs of really lame movies. At least all of our movies kick total ass." Indeed, it is important to remember that such complaints over the treatment of vintage adult films have generated far more controversy within fan cultures than if these films were more "respectfully" remediated with the same frequency as mainstream Hollywood product. Like many other types of cult and exploitation cinema, the very fact that Golden Age adult films have generally received such shoddy treatment on home video has merely catalyzed fans' online discussion about different VHS and DVD editions from around the world, with the search for "original" uncut versions garnering screen grabs of different transfers and running times analyzed down to the second.

Because the "first-sale doctrine"—a legal precedent which allows buyers of physical media like books and videotapes to loan or resell these legally purchased objects to others without paying additional royalties to copyright holders—does not permit buyers of prerecorded videotapes to legally copy and sell the complete works contained therein, ABA's profit-motivated practices would seem to verge closer to *piracy* (defined by Hilderbrand as "commercial duplication and sale of knockoffs of readily available videos") than to *bootlegging* ("noncommercial practices of timeshifting, tape dubbing, importing and sharing media content that is not reasonably available commercially").[54] Yet, the fact that much of the label's stock-in-trade consists of texts that are *not* readily and reasonably available suggests video's capacity as an ethical preservation medium for film-born texts whose print materials are lost or inaccessible.

At the same time, however, there is a danger that when companies like ABA piece together composite transfers from multiple sources, their attempts to "restore" a lost original may actually assemble versions that never previously existed. An on-screen preface to ABA's aforementioned *Anyone But My Husband* composite version, for example, claims that this iteration "contains rare scenes which were even cut from the theatrical version of the film" (or, more likely, cut from the specific theatrical release print from which ABA sourced their DVD, not from Roberta Findlay's 35-mm master version). As Janna Jones and Giovanna Fossati note, films that are already considered culturally significant and readily accessible tend to have far more contextual information available to guide the reconstruction process, but when culturally neglected films are creatively reassembled, there is little widespread critical outcry (at least outside fan communities) over such distortions.[55] Take, for example, ABA's supposedly "widescreen uncut" version of Damiano's *The Story of Joanna* (1975), which may be transferred from a celluloid release print to preserve its correct aspect ratio, but is missing important dialogue and even has out-of-order scenes.[56] Even after fans comparing different video editions discovered these blatant changes, the label refused to reissue a corrected version. And when ABA attempted to reconstruct an uncut composite version of Alex de Renzy's *Babyface* (1977), they discovered that their various source materials differed so much that discerning an "original" version was virtually impossible: "For me to put together a new version using both cuts would have not only taken forever," says Catlin, "but it would have been completely distracting as the picture quality would change every 3 seconds. Not to mention I would be rewriting history in a way by using my own judgment on what to keep."[57] Yet, Casey Scott suggests that releasing actual "original" versions (if possible) would not necessarily serve the best interests of companies like ABA, Alternative Cinema, and many other small labels that promote their product as "uncut" or "restored" versions. Although they cannot claim definitive ownership over an orphaned film as a whole, a legal loophole allows them to digitally superimpose a new copyright notice into the on-screen credits of re-cut or otherwise altered versions, effectively staking legal ownership to their unique (but historically dubious) home video *iteration* of the film.[58]

ABA's unauthorized duplication and sale of "uncut" films that are either orphaned or in stasis may thus be an ethical preservation process in the sense of circumventing industrial copyright and self-censorship to recirculate otherwise inaccessible works in a state somewhat closer to the filmmaker's original intent, albeit in an aesthetically degraded condition appropriate to analog adult video's histories of eroticized access. Still, the label's very efforts to reconstruct hard-core cinema's uncensored past can be just as likely to spawn unethically reconstituted versions that serve as little more than historical fantasies, readily called into question by genre aficionados. Furthermore, while it may serve ABA's financial interests to mark their "rebellious" subcultural distinction from longstanding classics studios seemingly too afraid of obscenity laws to release uncut versions, Ramon Lobato suggests that there is a danger in romanticizing the unauthorized circulation of potentially copyrighted texts. By reproducing "a Cold War paradigm of enlightened freedom versus authoritarian opacity," such anti-corporate connotations, so often implied within celebratory discussions of fandom as a democratic force for revaluing culturally marginal texts, run the risk of equating *political* freedom with *market* freedom—and thus end up paradoxically upholding whatever monetary value the overall market will bear for a niche-interest text, regardless of the uncertain (sub)cultural value held by the questionably remediated film.[59]

Moving beyond bad faith: Vinegar Syndrome and Distribpix Inc.

For an older generation of cult video distributors specializing in vintage hard-core pornography, then, these films' long-time archival neglect justifies a profit-motivated preservational ethics based in speed of access over quality of transfer: the resulting video reissues may not look great, but waiting for higher-quality print elements to materialize would likely not only fail to bear fruit (in terms of both products and profits) in the long run, but also allow known prints/transfers to increasingly decay in the meantime. In a sense, these companies operate according to a business logic of making up for lost time, precisely because further delay in recapitalizing on the films' residual value could jeopardize both the existence of these historically marginalized texts and the companies' own economic bottom lines.

This sense of working against the inevitable temporality of filmic decay is expressed in the name of a younger video label, Vinegar Syndrome (named after the destructive accumulation of acetic acid in decaying cellulose acetate film, one of the film archivist's most common banes)—albeit a company which represents a more sincerely recuperative turn toward vintage adult films than represented by SWV and

ABA releases. Whereas earlier cult video companies (and their more recent imitators like Alternative Cinema) are far more likely to flaunt the "bad taste" of the politically incorrect sexual depictions in their distributed films—thereby exacerbating hard-core pornography's disrepute at the same time as they seek to profit off it—these older taste strategies are not shared by all up-and-coming labels. In this section, I examine Vinegar Syndrome and Distribpix Inc. as two vintage labels that have recently collaborated in attempting to foster a fresh appreciation of hard-core cinema as more than just "porn," but rather as an aesthetically and historically significant genre in its own right. Their "post-porn" approach to vintage hard core—from releasing Criterion-quality DVD/Blu-ray editions of genre classics to programming several series of hard-core features in 35 mm at prestigious venues like New York's Anthology Film Archives—speaks to a more earnest investment in these films than, say, Mike Vraney's paracinematic celebration of "terrible" films as ironically wonderful artifacts.

As David Andrews argues, cult discourses around adult cinema tend to evoke bad-faith reading strategies, whether by downplaying the genre's autoerotic appeals or by ironically sacralizing films through tongue-in-cheek descriptors like "genius" and "masterpiece." Even "when hardcore has the patina of age ... this variety of porn is more easily defended as just another ironic consumer pleasure," he says, "as it has become more opaque and less obviously masturbatory."[60] Yet, as I have argued throughout this book, separating autoerotic appeals from aesthetic ones is impossible in the case of vintage pornography, as this younger generation of video labels more openly acknowledges by sincerely reassessing the genre without automatic recourse to bad faith. Nevertheless, their high-cultural touchstones like the Criterion Collection and Anthology Film Archives imply that their aspirational strategies are not intended to "mainstream" vintage hard-core features to the point that such films might begin carrying present-day pornography's subculturally devalued connotations of "feminized" and passive consumption (as described in Chapter 1). Rather, their allusions to high-cultural reading strategies are aimed at both satisfying existing vintage porn fans while also crossing into a broader, more "legitimate" subculture of culturally omnivorous cinephiles.

Founded in January 2013 by print collector Joe Rubin and his business partner Ryan Emerson, Vinegar Syndrome initially began as a subsidiary of the Process Blue film scanning and restoration firm (since renamed OCN Digital Labs), which they cofounded in 2011. Although the company launched during a stagnating DVD market, the cost of 2K (and later, 4K) digital scanning had dropped significantly over the decade between when SWV made its film-to-DVD transfers and when young upstarts like Rubin entered the fray. After a successful Kickstarter campaign to crowd-fund the label's first release—a DVD/Blu-ray edition of three previously "lost" Herschell Gordon Lewis sexploitation films (which Vraney had previously claimed would never be released, due to decades of unpaid lab storage fees)—gauged plenty of potential customer interest and garnered publicity for the fledgling label, the company quickly began releasing uncut and digitally restored editions of both non-explicit exploitation films and hard-core adult films, but soon found the latter becoming its biggest sellers.[61]

Espousing a philosophy closer to FIAF standards, Rubin views the preservation of original celluloid elements as his utmost goal, with the DVD label serving as a means of not only increasing awareness of neglected films, but also a pragmatic means of funding his ongoing preservation efforts. As he told the *New York Times*, he considers himself a preservationist, not a part of the porn industry.[62] He makes clear his generational debt to the work of earlier labels, explaining that he grew up watching SWV and ABA releases, whom he credits as "pioneers" but criticizes for their low-quality transfers. Indeed, I would suggest that if these earlier companies' degraded prints and transfers reinforced niche viewers' oppositional pride in subcultural marginality from more mainstream taste cultures, Vinegar Syndrome's superior treatment of its remediated films aspires to spread these texts beyond existing fan cultures, toward wider (and more profitable) recuperation. Rubin's 2015 launch of Etiquette Pictures, a sibling video label devoted to experimental, documentary, and other independent works falling outside the realm of adult/exploitation cinema, further attests to the catholic tastes and recuperative strategies behind his preservational efforts.

Although admitting that he cannot control how his customers actually use his films, he personally rejects viewing vintage adult cinema as kitschy or ironic fodder to be consumed with a "sneering superiority" over the texts and their historical audiences. In this respect, his label differs from SWV and other companies, with even middling-quality release prints receiving significant digital restoration before their DVD release in the correct aspect ratio. Much as Criterion Collection releases often feature interviews with academics and prominent critics, Vinegar Syndrome has enlisted leading adult film scholars Eric Schaefer and Linda Williams for video interviews on several of its releases.[63] Likewise, Rubin refuses to cut or alter the content of films for DVD reissue—even if means retaining sexual content that might run afoul of local obscenity laws—believing that distributors have no right to tamper with filmmakers' creations. Vinegar Syndrome's ethical approach quickly gained praise from even famed preservationists (or "starchivists," to use one scholar's phrase) like Robert A. Harris, who remarked, "Right out of the gate, even with low-budget productions, their quality is superb, and actually far better than much of the work Universal has done on their Hitchcock films."[64] Although Rubin notes that, unlike Hitchcock's films, many of his customers would not have a comparative reference point for such changes, since most of the films he releases are otherwise so marginal and inaccessible to begin with, his ethical responsibility as a preservationist precludes historically inaccurate modifications. Yet, this also means that, compared with ABA's questionable legal practices, Rubin's label must be more careful with securing distribution rights or establishing chain of title for the films themselves. Unlike ABA, for example, Vinegar Syndrome acquired official permission from Alex de Renzy's estate to scan and distribute rare uncut versions derived from the filmmaker's original camera negatives, not unlike its similar arrangements with living filmmakers like Bob Chinn.

In Rubin's estimation, Vinegar Syndrome's main customers are 35-to-40-year-old men who likely first saw Golden Age adult films during their youth (such as through degraded VHS copies), many of whom are also cult/exploitation film fans. He does not presume that more people have become interested in vintage adult films in recent years, but rather that online communities have allowed fans to find each other, swap information, and create wider publicity for recent reissues. Perhaps the majority of discussion topics on online fan forums, for example, are requests for help in identifying a particular film seen (often surreptitiously) during adolescence. Since coming-of-age memories and potentially distorted remembrances of specific scenes or actors frame so many of these primarily homosocial fan exchanges, the possibility that the cinematic subjects of these formative sexual memories may have been edited out or excised and compiled elsewhere on home video further fuels the search for latterly rediscovering and even reliving such epiphanic experiences. In the words of Ashley West, host of *The Rialto Report*—a podcast that serves as one of the most meticulously researched hubs for the recent resurgence of earnest and desensationalized 1970s–1980s hard-core genre fandom (so much so that many adult film veterans have provided the website with their first in-depth interviews in decades)—this brief historical window when a newly emerging hard-core cinema "tried to make real art ... was [also] a time that a lot of fans were young, so we remember this time as a golden era in our own lives as well."[65] He continues,

> I'm not one of the fans who believes that MOST of the films were good, however. I actually believe that most of them were pretty bad, but that doesn't bother me. I can enjoy pretty bad films as much as I enjoy good films, but the good ones are GENUINELY good, and I think they're definitely worthy of study or just sharing with as many people as possible.[66]

Although Rubin suggests that many buyers of his "X-rated" releases (his preferred term—a qualifier suggestive less of pornography's autoerotic potential than of a period-appropriate film-historical classification) are likely seeking the sex scenes above all, he hopes that culturally omnivorous cinephiles constitute a growing percentage of the label's base, with more adventurous viewers of art and cult films willing to cross over into earnest reception of adult cinema. In this respect, he echoes many other vintage porn fans in repeatedly invoking the 1970s as a time when even respectable publications regularly reviewed hard-core feature films that aspired to be more than just masturbatory program filler but also documents of an ongoing sexual revolution.[67] For Rubin, not only does this historically contextualized approach—a commingling of aesthetic appreciation and carnal appeal—inspire Vinegar Syndrome's larger aims, but also, he presumes, its existing customer base. That is, much like during the 1970s porno-chic era, for all of the patrons primarily seeking autoerotic fodder, there are others still taking these films seriously, flaws and all. Unlike many long-established adult classics studios, for example, which tend to either chapterize their DVDs by sex scene or stream their films on a scene-by-scene basis via VOD websites, Vinegar Syndrome's DVDs do not allow viewers to skip right to particular sexual numbers for masturbatory purposes. By instead chapterizing discs by reel (with an average of four-to-five reels per feature), Rubin encourages viewers to watch feature films in whole, while also highlighting the materiality of the original celluloid elements.

With a partnership through CAV Distributing Corporation (a DVD replication and wholesale distribution company which also handles other niche-interest DVD labels like Cult Epics, Synapse Films, and Grindhouse Releasing), Vinegar Syndrome's releases reach a small number of brick-and-mortar stores, but achieve most sales through major online retailers like Amazon.com, effectively mimicking SWV's distribution deal with Image Entertainment and thus avoiding ghettoization into adults-only outlets for its prepressed DVDs. As Rubin says, this ability to distribute through such mainstream retailers also conveniently allows customers to furtively purchase adult films through a more "legitimate" outlet than adults-only retailers, should they need to conceal the films and their content from significant others.

Vinegar Syndrome's hard-core offerings first appeared as part of its "Drive-In Collection" line of double-feature DVDs from various exploitation genres, but after several unhappy customers complained that hard-core titles were not clearly enough marked as such, many of its future hard-core offerings were moved into a separate "Peekarama" double-feature DVD line (named after a one-time San Francisco porn theater). To Rubin, it had been a deliberate choice—and one vocally supported by some of his customers—to use his label in desegregating hard-core films from other exploitation genres in an effort to not only help downplay the lingering cultural stigmas retarding serious aesthetic reassessment of hard-core feature films, but also to better evoke the historical programming of these varied genres within the same 1970s drive-in, grind house, and even neighborhood theaters (not just the culturally degraded storefront porn theater). Although some of Vinegar Syndrome's distributed films are unrepentantly misogynistic (e.g., several of the Avon films previously released by ABA), Rubin shares his competitors' view of Golden Age hard-core films as fascinating historical documents, but without wholly reducing them to simply "weird" artifacts, "politically incorrect" oddities, or "pornographic" implements.

In doing so, Vinegar Syndrome's operative strategy attempts to resurrect a critical moment in the 1970s when hard-core films and mainstream films seemed on the verge of legitimately merging—that is, before the adult industry's turn toward video-based production and distribution encouraged the so-called wall-to-wall and gonzo sex films which became the industry standard by the late 1980s and no longer garnered crossover critical evaluation as a cinematic genre in their own right. This view thus bolsters that of many vintage porn fans who celebrate the Golden Age of adult feature films with "real" stories/directors/actors—even as such fans tend to downplay not only the fact that many 1970s features were anonymously churned-out "loop carriers" but also that original narrative features have not wholly vanished from the world of present-day porn production. However much some fans may romanticize the industry's past, though, the complaints over his desegregation of hard-core from soft-core content suggest that some of Vinegar Syndrome's customers are unwilling to participate in Rubin's particular historically minded thought experiment.

Another long-tail method of encouraging niche-interest sales within the context of more "mainstream" taste valuations is using DVD and Blu-ray technology to "upscale" the content of aesthetically and politically questionable films through high-quality transfers and a mobile archive of bonus features appearing qualitatively closer to Criterion Collection standards than the relatively déclassé MOD release. Indeed, as Lynda Nead argues, "pornography" is traditionally "characterized by disparity between economic and cultural value, whereas erotic art is altogether a sounder product which confirms the parity between these two fields of value." Erotic art is certainly not immune to market forces, but when pornography begins to be sold for the same amount as "a well-produced glossy art book"—such as former porn magazine editor Dian Hanson's series of glossy TASCHEN coffee-table books—then these taste-based categories begin to significantly blur.[68] As one fan remarks, "I believe that potentially the type of customer that would purchase [*The Devil in Miss Jones* (1973)] or Kemal Horulu's LUSTFUL FEELINGS [1977] as opposed to CUM DUMPSTERS VOL. 29 would have no problem spending an extra $5-$10 on a film that's not just fuck scenes but a film made for theatrical exhibition."[69]

This strategy can be seen in the case of Distribpix Inc., whose generational debt to earlier video companies is far more literal, since the New York-based company began in 1965 as a sexploitation distributor headed by Arthur Morowitz and Howard Farber, and is now run by the former's son, Steven. By the late 1970s, the elder Morowitz owned the Sweetheart Theatre chain, which included five houses located in the Times Square area, where his company's films regularly played and from whose lobbies he began selling adult videotapes under the label "Video-X-Pix." Around this time, he also became a pioneer in the home video industry with his chain of Video Shack retail stores, founded in 1978 and initially stocked with a mix of adult and non-adult tapes (Figure 4.3).[70] Although Distribpix financed the production of 35-mm hard-core features until 1989 under the name Evart Enterprises, eventually becoming a major classics studio, it ceased regular operations until resurrected by Steven in 2002.

Steven began reissuing on DVD about "four or five movies a month" from the company's hard-core library, but these bare-bones editions, distributed under the Video-X-Pix shingle through porn specialists International Video Distributors (IVD), were largely indistinguishable from those of other classics studios. "Really, as far as the way things used to work out," Morowitz recalls, "we would just take a movie off a shitty [¾-inch] master and put it out."[71] Each disc contained the film itself, often imported from the 1980s era, full-screen telecine transfers (with a periodic on-screen watermark), with virtually identical DVD menus and no bonus features beyond a few trailers for the company's other films. These DVDs do include a disclaimer stating that each film was originally "produced for theatrical release. [...] It is the wish of the producers that you watch this film in it's [sic] entirety, without flipping through the scenes, or fast forwarding through the story." But despite this call for the films to be consumed as narratives, respecting the creators' artistic intentions, the disclaimer then notes that a scene selection menu chapterized by sexual number has been provided for the contemporary viewer's convenience.

In this respect, these DVDs suggest a tension between wanting to present the films *as films* and not just as masturbatory fodder, while also acknowledging the opportunities and expectations of selective access formed around digital video technologies. Much

Figure 4.3 Arthur Morowitz's Video Shack store (ca. 1980) at Broadway & 49th, New York City, adjacent to the Circus Theatre (right), part of the Sweetheart Theatres chain. Photo courtesy of Steven Morowitz.

as Rubin admits that some of his customers likely buy hard-core films for the sex scenes alone, then, Morowitz's disclaimer on these early DVDs invokes a pre-video historical exhibition context, when narrative-based adult films were more likely to be taken seriously by critics—and yet, the chapterization by sex scene inadvertently admits that many of these films' original theatrical patrons may have also dropped into the viewing experience in a more fragmentary way and only stayed until their autoerotic aims were satisfied.

After the revived company began earning new cash flow from these DVDs, Morowitz turned to a line of premium-priced "Platinum Elite" editions in 2009, each a multiple-disc set containing a digitally restored 2K transfer (in the correct aspect ratio) from the original camera negatives, plus commentary tracks, featurettes, detailed liner notes, menus chapterized by plot events, and other paratexts curated to each release. Whereas SWV packed its Image Entertainment special-edition DVDs with a miscellany of thematically related paratexts like trailers and ephemeral short subjects, turning each disc into what Mike Vraney—ever the connoisseur of vintage Americana—compared with a box of Cracker Jacks filled with mystery prizes, Morowitz's Platinum Elite line is closer to the Criterion Collection in only providing bonus paratexts that contextually expand upon the main text itself. "We're realizing our stuff is accepted more by a cult audience," he says, with the company serving not only "older guys … who saw this in the theater" but also a generation of "young people … from the film education movement." Consequently, "we take every part of it and put it into its *proper* historical context, which actually makes it a much more legitimate project. [...] It's kind of like the Criterion approach, but for classics."[72] The cult audience has certainly responded in kind, with representative praise like "When I saw the quality of the picture itself and the extras, I had to stop and make sure that the Criterion Collection hadn't started putting out XXX material without me knowing about it."[73] For a film to qualify for this upscale treatment, says Morowitz, "it needs to have some sort of importance, a good cast, [be] a great seller, or maybe it was cut/edited really bad[ly], etc.,"[74] such as *The Passions of Carol* (1975), *Blonde Ambition* (1981), and Radley Metzger's five hard-core films directed under the name Henry Paris (which had all been previously released by VCA in cut versions).

Although Morowitz continued using the Video-X-Pix and Platinum Elite monikers for these first few deluxe releases, he eventually foregrounded the company's original name for his ongoing series of qualitatively upscaled reissues. This reversion to "Distribpix" not only played upon the company's historical legacy, but also helped downplay the cheaper connotations of "video"—much as the name of Rubin's label likewise evokes a more deliberate focus on film-born texts and recuperative transfers from threatened celluloid elements, not the video-quality materials offered by labels like ABA. Likewise, the initial line of no-frills Video-X-Pix DVDs were not only retailed by competitors like Alternative Cinema and ABA, but also sold scene by scene through VOD websites, suggesting their relative disposability in comparison with the upscale editions bearing the Distribpix name. Compared with the company's older image propagated through the Video-X-Pix label, then, the rebranded label marked a (partial) repudiation of the bad-faith practices of competing classics studios—although Distribpix continues to sell their older line of "shitty" DVDs through IVD to help fund future upscale editions.

As Morowitz says, DVD sales continue to generate far more profits for Distribpix than VOD websites, especially as the latter were undercut by the rise of tube sites delivering pirated content. In fact, it was the very fact that the DVD market collapsed in 2008—coincident with the faster broadband speeds that allowed the rise of tube sites—which persuaded him to take a more connoisseurial, historically minded approach to Distribpix's film library in the first place. Yet, adults-only DVD distributors like IVD were hesitant to handle the resulting Platinum Elite editions because porn DVDs were so seldom marketed as boutique items that would justify above-average wholesale prices. Meanwhile, more "mainstream" DVD distributors like CAV (that is, "mainstream" in the sense of not being segregated into the adults-only market, albeit still specializing in niche-interest films) were initially hesitant to handle Distribpix's films because of its reputation as a hard-core-only company, but were willing to release hard-core films from mixed-genre labels like Synapse and Vinegar Syndrome.[75] "I sometimes wish there was no sex in the films," Morowitz remarks, "as I feel we would be taken more seriously" by distributors and critics alike.[76] Consequently, he began by self-distributing his Platinum Elite editions through the Distribpix website and an Amazon.com third-party storefront.

Following pressure from the adult video industry in the wake of the DVD market's decline, Amazon.com loosened its one-time restrictions on selling hard-core adult DVDs via third-party retailers, and the online retail giant currently accounts for the majority of Distribpix's sales at this time of writing. Morowitz suggests that the anonymity of online shopping through a catch-all retail giant like Amazon.com also encourages more sales from socioeconomically higher consumers than the regular customers of adults-only retailers—thus complementing Distribpix's sales of premium-priced editions. Metzger's Henry Paris films, for example, once comprised over 80 percent of Distribpix's Amazon.com sales alone, and the label eventually released more economical single-disc versions of each remastered Metzger feature in 2014. After several hectic years operating as a virtually one-man operation, Morowitz eventually began an emergent relationship with CAV that would see Distribpix "softening" its hard-core image by beginning to also release new transfers from its extensive library of sexploitation films under its "Distribpix Archive Collection" line, including films previously licensed to SWV in the mid-1990s. As he notes, one major benefit of using CAV to replicate and package some of his remastered films is that, unlike the earlier line of DVDs distributed by IVD, items supplied to retailers through a non-adults-only intermediary company are no longer listed on Amazon.com and elsewhere as being offered through a third-party seller, and thus are less likely to be flagged for removal from the websites of online retailers who would not otherwise directly carry hard-core adult films.

"Some of our movies perfectly connote themselves to be historically preserved" because of their artistic ambitions, Morowitz says, but "others are just fine as sex films." While he admits that some of the latter films might be the company's bigger sellers, the company's ownership of the original elements suggests a greater preservational responsibility than held by competing studios. From his interviews, it becomes clear that part of this stems from a personal investment in protecting and promoting the family legacy ("One of the things we have going for us is that most of our stuff is copyrighted"), but also restoring cultural value in a disreputable genre. There is also, he says, an element of urgency in securing the participation of a dying generation of 1970s-era filmmakers and actors, with these special editions helping serve as both tributes and correctives to decades of misinformation. At the same time, however, Morowitz seems somewhat ambivalent about the mixed profitability of these elaborate editions that require so much more upfront investment (e.g., $20,000 for the *Blonde Ambition* reissue): "Really, it's not even so much for the labor of love," he admits. "We're really excited to see if it's going to be commercially viable."[77]

Yet, despite taking the "Criterion approach," Morowitz was initially unable to release more than a handful of these deluxe editions—far fewer than, say, Vinegar Syndrome's considerably less elaborate but still audiovisually restored DVDs—at least until the company's new relationship with a more "mainstream" distributor in CAV expanded the company's distribution options. By late 2014, for instance, Distribpix had abandoned the "Platinum Elite" moniker and followed the lead of Vinegar Syndrome's "Peekarama" line by releasing its own series of "Sweetheart Theatres" double-feature DVDs, named after the elder Morowitz's Times Square venues and chapterized by reel. The company simultaneously developed a line of single-disc 2K remastered editions of its popular library titles, priced more affordably than its previous Platinum Elite editions and thus intended to be more attractive to would-be video wholesalers. In

Preservational Ethics, Cultural Distinctions, and Vintage Pornoisseurship   179

sum, Distribpix may have aimed for both critical and commercial crossover appeal with its upscale editions of notable Golden Age classics, but this was difficult to achieve without somehow distancing the company's present-day image from the stigma of hard-core pornography while also heeding the economic realities of the adult video industry.

A prime example is Distribpix's first Blu-ray (Figure 4.4)—and the first Blu-ray release for any canonical hard-core film—Metzger's *The Opening of Misty Beethoven* (1976). *Misty* holds a reputation as perhaps the most artfully accomplished hard-core adult film of the 1970s porno-chic era, celebrated as a work that may have failed to wholly merge the hard-core and mainstream film worlds, but still succeeded in raising the aesthetic bar to a level that later hard-core films have arguably never surpassed. Accordingly, the company attempted to capitalize on this reputation by similarly raising the bar for home video editions of hard-core adult films (and, not coincidentally, used this reissue as the first title to bear the reclaimed Distribpix name). Although Metzger's films had not originally been produced by Distribpix, but rather by his own production company, the advent of Blu-ray found the one-time Janus Films trailer editor and art

Figure 4.4 Promotional material for Distribpix's Blu-ray edition of *The Opening of Misty Beethoven* (1976), featuring technical specifications and special features unmatched by any previous video edition of a Golden Age hard-core film.

film importer in search of a video distributor for his own work. Although most of Metzger's soft-core and quasi-hard-core films from 1969 to 1975 (such as *The Lickerish Quartet* [1970], *Score* [1974], and *The Image* [1975]) were concurrently remastered on DVD and Blu-ray by the CAV-distributed labels Cult Epics and Synapse Films, Morowitz approached Metzger to handle his hard-core offerings, based on the quality of Distribpix's previous Platinum Elite releases. Featuring Process Blue's digital restoration of both the soft and hard versions, director and actor commentary tracks, a newly assembled 5.1 multichannel sound track (although some restorers would consider this an unethical addition, since the film was not originally released in stereo), deleted scenes, and multiple featurettes, the 2012 *Misty* reissue bridged the qualitative gap between the DVD/Blu-ray treatment given to soft-core and hard-core pictures, but arguably in a manner uncritically flattering of heterosexual men's creative-cum-sexual desires.

Misty is a retelling of George Bernard Shaw's *Pygmalion* (1913) by way of *My Fair Lady* (1964), with sex scenes standing in for musical numbers. This provides a well-known and even culturally respectable template for a film that is less a parody than an alternately witty, bawdy, and faithful incarnation of its source material. Arrogant sexologist Dr. Seymour Love (Jamie Gillis) first meets lowly prostitute Misty Beethoven (Constance Money) while conducting research for his latest book in a grimy porn theater in Paris's Place Pigalle. Wearing garishly overdone makeup and a Master Charge logo on her shirt, she is little more than "a sexual civil service worker" in Love's eyes, instrumentally rattling off prices for humdrum services. In an adjacent brothel, he encounters his friend and fellow cultural slummer Geraldine Rich (Jacqueline Beudant), a wealthy jetsetter seeking some *nostalgie de la boue* after an extravagant party held by the vapid, young publishing magnate Lawrence Layman (Ras Kean). Convinced they can refashion Misty into the latest "Goldenrod Girl," a sexual celebrity selected by Layman, Love and Rich begin training their new ingénue into someone with "the instinct to convert a trivial act, a mundane routine, a daily chore into something stimulating, creative, and above all, communicative."

Throughout the film, "authentic" desire is posited as a force that might overcome the bland instrumentality of not only Misty's initially uninspired sex work, but also Love's use of her for furthering his professional career. For Metzger, this sense of "authentic" desire was crucial to positioning his own picture as a higher class of adult film—that is, "something stimulating, creative, and above all, communicative." Not unlike *The Lickerish Quartet*'s depiction of a stag film brought into a palace, *Misty*'s transformation from a common whore (first shown attending a mediocre porno film shot in a bland apartment) to a glamorous courtesan participating in stylishly filmed sex scenes parallels *Misty*'s own attempt at distinguishing itself from the shoddy "one-day wonders" spilling into theaters during the 1970s porno-chic era (Figure 4.5). As Metzger himself notes on the commentary track, it is somewhat unfair to compare him with the less accomplished directors then breaking into the hard-core market, since he was already an experienced filmmaker with international connections through his distribution company Audubon Films. In this regard, it is notable that *Misty*'s cosmopolitan aesthetics more closely resemble those of European hard-core imports

Figure 4.5 At left, the quotidian mise-en-scène, flat composition, and overall cheap look of the porn film shown playing at the Place Pigalle theater during *Misty Beethoven*'s opening credits. At right, Metzger's opulent settings, multiplanar action, and soft-focus cinematography on display during Misty's training to be the "Goldenrod Girl."

like *Sensations* (1975), *Felicia* (1975), and *The Kinky Ladies of Bourbon Street* (1976) than the cheaper varieties of hard-core films then losing market share in the US. As Kevin Heffernan observes, a 1976 federal repeal of tax-shelter laws meant that the adult film industry's silent investors could no longer fund low-budget film productions as a means of writing off their declared income from other industries. Consequently, in addition to 16-mm one-day wonders becoming even scarcer, the industry consolidated in the late 1970s toward a handful of notable studios (such as Distribpix, et al.) that produced a smaller annual slate of larger budgeted hard-core features, mostly shot and released in 35 mm.[78]

Love frames his blatant chauvinism toward Misty in less overtly sexist terms than *My Fair Lady*'s woman-hating Henry Higgins, bespeaking a modest feminist-era shift in accepting sexually liberated women if, like the aptly named Rich, they know how to turn sex into something more artful than proletarian drudgery. Yet, as Linda Williams argues, *Misty* problematically retains its source material's emphasis on the male expert's power in bestowing knowledge upon an honest but hapless woman, culminating in heterosexual union once the woman has risen to the "proper" station. When Love answers Misty's frustrated complaint that "men stink" with the response "Well, they think you stink; in fact, it's one of the most perfectly balanced equations in nature," his comeback neglects Misty's unequal subordination to the demands of straight male pleasure. Although, in classical style, both characters may be changed by the narrative's end—Misty has taken over Love's sexology practice, while the doctor sits nearby wearing BDSM-submissive gear—this role reversal is premised on Misty's assumption of male tastes.[79] Love's mission to combine sensual pursuits with high-class artistry thus mirrors Metzger's own aesthetic aims, with the success of these aspirations ultimately flattering male expertise while casting aside those denigrated women/films who fail to transcend. With hard core's more fragmentary forms less assimilable to the upwardly classed criteria of artworthiness that Love, Metzger, and most cinephiles privilege, it is no surprise that *Misty* has received a Blu-ray release that might cross over between the non-mutually exclusive categories of (male) porn consumers and film buffs alike.

Indeed, to fund the pressing of a Blu-ray edition instead of just the DVD format used in previous Platinum Elite editions, Morowitz began the "Project Misty" Kickstarter campaign, with a goal of raising $10,000. As with Vinegar Syndrome's similar campaign to release its Lewis films, this initiative let fans directly invest in bringing a much-desired title to the market. In addition to several tiers of rewards for donations, names of especially generous project backers would be immortalized in liner notes or disc credits, allowing fans to become visible additions to the cultural history of their chosen objects—even without otherwise interacting with a wider fan community. This possible desire *not* to interact with other fans is especially acute with sexually explicit films which one might wish to exclusively consume in the privacy of one's home. Indeed, as Chuck Tryon notes, crowd-funding campaigns may not be rooted in fan "communities" in a traditional sense, since these efforts are primarily dependent on individualistic consumption preferences that necessitate little horizontal interaction between fans, but they can still offer communitarian support to independents.[80] And yet, because *Misty* is a hard-core film, Kickstarter quickly canceled Distribpix's initiative, forcing the company to successfully crowd-fund its project elsewhere. (All this despite the *Misty* release including both the soft and hard versions, whereas the largely soft-core Lewis set also contained the hard-core white coater *Black Love* [1971], which ironically raised no objections from Kickstarter.) Despite the obstacles initially thrown up against the reissue, fans' personal and economic investment in producing high-quality treatments of adult films marks a notable shift in these texts' cultural standing on home video. Once largely viewed as interchangeable tools for anonymous acts of autoeroticism, these films have become highly valued objects that fans will proudly put their names on through crowd-funding efforts expanding the range of niche titles given privileged status amid the long tail.

Yet, much as the sheer number of male names among the over 160 "Project Misty" backers speaks to the genre's historically male-dominated viewing demographic, the project's overall recuperative appeals to traditionally bourgeois standards of artworthiness for legitimacy—especially the figure of Metzger as male auteur, a figure not unlike the male aesthete/expert within the film itself, as reinforced through the Criterion-quality overall package—firmly promote the *his* in "history." In other words, since cultism, cinephilia, and film criticism have all been historically centered around the male auteur, there is a danger that the many superlatives hoisted onto a standout hard-core film ("the greatest adult film of all time," "the apex of porno chic," "master director Radley Metzger," "the golden standard," and "one of the most arousing films ever created" all appear on the back cover) in an effort to reclaim it as erotic art end up unwittingly celebrating hetero-male sexual and aesthetic tastes, on the part of both filmmaker and fans, in the same broad motion. After all, even cultural omnivores, from cineastes to academics, tend to fall back on middlebrow or high-cultural qualifiers (e.g., formalism, historical value, and references to canonical art movements) as justification for trying to take ostensibly "low" culture seriously.[81]

Compare this masculinist ethos, then, with the retrospectively feminist reading suggested by the 2009 Platinum Elite DVD reissue of *Deep Inside Annie Sprinkle* (1981), starring, written, and directed by the eponymous porn star (although the Distribpix website, among others, chauvinistically attributes more directorial credit to the film's assistant director, sexploitation veteran Joe Sarno). While not a coherently plotted feature like *Misty Beethoven*, numerous scholars have suggested that this film marked a significant turning point for Sprinkle between her earlier, male-dominated porn career (which began in 1973) and her later "post-porn"[82] career as a performance artist and sexologist. The film has not only proven a strong seller for Distribpix since its home video debut in 1982 but has retroactively gained a veneer of artworthiness as a precursor to Sprinkle's later work, especially her 1997-2001 one-person theater performance *Annie Sprinkle's Herstory of Porn: Reel to Real*.

The film opens with Sprinkle herself directly addressing the viewer, welcoming him/her to learn more about the star as a prelude to the film's series of vignettes—each allegedly based on Sprinkle's fantasies and/or real-life sexual experiences, and each themed around a particular sexual variation (e.g., breasts, anal sex, urolagnia, girl-on-girl sex, masturbation). According to her DVD commentary, Sprinkle's decision to effectively play herself (and to cast her actual friends and lovers as her scene partners) and to repeatedly break the fourth wall was rooted in a desire to move away from acting out a fictional character and instead evoke the viewer's erotic investment by documenting her "authentic" pleasures. To this end, Sprinkle opens the film by showing us actual family photos of herself as a child and then stressing her mundane, sexually inexperienced youth as teenager Ellen Steinberg.

As Linda Williams says, this unconventional biographical strategy—a precursor to Sprinkle's development of "docu-porn" through her collaborative conceptualization of Gerard Damiano's *Consenting Adults* (1982) and her later codirecting of queer porn videos like *Linda/Les & Annie: The First Female-to-Male Transsexual Love Story* (1989)—mimics the intimacy established between whore and client, but with cinema mediating this contact by rendering each side of the imagined transaction absent from the other. Furthermore, Williams describes Sprinkle's injection of kink into many of the sexual numbers (e.g., showing the viewer how to digitally penetrate a man's anus before he genitally does likewise to her) as subtly queering heterosexual pornography's visual conventions.[83] Indeed, Sprinkle's interpellation of the implicitly masturbating viewer[84] foregrounds that *she* is the sexually controlling agent in each scenario, and that, unlike most heterosexual pornography, visual evidence of *her* pleasure is of paramount importance. In a solo masturbation scene with a vibrator, for example, she remarks, "I can feel your eyes all over ... my pussy," inviting the viewer to "just tingle yourself like this with me," until the scene culminates with what Sprinkle thinks may be the first female ejaculation captured in a work of mainstream adult cinema. Judging by one of Sprinkle's oft-repeated anecdotes, this direct address to the viewer even carried over to the film's promotional tour, with Sprinkle herself using an Ohio drive-in theater's in-car speaker system to instruct patrons to talk back to her using a combination of honks and blinkers to signal their sexual preferences (straight, gay, kinky, or otherwise).

Such participatory strategies would be foregrounded in her later performance pieces, including *Deep Inside Porn Stars* (1984), *Post-Porn Modernist* (1990-1995), and *Annie Sprinkle's Herstory of Porn*. The latter show, directed by Emilio Cubeiro (who also directed *Post-Porn Modernist*), is especially noteworthy here, because it traces Sprinkle's career from her own perspective as she performs before an extensive array of clips (often making comments similar to the annotated filmography in her book *Post-Porn Modernist*), with each of seven career phases signaled by a different theatrical venue, projectionist, and a change of persona/costume by Sprinkle—indicating how cultural distinctions between porn, art, and art-porn are largely dependent on the reception context and perceived agency of the participants.

The first phase, for instance, supposedly takes place at the "Pink Pussycat Sinema," with Sprinkle sporting pigtails, a schoolgirl outfit, and a "naïve bimbo" voice—all of which mirror her character in her early film *Teenage Deviate* (1976), shown as she explains how she first got into pornography. The next phase (at the Hell Hole Room in the basement of the Mitchell Brothers' San Francisco theater) finds Sprinkle in a leather dominatrix costume as she explains her move into films that allowed her to experiment with her preferences for rough sex, such as *Night of Submission* (1976), *The Devil Inside Her* (1977), and *Kneel Before Me* (1983), and how some of these "outright violent, and in retrospect, very misogynist" representations (including one in which the male performers in a gang-rape scene "got rougher than I had anticipated. I got a bit bruised up, and almost really got hurt. I got kind of scared") strengthened her resolve to move away from the conventions of heterosexist porn.[85] The third phase of *Herstory of Porn*, just before she transitions to her second-act, video-era "post-porn" career, concludes with three of the scenes from *Deep Inside Annie Sprinkle* that exemplify not only what she calls "the beginning of a new era, pornography made by women," but also that film's moments of direct address. During a clip of the aforementioned masturbation scene, for example, the onstage Sprinkle (Figure 4.6) produces an identical vibrator, with which she "masturbates" the genitals of her on-screen self while explaining how earlier adult films were unconcerned with documenting real female orgasms.

Perhaps the quintessential scene in *Deep Inside* depicts Sprinkle standing outside the Orleans Theatre in Times Square (also where this third phase of *Herstory* is set), which was part of the Sweetheart Theatres chain owned by Arthur Morowitz and features an "Annie Sprinkles [*sic*] Erotic Film Festival" on the marquee, including other Distribpix films like *Teenage Deviate*, *Slippery When Wet* (1976), and *Jack 'n' Jill* (1979)—although the nonexistent fourth film, *Teenage Grandmother*, was Sprinkle's in-joke. In *Herstory of Porn*, the onstage Sprinkle mimes this on-screen double's monologue about how she visits adult theaters and has sex with patrons of her own films. Sure enough, *Deep Inside*'s Sprinkle enters the Orleans, sits down, and begins fucking spectators as *Slippery When Wet* plays on the screen before them. During this clip in *Herstory*, the onstage Sprinkle likewise sits in a row of theater chairs positioned before the projection screen, even turning around to shush her on-screen analogue (Figure 4.7). This recursive doubling (or tripling, if you count the *Slippery When Wet* footage playing on the movie screen) calls into question the veracity of the many personas that the on-screen and onstage Sprinkle performs, unsettling any clear sense of woman as an essentially (over)sexualized figure.[86] Describing a performance of *Herstory*, for example, Marla Carlson observes that "There is no particular reason to believe that Sprinkle is telling a life story any more authentic or less pornographic than the films she shows"—a statement that could apply as easily to the supposedly autobiographical fantasies depicted in *Deep Inside Annie Sprinkle* as well.

Preservational Ethics, Cultural Distinctions, and Vintage Pornoisseurship   185

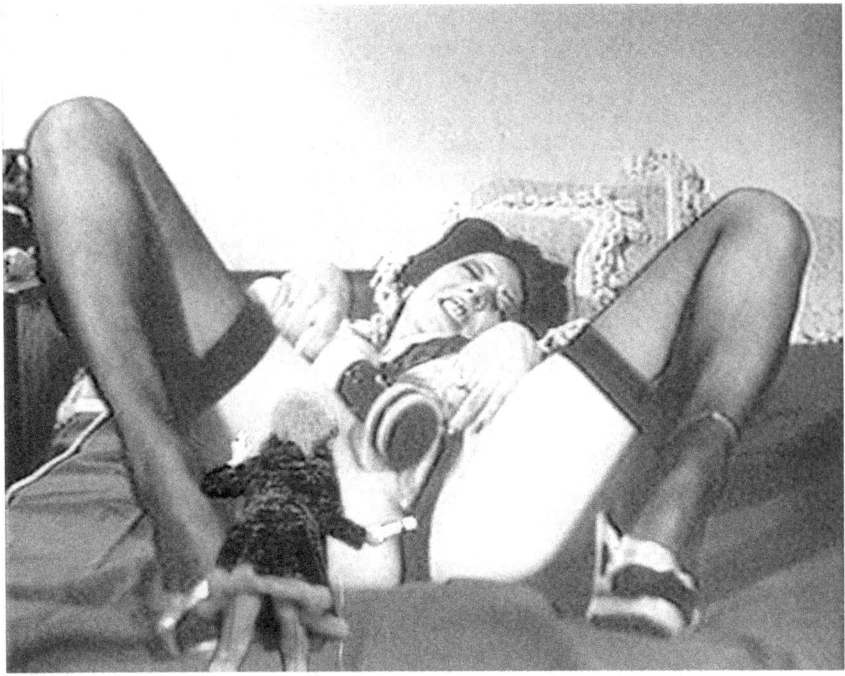

Figure 4.6 In *Annie Sprinkle's Herstory of Porn* (1999), the onstage Sprinkle uses a similar vibrator to "masturbate" her on-screen self while explaining how *Deep Inside Annie Sprinkle* (1981) was the first mainstream porn film to show female ejaculation.

Figure 4.7 In *Annie Sprinkle's Herstory of Porn*, Sprinkle (left) mimes along to her on-screen analogue during a clip originally filmed at the Orleans Theatre in her 1981 directorial debut; and (right) shushes her younger on-screen self while also seated in theater seats.

Like *Deep Inside*'s on-screen use of *Slippery When Wet*, then, Sprinkle's *Herstory* does not surrender its power to pornographically arouse, while, at the same time, Carlson finds that

> Sprinkle continues to insist that she did it all voluntarily and enjoyed it, yet she wants to present her work and life *after* 1980 as clearly superior to this early phase, both ethically and sexually. If she presents no negative side at all to the early work, then there is no reason to prefer the latter. On the other hand, if she presents it in too negative a light and voices too much regret, she opens the door to the claim that women are inevitably violated, degraded, and silenced by pornography.[87]

Although Sprinkle herself once may have concurred with Carlson's reading of her early films in some ways ("On the one hand, I can't really recommend any of them, because they're mostly pretty silly, unaesthetic, and immature, and several are even rather violent and misogynistic" fantasies, she notes in her *Post-Porn Modernist* filmography), Sprinkle now prefers upholding the personal and historical value of her earlier films as more "youthful" and (politically) "naïve" compared with her more "mature" (feminist/ empowered) later films ("On the other hand, I really am proud of all the movies I made. They have a wonderful nostalgic quality").[88] As she clarifies today, "I wanted to pursue my own fantasies and desires, instead of participating in men's. But this was a gradual shift. One [career phase] wasn't better or worse. This was a process of evolution and aging, and growing as an artist/performer."[89] Looking back from the more mature perspective of a creative practitioner whose work consistently combines both art and porn (to the exclusion of neither), it thus makes perfect sense that *Deep Inside*'s own creative strategies of on/off-screen doubling are heralded through reenactment as a prefiguration of what was soon to come.

Herstory of Porn's retrospective mise en abyme thus brings us back to Distribpix's Platinum Elite reissue of *Deep Inside Annie Sprinkle* as another site for documenting this "herstory" of an increasingly feminist (and eventually ecosexual/ecofeminist) career in and out of sex work, and the aesthetic-cum-political distinctions to be drawn between different periods of her mediated life. Whereas ABA, for example, still sells many of the hard-core roughies described by Sprinkle as containing violent and misogynistic fantasies, echoing that label's ethically questionable preservation practices, Distribpix drew (intentionally or not) upon Sprinkle's current reputation as an artist to give its upscale *Deep Inside* package an imprimatur of cultural/historical value that the company's other sex-heavy vignette films might appear to lack. That is, much as this reissue marks Steven Morowitz's attempt at distancing his company from his one-time bad-faith approach to the first line of Video-X-Pix DVDs (even as the company still sells these déclassé editions of films like *Teenage Deviate* and *Slippery When Wet*), Sprinkle's performance in *Herstory* similarly distances herself from the political and aesthetic naivety of her early porn films, while still using those early films as raw material for her creative practice. (Tellingly, Sprinkle's website describes the Platinum Elite edition of *Deep Inside* as "the best of the mainstream golden age porn movies I ever made … a porn connoisseur[']s wet dream," whereas the Video-X-Pix DVD of *Teenage Deviate* retains its respective value as a "film you can probably jerk off to."[90])

In the absence of critical commentary, Sprinkle explained to me, the politically problematic scenes in her early films are best seen in the context of their overall narrative function—whereas she disparages compilations like ABA's *The Kinky World of Annie Sprinkle* for stringing together poor-quality versions of her less "vanilla" scenes without any accompanying justification. In her estimation, pornography serves a similar cultural purpose as performance art in its capacity to provoke political discussion, so it is important to create a historical archive of uncut Golden Age films before they fall into decay—and yet, she believes that video distributors should also be mindful about the political implications of the films they re-release into the marketplace. As she states at *Herstory*'s conclusion, "The same image may appear beautiful one day, and ugly the next … be liberating one year, and offensive later." Although she acknowledges a certain nostalgia for the 1970s as an era in which any fantasy could be explored in mainstream adult cinema—underage characters and rape/incest themes, for example, might be seen (in my estimation) as the respective cinematic analogues to "ageplay" and "edgeplay," two well-documented forms of sexual role play—she suggests that the industry's latter-day censorship of less heteronormative Golden Age scenes is perhaps an unavoidable byproduct of wider political progress for women.[91]

As Carlson observes, Sprinkle's running commentary across *Herstory*'s first act humorously sends up mainstream porn conventions (indeed, the text on *Herstory*'s VHS box even compares the show with *Mystery Science Theater 3000* [1988–1999]), whereas the clips presented in the show's second act demonstrate her post-porn videos "contain[ing] their own irony rather than merely enabling it." For feminist viewers, then, Sprinkle's own tongue-in-cheek strategies toward framing her early, more misogynistic films as mockably "bad" might render them easier to digest as a point of comparison with her later work, even as Carlson says there is a resulting danger that viewers will not so easily recognize her post-porn videos' internalized irony and instead accept the later videos as more reliably "authentic."[92] Although her more confident and aggressive persona in *Deep Inside* is no less constructed than the naïve schoolgirl starlet role that she associates with her earlier films (as the 1981 film itself foregrounds through reference to her unassuming youth), *Herstory* emphasizes that her directorial debut with *Deep Inside* marks the point where her filmic work truly deserves to be taken seriously. In this respect, the Platinum Elite edition still leans on the filmmaker's original authorial vision for its claims to legitimacy, but her prominent use of *Deep Inside* in her later performance work complicates the simpler conflation of historical value, auteurism, and artworthiness seen in the *Misty Beethoven* reissue.

In addition to receiving a remastered transfer from the 35-mm negatives, for instance, one of the edition's major selling points was its restoration of a famed "golden shower" (urolagnia) scene that Distribpix had cut from previous video editions (but was later included in *Herstory*)—allegedly because the company feared obscenity prosecutions that were threatened during the film's run at the highly profitable Pussycat Theater chain, which, as mentioned earlier, had styled itself as a respectable, upscale chain for the couples' market.[93] Sprinkle's proclivity for golden showers had become notorious by 1981 ("The Golden Girl of Porn!" boasts the tagline on the film's original poster), retrospectively coloring the meaning of her chosen *nom de porn*[94]—so by restoring this scene in 2009, the Platinum Elite edition effectively aided in restoring historical meaning to her authorial persona. Indeed, in her DVD commentary (Figure 4.8), Sprinkle compares the golden shower scene with "painting" her real-life lover Mal O'Ree with liquid, again suggesting the scene's potentially creative connotations.

Sprinkle's recording of a video commentary for the film, allowing her to remain visually inset in the corner of the screen throughout the set's second disc, further loops back to her prominent use of the film in *Herstory*'s feminist historiography. The moments in *Deep Inside* when Sprinkle markedly breaks the fourth wall (such as the masturbation and Orleans Theatre scenes) thereby become uncannily recalled through the on-screen DVD commentary's rough replication of the show's onstage/on-screen doubling; the image of Sprinkle seated in the inset during the Orleans scene, sporting a similar wardrobe and amply displayed décolletage, for example, especially recalls her seated position in the prop theater seats during the same scene in *Herstory* (Figure 4.9). Likewise, her running commentary includes discussion of how the feminist movement allowed women to assert their drives for sexual pleasure; how the AIDS pandemic

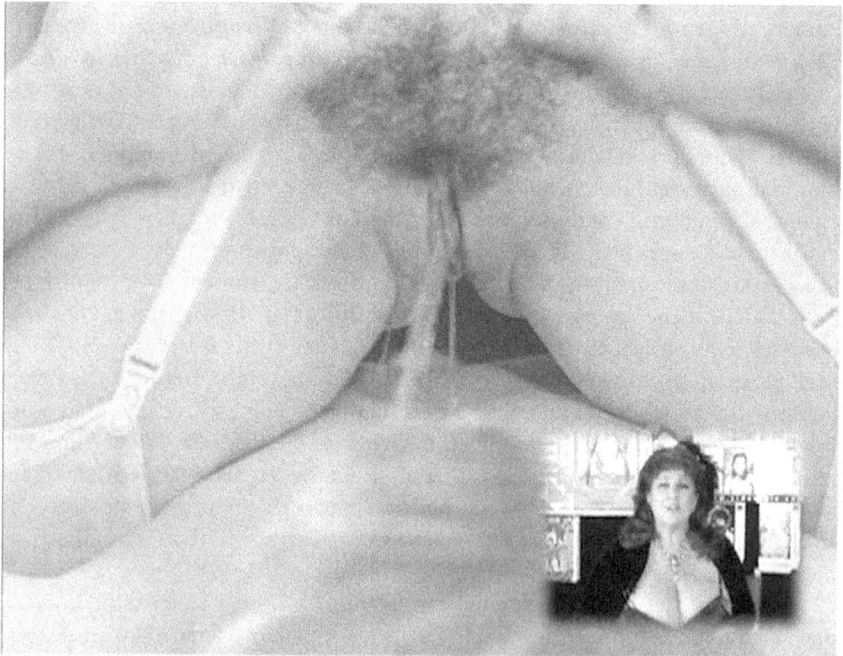

Figure 4.8 Sprinkle describes the once-censored "golden shower" scene in painterly terms during her on-screen commentary track on Distribpix's *Deep Inside Annie Sprinkle* DVD.

Figure 4.9 When visually inset during the on-screen DVD commentary track for *Deep Inside Annie Sprinkle*, Sprinkle's position recalls her mode of feminist historiography performed several years earlier in *Annie Sprinkle's Herstory of Porn* (compare with Figures 4.6 and 4.7).

killed some of her on-screen lovers; how queer subcultures influenced her on-screen sex performances; and how hetero-male depictions of interfemale sex differ from actual lesbian porn. While there are important differences between Sprinkle's on-screen DVD commentary (especially with prompts coming from off-screen male interviewees like Ashley West) and her far more animated, in-person *Herstory* theater piece—although watching the recorded version of *Herstory* on video flattens out some of the live show's productive tension between her on-screen and onstage selves—a viewer versed in her post-porn work will likely find the DVD commentary consistent with her more recent attempts at deconstructing her mainstream hard-core past.

What this particular Distribpix edition elicits, then, is a tension between what we might consider two connotations of the term "post-porn." These connotations are far from mutually exclusive, of course (as Sprinkle's work suggests), but they do have the potential to carry certain gendered valences. The first connotation attempts to distance mainstream Golden Age films from hard-core pornography's cultural denigration through conventional appeals to aesthetic and historical value, such as the value of narrative, genre, and authorial vision. As self-proclaimed "pornoisseur" Jacques Boyreau writes,

> Post-porn does not seek the comforts of ambiguity by separating healthy versus unhealthy porn. Nor am I talking about a porn-less world. Post-porn is, above all, a rebound from the clawing heap of polemology about porn. [...] Part of being a pornoisseur is that you appreciate cold assessments on a hot day. You err on the turf of the aesthete

recognizing that being "Turned On and Fucked Up [By Art] are not the same."[95] Unlike an earlier generation of video distributors only too willing to posit Golden Age films as mockable and/or spankable as simply "porn," this non-ironic stance is exemplified by Vinegar Syndrome and especially Distribpix—with the *Misty Beethoven* reissue as the prime case, given Metzger's status as perhaps the easiest adult filmmaker to claim as a "legitimate" auteur. Aesthetic traditionalism and gender traditionalism threaten to converge in this bourgeois emphasis on the redeemable "quality" of certain films from a "chic" period dominated by male filmmakers.

Compare that, though, with the second connotation of "post-porn," as popularized by Sprinkle and the other sex-positive feminist, queer, and genderqueer artists and activists following in her wake.[96] In her documentary *Mutantes (Punk, Porn, Feminism)* (2009), post-porn practitioner Virginie Despentes traces contemporary post-porn culture's early development from pioneers like Sprinkle to a younger generation of politically engaged performance and video artists in the US and Western Europe. As the documentary's title suggests, however, this younger generation is very much invested in punk and DIY culture, both of which are less easily recuperable to bourgeois aesthetic valuations. Evoking an aesthetics based more in shock and disorder than in conservative standards of beauty and skill, this second vision of post-porn aims to create new spaces for agency and pleasure within the realm of pornographic representation by decentering the dominant hetero-male pornographic gaze and thereby rejecting the heteronormative cultural mainstream with which the Golden Age hard-core feature attempted to merge. With its glossy 35-mm production values, poised on the cusp of her artistic turn toward cheaper but more politically engaged videos, *Deep Inside Annie Sprinkle* and its Platinum Elite reissue constitute the hinge between these two connotations, exploring kink (e.g., the once-excised golden shower scene) within the bounds of hetero-male genre conventions, while also paving the way for the later, more radically queer work that has nevertheless helped retrospectively reclaim the value of this relatively mainstream historical precursor.

Recursive distribution methods and diminishing physicality

Yet, if labels like Distribpix represent small pockets of the adult film industry finally catching up with the Criterion Collection and other high-cultural boutique labels that specialize in elaborate reissues marketed to fans as ownable art objects, this belated shift was ironically timed, since many content providers increasingly shifted away from physical media formats following the industry-wide DVD decline in 2008. As Chuck Tryon argues, Hollywood began encouraging *platform mobility* (the ability for the same media content to be ubiquitously accessible across multiple, mobile technologies) as a means of reasserting control over the forms of *content mobility* (the ability to circulate media content among multiple users) that the first-sale doctrine initially tendered to timeshifting formats like VHS. When home video first appeared as a consumer market in the 1970s, for example, the major film studios initially resisted releasing their content on prerecorded tapes since, unlike the film industry's historical business model of offering access to content for each ticket sold, the first-sale doctrine would allow purchasers of a videocassette to make unlimited use of the contained content (such as renting or selling the tape to others). With the advent of streaming VOD through online venues like iTunes and Amazon Prime over the past ten years, however, the industry recovered the potential to monetize each nontheatrical viewing through the pay-per-view business model it always wanted. If consumers were becoming less likely to purchase permanent access to a given film by acquiring a physical DVD, then the resurgence of a rental-based market in which distributors themselves circumvented the first-sale doctrine by granting limited-time streaming access would (in theory) allow them to maintain more control over the legal uses of their content. Furthermore, Tryon suggests that this shift away from physical media loaded with DVD/Blu-ray bonus features has made media consumption more casual, undercutting the perceived value of the text itself when it is no longer purchased as an object to be permanently placed in one's home.[97]

For my purposes, though, it is important to emphasize that this shift away from the commonality of purchasing films as physical media objects resembles less of an entirely new business model than it resembles the 1980s video rental market which existed prior to the sell-through market that became standard industry practice with the 1990s rise of DVD—albeit with the first-sale doctrine now far less operative (except in the case of download-to-own titles). In the meantime, of course, physical media have not vanished but may have to increasingly rely on elaborate bonus features and other paratexts to differentiate themselves from VOD movies whose casual access might threaten to call the text's cultural value into question. This also means that physical media will gradually return to the remit of specialized collectors willing to pay a higher premium for the luxury of owning the text-as-object.

As has been true of so many technological shifts, the adult video market foreshadowed these distribution methods, whether by offering pay-per-view movies since the early 1970s; selling prerecorded tapes to collectors at premium prices beginning that same decade (as Arthur Morowitz did at his theaters and Video Shack chain), years before the sell-through market promoted priced-to-own tapes/discs (Figure 4.10); and pioneering online streaming video in the 1990s, before that viewing method became de rigueur. As mentioned earlier, for example, most classics studios anticipated the overall film industry's present-day distribution strategies by offering subpar transfers of their catalogues through subscription-based and pay-per-view VOD websites—albeit with narrative films typically fragmented into individually purchasable scenes for masturbatory use.

On the one hand, then, Criterion-quality DVD/Blu-ray packages like Distribpix's Platinum Elite editions are more likely positioned to be sold as premium-priced collectors' items in a marketplace where sell-through sales of physical media are again becoming less common, much as pre-1990s porn fans with less blatantly casual/autoerotic investments in the genre were once willing to shell out more money (up to $80–100 per tape) than the average renter in order to gain tape ownership. On the other hand, whereas the value of a given text may seem to decline when it can be casually streamed on-demand by the average viewer, the decline of physical media can simultaneously increase the physical object's very desirability among more devoted niche audiences. As Tryon notes, for example, collector cultures may feel far more

Figure 4.10 Interior of Video Shack store in early 1980s, with prerecorded tapes displayed in glass cases or behind the counter, protected from potential theft due to their premium prices of up to $80 per tape. Photo courtesy of Steven Morowitz.

threatened by a shift away from physical media than other viewers, unless those fan-collectors can figure out a way to hack and archive streaming content in more physical forms.[98] And yet, because pornography is a genre whose texts have long been more commonly associated with interchangable masturbatory utility than cultural value as a variegated genre, these tensions between the physicality of the ownable media text and the physicality of the text's potential uses become all the more acute in the case of adult cinema.

After all, hard-core adult cinema is a genre whose platform mobility is distinctly limited by certain legal and cultural prohibitions. Unlike the non-adult entertainment industry's widespread promotion of VOD as capable of delivering content into both homes and mobile devices on the go, pornography's continuing disrepute tends to circumscribe its potential mobility beyond relatively private places. This is one reason why the DVD market's decline hit the porn industry especially hard, with even major studios like Vivid Entertainment seeing DVD sales down up to 80 percent since 2008, largely blamed on piracy by streaming tube sites.[99] In fact, Steven Morowitz observes that this downturn has led major porn studios like Zero Tolerance to decrease their production of video content and shift toward producing sex toys (often modeled off the body parts of star performers), since plastic specialty goods cannot be pirated like digital audiovisual material—a fascinating instance of an erotic object's quite literal physicality serving as a form of industrial self-defense.[100]

In any case, whether or not it is used for masturbatory purposes, adult cinema is still more likely consumed behind closed doors than in public—potentially bolstering its reputation as a genre reserved for niche reclamation by devoted fans—and thus marks an important exception to many wider industry trends. Indeed, the porn industry may have pioneered the wider entertainment industry's recent turn toward VOD distribution, but it has enjoyed few of the economic benefits—partly because most long-established adult studios' own inferior treatment of their vintage libraries has helped doom so many Golden Age films to the appearance of only being worthy of casual/devalued consumption instead of worthy of consideration as a historically important and even artworthy genre. Moreover, despite the corporatized porn industry's moves toward asserting copyright control over its content, it has remained especially subject to piracy, bootlegging, and other forms of unauthorized distribution because its products are already culturally segregated for exclusive sale (a) to adult viewers; (b) for private consumption; and (c) in countries or jurisdictions where porn is legal—and these same prohibitions have merely served to catalyze the circumventing of legal access. Like the aforementioned self-censorship of its older texts, then, we repeatedly find that the porn industry's inability to be culturally regarded as just another media industry means that the genre it propagates continues to face obstacles to cultural reclamation precisely *because* of the industry's latter-day moves to operate legitimately within the law, not in spite of them.

As discussed above, unauthorized digital distribution has been a boon to fans of Golden Age pornography who seek texts that have been otherwise orphaned, censored, or left behind on outdated analog formats. Some fans may collect early VHS and Beta tapes to increase their collections, while others may rely on torrent and tube sites to download digitized files of hard-to-find films. Joe Rubin, for example, says he is not above using cinephile-oriented torrent sites like Cinemageddon and Karagarga, provided these sites adhere to their stated aims of offering access to out-of-print films, not commercially available ones. After all, Rubin first learned about and saw the offbeat drama *Good Luck, Miss Wyckoff* (1979) through Cinemageddon, which impressed him enough to track down the rights holders and officially release it on Blu-ray/DVD through Vinegar Syndrome—a rare instance of a film's original owners eventually profiting from the renewed attention garnered via unauthorized distribution. To implicitly endorse torrent sites' "proper" function of circulating unavailable or unmarketable films, the company also launched VS Direct, a website section boasting a rotating selection of digitally restored but otherwise unreleased films, available for torrent and download as a reward for customers who have bought the company's physical discs.

Although some vintage porn discussion forums outright ban or delete links to publicly viewable tube and torrent sites—perhaps out of fears that porn industry lawyers will send shutdown notices endangering the survival of fan websites—others allow private members to quietly circulate such content among each other. Since streaming online video (especially from tube sites) lacks bonus features and tends to encode films in grainy or pixelated quality, Susanna Paasonen suggests that the experience of watching it can even conjure memories of consuming VHS and other outdated media formats, especially since older adult films on DVD remain so often sourced from VHS-era telecine transfers today.[101] While this quality might be nostalgically attractive for some fans, it also has the potential to reverse the restorative work done by companies like Vinegar Syndrome and Distribpix—hence Rubin's initial inclination to directly supply torrent sites with high-quality files of restored films that would be unlikely to sell (or legally impractical to sell, due to music licensing costs) on DVD anyway. After all, the online circulation of "lossy," highly compressed rips of carefully restored movies merely reinforces the longstanding denigration of home video in comparison with celluloid,[102] which does no favors to those attempting to rehabilitate Golden Age adult cinema through allusions to its pre-video critical moment of crossover into wider theaters—especially if the ephemerality of here-today-gone-tomorrow tube or torrent videos shows how traditional archival practices have not become irrelevant in the Internet age.[103]

For a younger generation of independent labels coming into the marketplace during an industry-wide turn away from physical media, a reasonable compromise could be found in establishing their own VOD sites, albeit with important qualitative distinctions from both illicit torrent sites and competing classics studios' existing VOD content. As this book went to press, Vinegar Syndrome and Distribpix each began launching their own subscription-based VOD websites dedicated to 1960s–1980s adult cinema: Exploitation.tv and Sexploitation Nation (respectively). Instead of simply releasing less marketable films to torrent sites or replicating the older generation of Distribpix films still available on VOD sites under the Video-X-Pix shingle, Sexploitation Nation films would be newly transferred in 1080p HD and also include previously unavailable vault titles alongside scans of archival material. Moreover, by including both 1960s sexploitation and 1970s–1980s hard-core films under its auspices, Distribpix would be better able to leverage its half-century of longevity as not just a "porn" studio; much as Exploitation.tv (launched in September 2015) offers generically diverse films from both the Vinegar Syndrome and Etiquette Pictures catalogues (in addition to genre films from a handful of partner studios), not just pornographic films. Yet, much as Rubin initially resisted segregating Vinegar Syndrome's hard-core and soft-core DVD offerings, Exploitation.tv situates all of its hard-core adult films within more established genre categories (e.g., "action," "arthouse," "comedy," "drama," "horror," and "thriller"), thus avoiding the knee-jerk marginalization of porn-specific genre terms.

Unlike most other VOD sites, Rubin planned that Exploitation.tv (which was made possible by a $75,000 crowd-funding campaign) would also distinguish itself by including critical essays on specific directors and stars, featured films each week, and scans of rare promotional artifacts and behind-the-scenes content. Presenting newly transferred films in full as whole texts, instead of merely available on a scene-by-scene basis, would follow Vinegar Syndrome's DVDs in emphasizing the films' exclusivity and quality as complete narratives. This emphasis on the deliberate curation of historical/educational value thereby mimicked the sort of value-added DVD/Blu-ray bonus features which might otherwise be lost with the switch from physical to intangible media; that is, these archival and critical materials would help compensate for the implication that streaming-only formats might compound the devaluation of these already less-marketable films. With curated playlists and exclusive streaming-only content, Exploitation.tv would also mimic the Criterion Collection's 2011 decision to license its films to the Hulu Plus subscription service while nevertheless maintaining physical discs as its "core business."[104] Although Rubin hoped that eschewing a download-to-own option in favor of streaming-only formats would help prevent the unauthorized torrenting of Exploitation.tv films, he did acknowledge that streaming-only titles that proved uncommonly popular could demonstrate the viability of a later DVD release.

In Rubin's eyes, if the bulk of his existing customers of hard-core films are in search of sex scenes instead of a more cinephiliac appreciation of adult narratives as a whole, then most customers would likely prefer streaming formats as quicker and easier to access discretely, without the material accumulation accompanying sales of a physical video format. This market logic seemingly concurs with Tryon's observations about VOD consumption as increasingly casual use. For Rubin, cinephiles may indeed complain over the death of physical media (as many of his loyal customers do on the company's Facebook news page whenever a new non-physical release is announced), but once they realize the easier accessibility of the uncut, high-definition streaming text, he thinks that genre fans will stop fetishizing the ownership of factory-pressed tapes and discs as endangered material objects and instead refocus their proper attention on the texts themselves.

And yet, I would argue that when we consider the fan quoted earlier who claims that the "XXX stuff ... I leave out for guests to see" are *real movies* (in contrast to the status of "porn" as a hidden-away masturbatory aid), the spatial situation of physical media in fans' homes reveals itself to be a more text-centric demonstration of discerning taste than, say, some exploitation film fans' superficial fetish for 1980s VHS box covers. While certain vintage porn fans have long collected dusty old videocassettes in order to own more complete versions of otherwise censored texts, the sudden accessibility of uncut, digitally restored, streaming versions will not likely replace the mnemonic value attached to ownership of a rare ephemeral object. After all, as I argued in Chapter 2, the ability to tangibly grasp and keep outdated objects—including even recent DVDs and Blu-rays as they become increasingly residual in the age of intangible media—is more likely to reenact the eroticized longings for pastness that are central to vintage pornography's retrospective appeal. Furthermore, if cloud-based VOD providers do not allow fans to download and recirculate content among each other, then these films' continuing availability will be dependent on the future survival of these online distribution companies. Since there are no guarantees that any VOD company will remain a permanent industry player, the ownership of their distributed films may one day become no less up for grabs than it was in the adult video industry's chaotic early years—thus making fan-collectors' various means of unofficial circulation all the more important in maintaining access to rare texts.

If the wider entertainment industry has witnessed a growing shift away from physical media in the home market, this has been accompanied by a shift away from celluloid in the theatrical market as well. Over the 2000s, the major Hollywood studios sponsored a Digital Cinema Initiative (DCI) aimed at replacing analog projection and 35-mm release prints with digital projectors and Digital Cinema Packages (DCPs) contained on portable hard drives. This initiative was intended to eliminate the high cost of striking and shipping prints for saturation released films—but also to help control piracy and consolidate power over a theatrical market in a state of perpetual panic over falling admissions. These efforts to standardize distribution and exhibition between major studios and the large national theater chains with whom they have been vertically integrated since the 1980s further marginalized art houses and repertory theaters seeking different fare than major-studio-distributed DCPs.[105] Indeed, for Hollywood classics not available as DCPs, studio representatives now typically give repertory exhibitors the limited option of either screening a heavily battered 35-mm release print from the studio vaults (if one is even available) or digitally projecting the remastered Blu-ray version of said film (provided that repertory house has made the sometimes prohibitively expensive switch to digital projection).

Despite the fetishization of celluloid among cinephiles and preservationists, the qualitative differences between home video formats and theatrical formats have thereby become all the more blurred in recent years. As Leo Enticknap argues, preservational codes of ethics to both preserve and project on celluloid are quickly becoming irrelevant as 35-mm film stock and 35-mm projectors are being quickly phased out at the time of writing, forcing archivists and exhibitors toward more pragmatic digital solutions, much as an earlier generation of archivists had to switch from working with nitrate to acetate stock when the former was no longer manufactured.[106] Repertory screenings of older films on celluloid may increasingly appear inferior to the projected Blu-ray, forcing fans to grudgingly accept (home) video's unseating of film even within theatrical settings. On the other hand, large theater chains have increasingly used their digital projection capabilities to foster special fan-oriented screenings and simulcasts of niche-interest titles and populist favorites that are seldom revived on the big screen, thereby turning even multiplex theaters into in-person communal spaces akin to an earlier generation's cultish love of repertory midnight movies. Digital cinema has thus allowed mainstream theaters to encroach on repertory theaters while the latter have had to increasingly make-do with formats primarily designed for home video use.

Such industry-wide overlaps between digital cinema's use both in theaters and at home would seem irrelevant to Golden Age adult cinema's latter-day private and domestic consumption—but there are notable exceptions. After Anthology Film Archives, the venerable New York avant-garde repertory house, screened back-to-back series of Russ Meyer films and Something Weird-sourced sexploitation films in 2013, for example, Casey Scott approached curator Andrew Lampert to program a Golden Age hard-core series as the next logical step in tracing adult cinema's historical progression. Anthology inaugurated "In the Flesh" in December 2013 as a quarterly series devoted to hard-core genre films. Cosponsored by Distribpix and Vinegar Syndrome (who also typically supplied the prints), Anthology stipulated that the series had to be shown on 35 mm, framed by discussions of historical/educational value, and each screening had to feature special guests like filmmakers and performers willing to publicly discuss their on-screen work. Because Distribpix is one of the few classics studios with well-documented files establishing their outright ownership of prints and rights, Scott selected several notable films from their library—including *High Rise* (1973), *Through the Looking Glass* (1976), *Take Off* (1978), and *Wanda Whips Wall Street* (1982) for the first series—and invited guests from the New York area.

Unlike, say, crowd-funding initiatives in which fans may not directly interact with each other, this recurring series was a rare case of hard-core films receiving prominent and sustained revival outside the realm of home consumption. The title "In the Flesh" evokes this sense of personal encounter between fellow viewers, especially with the filmmakers present in the flesh as well (Figure 4.11)—while the use of archival 35-mm prints reinforces this notion of *physicality* in an era increasingly marked by moves away from physical media. Moreover, much as a "Gay Pride"-themed iteration of the series in June 2014 focused on openly gay filmmakers who made straight porn films (such as Chuck Vincent and the Amero Brothers), Scott notes that the fluidity of desire—including his own positionality as a gay man turned on by straight porn—allowed the series to appeal to many sexual demographics.[107] He observes that the well-attended series' audience consisted of a diverse mix of straight and gay cinephiles and porn

Figure 4.11 From left, Vinegar Syndrome cofounder Joe Rubin, director Larry Revene, and star Jane Hamilton discuss the Distribpix film *Wanda Whips Wall Street* (1982) at the "In the Flesh" film series, Anthology Film Archives, December 8, 2013. Photo courtesy of Steven Morowitz.

fans, both young and old, curious and experienced. The most common refrain among viewers was that, unlike the predominant directions taken by hard-core cinema before and after the Golden Age, these were "real movies" worth watching as long as they were aesthetically and historically interesting.[108]

Much like Distribpix's own strategies of upscale presentation for its Platinum Elite line and remastered single-disc editions, then, Anthology's series of Distribpix films gained a sense of legitimacy through its artistically reputable venue, the imprimatur of historical/educational significance, and the open participation of veteran discussants. Scott even sent

> professional invitations to all surviving cast and crew in the tri-state area that I could find, which could be turned in at the box office for free admission for two. [...] I received a few RSVP's from people who were either excited to attend or couldn't attend because any publicity surrounding their appearances would result in termination from their jobs. It's still that kind of a world we live in, folks, where appearing in or working on an X-rated film decades ago will be held against you. Because the invites were intended to make it easier for cast and crew to attend discreetly, I won't reveal who did attend, and the series has a permanent policy about surprise guest audience members: what happens at "In the Flesh" stays at "In the Flesh."[109]

Yet, as much as discretion allowed former cast and crew to attend the series as anonymous audience members instead of onstage presenters, at least one male viewer was kicked out for masturbating during a screening, suggesting how the various uses of these texts have not wholly collapsed the respective benefits of theatrical and domestic consumption.

Steven Morowitz took the opportunity to record interviews and commentaries with the guest actors and filmmakers, providing an incentive to incorporate such material into his next line of remastered DVD editions, and was so impressed by the series' success that he considered striking several new prints of selected films to tour the repertory circuit, one of the last bastions of film-on-film.[110] In this respect, a fan-friendly series like "In the Flesh" helped spur future video releases, suggesting a growing convergence between repertory potential and economic potential for this slowly revalued genre. Ironically, however, each copy of early Platinum Elite editions of *Maraschino Cherry* (1978) and *Blonde Ambition* contained 35-mm film strips snipped from release prints of the corresponding film, suggesting that Distribpix's presumed inability to capitalize on repertory screenings of its library had once turned the destruction of old vault prints into a paratextual selling point for the company's digitally remastered home video editions.

This is yet another small example of how, as I have suggested throughout this book, adult cinema's threatened destruction, particularly as an ephemeral form associated with decaying celluloid, remains inseparable from its continuing desirability as a vintage commodity (even in remediated forms). If this sacrifice of old celluloid prints to the potential profitability of high-quality video reissues echoes the major Hollywood studios' recent, post-DCI strategies for remarketing digital versions of their older films instead of 35-mm copies, then Distribpix's use of successful 35-mm repertory screenings to help fuel interest in its main video business further evokes the overall film industry's goal of blurring the qualitative lines between theatrical and home video exhibition. Indeed, since far more people will be able to purchase a newly remastered DVD reissue than attend a repertory screening of even a newly struck 35-mm print, Distribpix can use these limited opportunities for more communal, in-person fandom to market its primary sales of digital video formats. And yet, I would argue that the reclamation of vintage adult cinema as a genre worthy of serious aesthetic consideration truly deserves the more widespread return of public exhibition opportunities that can provoke interpersonal conversation that moves beyond embarrassment or bemusement at finding oneself watching hard-core pornography among a room full of strangers.

For many viewers, then, the physicality of Golden Age adult cinema's repertory revival may adhere as much in the physical presence of fellow viewers/fans and veteran filmmaking personnel as in the physical presence of 35-mm celluloid. And yet, despite these video labels' efforts to contextualize these films within a past historical period in which autoeroticism within adult theaters was common, the masturbating Anthology patron begs the question of how certain forms of physicality might still remain disciplined through this attempted cultural recuperation of the films (in the words of Anthology's program) "as they were intended to be seen." As film-born pornographic cinema becomes reappraised, this already denigrated figure may become increasingly marginalized as Golden Age porn's "bad fan," shunted off into the domestic sphere where physical media are themselves becoming less common. In this respect, access to the physicality of the repertory experience necessitates relinquishing the physicality of other pleasures—even when the latter may be quite consistent with a film's original authorial or generic intent (as the Orleans Theatre scene in *Deep Inside Annie Sprinkle* so clearly depicts)—much as the production of sacralized cultural spaces has long relied on the presumption of distanced aesthetic contemplation.[111]

If, as Rubin suggests, porn consumers primarily seeking sex scenes over connoisseurship of the narratives as a whole may be more apt to use streaming media for casually autoerotic purposes than physical media fans who want to own complete films, then the video market's overall shifts toward VOD content may pose particular obstacles for the genre's recuperation as more than just "porn." Of course, in his day-to-day life, the masturbating Anthology patron may not be any less connected to other fans through online fan communities and the like; nor does the act of going so far as to masturbate in an acclaimed repertory theater suggest that he is more of a "casual" porn viewer than anyone else (in fact, we might even speculate that the opposite is true). What we can safely say, however, is that, even as Golden Age features begin receiving a measure of overdue critical reappraisal and even expanded canonization— not only through more ethically respectful home video reissues but also through the anachronistic resurrection of theatrical exhibition for a genre so often associated today with nontheatrical pleasures—the physicality of vintage pornography's various uses and incarnations will remain a point of contention for some and even become a site of cultural privilege for others.

Conclusion

As early as 1974, critics said of iconic *Deep Throat* (1972) star Linda Lovelace, "it is a sure thing that those of her fans who are still alive in 2006 will spend part of their Social Security check to see her."[1] Ironically, this prediction has proven only too true, whether through continuing sales of her starring vehicles on DVD, the various books and films based upon her experience, and the many academic analyses of her brief career—all of which did unfortunately little to materially benefit Lovelace herself during a life marked by periods of spousal abuse, economic poverty, and poor health, finally cut short by a car accident in 2002. After all, it is as much *Deep Throat*'s one-time notoriety as the paragon of pornography's move into the cultural mainstream as its oft-told cautionary backstory among antiporn feminists that continues to fuel its status as an *urtext* for the "sex wars" that followed. The question of Lovelace's active agency as a poster child, first for 1970s "porno chic" and later for antiporn crusaders, continues to be debated (and need not be rehashed here), but regardless of where the unknowable truth lies, it remains enough to say that she did not fare well from her involvement with either movement. Antiporn activists exploited her more as the image of a fallen woman than as a fellow feminist like them—and after being held at arm's length in the service of a particular political agenda, she was cast away. "Between Andrea Dworkin and Kitty MacKinnon," Lovelace lamented shortly before her death, "they've written so many books, and they mention my name and all that, but financially they've never helped me out. When I showed up with them for speaking engagements, I'd always get five hundred dollars or so. But I know they made a few bucks off me, just like everybody else."[2]

What remains crucial to remember, then, is that regardless of whatever residual (sub)cultural or economic value that vintage pornographic cinema may accrue, the sex workers in front of the camera—that is, those whose lives are most often altered by their visible participation in erotic labor—typically see few residuals from these textual afterlives. Moreover, by leaving less of a financial paper trail, this practice has important implications for the accounting done by historians as well; as *The Devil in Miss Jones*'s (1973) star Georgina Spelvin observes, "There are so many films out there that have been made of cutting-room trash, with different names—and since I never received a royalty, not one penny, from any film I ever made, I cannot tell you what I did or did not do."[3] A handful of Golden Age performers have enjoyed long careers within the adult film industry, though most were unable to substantially cross over to non-adult cinema. As in the non-adult film industry, a gendered double standard also found easier career longevity for male stars—as attested by the many 1980s era *Adult Video News* letters to the editor complaining that the period's most prolific male performers were merely holdovers from the 1970s, with genre fans hoping for a fresh crop of younger male personalities.

Other (female) performers may have continued indirectly eking out the ancillary benefits of fame (e.g., book deals, escorting, paid appearances at strip clubs and fan conventions), but they seldom directly profit from the unexpectedly long afterlives of their remediated movies themselves. Indeed, Mireille Miller-Young explains, porn performers commonly use these forms of ancillary employment to make a living wage and avoid becoming "overexposed" through making too many films in too short a period. Being considered "old" in the porn industry, then, has less to do with a performer's actual age than the frequency of his/her work.[4] If "vintage-ness" adheres in the allure of careers and films that may have burned brightly for a brief period and then vanished from the more recent screen, then the pathos of historical loss that fans retrospectively project onto the corpus cannot be wholly separated from the practical realities of lost earning power for the industry's most vulnerable workers—especially when their paths into and out of the industry share many of the "arguably degrading, depressing, and potentially dangerous or traumatizing" traits of minimum-wage service jobs.[5] After all, as Casey Scott observed in the previous chapter, one's decades-old participation in an adult film can have negative repercussions upon one's social standing, long after the event, when the films live on as mnemonic reminders of sexual deeds that some might prefer remain consigned to obscurity.

This tension can, for example, be found at the Erotic Heritage Museum in Las Vegas, initially founded as a nonprofit institution in 2008 by Dr. Ted McIlvenna of the Exodus Trust and the Institute for the Advanced Study of Human Sexuality (IASHS), a San Francisco-based graduate program in sexology, from which former porn stars like Annie Sprinkle and Sharon Mitchell have earned doctorate degrees in human sexuality. Housed in a 17,000-square-foot former sex accessory store in a city that plays annual host to the AVN Awards and Adult Entertainment Expo, the US porn industry's biggest events, the museum holds educational exhibits (Figure C.1), many curated from the Exodus Trust's archives, illustrating the history of both erotic art and more commercial pornographic materials, plus a research library, sexual health workshops, an erotic film screening series, and so on.

The museum also prominently bears the name of founding patron Harry Mohney over its own. Mohney made a fortune from adult theaters and bookstores, the adult film distribution company Entertainment World International, the production company Caribbean Films, the adult video distributor Wild World of Video, and the Déjà Vu strip club empire (one of which is located directly next door to the museum). He allegedly donated the building in gratitude for McIlvenna's years of legal testimony on his behalf in obscenity trials over pornography's cultural value. Yet, with Mohney repeatedly named in lawsuits by Déjà Vu dancers (including a class-action suit settled for $11.3 million in 2010) over alleged threats against unionization, violations of minimum wage laws, and "managers routinely withhold[ing] money from dancers, improperly classifying them as independent contractors instead of employees,"[6] the systemic treatment of his company's low-level sex workers, recalling that of many other

Figure C.1 A 2008 temporary exhibit at the Erotic Heritage Museum in Las Vegas, commemorating Distribpix's release of the *Deep Inside Annie Sprinkle* (1981) Platinum Elite DVD, featuring ephemera related to the film and Sprinkle's on-screen video commentary. Photo courtesy of Steven Morowitz.

corporatized service industries, stands as a stark reminder of whose backs the Erotic Heritage Museum is built upon. (In this respect, it differs from New York's Museum of Sex, founded in 2002 with bylaws refusing "financial backing from anyone in 'the adult entertainment industry.'"[7])

If, as I noted in the previous chapter, pornography's reputation as little more than disposable masturbatory fodder is tied to its supposed alignment with crass commercialism instead of erotic art, then these legal complaints toward the Erotic Heritage Museum's major benefactor unfortunately suggested that the residual value of its holdings was primarily economic, not cultural. Indeed, Mohney even sued the museum's former curator in 2011, alleging that the latter incorrectly appraised a collection of 16-mm porn films and related ephemera that the mogul had donated to the museum as a charitable tax deduction. Yet, because of supposedly "false information in the appraisals [claiming] that Mohney owned copyrights and distribution rights to the films" (which, as I explained in the last two chapters, is not surprising, given the difficulty of definitively establishing the legal provenance of most adult films), the Internal Revenue Service raised red flags and again proved itself one of Mohney's longtime banes.[8] The museum unceremoniously closed in

February 2014, during a dispute between Mohney and McIlvenna over several years of unpaid rent, which McIlvenna claims was never an agreed-upon precondition for using the building. He also complained that Mohney "wants to use the museum to promote his business interests, rather than nonprofit and education work."[9] Mohney later reopened the museum as a for-profit corporation in June 2014, with a selection of exhibits on loan from the Exodus Trust (minus the research library and student interns), but with McIlvenna relieved of his former role in the museum's leadership.[10]

Nevertheless, by intending to create a permanent and publicly accessible site conferring the title of "heritage" upon pornography, McIlvenna's museological mission did mark a significant attempt to reassign cultural value to the disreputable genre by classifying it as a form of "folk art." In this regard, it is consistent with the mission of the IASHS's earlier incarnation, the National Sex Forum (NSF), which Eithne Johnson describes as an educational-therapeutic program in humanistic sexology (begun in 1968), in which cofounders McIlvenna and Laird Sutton immersed subjects in multimedia installations (informally dubbed the "Sexarama") featuring sexually explicit audiovisual content. These "Sexual Attitude Restructuring" sessions—still used at the IASHS to this day—first bombarded subjects with commercially made hard-core imagery to "desensitize" viewers to explicit sex, while a second round of content would "resensitize" subjects via sexually explicit films produced by the NSF itself. As Johnson notes, the latter films were no less explicit than the commercially made ones (and were indeed intended to arouse, even to the point of coupling in the Sexarama room itself), but were intended to evoke "erotic art" over "pornographic" fodder, depicting unsimulated sex in the context of love, happiness, and educational sobriety instead of just crude fucking.[11] Regardless of this therapeutic method's uncertain efficacy (to say nothing of its presumed distinctions between the erotic and the pornographic), it is difficult not to see the Erotic Heritage Museum as likewise using an immersive physical space for multimedia displays of all manner of sexually explicit material for similar goals of "resensitizing" visitors to a more liberalized range of human sexual behaviors through this "folk art"—especially if the Exodus Trust's large pornography collection was originally accrued in part to aid the NSF/IASHS's Sexual Attitude Restructuring experiments.

The museum's exhibit on pornographic cinema, for example, is heavily weighted toward examples of now-vintage pornography in particular (partly a product of the Exodus Trust's peak acquisition years), containing artifacts like Alex de Renzy's 16-mm camera, a replica of a porn film set, and a video installation in which visitors walk into a circular partitioned area housing eight screens, each one simultaneously showing a selected scene from the early stag *A Free Ride* (1915), *Deep Throat*, *Behind the Green Door* (1972), and several more recent offerings. Each looped scene is a brief but visually spectacular extract from the surrounding narrative— such as the psychedelically colored, superimposed cumshots at the finale of *Green Door*—suggesting a sample of canonical films, but without conveying the narrative justification that genre aficionados so often evaluate as crucial to revaluing hard-core films as more than mere benchmarks in the history of on-screen sex.[12] For the less uninitiated, most of these films perhaps need little introduction, with the museum likely presuming that a stag film and several of the biggest first-wave porno-chic hits would already be familiar to many visitors, at least by reputation. After all, as I have suggested throughout this book, vintage pornography may today be marketed as a niche category like any other fetish, but its constitutive texts once occupied a more tenuous proximity to the cultural mainstream—from (illegal) stags screened at respected fraternal clubs, to sexploitation's capitalization on industry-wide changes culminating with the X rating, to the notoriety of Golden Age features as required viewing for the culturally hip. In any case, the museum's choices for exhibited clips are less of a stretch in the "heritage" department than, say, clips from De Renzy's notorious but fan-acclaimed *Femmes de Sade* (1976), whose original theatrical poster is displayed nearby but might not prove a productively "resensitizing" text due to its fictional scenes of sexual violence.

Among the museum's most notable "acquisitions" was Jane Hamilton—better known as Golden Age porn star Veronica Hart—who worked as the museum's director of new media from 2010 to 2013. Also serving as a museum docent, Hamilton's long career in the industry as both an actor and filmmaker made her one of the institution's most public faces. While her on-screen career as a sex performer at the tail end of the Golden Age only lasted from 1980 to 1984 (though new compilation videos of her early scenes have continued appearing, even as recently as 2009), she quickly became renowned as "the finest pure actress of the early eighties,"[13] starring in Chuck Vincent's auteur vehicles like *Roommates* (1981) and often cast as strong, intelligent, "classy" women in films like *A Scent of Heather* (1980), *Amanda by Night* (1981), *Pandora's Mirror* (1981), and *Center Spread Girls* (1982). She is also a charter member of Club 90, a feminist consciousness-raising group for female porn stars, also including Annie Sprinkle, Gloria Leonard, Candida Royalle, Veronica Vera, Sue Nero, and Kelly Nichols—who together staged the influential performance piece *Deep Inside Porn Stars* in 1984.[14] She has continued acting in nonsex roles both within and beyond the adult industry (including a cameo in *Boogie Nights* [1997] and a starring role in the off-Broadway play *The Deep Throat Sex Scandal* [2013]), in addition to producing and directing several dozen adult features for VCA (including the Golden Age homages *Barbara Broadcast Too!* [2003] and *Misty Beethoven: The Musical!* [2004]), working as a production manager for *Adam Film World* alumnus-turned-filmmaker James Avalon, and most recently, teaching sexual health and intimacy courses in China.

This illustrious reputation was no doubt a boon to the museum's edifying mission, while also allowing Hamilton to effectively serve as a sort of "living history" exhibit, adding to the overall ambience while discussing her long and multifaceted career with visitors. On the one hand, both she and the museum could mutually benefit from the ancillary value of her porn career. On the other hand, because none of her own films as "Veronica Hart" were represented by inclusion in the museum itself, despite their high renown among genre aficionados (Figure C.2), the museum's limited representation of adult cinema's history simultaneously complicated the perceived value of her fan-culturally celebrated oeuvre.

Figure C.2 Detail from 1985 Caballero Control Corporation home video catalogue promoting Veronica Hart in one of her most acclaimed films, *Amanda by Night* (1981), for which she won an Adult Film Critics Award for Best Actress (author's collection).

As Hamilton told me, the Erotic Heritage Museum's most important purpose is providing a healthy, sex-positive forum for anyone to feel welcome. She does, however, note that the Exodus Trust's general reliance on relatively outdated technologies for its exhibits is more befitting of a museum setting than an active site for teaching and research, potentially limiting the more innovative cultural interventions that the institution might one day foster. For her, pornography is important to preserve as part of our cultural heritage, regardless of its oft-questionable aesthetic value, and the museum's broad scope is notable for being more inclusive than simply covering more "legitimate" forms of erotic art—especially when the adult industry itself does a "horrible job" at preserving its past.

Still, she readily admits that one of the main proofs that pornography is culturally valid is that it makes so much money—even as the present-day porn industry's reliance upon safely profitable conventions has made it very difficult for her to raise funds to make the kinds of adult films she would like to see: those in which explicit sex is portrayed as an important and healthy part of characters' lives (not unlike the NSF's self-produced films), but without sex completely dominating their lives or being narratively conjoined to the tropes of violence and degradation found in the recent spate of hard-core art films. As much as she might lament the fact that many of her best-known films as a star performer are only available on video today in poor-quality DVD editions, she prefers producing new work.[15] Small wonder, then, that she eventually gave up the museum job for more creative opportunities—even if, like the museum itself, future opportunities for more progressive projects remain uncertain due to the vagaries of funding, ownership, and so on.

Regardless, other former porn stars were not as lucky. Take Wade Nichols, whose memorable starring role in Armand Weston's aptly named Hollywood spoof *Take Off* (1978) appeared at Anthology's "In the Flesh" series, along with the Veronica Hart star vehicle *Wanda Whips Wall Street* (1982). Nichols, whose heartthrob good looks saw him successfully transition from gay escort to porn star to disco singer and even to soap opera actor, died in 1985, reportedly committing suicide at age thirty-nine after contracting AIDS the previous year. Often ranked among the best Golden Age adult features ever made, yet practically unknown to all but genre fans, *Take Off* stands as a notable example of a film that participates in indirectly canonizing Hollywood films through decade-specific parodies, while the film's own marginal status bespeaks pornography's difficulty in gaining admittance to the cultural canon. Based on Oscar Wilde's *The Picture of Dorian Gray* (1890), a novel published shortly before the first stag films appeared, *Take Off* opens at a Gatsbyesque party where two present-day guests, Linda (Leslie Bovee) and Roy (Eric Edwards), abscond together into the mansion for sex and then discover a 1920s-era stag film depicting a woman fucking an old man in a meadow—an image that will soon gain tremendous significance as we learn that, not unlike the magical stag reel in *The Lickerish Quartet* (1970), it carries certain enchantments.

"This must be a collector's item" due to its age, Linda remarks, with Roy observing that the on-screen sex acts are "practically an instant replay" of what they have just done in 1978. Much as I have described the retrospective allure of stags and vintage pornography in general as rooted in the curiosity and collectability of the outdated and ephemeral text, their carnal appeal continues to reside in sexual acts that have not themselves drastically changed between then and now. Indeed, as a feature film from near the end of the so-called vintage era, *Take Off* itself has since acquired a similar quality—perhaps not as markedly anachronistic to us today as a 1920s stag reel, but still evoking a combination of pathos at the loss of a past era and viscerality in delivering an eroticism transcending the historical gulf. And yet, as much as one might attempt to foreclose that historical/aesthetic distance through autoeroticism, the gulf inevitably remains insurmountable, except in the realm of fantasy—a reminder of how vintage pornography's affectivity can also implicate oneself in the register of pathos.

The party's mysterious host, Darrin Blue (Nichols), soon reveals himself to Linda, and they drive away into the countryside together as he solemnly notes, "I've had enough parties to fill a lifetime." He begins telling her his story through flashbacks, opening with his seduction by a sexually liberated older woman, Henrietta Wilde (Georgina Spelvin), during the 1920s; the film seamlessly transitions into sepia tones and ragtime accompaniment as Darrin's 1970s Mercedes turns a corner and Henrietta's 1928 Rolls Royce comes around the corner in the opposite direction. Obsessed with aging, she tells her young beau that he takes his youth and beauty for granted. "The true mystery of the world is in the visible, not the invisible," she explains. "It's in the things you can see … and touch"—a philosophy as consistent with Wildean aestheticism as pornography's generic impetus toward capturing the visible proof of sexual pleasure. While their recently shot stag footage (Figure C.3) may not yet bear the desirable veneer of historicity that audiences in later decades could appreciate and even fetishize, Henrietta's longing to preserve those on-screen bodies luminously dancing in sexual congress, even as the film itself is destined to fade and decay, at least foreshadows vintage adult cinema's present-day potential to be taken up as both art and porn. Darrin does not subscribe to her decadent views until he later sees himself projected alongside her in the stag reel, which was secretly filmed by her driver. He then makes a pact to stay eternally youthful while his on-screen image in the stag film, left to him by the recently vanished Henrietta, grows old in his place. "At first he thought it was simply that the film had begun to show the normal signs of wear and tear," Darrin's third-person narration recalls—a comparison between personal and artifactual aging that has grown more poignant in light of Nichols's untimely death. Likewise, Henrietta's desire to cinematically capture a powerfully erotic moment within that meta-object of desire recalls the historian/fan's own erotic encounters with ephemera that seem to imaginatively bridge across a history of erotic fantasies and documented realities. Much as Henrietta, discussing her stag reel, once said that one is "left with nothing but memories" when one grows old, *Take Off*'s own status as a cinematic memory of Nichols has remained subject to gradual degradation and decay pending Distribpix's DVD release of a new 2K restoration.

The remainder of *Take Off* unfolds through a series of flashbacks to Darrin's sexual adventures across the decades, each one a spoof of iconic Hollywood films (1930s gangster films, 1940s Humphrey Bogart films, 1950s juvenile delinquent films, and 1960s hippie films) leading back up to the film's own late 1970s present. This narrative

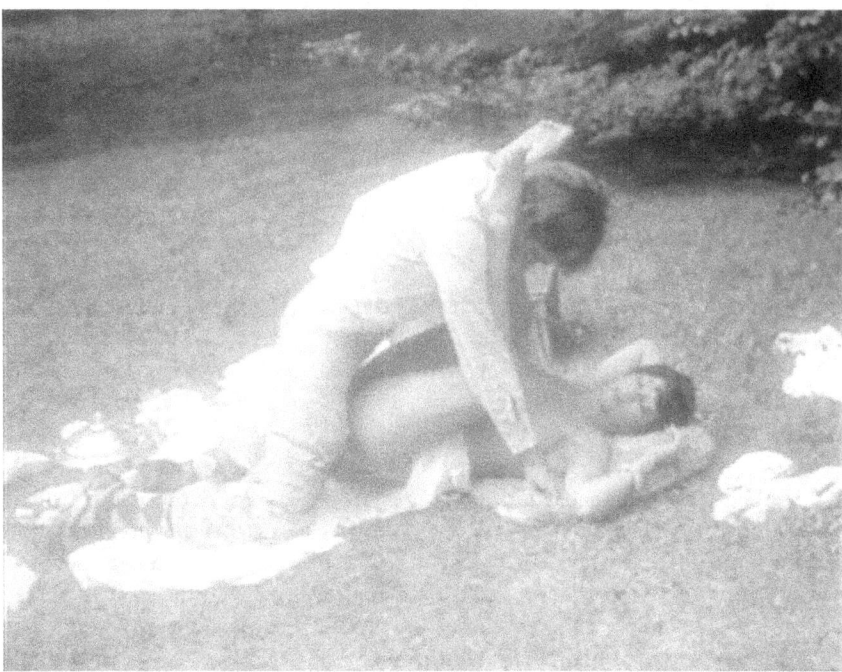

Figure C.3 A sepia-toned image of the young Darrin Blue (Wade Nichols) and Henrietta Wilde (Georgina Spelvin) performing for the stag movie camera in the 1920s segment of *Take Off* (1978).

conceit is not unlike the organization of decade-specific vintage porn DVDs and website sections discussed in my first chapter, while also recalling hard-core stags' ability to "desecrate" the Hollywood fantasies made during their respective pre-legalization periods. Yet, the increasingly melancholy Darrin, whose pact has cursed him to a life without lasting love and human connection, finally realizes during a 1960s acid trip that "lack of change is the real death"—a line that also resonates with the film's attention to changing sexual mores over the decades. From the aforementioned 1920s stag film, to a scene depicting 1950s greasers wowed by *Playboy*'s permissibility, to a 1960s hippie chick attempting to give her mother advice about fellatio and clitoral orgasms, *Take Off*'s parodic depictions of the decades before the "permissive 1970s" invites its late 1970s audience to laugh at how far we've come. Much as critics have often (erroneously) described the post-1970s legalization of hard-core cinema as a historical endpoint in sex's own cinematic "coming of age," *Take Off* thus presents itself as a product of that very culmination—hence, Darrin's decision to finally break the spell by again filming himself having sex, this time with Linda. Now magically restored to his proper age, Darrin reunites with his lost love Henrietta, and the two elderly folks leave the mansion to live happily (if temporarily) ever after. The film ultimately depicts cinema as a machine whose ability to magically capture and preserve memories has a potential dark side—an irony likely not lost on those past cast and crew who were unable to attend its "In the Flesh" screening—with the film's own comedic tone retrospectively sitting in stark contrast to its star's early demise. Darrin may have finally realized that personal and historical change is inevitable, but this role also reminds us of the real death that Nichols, like his now-aged character, would encounter only a few short years later, leaving his own youthful visage preserved in the relative cultural obscurity of the Distribpix vaults.

As frozen testaments to deceased stars, Golden Age adult films like *Take Off* can thus remind us today of not only a lost moment of attempted crossover between pornography and Hollywood (Nichols himself would succeed in landing a regular role on the long-running television soap *The Edge of Night* [1956–1984], under the alternate name Dennis Parker), but also a time before home video, AIDS, the Internet, and all those other factors impacting the contemporary porn industry and comparatively coloring the vintage-ness of what came before. And indeed, as the twentieth century's alternative index for changing cultural restrictions on cinematic sex, all forms of vintage adult cinema bear a similar nostalgic tension between a not-wholly-better now and a not-wholly-lost then. As Jeffrey Escoffier notes, for example, watching old porn movies—especially all-male pornography nostalgically marketed today as "pre-condom classics"—featuring sex without condoms can provoke ambivalence in present-day viewers by reading "either as 'fantasy' or as the sign of an imminent disaster."[16] Gregory Storms argues that the periodizing term "pre-condom" may allow older forms of gay pornography to remain far less denigrated than contemporary bareback porn's fetishization of potential HIV infection, but the very term implicitly invokes the specter of HIV/AIDS, eroticizing the fact that "actors [such as Nichols] engaging in condom-less anal sex in precondom films made in the 1970s and 1980s were at risk of contracting HIV, regardless of whether it was a known risk at the time."[17]

The decimation from AIDS of an entire youthful generation of early gay filmmakers has had crucial historiographic implications, as the relative dearth of survivors has made the legal provenance of many all-male porn films especially difficult to ascertain. Furthermore, unlike the all-male porn industry, the heterosexual porn industry's continuing resistance to mandatory condom use (even to the point of shooting overseas to avoid recent California laws mandating condom use in porn production)[18] proves that it has still failed to sufficiently learn from the fates of Nichols and other performers like him. Moreover, I suggested in the previous chapter that the mainstream porn industry's self-censorship of Golden Age content like fictionalized rape/incest scenes or adult actors depicted as underage characters may be a strategy for legal self-defense and a concession to the political impact of second-wave feminism—but it is simultaneously (for better or worse) a self-defeating surrender of creative freedom for what types of stories the genre can or cannot tell, and an implicit bolstering of the spurious antiporn position that such depictions necessarily have a real-life capacity to harm. It is all the more ironic and even tragic, then, that the heterosexual porn industry's main objection to mandatory condom use—the supposition that visible condoms would shatter the genre's pornotopian illusion of consequence-free sex—stubbornly retains this far less significant generic signifier of "harmless fantasy" at the undeniable risk of performers' *actual lives*.

Yet, if my comments in this Conclusion serve as a pessimistic reminder of the lived costs for those performers whose indexical bodies are lent to the genre's enactment of erotic fantasies, these remarks are not meant to be read as defensive backpedalling over previous chapters that some readers might see as an apologia for some forms of vintage pornography. Rather, because pornography is (for better or worse) a more politically freighted filmic genre than any other, it remains important not to lose sight of the more concrete ramifications—above and beyond any highly questionable claims about the media effects of viewing such material—that the cultural marginalization of sex workers and other minorities can have upon those participants and viewers who have turned to the genre for more than just getting off.

Indeed, the fact that Nichols himself was gay—and continues to have a notable gay following—but performed "straight-for-pay" in heterosexual films (*Take Off*, for example, replaces the homoerotic relationships in Wilde's novel with Darrin and Henrietta's straight romance, but Nichols's star persona injects a sense of queerness into the proceedings) also suggests how vintage pornography's survival allows alternative histories of past and present desires to unfold, spurred on by a sense of temporal distance from the present that can encourage both critical reflection and a longing to collapse the historical gap through one's own bodily pleasures. This book, after all, may have predominantly focused on hetero-male texts and readings, but vintage pornography's more recent appropriation by feminist and queer viewers suggests the continuing importance of these textual afterlives as their interpersonal fan uses also become more diverse.[19] Moreover, if the remarketing of some vintage pornographic forms may draw upon discourses of nostalgia to uphold culturally overdetermined, retrograde gender norms in some regards, then vintage pornography's alluring investment in the vagaries of "erotohistoriography" can also open creative spaces for historically revisionist and/or queer investments, precisely by fostering an eroticism that springs less from specific sexual acts or identities than from fetishizing the culturally *underdetermined* notion of pastness itself.[20]

The fact that *Take Off*'s 1978 present day has, by the early twenty-first century, already passed into the seemingly "vintage" realm also draws attention to what we might consider the sliding ground of nostalgization as history continues to unfold. I would go so far as to say that, despite the close ties I have described between the vintage and analog/celluloid formats, the very term "vintage" may now be gaining increased discursive importance as it becomes no longer possible to simply posit a pre-video/post-video distinction as the dividing line between so-called vintage and contemporary porn. Much as "Golden Age" is useful as a historically localized term for film-born hard-core narratives from the 1970s and early 1980s but does not encompass all forms or functions of so-called vintage pornography, we may eventually find that what becomes gradually designated as "vintage" texts will come to include today's video-born online videos. That is, as the aesthetic primitivism of pixelated, consumer-grade digital video recordings of nonprofessional sex starts to become seen as "vintage" in future decades, the idea of vintage-ness may well readmit many of the formal qualities endemic to early-twentieth-century stag films, not just the more polished products of the 1960s sexploitation and 1970s porno-chic eras. Likewise, even professionally shot-on-video porn from the "Silver Age" and beyond will likely come to gain a sense of vintage-ness marked less by recording/distribution medium than by the presence of specific performers and temporal signifiers of bygone eras—as we can already see occurring in the inclusion of 1990s porn on some vintage websites. (The website Vintage Erotica Forums, for example, restricts discussion and file sharing to pre-1995 content at the time of this writing.) As Alpha Blue Archives' Jacy Catlin predicts,

> I think we could expect to see a few die hard fans of the nowadays porn seeking out titles that are currently right under our noses in 10–20 years. The big difference is that in 10–20 years [contemporary gonzo pornographer] Max Hardcore and Vivid [V]ideo will still be around, and probably have some sort of "classics" line. Most people will be nostalgic for videos they saw on the internet. Those files will still be around in newsgroups, etc. Many 70's films on the other hand were made for fast cash by short lived partnerships by people who no longer have anything to do with the industry.[21]

What this comment suggests, then, is that vintage pornography's constitutive texts may increasingly include materials from the industry's post-1980s corporatization, including texts whose legal provenance and preservational status are far less vague than so much of the material produced before and during the Golden Age. Nevertheless, the copyright issues discussed in the previous two chapters may become more acutely important as older films are more widely reappraised and larger residual profits become at stake.

As the niche category of vintage pornography increasingly encompasses video-born texts, celluloid will doubtless continue to carry powerfully nostalgic and aestheticized associations—but the addition of more and more video-born texts to the corpus may have the benefit of admitting the more diverse and far less heterosexist pornographies (such as feminist and queer porn) that the low cost of post-Golden Age video production helped proliferate. As much as the 1970s-era films that once inched toward mainstream appeal during the first porno-chic wave are increasingly becoming angled toward mainstream reappraisal in our current, second wave of porno chic, a gradual diminishment of long-standing biases against video may help prevent the genre's pioneering moves toward more politically progressive work from becoming unduly marginalized in the historical record—a genealogy that I pointed toward in the parallels between Distribpix's *Deep Inside Annie Sprinkle* (1981) reissue and post-porn feminist art like *Annie Sprinkle's Herstory of Porn* (1999). If younger video companies are partnering with each other to reissue vintage adult cinema as more valuable historical texts than the seemingly disposable, interchangeable, and disreputable products that older video companies found unworthy of proper preservation, then the possibilities for wider cultural recuperation of these reissued texts can only increase. And yet, we must remain cognizant that video companies may perform increasingly preservational labor through today's more cost-effective digital scanning and restoration technologies, but they are not "archives" in a proper sense—for they are neither formally open to outside researchers, nor likely to invest their independent capital without the ability to distribute and monetize the resulting remediations.

As Peter Alilunas argues, studying pornography as a historian requires the use of "trace historiography," in which research must proceed through surviving ephemera (including materials collected and saved by the researcher him/herself) because little paper trail has remained beyond those materials that might gain some residual economic value.[22] In effect, pornography emphasizes the "streetwalker" in Giuliana Bruno's famous metaphor that researching historically lost or neglected cinema is akin to "streetwalking on a ruined map,"[23] for the fact of a whole genre's archival neglect foregrounds any text's promiscuous route through history when cultural value is inherently open to contestation. Take, for instance, Jacqueline Stewart's discussion of a trove of Jim Crow-era race films discovered in a Tyler, Texas warehouse in 1983, after having been spared from the demolition of Dallas's Film Exchange Building. Archival discourses attempted to both acknowledge the historical value of these little-known films (which, tellingly, were found commingled with exploitation films and had initially been overlooked as "pornographic" on the basis of their lurid titles), while steeling contemporary viewers toward their potentially offensive racial representations—in any case, framing the films as a significant glimpse into a "lost" past, despite their inability to offer any more than a minute fraction of the era's Black cultural production.[24]

Vintage pornography's inevitably limited glimpses into a "lost" sexual past operate in a similar way—but unlike these Black-produced race films' eventual archivization by predominantly white institutions like Southern Methodist University, heterosexual adult cinema's surviving texts have largely remained in the hands of their originally intended demographic: heterosexual men. Like Stewart, then, I strongly agree that such marginal cinemas deserve to be revalued, yet it remains crucial for us to remember that vintage adult cinema often espoused culturally dominant values—both then and now—such as the celebration of heterosexual male prowess. That is, when hetero-male-run commercial labels that specialize in vintage pornography are prone to framing seemingly outdated films in ways ranging from politically incorrect celebrations of prefeminist "bad taste" to more sincere appreciations of male authorial skill, we must be carefully attuned to how these texts continue to circulate in a culture that has seen a far more pervasive backlash against the advances of second-wave feminism than against the struggle for racial civil rights that helped render race films more obviously obsolete. Vintage pornography's lingering status as outdated but not wholly obsolete texts thereby remains firmly tied up with notions of subcultural value, even as some of the subcultures appropriating such films may today constitute more diverse demographics and reception practices than the films' creators originally intended. Much as film preservationists often invest in untenable fantasies about approximating a film's original exhibition context but must also make concessions to the needs and expectations of present-day audiences,[25] vintage pornography's value today resides its ability to viscerally stimulate our awareness of both similarities and differences between past and present audiences. Moreover, this ongoing dialogue between historical moments and viewers is fuelled by a productive tension between cultural remembrance and cultural forgetting—two complex forces that posit fans, historians, and archives as active players shaping the legacies of our society's cinematic-cum-sexual past.

And yet, as I have suggested, none of these players are immune from reencountering that past in profoundly embodied ways due to a desirous tension between cultural visibility and invisibility that metatextually echoes the viewing dynamics of the genre itself. Hence, the anxieties that some academics may continue to face when studying the history of a genre that resolutely refuses to be safely consumed under the guise of critical/aesthetic/ironic distance or the seemingly dispassionate connotations of empirical/archival research. By the same token, when some academics smugly assert that pornography is unworthy of exploring as a variegated historical genre because it is supposedly "boring" or aesthetically "inferior," such claims could just as easily be made about any other genre—and likely derive from either disingenuous efforts at intellectual self-defense against the genre's carnal appeal or from not knowing the genre's sheer diversity well enough to find and appreciate texts that might pleasurably resonate with one's own desires. As I have suggested throughout this book, we might better drop such defenses and attend to how a variety of actants—from fans/collectors to historians to archivists/preservationists to home video distributors—all have a shared stake, advertently or not, in prolonging and recharging the erotic appeal of vintage pornography by bringing these archival texts into and out of our historical focus today in ways echoing the films' own peek-a-boo display of exposed flesh.

Much as the shift from 1960s sexploitation to 1970s hard-core films indexed a gradual move from excessive fantasies to permissive realities, we might now find the archival life of adult cinema moving from vague reveries about a nebulously "lost" corpus to a genre made increasingly permissible for serious appreciation. If the revival of vintage pornography derives part of its continuing fascination as both fantasies and documents of sexual-historical transition, then it seems fitting that this phenomenon is itself currently undergoing a transitional phase—of which this book offers a mere snapshot. These changes are both cultural and technological—from the online networks that allow fans to more easily find each other and circulate hard-to-find texts, to the physical and streaming media formats that video distributors are exploring to upscale the critical reputation of a denigrated genre. And yet, as vintage pornography's seductive connotations of historical loss and neglect perhaps become more difficult to maintain in the wake of its growing restoration and recuperation beyond just subcultural denizens, it remains to be seen how the phenomenon may have to adjust its discursive appeals to accommodate changes that may alter the affective allure of the degraded text but can only help to better restore these films to their rightful place as important (if fantastic) touchstones in our sexual-cultural histories. In other words, if the eroticization of pastness in vintage pornography relies upon these texts tantalizingly coming both into and out of cultural visibility like the very tease of exposed flesh within them, then their more concerted return to accessibility and even cultural recuperation may threaten a significant measure of their underlying appeal as a fetishized niche.

Even within the formal archival world—one of the quintessential bastions of cultural conservatism—these changes are slowly emerging. Members of the Association of Moving Image Archivists have discussed inaugurating a pornography special-interest group dedicated to the special archival issues that such materials raise, while the 2014 edited collection *Porn Archives* features a thorough bibliography of porn-related research collections.[26] At the time of this writing, there are even growing calls to add a representative film from the 1970s porno-chic craze to the National Film Registry; after all, prudery aside, it would be hard to dispute a film like *Deep Throat*'s eminent qualifications as either "culturally, historically, or aesthetically significant" to our understanding of American film history and popular culture more generally. More concretely, spring 2015 saw the first meeting of the Society for Cinema and Media Studies' Adult Film History special-interest group, a research and support network for adult film historians. First proposed by Eric Schaefer, the group's aims include pooling archival and bibliographic resources; developing a series of "best practices" guidelines for the archiving and historiography of adults-only materials; and an initiative by Peter Alilunas to collect and digitize orphaned or ephemeral materials through the University of Oregon's Digital Scholarship Center.

Much as I noted above about the Erotic Heritage Museum, however, problems of curation and access are likely to remain rampant: like the obvious shortcomings of selecting a single film to represent a whole genre, the research collections heralded by traditional archivists can easily neglect the genre's historical diversity by prioritizing access to a handful of works that misleadingly come to stand in for a far more complex realm of historical/erotic fantasies—a selectivity that inadvertently bears certain similarities to antiporn activists' tendencies to misleadingly highlight the most misogynistic and least defensible examples of pornography as supposedly representative of the form as a whole. As long as so much pornography bears an entrenched investment in its own cultural marginality for generating its visceral thrills, the genre's position of prestige within official archives will likely remain provisional. It is, after all, the very diversity of its erotic appeals—some more politically and/or aesthetically suspect than others—that garners the genre's less redeemable connotations of "bad taste" among more conservative cultural custodians. In this sense, historically diverse pornographic materials may gradually find their way into official archives—as they already have for decades—but only some may become highlighted for preservation and publicity, thereby relegating less historically narrativizable texts to archival purgatory. Perhaps, then, it is ultimately a disguised blessing that taste politics have kept pornography from becoming too easily assimilated into the archival establishment's own politically conservative reputation as privileged sites of homogenized cultural "heritage."

Meanwhile, on the flip side of these physical archives, digital technologies may have made it more economical to transfer, restore, and recirculate analog texts, but they have also made some of pornography's would-be custodians more complacent about possibilities for future access. Indeed, as Linda Williams astutely argues, scholars too often presume that pornography's digitization into online formats equals utopian opportunities for long-term cataloguing and preservation, despite how the vagaries of digital storage methods and format shifts belie the fantasy that "present ubiquity translates to future permanence." The Internet's contents as a digital "archive" are ultimately no more reliably catalogued, preserved, and permanently accessible than the fan–collector's private stash of paper ephemera and out-of-print VHS tapes, or the home video distributor's oft-degraded repository of old film and video elements.[27]

In this respect, as much as contemporary video technologies may be encouraging the unofficial archivization of a vast swath of vintage pornography that was previously far less publicly accessible, these same technologies will perhaps ensure a continuing tension between cultural remembrance and cultural forgetting, inadvertently remediating vintage-ness's pathos of historical loss through their very limitations as preservational media. Much as *Take Off*'s stars are no more pristinely preserved on DVD today than on Darrin Blue's decaying stag reel, adult cinema's material traces will no doubt continue to spur erotic longings among fans, collectors, and historians for the foreseeable future, especially as the sheer number of texts sliding under the auspices of "vintage" appreciation continues to accumulate with passing years. Ultimately, the task of archiving these innumerable texts will become no less challenging as the genre's history of documented fantasies continues to unfold over the coming decades, but perhaps we are now seeing that cultural labor—and the labor of sex workers themselves—slowly becoming regarded as all the more worthwhile.

Notes

Introduction

1. Tim Lucas, *Throat Sprockets* (New York: Dell, 1994), 4, 5.
2. Laura Kipnis, "She-Male Fantasies and the Aesthetics of Pornography," in *More Dirty Looks: Gender, Pornography, and Power*, ed. Pamela Church Gibson (London: British Film Institute, 2004), 211–12.
3. On the aesthetic appreciation of age and decay, see David Lowenthal, *The Past Is a Foreign Country* (Cambridge, UK: Cambridge University Press, 1985), chap. 4.
4. Linda Williams, *Screening Sex* (Durham, NC: Duke University Press, 2008), 14, 48, 132–33.
5. See Jay David Bolter and Richard Grusin, *Remediation: Understanding New Media* (Cambridge, MA: MIT Press, 2000).
6. Ramon Lobato, *Shadow Economies of Cinema: Mapping Informal Film Distribution* (London: British Film Institute, 2012), 16, 18.
7. Sarah Thornton, *Club Cultures: Music, Media, and Subcultural Capital* (Middletown, CT: Wesleyan University Press, 1996), 68, 118.
8. Aleida Assmann, "Canon and Archive," in *Cultural Memory Studies: An International and Interdisciplinary Handbook*, eds Astrid Erll and Ansgar Nünnung (Berlin: Walter de Gruyter, 2008), 97–107. Also see Franco Moretti, "The Slaughterhouse of Literature," *Modern Language Quarterly* 61, no. 1 (2000): 207–27; Lobato, *Shadow Economies of Cinema*, 32–37.
9. Michel Foucault, *The History of Sexuality, Vol. 1: An Introduction*, trans. Robert Hurley (New York: Vintage, 1990), 84.
10. Paul Connerton, "Seven Types of Forgetting," *Memory Studies* 1, no. 1 (2008): 59–71.
11. Lucas Hilderbrand, "Historical Fantasies: 1970s Gay Pornography in the Archives," in *Porno Chic and the Sex Wars: American Sexual Representation in the 1970s.*, eds Carolyn Bronstein and Whitney Strub (Amherst: University of Massachusetts Press, 2016). See also Tim Dean, *Unlimited Intimacy: Reflections on the Subculture of Barebacking* (Chicago: University of Chicago Press, 2009), 109.
12. Ryan Powell, "Man Country: A Social History of Seventies Gay Cinema" (Ph.D. diss., King's College London, 2010), chap. 4. Also see Janet Staiger, *Perverse Spectators: The Practices of Film Reception* (New York: New York University Press, 2000), chap. 8; José B. Capino, "Seminal Fantasies: Wakefield Poole, Pornography, Independent Cinema, and the Avant-Garde," in *Contemporary American Independent Film: From the Margins to the Mainstream*, eds Chris Holmlund and Justin Wyatt (New York: Routledge, 2005), 155–73; William E. Jones, *Halsted Plays Himself* (Los Angeles: Semiotext(e), 2011); Cindy Patton, *L.A. Plays Itself/Boys in the Sand*, Queer Film Classics (Vancouver: Arsenal Pulp Press, 2014).
13. Eric Schaefer, "Dirty Little Secrets: Scholars, Archivists, and Dirty Movies," *The Moving Image* 5, no. 2 (2005): 81–82.

14 David Andrews, "Toward a More Valid Definition of 'Pornography,'" *Journal of Popular Culture* 45, no. 3 (2012): 459–61. Quote at 459 (original italics).
15 See Martin Barker, "The 'Problem' of Sexual Fantasies," *Porn Studies* 1, no. 1–2 (2014): 143–60.
16 Elena Gorfinkel, "'Indecent Desires': Sexploitation Cinema, 1960s Film Culture, and the Adult Film Audience" (Ph.D. diss., New York University, 2008), 365–68, 371–72. Personally, I find sexploitation's soft-core visual strategies of intimation and hesitation more cinematically engaging than hardcore's explicit spectacle, while the former's sometimes politically repugnant narratives can be easier to watch precisely because of softcore's added potential for disavowing its verisimilitude.
17 For example, see Eddie Muller and Daniel Faris, *Grindhouse: The Forbidden World of "Adults Only" Cinema* (New York: St. Martin's Griffin, 1996), 140–49; and the conclusion of the documentary *American Grindhouse* (2010).
18 David Andrews, *Soft in the Middle: The Contemporary Softcore Feature in Its Contexts* (Columbus: Ohio State University Press, 2006), 187.
19 Jim Holliday, *How to Build Your X-Rated Video Library* (Beverly Hills, CA: Skull Mountain Publishing, 1980), 23.
20 William Rotsler, *Contemporary Erotic Cinema* (New York: Penthouse/Ballantine, 1973), 12–13. Original italics.
21 Amelie Hastie, *Cupboards of Curiosity: Women, Recollection, and Film History* (Durham, NC: Duke University Press, 2007), 27.
22 Joseph W. Slade, "The Porn Market and Porn Formulas: The Feature Film of the Seventies," *Journal of Popular Film* 6, no. 2 (1977): 177.
23 Richard Merkin, "Vintage Vamp: A History of Pornographics," *High Society*, March 1977, 78–79.
24 Brian McNair, *Porno? Chic! How Pornography Changed the World and Made It a Better Place* (New York: Routledge, 2013), 40–52, 56. The phrase "porno chic" was itself coined in Ralph Blumenthal, "Porno Chic," *New York Times Magazine*, January 21, 1973, 28–34.
25 Feona Attwood and Clarissa Smith, "Emotional Truths and Thrilling Slide Shows: The Resurgence of Antiporn Feminism," in *The Feminist Porn Book: The Politics of Producing Pleasure*, eds Tristan Taormino, Celine Parreñas Shimizu, Constance Penley, and Mireille Miller-Young (New York: The Feminist Press, 2013), 44–45.
26 Richard A. Peterson and Roger M. Kern, "Changing Highbrow Taste: From Snob to Omnivore," *American Sociological Review* 61, no. 5 (1996): 904.
27 In *Boogie Nights*, for example, film-within-the-film footage of a documentary about the Holmes-inspired Dirk Diggler character was largely inspired by Julia St. Vincent's hagiographic documentary *Exhausted: John C. Holmes, The Real Story* (1981), with Anderson even replicating several interviews and film clips from St. Vincent's film.
28 McNair, *Porno? Chic!*, 13, 84, 90, 111.
29 Susanna Paasonen and Laura Saarenmaa, "The Golden Age of Porn: Nostalgia and History in Cinema," in *Pornification: Sex and Sexuality in Media Culture*, eds Susanna Paasonen, Kaarina Nikunen, and Laura Saarenmaa (Oxford: Berg, 2007), 25–26, 29–30.
30 See, for example, the interviews in Jill C. Nelson, *Golden Goddesses: 25 Legendary Women of Classic Erotic Cinema, 1968–1985* (Duncan, OK: BearManor Media, 2012), 545, 593, 739–40, 900.

31 Tim Connelly, quoted in Legs McNeil and Jennifer Osbourne with Peter Pavia, *The Other Hollywood: The Uncensored Oral History of the Porn Film Industry* (New York: HarperCollins, 2005), 368.
32 David Church, *Grindhouse Nostalgia: Memory, Home Video, and Exploitation Film Fandom* (Edinburgh: Edinburgh University Press, 2015).
33 Jeffrey Sconce, "'Trashing' the Academy: Taste, Excess, and an Emerging Politics of Cinematic Style," *Screen* 36, no. 4 (1995): 371–93.
34 Susanna Paasonen, *Carnal Resonance: Affect and Online Pornography* (Cambridge, MA: MIT Press, 2011), 142–43.
35 Nathan Scott Epley, "Pin-Ups, Retro-chic, and the Consumption of Irony," in *Pornification*, 51–56. Also see Jacinda Read, "The Cult of Masculinity: From Fan-Boys to Academic Bad-Boys," in *Defining Cult Movies: The Cultural Politics of Oppositional Taste*, eds Mark Jancovich, Antonio Lázaro Reboll, Julian Stringer, and Andy Willis (Manchester: Manchester University Press, 2003), 62–63.
36 See Henry Jenkins, *Textual Poachers: Television Fans & Participatory Culture* (New York: Routledge, 1992), 12–19.
37 Alan McKee, Katherine Albury, and Catharine Lumby, *The Porn Report* (Carlton: Melbourne University Press, 2008), 81–82.
38 Feona Attwood, "'Other' or 'One of Us'?: The Porn User in Public and Academic Discourse," *Participations: Journal of Audience and Reception Studies* 4, no. 1 (2007): http://www.participations.org/Volume%204/Issue%201/4_01_attwood.htm.
39 Cornel Sandvoss, *Fans: The Mirror of Consumption* (Cambridge, UK: Polity Press, 2005), 2.
40 Paasonen, *Carnal Resonance*, 67, 218. Common stereotypes of the autoerotically aroused, inward-turning, irrational reader immersed in fantasy worlds date back to stereotypes of eighteenth- and nineteenth-century female readers of novels (218). Also see Walter Kendrick, *The Secret Museum: Pornography in Modern Culture* (New York: Viking, 1987), 84–93, 232.
41 Jane Gaines, "Machines That Make the Body Do Things," in *More Dirty Looks*, 31–32, 35.
42 Sandvoss, *Fans*, 48, 97–98.
43 Simon Lindgren, "Widening the Glory Hole: The Discourse of Online Porn Fandom," in *Porn.com: Making Sense of Online Pornography*, ed. Feona Attwood (New York: Peter Lang, 2010), 178–83.
44 Lucas, *Throat Sprockets*, 97, 167.
45 Linda Williams, "Second Thoughts on *Hard Core*: American Obscenity Law and the Scapegoating of Deviance," in *More Dirty Looks*, 172.
46 Paasonen, *Carnal Resonance*, 23.
47 Consequently, I do not analyze Vintage Erotica Forums, one of the largest online fan communities (in terms of active members and uploaded content) devoted to this niche, since one must be a registered user to access the contents of each forum. The website's general functions and dynamics are, however, represented in my examples taken from more publicly accessible websites.
48 Linda Williams, *Hard Core: Power, Pleasure, and the "Frenzy of the Visible"* (Berkeley: University of California Press, 1999), 2.

Chapter 1

1. Joan Hawkins, *Cutting-Edge: Art-Horror and the Horrific Avant-Garde* (Minneapolis: University of Minnesota Press, 2000), 5–7. On the blurred class and taste distinctions in Metzger's pre-hard-core career, see Elena Gorfinkel, "Radley Metzger's 'Elegant Arousal': Taste, Aesthetic Distinction, and Sexploitation," in *Underground U.S.A.: Filmmaking beyond the Hollywood Canon*, eds Xavier Mendik and Steven Jay Schneider (London: Wallflower Press, 2002), 26–39.
2. Russell Sheaffer, "Smut, Novelty, Indecency: Reworking a History of the Early-Twentieth-Century 'Stag Film,'" *Porn Studies* 1, no. 4 (2014): 346–59.
3. David Andrews, "What Soft-Core Can Do for Porn Studies," *The Velvet Light Trap*, no. 59 (2007): 55–58. Quote at 56.
4. Zabet Patterson, "Going On-Line: Consuming Pornography in the Digital Era," in *Porn Studies*, ed. Linda Williams (Durham, NC: Duke University Press, 2004), 106.
5. Giuliana Bruno, *Atlas of Emotion: Journeys in Art, Architecture, and Film* (New York: Verso, 2002), 103. Original italics.
6. Susanna Paasonen, *Carnal Resonance: Affect and Online Pornography* (Cambridge, MA: MIT Press, 2011), 107–8.
7. Emily Shelton, "A Star Is Porn: Corpulence, Comedy, and the Homosocial Cult of Adult Film Star Ron Jeremy," *Camera Obscura* 17, no. 3 (2002): 129–30.
8. David Andrews, *Soft in the Middle: The Contemporary Softcore Feature in Its Contexts* (Columbus: Ohio State University Press, 2006), 190. Also see Chuck Kleinhans, "The Change from Film to Video Pornography: Implications for Analysis," in *Pornography: Film and Culture*, ed. Peter Lehman (New Brunswick, NJ: Rutgers University Press, 2006), 154–67.
9. See Andrew Ross, *No Respect: Intellectuals and Popular Culture* (New York: Routledge, 1989), 195–96; Linda Williams, *Hard Core: Power, Pleasure, and the "Frenzy of the Visible"* (Berkeley: University of California Press, 1999), 246–64; Jane Juffer, "There's No Place Like Home: Further Developments on the Domestic Front," in *More Dirty Looks: Gender, Pornography, and Power*, ed. Pamela Church Gibson (London: British Film Institute, 2004), 45–58.
10. Joseph W. Slade, "Eroticism and Technological Regression: The Stag Film," *History and Technology* 22, no. 1 (2006): 32–33.
11. Al Di Lauro and Gerald Rabkin, *Dirty Movies: An Illustrated History of the Stag Film, 1915–1970* (New York: Chelsea House, 1976), 52.
12. Thomas Waugh, "Homosociality in the Classical American Stag Film: Off-Screen, On-Screen," *Sexualities* 4, no. 3 (2001): 285.
13. Raymond Street, "Stag Movie Rackets are Growing," *Bare* 1, no. 2 (1959): 6; H. C. Shelby, *Stag Movie Review* (Canoga Park, CA: Viceroy Books, 1970), 13; and *The Report of the Commission on Obscenity and Pornography* (New York: Bantam Books, 1970), 139. The documentary *American Stag* (2006) also features interviews with several itinerant stag exhibitors about their former occupation.
14. Di Lauro and Rabkin, *Dirty Movies*, 48, 51.
15. Williams, *Hard Core*, 65, 67.
16. Ibid., 80. In this sense, the male stag audience was left "not 'gazing'—the sense of omnipotent mastery, but 'looking'—in the sense of a vulnerable fascination" (294–95). Cf. Laura Mulvey, "Visual Pleasure and Narrative Cinema," *Screen* 16, no. 3 (1975): 6–18.

17 Paasonen, *Carnal Resonance*, 186–87, 189, 190–92, 202. Also see André Bazin, "The Ontology of the Photographic Image," trans. Hugh Gray, *Film Quarterly* 13, no. 4 (1960): 8; Roland Barthes, *Camera Lucida: Reflections on Photography*, trans. Richard Howard (New York: Hill and Wang, 1981); Christian Keathley, *Cinephilia and History, or The Wind in the Trees* (Bloomington: Indiana University Press, 2006), 34.
18 Williams, *Hard Core*, 77–78; Slade, "Eroticism and Technological Regression," 30. See also Tom Gunning, "The Cinema of Attractions: Early Film, Its Spectator, and the Avant-Garde," in *Early Cinema: Space, Frame, Narrative*, ed. Thomas Elsaesser (London: British Film Institute, 1990), 56–62.
19 Slade, "Eroticism and Technological Regression," 39–40.
20 Williams, *Hard Core*, 73, 80.
21 Waugh, "Homosociality in the Classical American Stag Film," 280, 285. The "threat" of homoeroticism is also blamed for the disproportionate focus on female genitals (and female nudity in general) over that of their on-screen male partners (276).
22 Williams, *Hard Core*, 72, 74. Original italics.
23 Di Lauro and Rabkin, *Dirty Movies*, 55–57, 59.
24 Saturnalia mail-order catalogue, ca. late 1950s (author's collection).
25 Eric Schaefer, "Plain Brown Wrapper: Adult Films for the Home Market, 1930–1969," in *Looking Past the Screen: Case Studies in American Film History and Method*, eds Jon Lewis and Eric Smoodin (Durham, NC: Duke University Press, 2007), 207.
26 Dave Thompson, *Black and White and Blue: Adult Cinema from the Victorian Age to the VCR* (Toronto: ECW Press, 2007), 4.
27 See Amy Herzog, "In the Flesh: Space and Embodiment in the Pornographic Peep Show Arcade," *The Velvet Light Trap*, no. 62 (2008): 29–43.
28 Eric Schaefer, "Gauging a Revolution: 16 mm Film and the Rise of the Pornographic Feature," *Cinema Journal* 41, no. 3 (2002): 4, 7, 17.
29 Di Lauro and Rabkin, *Dirty Movies*, 112.
30 Roger Blake, *The Porno Movies* (Cleveland: Century Books, 1970), 52.
31 Chuck Kleinhans, "Pornography and Documentary: Narrating the Alibi," in *Sleaze Artists: Cinema at the Margins of Taste, Style, and Politics*, ed. Jeffrey Sconce (Durham, NC: Duke University Press, 2007), 96–120. Similar documentaries appeared in the all-male porn market as well, such as *The AMG Story* (1970) and *Erotikus: A History of the Gay Movie* (1974), each tracing the history of gay erotica from physique photos to nascent hard-core films by pioneers like Bob Mizer, Wakefield Poole, and Fred Halsted. See Jeffrey Escoffier, *Bigger than Life: The History of Gay Porn Cinema from Beefcake to Hardcore* (Philadelphia: Running Press, 2009), 58–59, 78–79.
32 Amos Vogel, *Film as a Subversive Art* (New York: Random House, 1974), 224.
33 See, for example, Jim Holliday, *Only the Best: Jim Holliday's Adult Video Almanac and Trivia Treasury* (Van Nuys, CA: Cal Vista Publications, 1986).
34 Williams, *Hard Core*, 5, 45.
35 See, for example, the lengthy filmographies in Thompson, *Black and White and Blue*, 273–301; Jason S. Martinko, *The XXX Filmography, 1968–1988* (Jefferson, NC: McFarland, 2013), 319–41.
36 "Main," RetroRaunch, accessed April 17, 2011, http://retroraunch.com/main.htm.
37 This market is actually far from "amateur" in its influences and industrial organization, spawning its own set of well-known "professional-amateur" star performers (Paasonen, *Carnal Resonance*, 71–114).

38 Fred Chappell, "Twenty-Six Propositions about Skin Flicks," in *Man and the Movies*, ed. W. R. Robinson with George Garrett (Baton Rouge: Louisiana State University Press, 1967), 55.
39 Linda Williams, *Screening Sex* (Durham, NC: Duke University Press, 2008), 25–42.
40 Thompson, *Black and White and Blue*, 4–5, 43. Quote at 43.
41 "Frequently Asked Questions," RetroRaunch, accessed April 17, 2011, http://retroraunch.com/faq.htm.
42 Retro Porn Archive, accessed November 14, 2010, http://www.retropornarchive.com.
43 Frederick S. Lane III, *Obscene Profits: The Entrepreneurs of Pornography in the Cyber Age* (New York: Routledge, 2000), 225–26.
44 Hester Nash, "On How a Longtime Interest in Vintage Porn Launched a Unique Site on the Internet," in *Naked Ambition: Women Who Are Changing Pornography*, ed. Carly Milne (New York: Carroll & Graf, 2005), 216.
45 "Tour," RetroRaunch, accessed April 17, 2011, http://retroraunch.com/tour0.htm.
46 Nash, "On How a Longtime Interest in Vintage Porn," 207. As Nash continues, "Even the newsreels and documentaries [of the pre-1960s era] are weirdly disconnected from real human emotion. But hardcore porn of the period pretty much cuts through the bullshit and right to the humanity of the people in a way that little else from that time does" (214).
47 Schaefer, "Gauging a Revolution," 14.
48 "1940's," Good Old XXX, accessed April 12, 2011, http://www.goodoldxxx.com/tour.php?nats=&section=13. For example,

> Society might have been a little slow at adopting fun sexual attitudes, but they were slowly getting there. We still have a few decades before people really get the sticks out of their asses, so I had to be a little bit discrete during the 40s. There was something about this sexual repression that really drove the ladies mad with desire though. Maybe it was a way for them to forget World War II, but these lonely housewives and ladies let out their frustrations by getting in front of the camera and fucking it all away.

49 Retro Lady: Sex from 1870 Till 1970, accessed April 17, 2011, http://www.retrolady.com.
50 *Grandpa Bucky's Naughty Triple XXX Stags, Loops, & Peeps, Volume 7* DVD (Something Weird Video, 2006). Original italics. In another example, the DVD back cover of Volume 13 reads, "Though Presidents changed, wars were fought, aviation was conquered, man walked on the moon, and the atom was split, fucking and sucking sure remained the same!"
51 Michel Foucault, *The History of Sexuality, Volume 1: An Introduction*, trans. Robert Hurley (New York: Vintage Books, 1990), 47–49.
52 Retro Porn Archive.
53 RetroRaunch, for example, offers this tongue-in-cheek disclaimer: "RetroRaunch takes no responsibility for distress caused by seeking naked pictures of your grandmother" ("Tour"); while the DVD box for Volume 14 of the *Grandpa Bucky's* series asks "And just which of these copulating couples were your grandparents?"
54 "Tour," RetroRaunch. As another site says, "No stale screwing scenes, coked-up porn stars, or similar nonsense. One gets the impression that these folks are pretty fucking excited to be on camera and pretty excited to be, well, fucking on camera"

("The Films," Delta of Venus, accessed April 17, 2011, http://www.deltaofvenus.com/intro/tour3.php).
55 Missy, "Vintage Cuties Review," Porn Inspector, accessed April 17, 2011, http://www.porninspector.com/reviews/review/vintage-cuties/. In a different review, the reviewer "liked knowing the fuller figured ladies were respected, revered, and appreciated in this time frame," going on to celebrate the women's "full bosom area, and you know it wasn't silicone then" (Monty Woods, "Vintage Taboo Review," Porn Inspector, accessed April 17, 2011, http://www.porninspector.com/reviews/review/vintage-taboo/).
56 Retro Porn Archive.
57 For example, according to Dennis Harvey of the *San Francisco Bay Guardian*, "What's really surprising about them is that while the scenarios are predictable fantasy ones … the sex acts are a lot more diverse than they would have been in standard American porn, then and now" (quoted on back cover of *The Good Old Naughty Days* DVD, Strand Releasing, 2003).
58 Williams, *Hard Core*, 92. Original italics.
59 Thomas Waugh, *Hard to Imagine: Gay Male Eroticism in Photography and Film from Their Beginnings to Stonewall* (New York: Columbia University Press, 1996), 309, 311–12, 316, 318–19, 321. Quote at 318.
60 Matt Haber, "Taking Pornography Low Tech," *New York Times*, October 1, 2010, accessed April 24, 2011, http://www.nytimes.com/2010/10/03/fashion/03porn.html.
61 See Laura Kipnis, "She-Male Fantasies and the Aesthetics of Pornography," in *More Dirty Looks*, 207–09. Sherman's work can be recognized as not only a form of art performance, but also an example of critical fandom. Not surprisingly, she was one of several artists profiled in the premiere issue of *Jacques*.
62 See David Church, *Grindhouse Nostalgia: Memory, Home Video, and Exploitation Film Fandom* (Edinburgh: Edinburgh University Press, 2015), chaps. 3–4 (esp. 206–14).
63 Despina Kakoudaki, "Pinup: The American Secret Weapon in World War II," in *Porn Studies*, 344.
64 Maria Elena Buszek, *Pin-Up Grrrls: Feminism, Sexuality, Popular Culture* (Durham, NC: Duke University Press, 2006), 244, 282, 300, 321, 345, 347 (quoted). For Buszek, Page's over-the-top poses and lighthearted approach to the sadomasochistic content of her most famous photo sessions exposed 1950s erotic photography as a potential medium for women's expression. Overall, Page would "provide one of the most imitated models for feminist appropriations of the [pin-up] genre" due to "[h]er visibility and popularity as a transgressive alternative to the pointedly nonthreatening [*Playboy*] Playmate" (247). On the related resurgence of neo-burlesque as a potential means of female empowerment that champions vintage-ness for subcultural capital, see Debra Ferreday, "'Showing the Girl': The New Burlesque," *Feminist Theory* 9, no. 1 (2008): 47–65.
65 Despite its subcultural uses, however, this (re)appropriative reading strategy has not been immune to commodification, as seen in retro-clothing designer Tatyana Khomyakova's upscale chain of Bettie Page fashion boutiques (founded in 2007), or the "officially licensed" Bettie Page merchandise (including fashion, costumes, fragrances, and jewelry) marketed by CMG Brands.
66 See Feona Attwood, "No Money Shot? Commerce, Pornography, and New Sex Taste Cultures," *Sexualities* 10, no. 4 (2007): 441–56. Attwood, however, claims that

alt-porn websites make their taste distinctions through a "lack of emphasis on a 'dirty' porn body that is available for penetration" (446). This may indeed be true for soft-core websites like SuicideGirls, but it downplays the place of hard-core alt-porn competitors like Burning Angel and its imitators.
67 Andrews, *Soft in the Middle*, 190–91.
68 Williams, *Hard Core*, 110, 176.
69 Joanne Hollows, "The Masculinity of Cult," in *Defining Cult Movies: The Cultural Politics of Oppositional Taste*, eds Mark Jancovich, Antonio Lázaro Reboll, Julian Stringer, and Andy Willis (Manchester: Manchester University Press, 2003), 39.
70 See Andreas Huyssen, *After the Great Divide: Modernism, Mass Culture, Postmodernism* (Bloomington: Indiana University Press, 1986), 44–62; Sally Robinson, "Feminized Men and Inauthentic Women," *Genders*, no. 53 (2011): http://www.genders.org/g53/g53_robinson.html.
71 Mark Jancovich, "Naked Ambitions: Pornography, Taste, and the Problem of the Middlebrow," *Scope* (June 2001), accessed March 17, 2011, http://www.scope.nottingham.ac.uk/article.php?issue=jun2001&id=274&section=article.
72 In its compilation of French stags, the box-cover text on the *Vintage Erotica: Anno 1930* DVD (Cult Epics, 2000) begins: "Artists have explored the erotic image since the beginning of time," citing Hindu temples, cave paintings, and ancient scrolls as other examples. Yet, this is not to say that all stag collections archive their films in very meticulous ways; the *Grandpa Bucky's* series, for example, features both whole films and fragments of stags, mostly lacking titles and dates. "Of course, I put this together the way I think lately, namely in no goddamn order," admits the box of Volume 14. "Fortunately, the wonderful hairdos on display instantly peg what decade it was made in."
73 Barbara Klinger, *Beyond the Multiplex: Cinema, New Technologies, and the Home* (Berkeley: University of California Press, 2006), 87.
74 The site tour continues: "The French Revolution brought us a whole new perspective on sex. These paintings included sex with animals, orgies, and other sexual fantasies" ("Erotic Art," Erotic Past, accessed April 14, 2011, http://www.eroticpast.com/art.html).
75 "Main," RetroRaunch.
76 "An Introduction," Delta of Venus, accessed April 17, 2011, http://www.deltaofvenus.com/main.php.
77 "Maximum visibility" is the principle by which certain body parts, sexual positions, and generic conventions are privileged in porn, seemingly allowing the body to visibly "confess" its pleasure (Williams, *Hard Core*, 48–49).
78 Laura U. Marks, *The Skin of the Film: Intercultural Cinema, Embodiment, and the Senses* (Durham, NC: Duke University Press, 2000), 162–63.
79 Missy, "Good Old XXX Review," Porn Inspector, accessed April 17, 2011, http://www.porninspector.com/reviews/review/good-old-xxx/.
80 Lucas Hilderbrand, *Inherent Vice: Bootleg Histories of Videotape and Copyright* (Durham, NC: Duke University Press, 2009), 65–71.
81 Hawkins, *Cutting Edge*, 47–49.
82 Shelton, "A Star Is Porn," 124, 127, 129–30, 135. Quote at 124.
83 Jane Gaines, "Machines That Make the Body Do Things," in *More Dirty Looks*, 39.
84 Klinger, *Beyond the Multiplex*, 88.
85 Andrews, *Soft in the Middle*, 29–30.

86 Lynda Nead, "'Above the Pulp-Line': The Cultural Significance of Erotic Art," in *More Dirty Looks*, 218.
87 Linda Williams, "'White Slavery' versus the Ethnography of 'Sexworkers': Women in Stag Films at the Kinsey Archive," *The Moving Image* 5, no. 2 (2005): 129. Although they were silent in their original form, most stag films sold today have some musical accompaniment, often evoking the period of the film's estimated production. A notable exception is *The Good Old Naughty Days [deconstructed]* (2009), a compilation of stag film excerpts that multimedia artist Cécile Babiole used digital postproduction effects to abstract and fetishize into the equivalent of miniature music videos, featuring electronic dance music. Consequently, the nostalgic tenor of the original *Good Old Naughty Days* is unmistakably shifted into the digital present on the level of both sound and image.
88 See Jane Juffer, *At Home with Pornography: Women, Sex, and Everyday Life* (New York: New York University Press, 1998); Clarissa Smith, *One for the Girls! The Pleasures and Practices of Reading Women's Porn* (Bristol: Intellect Books, 2007).
89 Williams, *Hard Core*, 233; Williams, "White Slavery," 118.
90 Susan Sontag, "Notes on 'Camp,'" in *The Cult Film Reader*, eds Ernest Mathijs and Xavier Mendik (Maidenhead, UK: Open University Press-McGraw-Hill Education, 2008), 43.
91 Missy, "Vintage Cuties Review" (italics mine).
92 Herzog, "In the Flesh," 41.
93 See Jennifer M. Barker, *The Tactile Eye: Touch and the Cinematic Experience* (Berkeley: University of California Press, 2009), 23–24; Laura U. Marks, *Touch: Sensuous Theory and Multisensory Media* (Minneapolis: University of Minnesota Press, 2002), 100–01; Elena Gorfinkel, "Arousal in Ruins: *The Color of Love* and the Haptic Object of Film History," *World Picture*, no. 4 (2010): http://www.worldpicturejournal.com/WP_4/Gorfinkel.html.
94 See Adrian Martin, "What's Cult Got to Do with It? In Defense of Cinephile Elitism," *Cineaste* 34, no. 1 (2008): 39–42.
95 Paul Willemen, "Through the Glass Darkly: Cinephilia Reconsidered," in *Looks and Frictions: Essays in Cultural Studies and Film Theory* (Bloomington: Indiana University Press, 1994), 227.
96 Susan Felleman, *Art in the Cinematic Imagination* (Austin: University of Texas Press, 2006), 47–48, 55.
97 Thomas Elsaesser, "Cinephilia or the Uses of Disenchantment," in *Cinephilia: Movies, Love, and Memory*, eds Marijke de Valck and Malte Hagener (Amsterdam: Amsterdam University Press, 2005), 41. Italics in original.
98 Williams, *Hard Core*, 164.
99 Lisa Downing, *Desiring the Dead: Necrophilia and Nineteenth-Century French Literature* (Oxford: Legenda, 2003), 52–54, 58.
100 Dennis Giles, "Pornographic Space: The Other Place," in *The 1977 Film Studies Annual: Part 2* (Pleasantville, NY: Redgrave, 1977), 56–57. Williams argues that Giles's theory more specifically fits stag films than later, more elaborate, feature-length hard-core films that allow "other points of secondary, fictional identification beyond those merely of phallus or hole" (*Hard Core*, 83).
101 Giles, "Pornographic Space," 60. Italics in original.
102 Ibid., 63–64. Italics in original.

103 Williams, *Hard Core*, 294 (italics mine).
104 Cornel Sandvoss, *Fans: The Mirror of Consumption* (Cambridge, UK: Polity Press, 2005), 126.
105 Marks, *The Skin of the Film*, 191.
106 Elizabeth Freeman, *Time Binds: Queer Temporalities, Queer Histories* (Durham, NC: Duke University Press, 2010), 95–96, 120, 123. Quote at 95.
107 Marks, *The Skin of the Film*, 170–72, 183–85; Barker, *The Tactile Eye*, 24.
108 Paasonen, *Carnal Resonance*, 190–92.
109 Dany Nobus, "Over My Dead Body: On the Histories and Cultures of Necrophilia," in *Inappropriate Relationships: The Unconventional, the Disapproved, and the Forbidden*, eds Robin Goodwin and Duncan Cramer (Mahwah, NJ: Lawrence Erlbaum Associates, 2002), 188.
110 Elena Gorfinkel, "'Dated Sexuality': Anna Biller's *Viva* and the Retrospective Life of Sexploitation Cinema," *Camera Obscura* 26, no. 3 (2011): 97–98.
111 Gertrud Koch, "The Body's Shadow Realm," trans. Jan-Christopher Horak and Joyce Rheuban, *October*, no. 50 (1989): 29.
112 Thompson, *Black and White and Blue*, 100.
113 Paasonen, *Carnal Resonance*, 78–79.
114 Slade, "Eroticism and Technological Regression," 47n82; Thompson, *Black and White and Blue*, 166–75. Di Lauro and Rabkin claim there is evidence that hardcore inserts actually were filmed by unscrupulous local distributors, "with lookalikes finishing what Harlow and Gable started" (*Dirty Movies*, 73).
115 Slade, "Eroticism and Technological Regression," 47n82.
116 Mark Jancovich, "Cult Fictions: Cult Movies, Subcultural Capital, and the Production of Cultural Distinctions," *Cultural Studies* 16, no. 2 (2002): 315–17.
117 Elena Gorfinkel, "The Future of Anachronism: Todd Haynes and the Magnificent Andersons," in *Cinephilia: Movies, Love, and Memory*, 153, 160.
118 Elsaesser, "Cinephilia or the Uses of Disenchantment," 32.
119 Jason Sperb and Scott Balcerzak, "Introduction: Presence of Pleasure," in *Cinephilia in the Age of Digital Reproduction, Vol. 1*, eds Scott Balcerzak and Jason Sperb (London: Wallflower Press, 2009), 8.
120 Adrian Martin, "Beyond the Fragments of Cinephilia: Towards a Synthetic Analysis," in *Cinephilia in the Age of Digital Reproduction, Vol. 1*, 48.
121 Matt Hills, *Fan Cultures* (London: Routledge, 2002), 5; Alan McKee, "The Fans of Cultural Theory," in *Fandom: Identities and Communities in a Mediated World*, eds Jonathan Gray, Cornel Sandvoss, and C. Lee Harrington (New York: New York University Press, 2007), 94–97.
122 Jason Sperb, "Be Kind … Rewind/or, the A-Zs of an American *Off-Modern Cinephilia*," in *Cinephilia in the Age of Digital Reproduction, Vol. 2*, eds Scott Balcerzak and Jason Sperb (London: Wallflower Press, 2012), 80; original italics.
123 Willemen, "Through the Glass Darkly," 238, 242, 245, 256.
124 For a discussion of slow cinema's regressive orthodoxy, see Steven Shaviro, "Slow Cinema vs. Fast Films," *The Pinocchio Theory* (blog), posted May 12, 2010, accessed October 8, 2014, http://www.shaviro.com/Blog/?p=891.
125 Willemen, "Through the Glass Darkly," 243, 255; Keathley, *Cinephilia and History*, 38–39.
126 Chappell, "Twenty-Sex Propositions about Skin Flicks," 56–58.

127 Keathley, *Cinephilia and History*, 31–32.
128 Jeffrey Sconce, "'Trashing' the Academy: Taste, Excess, and an Emerging Politics of Cinematic Style," *Screen* 36, no. 4 (1995): 383–84, 387; Keathley, *Cinephilia and History*, 41, 44, 117, 128–29. On the potential elitism of paracinematic readings, see Jancovich, "Cult Fictions," 311–12.
129 James Morrison, "After the Revolution: On the Fate of Cinephilia," *Michigan Quarterly Review* 44, no. 3 (2005): 413. Also see Keathley, *Cinephilia and History*, 21; Charles Tashiro, "Videophilia: What Happens When You Wait for It on Video," *Film Quarterly* 45, no. 1 (1991): 7–17. Andreas Huyssen similarly observes that "modernization itself created the auratic effect to begin with. Today, it is digitalization that makes the 'original' photograph auratic," as he notes in "Present Pasts: Media, Politics, Amnesia," *Public Culture* 12, no. 1 (2000): 30.
130 Keathley, *Cinephilia and History*, 122.
131 Sconce, "'Trashing' the Academy," 372; Jeffrey Sconce, "Introduction," in *Sleaze Artists*, 4; Keathley, *Cinephilia and History*, 33–34. Also see Roland Barthes, "The Third Meaning," in *Image/Music/Text*, trans. Stephen Heath (New York: Hill and Wang, 1977), 52–68.
132 Andrews, *Soft in the Middle*, 195–96.
133 Jennifer Wicke, "Through a Gaze Darkly: Pornography's Academic Market," in *More Dirty Looks*, 183.
134 David F. Friedman, interviewed by John McCarty, in *The Sleaze Merchants: Adventures in Exploitation Filmmaking* (New York: St. Martin's Griffin, 1995), 69.

Chapter 2

1 Carolyn Steedman, *Dust: The Archive and Cultural History* (New Brunswick, NJ: Rutgers University Press, 2002), 75.
2 Walter Kendrick, *The Secret Museum: Pornography in Modern Culture* (New York: Viking, 1987), 70–71.
3 For a collectors' pricing guide to the *Adam* periodicals discussed in this chapter, for example, see Scott Aaron Stine, "Index & Current Market Values for *Adam* Magazine (1956–1979)," *Filthy Habits: Hardcore & Sexploitation Fare from the 1960s & 1970s*, Spring 2003, 34–41.
4 Mary Desjardins, "Ephemeral Culture/eBay Culture: Film Collectibles and Fan Investments," in *Everyday eBay: Culture, Collecting, and Desire*, eds Ken Hillis, Michael Petit, and Nathan Scott Epley (New York: Routledge, 2006), 32.
5 David M. Earle, *Re-covering Modernism: Pulps, Paperbacks, and the Prejudice of Form* (Burlington, VT: Ashgate, 2009), 6.
6 Lynda Nead, "'Above the Pulp Line': The Cultural Significance of Erotic Art," in *More Dirty Looks: Gender, Pornography, and Power*, ed. Pamela Church Gibson (London: British Film Institute, 2004), 217.
7 David Lowenthal, *The Past Is a Foreign Country* (Cambridge, UK: Cambridge University Press, 1985), 153.
8 Elizabeth Edwards, "Photographs as Objects of Memory," in *The Object Reader*, eds Fiona Candlin and Raiford Guins (London: Routledge, 2009), 334–37.

9   Elena Gorfinkel, "'Dated Sexuality': Anna Biller's *Viva* and the Retrospective Life of Sexploitation Cinema," *Camera Obscura* 26, no. 3 (2011): 96.
10 Amelie Hastie, *Cupboards of Curiosity: Women, Recollection, and Film History* (Durham, NC: Duke University Press, 2007), 8–9, 78, 193.
11 Phil Wickham, "Scrapbooks, Soap Dishes, and Screen Dreams: Ephemera, Everyday Life, and Cinema History," *New Review of Film and Television Studies* 8, no. 3 (2010): 317–19.
12 Vivian Sobchack, "Chasing the Maltese Falcon: On the Fabrications of a Film Prop," *Journal of Visual Culture* 6, no. 2 (2007): 239, 240. Original italics. On the inseparability of fans and collectors, also see Lincoln Geraghty, *Cult Collectors: Nostalgia, Fandom, and Collecting Popular Culture* (London: Routledge, 2014).
13 Jean Baudrillard, "The System of Collecting," in *The Cultures of Collecting*, eds John Elsner and Roger Cardinal (Cambridge, MA: Harvard University Press, 1994), 20. Italics mine.
14 Sobchack, "Chasing the Maltese Falcon," 239.
15 As a handy guidebook to sexploitation movie magazines, see Tom Brinkmann's *Bad Mags: The Strangest, Sleaziest, Most Unusual Periodicals Ever Published!, Volume 1* (London: Headpress, 2008), although I was introduced to these publications by my co-panelist Austin Miller, "Wild Screen Reviews: Reconceiving the Sexploitation Film in Adults-Only Publications, 1963–1969" (paper presented at the annual conference of the Society for Cinema and Media Studies, Los Angeles, CA, March 17–21, 2010). For magazines that do not provide a given issue's publication month, I have substituted the volume and issue numbers for reference purposes.
16 Notable examples include Kathryn Fuller, *At the Picture Show: Small-Town Audiences and the Creation of Movie Fan Culture* (Washington, DC: Smithsonian Institution Press, 1996); Shelley Stamp, *Movie-Struck Girls: Women and Motion Picture Culture after the Nickelodeon* (Princeton, NJ: Princeton University Press, 2000); Marsha Orgeron, "Making *It* in Hollywood: Clara Bow, Fandom, and Consumer Culture," *Cinema Journal* 42, no. 4 (2003): 76–97; Marsha Orgeron, "'You Are Invited to Participate': Interactive Fandom in the Age of the Movie Magazine," *Journal of Film and Video* 61, no. 3 (2009): 3–23; Anthony Slide, *Inside the Hollywood Fan Magazine: A History of Star Makers, Fabricators, and Gossip Mongers* (Jackson: University Press of Mississippi, 2011).
17 *The Report of the Commission on Obscenity and Pornography* (New York: Bantam Books, 1970), 95–97; William Rotsler, *Contemporary Erotic Cinema* (New York: Penthouse/Ballantine, 1973), 176, 183–84; Kenneth Turan and Stephen F. Zito, *Sinema: American Pornographic Films and the People Who Make Them* (New York: Praeger, 1974), 16, 228.
18 Bill Osgerby, *Playboys in Paradise: Masculinity, Youth, and Leisure-Style in Modern America* (New York: Berg, 2001), 162 (original emphasis). Also see John D'Emilio and Estelle B. Freedman, *Intimate Matters: A History of Sexuality in America*, 2nd ed. (Chicago: University of Chicago Press, 1997), chap. 13.
19 Elizabeth Fraterrigo, Playboy *and the Making of the Good Life in Modern America* (New York: Oxford University Press, 2009), 157.
20 *The Erotic Screen: A Probing Study of Sex in the Adult Cinema* (Los Angeles: Private Collectors, 1969), 201.
21 See Eric Schaefer, *"Bold! Daring! Shocking! True!" A History of Exploitation Films, 1919–1959* (Durham, NC: Duke University Press, 1999), chap. 8.

22 "*Mundo Depravados*," *Adult Movies Illustrated* 3, no. 1 (1969): n.p.
23 Rotsler, *Contemporary Erotic Cinema*, 132–33.
24 David Andrews, *Soft in the Middle: The Contemporary Softcore Feature in Its Contexts* (Columbus: Ohio State University Press, 2006), 53–54, 58–59.
25 Elena Gorfinkel, "The Body's Failed Labor: Performance Work in Sexploitation Cinema," *Framework* 53, no. 1 (2012): 84.
26 On the advertising appeals of sexploitation films, see Eric Schaefer, "Pandering to the 'Goon Trade': Framing the Sexploitation Audience through Advertising," in *Sleaze Artists: Cinema at the Margins of Taste, Style, and Politics*, ed. Jeffrey Sconce (Durham, NC: Duke University Press, 2007), 19–46.
27 Slide, *Inside the Hollywood Fan Magazine*, 86–90, 179; Mary Desjardins, "Systematizing Scandal: *Confidential* Magazine, Stardom, and the State of California," in *Headline Hollywood: A Century of Film Scandal*, eds Adrienne L. McLean and David A. Cook (New Brunswick, NJ: Rutgers University Press, 2001), 209, 215, 218.
28 Gorfinkel, "The Body's Failed Labor," 86–87.
29 "*Casting Call*," *Adam Film World*, April 1971, 15.
30 Linda Williams, *Screening Sex* (Durham, NC: Duke University Press, 2008), 7.
31 On the taste/class distinctions between these publications, see Laura Kipnis, *Bound and Gagged: Pornography and the Politics of Fantasy in America* (New York: Grove Press, 1996), chap. 4; Osgerby, *Playboys in Paradise*, 193–94; Fraterrigo, *Playboy and the Making of the Good Life in Modern America*, 208–9.
32 See Barbara Ehrenreich, *The Hearts of Men: American Dreams and the Flight from Commitment* (New York: Anchor, 1983); Osgerby, *Playboys in Paradise*; Fraterrigo, *Playboy and the Making of the Good Life in Modern America*.
33 Carrie Pitzulo, *Bachelors and Bunnies: The Sexual Politics of* Playboy (Chicago: University of Chicago Press, 2011), 80–81.
34 David M. Earle, *All Man! Hemingway, 1950s Men's Magazines, and the Masculine Persona* (Kent, OH: Kent State University Press, 2009), 2.
35 "Pornography Is Here to Stay," *Banned* 1, no. 1 (1963): 7. Like *Playboy*, *Adam* also faced several obscenity charges during its first years of publication.
36 Pitzulo, *Bachelors and Bunnies*, 66–67.
37 *The Report of the Commission*, 112.
38 *The Erotic Screen*, 237; Brinkmann, *Bad Mags*, 141.
39 Roger Blake, *The Porno Movies* (Cleveland: Century Books, 1970), 207.
40 Paul Smith, "*The Aqua-Nudes*," *Knight*, July 1964, 84. Such practices also extended into the 1970s porno-chic era, since 8-mm excerpts from popular theatrical hits like *Deep Throat* (1972) and *Behind the Green Door* (1972) were made available for home use, joining the existing market for 8-mm hard-core loops.
41 David F. Friedman with Don de Nevi, *A Youth in Babylon: Confessions of a Trash-Film King* (Buffalo, NY: Prometheus Books, 1990), 326.
42 Orgeron, "Making *It* in Hollywood," 79.
43 "*Hot Spur*," *Adult Movies Illustrated* 3, no. 1 (1969): n.p.
44 "Makeup Special," *Adult Movies Illustrated* 1, no. 3 (1968), n.p.; L. T., letter to the editor, *Art Films Review* 2, no. 2 (1968): n.p.
45 John Harrison, *Hip Pocket Sleaze: The Lurid World of Vintage Adult Paperbacks* (London: Headpress, 2011), 86–87, 106. Also see Brinkmann, *Bad Mags*, 200–1.
46 Robert Silverberg, quoted in Peter Stanfield, *Maximum Movies—Pulp Fictions: Film Culture and the Worlds of Samuel Fuller, Mickey Spillane, and Jim Thompson*

(New Brunswick, NJ: Rutgers University Press, 2011), 46–47. Also see James Harvey, *Pornography for Fun and Profit* (Los Angeles: Edka Books, 1967), 78–79.

47 Stephen J. Gertz, "Sexed-Up Literary Classics," *Booktryst* (blog), posted April 21, 2011, accessed April 13, 2013, http://www.booktryst.com/2011/04/sexed-up-literary-classics.html. Quote from front cover of *The Adult Sexual Version of around the World in 80 Days* (Los Angeles: Calga Publishers, 1971).

48 John W. Sargent, letter to the editor, "Dear Adam," *Adam*, July 1965, 66. Ironically, *Adam Film World* would later profile the Nazi-themed sexploitation film *Love Camp 7* (1969) at length in its July 1969 issue.

49 Jake Barnes, "Fifteen of the Worst Movies Ever," *Adam*, February 1966, 62–64; An O. U. Playboy, letter to the editor, "Dear Adam," *Adam*, July 1966, 82.

50 Mamie Van Doren, "When Legalized Abortions?" *Adam*, September 1965, 42–44.

51 Slide, *Inside the Hollywood Fan Magazine*, 9.

52 William Rotsler, "Notes of a Sex Film Photographer," *Knight*, October 1970, 16, 18–20.

53 Kinohi Nishikawa, "Reading the Street: Iceberg Slim, Donald Goines, and the Rise of Black Pulp Fiction" (Ph.D. diss., Duke University, 2010), 47.

54 Relevant biographical sources include David Hine, "Bill Rotsler: King of the Pornos," *Adam Special Report #8: The Erotic Photographers*, November 1971, 4–19; Terry Carr and Stephanie Bernstein, "*Vertex* Interviews William Rotsler," *Vertex: The Magazine of Science Fiction*, October 1974, 36–38; Peter J. Heck, "Science Fiction: Short But Sweet," *Newsday*, April 30, 1978, D23; James Van Hise, "An Interview with Bill Rotsler," *Enterprise*, June 1984, 19, 21; Bill Warren, "William Rotsler's Women," *Psychotronic Video*, Summer 1994, 65–66; William Rotsler, letter to Bill Bowers, July 7, 1997, The William Rotsler Virtual Museum, accessed April 8, 2013, http://williamrotsler.com/letters/rotslerbentlance.pdf.

55 On this complex censorship history, see Jon Lewis, *Hollywood v. Hard Core: How the Struggle over Censorship Saved the Modern Film Industry* (New York: New York University Press, 2000). *Jacobellis v. Ohio* also notably affected the adults-only publishing market, since the national "community-standards test unduly favors the established national publisher or distributor of material as compared with his smaller, less established counterpart" (*The Report of the Commission*, 422).

56 Justin Wyatt, "Selling 'Atrocious Sexual Behavior': Revising Sexualities in the Marketplace for Adult Film of the 1960s," in *Swinging Single: Representing Sexuality in the 1960s*, eds Hilary Radner and Moya Luckett (Minneapolis: University of Minnesota Press, 1999), 108, 112.

57 Turan and Zito, *Sinema*, 13.

58 "Scenes You'll Never See," *Banned* 1, no. 1 (1963): 22–29; "*Sinderella and the Golden Bra*," *Banned* 1, no. 5 (1965): 12–19; "The Foreign Scene," *Banned* 1, no. 5 (1965): 28–33; "Storm in a 'B' Cup," *Knight*, July 1964, 65.

59 "The Psychic Lover," *Adam Film Quarterly*, December 1968, 13.

60 A. J. Smith, "Decline and Fall of the Movie Censor," *Adam* 6, no. 5 (1962): 17, 54. Quote at 54.

61 "An American Dream," *Adam Film Quarterly*, June 1967, 14.

62 Pat Ballen, "Cool Hand Luke," *Adam Film Quarterly*, November 1967, 34, 37.

63 Frank Thistle, "Ingmar Bergman: Cinema Sultan of the Sex Shockers," *Adam Film Quarterly*, November 1967, 81; William Rotsler, "There's a New Kind of Film: The Underground Movement," *Adam Film Quarterly*, November 1967, 55, 68 (original emphasis). For contemporaneous links between sexploitation and underground

cinema drawn by a magazine at the other end of the taste spectrum, see James Lithgow and Colin Heard, "Underground U.S.A. and the Sexploitation Market," *Films and Filming*, August 1969, 24–29.
64 Bill New, "*Notte Erotique*," *Adam*, July 1965, 60. Also see "Celluloid Sexport," *Adam* 8, no. 3 (1964): 64.
65 Thomas Dove, "How to Make a Nude Movie," *Adam* 7, no. 6 (1963): 12, 15; Schaefer, "Pandering to the 'Goon Trade,'" 23.
66 Hilary Preston, "The Nudists Take the Blame," *Banned* 1, no. 1 (1963): 64.
67 Joseph Carbondale, "Those Naughty Nudes," *Adam* 8, no. 5 (1964): 13.
68 Dove, "How to Make a Nude Movie," 17; Ron Vogel and Bill New, "*Surftide 77*," *Adam* 6, no. 7 (1962): 65 (quoted).
69 Andrews, *Soft in the Middle*, 60.
70 See Mark Betz, "Art, Exploitation, Underground," in *Defining Cult Movies: The Cultural Politics of Oppositional Taste*, eds Mark Jancovich, Antonio Lázaro Reboll, Julian Stringer, and Andy Willis (Manchester: Manchester University Press, 2003), 202–22.
71 "*Playgirls International*," *Adult Movies Illustrated* 3, no. 1 (1969): n.p.; *The Erotic Screen*, 227, 236; and "*Pussycats Paradise*," *Art Films Review* 2, no. 2 (1968): n.p. (quoted).
72 James Naremore, *More than Night: Film Noir in Its Contexts* (Berkeley: University of California Press, 2008), 193.
73 William Rotsler, *Adam Film Quarterly*, July 1966, 56. Original emphasis.
74 "*Oddo*," *Adam Film Quarterly*, November 1967, 13, 16.
75 *The Report of the Commission*, 93.
76 Alfred K. Allan, "The Horror Films," *Adam Film Quarterly*, July 1968, 22–27, 76–80, 86–87; Alfred K. Allan, "The Cliffhangers," *Adam Film Quarterly*, July 1968, 36–39, 68–70, 92–95; Alfred K. Allan, "The Horse Operas," *Adam Film Quarterly*, September 1968, 46–52, 84–87; Alfred K. Allan, "Crime in the Movies," *Adam Film Quarterly*, February 1969, 20–25, 90–96; Alfred K. Allan, "Blood on the Screen: The War Movies," *Adam Film World*, September 1969, 20–25; Dan Rhys, "Sex in the Saddle," *Adam Film World*, November 1969, 20–25, 94–97.
77 Sheldon Stewart and Burch Robbins, "Sex on the Screen," *Adam Film Quarterly*, June 1967, 42–61, 68–69, 76–77; Eugene Bradley, "What Follows *The Fox?*" *Adam Film Quarterly*, September 1968, 36–41; Brent Howard, "Hollywood's Sexual State of Mind," *Adam Film Quarterly*, December 1968, 82–87; "*Girl on a Motorcycle*," *Adam*, February 1969, 50–53; Dan Rhys, "Sex in the Movies: Then and Now," *Adam Film World*, July 1969; Robert Bruno, "Look Ma—No Clothes!" *Adam Film World*, July 1969, 62–64, 68, 70.
78 Gabe Essoe, "The Fabulous Flynn," *Adam Film Quarterly*, December 1968, 20–24, 90–95.
79 Gabe Essoe, "A New Gable Cult Flexes Its Muscles," *Adam Film Quarterly*, September 1968, 22.
80 Orgeron, "'You Are Invited to Participate,'" 19.
81 "*Island Love-In*," *Art Films Review* 2, no. 2 (1968): n.p.
82 "The Rope and the Flesh," *Adult Movies Illustrated* 3, no. 1 (1969): n.p.
83 Adrienne L. McLean, "'New Films in Story Form': Movie Story Magazines and Spectatorship," *Cinema Journal* 42, no. 3 (2003): 12, 14. Quote at 12.

84 "*My Brother's Wife*," *Adult Movies Illustrated* 3, no. 1 (1969): n.p.
85 C. Davis Smith and Michael Bowen, DVD commentary track on *The Sexploiters* (1965), Retro-Seduction Cinema, 2011.
86 "*Island Love-In*," n.p.
87 "*The Muthers*," *Adam Film Quarterly*, February 1969, 29.
88 William Rotsler, "How to Make a Sex Film," *Adam Film World*, October 1972, 66.
89 "*Motel Confidential*," *Art Films Review* 2, no. 2 (1968): n.p.
90 "*Hot Skin and Cold Cash*," *Adam Film Quarterly*, April 1968, 13.
91 "*Island Love-In*," n.p.
92 "*The Warm, Warm Bed*," *Art Films Review* 2, no. 2 (1968): n.p.
93 "*The Game People Play*," *Adam Film Quarterly*, November 1967, 42.
94 Rotsler, *Contemporary Erotic Cinema*, 48–49.
95 "*The Swingers*," *Adam Film Quarterly*, September 1968, 35.
96 Desjardins, "Systematizing Scandal," 211–12. Quote at 212.
97 "*The Playpen Girls*," *Art Films Review* 2, no. 2 (1968): n.p.
98 Rotsler, *Contemporary Erotic Cinema*, 4, 14, 50, 58–61, 68, 245.
99 A comprehensive run of *ARTISEX* is held at the Kinsey Institute for Research in Sex, Gender, and Reproduction, where I consulted them. However, I first encountered this singular publication discussed in Elena Gorfinkel, "'Indecent Desires': Sexploitation Cinema, 1960s Film Culture, and the Adult Film Audience" (Ph.D. diss., New York University, 2008), chap. 3.
100 Eric Schaefer, "Gauging a Revolution: 16 mm Film and the Rise of the Pornographic Feature," *Cinema Journal* 41, no. 3 (2002): 18–21; Schaefer, "Pandering to the 'Goon Trade,'" 36–41. Also see Wyatt, "Selling 'Atrocious Sexual Behavior,'" 108–12.
101 "*The Animal*," *Adam Film Quarterly*, July 1968, 17, 20.
102 "Producer Profile: David Friedman," *Wildest Films* 1, no. 1 (1965): n.p.; Rotsler, *Contemporary Erotic Cinema*, 179–81; Turan and Zito, *Sinema*, 45–46, 106.
103 James Fulton, "Dirty Movies Are Dirtier than Ever," *Adam Film Quarterly*, February 1969, 74.
104 Also see Chuck Kleinhans, "Pornography and Documentary: Narrating the Alibi," in *Sleaze Artists*, 108–16. Despite most latter-day critics' inclination to find white coaters' sexual information amusingly outdated and their pedagogical alibis laughably disingenuous at best, these films' self-defensive tone of clinical seriousness at least models a far more earnest mode of reception—one not so different from the more serious vein of adult film genre criticism discussed in the next two chapters—compared to the jokey insincerity (a different type of self-defense) that many hard-core fictional narratives would internalize through easy appeals to low humor.
105 Eric Jeffrey Haims, quoted in Robert Bruno, "Making It—The Story of '101 Acts of Love,'" *Adam Film World*, February 1971, 69.
106 Schaefer, "Pandering to the 'Goon Trade,'" 41.
107 Kevin Heffernan, "Seen as a Business: Adult Film's Historical Framework and Foundations," in *New Views on Pornography: Sexuality, Politics, and the Law*, eds Lynn Comella and Shira Tarrant (Santa Barbara, CA: Praeger, 2015), 47–48. Also see Steven Ziplow, *The Film Maker's Guide to Pornography* (New York: Drake, 1977).

108 Dan Rhys, "M-J Productions Presents!" *Adam Film World*, January 1971, 56.
109 James Woodman, "Linda Lovelace," *Adam Film World*, June 1974, 12–13, 82; Nelson Wayman, "*Mona*," *Adam Film World*, June 1974, 26–27.
110 See Nishikawa, "Reading the Street"; Justin Gifford, *Pimping Fictions: African American Crime Literature and the Untold Story of Black Pulp Publishing* (Philadelphia: Temple University Press, 2013); Mireille Miller-Young, *A Taste for Brown Sugar: Black Women in Pornography* (Durham, NC: Duke University Press, 2014), 81–84.
111 See Gregory A. Waller, "An Annotated Filmography of R-Rated Sexploitation Films Released during the 1970s," *Journal of Popular Film and Television* 9, no. 2 (1981): 98–112.
112 Fraterrigo, *Playboy and the Making of the Good Life in Modern America*, 157; Roger H. Rubin, "Alternative Lifestyles Revisited, or Whatever Happened to Swingers, Group Marriages, and Communes?" *Journal of Family Issues* 22, no. 6 (2001): 720.
113 James V. Lawrence, "Are Our Sexpots for Real?" *Adam* 1, no. 12 (1957): 54–57; William Rotsler, "Are Sex Film Stars Really Swingers?" *Adam Film World*, August 1972, 18–23.
114 Rotsler, *Contemporary Erotic Cinema*, 191.
115 Philip Dakota, "Any Place, Any Time, Any Way," *Adam Film World*, October 1973, 39–41.
116 Rotsler, *Contemporary Erotic Cinema*, 51, 169, 194–95; Rotsler, "Notes of a Sex Film Photographer," 16, 19–20, 80.
117 Orgeron, "'You Are Invited to Participate,'" 4.
118 Gorfinkel, "The Body's Failed Labor," 84.
119 Rotsler, "How to Make a Sex Film"; Cord Heller, "How to Be a Porn Star, Part 1," *Adam Film World*, December 1975, 8–11, 76.
120 Hastie, *Cupboards of Curiosity*, 193.
121 Rotsler, interviewed by Warren, "William Rotsler's Women," 67.
122 Ibid., 69; "The House of Pain and Pleasure," *Adam Film Quarterly*, February 1969, 7 (quoted); Rotsler, letter to Bill Bowers.
123 Rotsler, interviewed by Hine, "Bill Rotsler," 17.
124 Rotsler, interviewed by Carr and Bernstein, "*Vertex* Interviews William Rotsler," 37–38; by Van Hise, "An Interview with Bill Rotsler," 15–18, 21. Also see Randall D. Larson, *Films into Books: An Analytical Bibliography of Film Novelizations, Movie and TV Tie-Ins* (Metuchen, NJ: Scarecrow Press, 1995), 3, 562.
125 "Astral Trip," *Adam Film Quarterly*, April 1968, 96–99.
126 Cord Heller, "Pornographer's Diary," *Adam Film World*, October 1972, 80–83, 98–99.
127 William Rotsler, "All-Time Favorite Porno Film Hits," *Adam Film World*, December 1975, 68–71, 88–90.
128 Charles D. Anderson, "Video Discs and Porno Movies for the Home," *Adam Film World*, February 1975, 28–31, 72.
129 Norman Bates, "The Videosex Scene: Shooting Your Own," *Adam Film World*, May 1980, 22–25.
130 "You," *Adam Film Quarterly*, February 1969, 32–35; *The Erotic Screen*, 26, 70.

Chapter 3

1. Carolyn Steedman, *Dust: The Archive and Cultural History* (New Brunswick, NJ: Rutgers University Press, 2002), 45.
2. Bill Landis and Michelle Clifford, *Sleazoid Express: A Mind-Twisting Tour through the Grindhouse Cinema of Times Square* (New York: Fireside, 2002), 37.
3. C. Davis Smith and Michael Bowen, DVD commentary track on *The Sexploiters* (1965), Retro-Seduction Cinema, 2011. Consequently, attempts to make critical distinctions between the qualifications of nude performance as professional "acting" and mere "action" adhered around these films, as discussed in Elena Gorfinkel, "The Body's Failed Labor: Performance Work in Sexploitation Cinema," *Framework* 53, no. 1 (2012): 84–86.
4. Thomas Dove, "How to Make a Nude Movie," *Adam* 7, no. 6 (1963): 16; Joseph Carbondale, "Those Naughty Nudes," *Adam* 8, no. 3 (1964): 16.
5. William Rotsler, "How to Make a Sex Film," *Adam Film World*, October 1972, 25.
6. "The Acid Eaters," *Adam Film Quarterly*, July 1968, 82.
7. Kenneth Turan and Stephen F. Zito, *Sinema: American Pornographic Films and the People Who Make Them* (New York, Praeger, 1974), 222. As Rotsler observed in his capsule review of *Street of a Thousand Pleasures* (1972), for example, "Almost every pretty girl you've ever seen in the magazines is in it!" William Rotsler, *Contemporary Erotic Cinema* (New York: Penthouse/Ballantine, 1973), 271.
8. Rotsler, *Contemporary Erotic Cinema*, 176–77.
9. Paolo Cherchi Usai, *The Death of Cinema: History, Cultural Memory, and the Digital Dark Age* (London: British Film Institute, 2001), 21, 25, 39, 101.
10. Ibid., 81.
11. Ibid., 89, 91. Quote at 91.
12. On the creative possibilities (and hazards) of writing film histories, also see Donald Crafton, "McCay and Keaton: Colligating, Conjecturing, and Conjuring," *Film History* 25, no. 1–2 (2013): 31–44. Admittedly, my own example of a fake film falls squarely into his category of "*conjuring*—summoning an apparition with scant or no connection to the facts" (33), which would qualify as no more than a hoax if passed off as actual historical scholarship.
13. Caroline Frick, *Saving Cinema: The Politics of Preservation* (Oxford: Oxford University Press, 2011), 65; David Pierce, *The Survival of American Silent Feature Films: 1912–1929* (Washington, DC: Council on Library and Information Resources and the Library of Congress, 2013).
14. Michael Bowen, personal communication, October 22, 2013.
15. Joe Rubin, personal communication, November 14, 2013. In this case, "complete" versions is relative, since these otherwise intact versions may still be missing opening or closing credits, a few seconds of material excised at reel changes, etc. These versions are, however, still considered complete enough to see the whole narrative and are not, for example, missing entire reels or only extant in very fragmentary forms.
16. James Kendrick, "Phantom Cinema: Illuminating the Structuring Absences of Film History," *Quarterly Review of Film and Video* 30, no. 1 (2013): 63, 65, 72. Quote at 65.
17. Darragh O'Donoghue, "Paradise Regained: *Queen Kelly* and the Lure of the 'Lost' Film," *Senses of Cinema*, no. 27 (2003): http://sensesofcinema.com/2003/27/queen_kelly/.

18 Ashley West, "Whatever Happened to Gigi Darlene?" *The Rialto Report*, May 11, 2014, accessed May 12, 2014, http://www.therialtoreport.com/2014/05/11/whatever-happened-to-gigi-darlene/. My thanks to Michael Bowen for additional information about Darlene.
19 Walter Kendrick, *The Secret Museum: Pornography in Modern Culture* (New York: Viking, 1987), 10, 238. Following Kendrick, Tim Dean observes that the very concept of "pornography" as a distinct classification emerged in the mid-nineteenth century as a function of such materials' segregation into restricted archives, so "there is no pornography without the institution of the archive." See "Introduction: Pornography, Technology, Archive," in *Porn Archives*, eds Tim Dean, Steven Ruszczycky, and David Squires (Durham, NC: Duke University Press, 2014), 3.
20 Eric Schaefer, "Dirty Little Secrets: Scholars, Archivists, and Dirty Movies," *The Moving Image* 5, no. 2 (2005): 80, 100.
21 Anthony Slide, *Nitrate Won't Wait: Film Preservation in the United States* (Jefferson, NC: McFarland, 1992), 94–95.
22 Peter Carlson, "'King of Porn' Empties Out His Castle," *The Washington Post*, August 24, 2002.
23 David Pierce, "Forgotten Faces: Why Some of Our Cinema Heritage Is Part of the Public Domain," *Film History* 19, no. 2 (2007): 128.
24 Lucas Hilderbrand, *Inherent Vice: Bootleg Histories of Videotape and Copyright* (Durham, NC: Duke University Press, 2009), 88.
25 Casey Scott, personal communication, January 24, 2014.
26 "Arrow Finds P.D. 'Deep Throat' in Connecticut; Company Says There Is No Such Thing," *Adult Video News*, July/August 1988, 18.
27 Mark Kernes, "Arrow, V.C.X. Settle 'Deep Throat'/'Debbie Does Dallas' Case," *Adult Video News*, October 21, 2011, http://business.avn.com/articles/legal/Arrow-V-C-X-Settle-Deep-Throat-Debbie-Does-Dallas-Case-451843.html.
28 Karen F. Gracy, *Film Preservation: Competing Definitions of Value, Use, and Practice* (Chicago: Society of American Archivists, 2007), 25–26, 49.
29 Eric Hoyt, "The Future of Selling the Past: Studio Libraries in the 21st Century," *Jump Cut*, no. 52 (2010), accessed May 22, 2014, http://www.ejumpcut.org/archive/jc52.2010/hoytStudioLibraries/index.html.
30 Gracy, *Film Preservation*, 30, 49, 196–99, 209.
31 Ibid., 72.
32 Ibid., 102, 104.
33 Steedman, *Dust*, 145. Original italics.
34 Sean Smalley, personal communication, September 19, 2014.
35 Janna Jones, *The Past Is a Moving Picture: Preserving the Twentieth Century on Film* (Gainesville: University Press of Florida, 2012), 114–16, 119, 123–24.
36 Lucas Hilderbrand, "Historical Fantasies: 1970s Gay Pornography in the Archives," in *Porno Chic and the Sex Wars: American Sexual Representation in the 1970s.*, eds Carolyn Bronstein and Whitney Strub (Amherst: University of Massachusetts Press, 2016).
37 "Horror with Some Sexy Scenes Seen Cashable by Omen-Reading Mishkin," *Variety*, December 10, 1969, 7.
38 Ad for *The Orgy at Lil's Place*, *Variety*, January 22, 1964, 25.
39 "Sexploiters Pushing into New & More Erotic Areas; Their Legal Cases Open New Vistas for Films," *Variety*, August 23, 1967, 7; and "Re-rate Trend Goes On," *Variety*, September 13, 1972, 26.

40 "*The Orgy at Lil's Place*," *ARTISEX*, April 10, 1968, 3. Mishkin himself wrote a letter to the editor of *ARTISEX* (published in the August 28, 1968 issue) to correct some of the editor's previously published misinformation about one of the films Mishkin imported and distributed, so he was certainly aware of the fanzine's existence.
41 "William Mishkin Motion Pictures, Inc.," *Independent Film Journal*, August 1, 1978, 23; Turan and Zito, *Sinema*, 53.
42 Jimmy McDonough, *The Ghastly One: The Sex-Gore Netherworld of Filmmaker Andy Milligan* (Chicago: A Cappella Books, 2001), 127.
43 Upon preservation, the print itself was found to be in far better condition than initially suspected. Several seconds of footage were missing here and there, creating a handful of abrupt splices, likely due to past projectionists mending breaks in the film strip, but significant omissions to the film's duration—including omissions to sexual scenes—were not apparent. An Eastmancolor sequence at the film's conclusion also contained little color fading.
44 Emily Cohen, "The Orphanista Manifesto: Orphan Films and the Politics of Reproduction," *American Anthropologist* 106, no. 4 (2004): 727.
45 Jones, *The Past Is a Moving Picture*, 132.
46 There are, nevertheless, a handful of dedicated collectors of 35- and 16-mm adult film prints—though, due to the resources needed to acquire and store such materials, they are less numerous than collectors of paper documents and other ephemera circulating on eBay and elsewhere. I discuss a notable example of one such collector-turned-entrepreneur later in this chapter.
47 Jonathan Gray, *Show Sold Separately: Promos, Spoilers, and Other Media Paratexts* (New York: New York University Press, 2010), 79.
48 Giovanna Fossati, *From Grain to Pixel: The Archival Life of Film in Transition* (Amsterdam: Amsterdam University Press, 2009), 95.
49 Jennifer Burns Bright and Ronan Crowley, "'A Quantity of Offensive Matter': Private Cases in Public Places," in *Porn Archives*, 103–26. As they note, items donated to the Kinsey Institute under the auspices of preservation can seemingly vanish into the closed stacks, becoming unsearchable in catalogues or inaccessible in person (120–21).
50 See Thomas Waugh, "Archaeology and Censorship," in *The Fruit Machine: Twenty Years of Writings on Queer Cinema* (Durham, NC: Duke University Press, 2000), 272–96; Linda Williams, "'White Slavery' versus the Ethnography of 'Sexworkers': Women in Stag Films at the Kinsey Archive," *The Moving Image* 5, no. 2 (2005): 130–31. As I noted in Chapter 1, this possibility of inadvertently witnessing one's ancestors in sexually compromising images is even teased in the contemporary marketing of stag films—though it is telling that none of these commercial video marketers seem to have similar fears of legal recrimination.
51 "Mission Statement of the Kinsey Institute," The Kinsey Institute, accessed October 15, 2013, http://www.kinseyinstitute.org/about/missionstatement.html.
52 David Squires, "Pornography in the Library," in *Porn Archives*, 85–86. This felt confluence of "dead" archival spaces and "live" sex also recalls my argument in Chapter 1 about the "necrophilic" appeal of vintage pornography.
53 Schaefer, "Dirty Little Secrets," 96.
54 Jones, *The Past Is a Moving Picture*, 13.
55 Steedman, *Dust*, 83.
56 Eric Schaefer, personal communication, July 24, 2013.

57 Jacqueline Stewart, "Discovering Black Film History: Tracing the Tyler, Texas Black Film Collection," *Film History* 23, no. 2 (2011): 161–63.
58 Ibid., 147–48, 151; Jones, *The Past Is a Moving Picture*, 160. Notwithstanding the other extant prints, I still consider the rediscovery and preservation of *The Orgy at Lil's Place* to be a small personal accomplishment, so I plead guilty to an investment in this narrative as well.
59 Frick, *Saving Cinema*, 84.
60 Schaefer, "Dirty Little Secrets," 98–99.
61 Jane M. Gaines, "Early Cinema's Heyday of Copying: The Too Many Copies of *L'Arroseur arrosé* (*The Waterer Watered*)," *Cultural Studies* 20, no. 2–3 (2006): 231, 237–38.
62 Peter Alilunas, "Smutty Little Movies: The Creation and Regulation of Adult Video, 1976–1986" (Ph.D. diss., University of Michigan, 2013), especially chaps. 1 and 2.
63 Dan Rhys, "M-J Productions Presents!" *Adam Film World*, January 1971, 56; Rotsler, *Contemporary Erotic Cinema*, 181; David Jennings, *Skinflicks: The Inside Story of the X-Rated Video Industry* (Bloomington, IN: AuthorHouse, 2000), chaps. 5 and 7, Kindle edition; Alan B. Bursteen, "International Pipeline," *Adult Video News Confidential*, January 1986, 19–20.
64 TVX Video Cassettes: X-Rated Motion Pictures on Video Tape catalogue (1979); collection of Peter Alilunas. One of the first prominent adult video companies, TVX was the brainchild of former sexploitation impresario David F. Friedman.
65 Roberta Findlay, quoted in *Golden Goddesses: 25 Legendary Women of Classic Erotic Cinema 1968–1985* (Duncan, OK: BearManor Media, 2012), 181.
66 There were, however, important exceptions as the hard-core industry later began restyling itself as a legitimate corporate enterprise in the late 1980s and 1990s. Founded in 1984, Vivid Entertainment became one of the industry's leading studios through its signing of rising star Ginger Lynn to an exclusive contract in exchange for residuals and other rights to control over her image. A luxury generally reserved for the industry's biggest stars, this system of paying residuals to a small roster of contracted stars still remains an exception to the standard per diem payment of performers. See Peter Alilunas, "Ephemerata: *Ginger's Private Party* Flyer (circa 1985)," *Film History* 26, no. 3 (2014): 144–55.
67 Ramon Lobato, *Shadow Economies of Cinema: Mapping Informal Film Distribution* (London: British Film Institute, 2012), 18.
68 Hilderbrand, *Inherent Vice*, 59.
69 Joshua M. Greenberg, *From Betamax to Blockbuster: Video Stores and the Invention of Movies on Video* (Cambridge, MA: MIT Press, 2008), 12, 95, 109.
70 Jim Holliday, *How to Build Your X-Rated Video Library* (Beverly Hills, CA: Skull Mountain Publishing, 1980), 14; Dick Goldhaber, "Swedish Erotica, Volume 50," *Adult Video News*, October 1983, 6 (quoted); Paul Fishbein, "The 'Perfect' Video Collection," *Adult Video News*, June 1984, 28; Paul Fishbein, "Interview: Caballero's Al Bloom," *Adult Video News Confidential*, April 1985, 14; Alex Thomas, "Erotica Collection, Volume 1," *Adult Video News Confidential*, May 1985, 20.
71 I. L. Slifkin and Paul Fishbein, "Sex Films: From Stag to Slick," *Adult Video News*, October 1983, 10–11.
72 Alvin Zbryski, "*Fantasy Peeps*: Sensuous Delights," *Adult Video News*, July/August 1984, 6.

73 Michael Midden, "*A History of the Blue Movie*," *Adult Video News*, April 1985, 12.
74 Thomas Lubicky, "Blue Memories II: The Classics," *Adult Video News*, October 1984, 12.
75 Steven Ziplow, *The Film Maker's Guide to Pornography* (New York: Drake, 1977), 15; Chuck Kleinhans, "The Change from Film to Video Pornography: Implications for Analysis," in *Pornography: Film and Culture*, ed. Peter Lehman (New Brunswick, NJ: Rutgers University Press, 2006), 156.
76 Jonathan Coopersmith, "Pornography, Technology, and Progress," *ICON* 4 (1998): 104.
77 Kleinhans, "The Change from Film to Video Pornography," 156–58; John Paone, "1985: Another AAAA Year for the Adult Film Industry," *Adult Video News Confidential*, January 1986, 8; John Paone, "Motion Pictures: A Lasting Quality," *Adult Video News*, October 1986, 18–20, 24; "Theatrical Video: Adult Movie Houses Live On in the Video Age," *Adult Video News*, February 1989, 10; Robert J. Stoller and I. S. Levine, *Coming Attractions: The Making of an X-Rated Video* (New Haven, CT: Yale University Press, 1993), 35, 37, 164, 208. On the present-day endurance of heterosexual adult theaters, see David Church, "'This Thing of Ours': Heterosexuality, Recreational Sex, and the Survival of Adult Movie Theaters," *Media Fields Journal*, no. 8 (2014): http://mediafieldsjournal.squarespace.com/this-thing-of-ours/.
78 Stoller and Levine, *Coming Attractions*, 163, 165, 229; Laurence O'Toole, *Pornotopia: Porn, Sex, Technology, and Desire* (London: Serpent's Tail, 1998), 104; Jennifer C. Nash, *The Black Body in Ecstasy: Reading Race, Reading Pornography* (Durham, NC: Duke University Press, 2014), chaps. 4 and 5. Although not popularly agreed upon, we might place an estimated end date for the "Silver Age" at around 1993, when the Mosaic web browser premiered. This browser popularized the World Wide Web's graphical capabilities, which the porn industry would quickly exploit, opening up a crucial new distribution method for adult content.
79 Jim Holliday, *Only the Best: Jim Holliday's Adult Video Almanac and Trivia Treasury* (Van Nuys, CA: Cal Vista Publications, 1986), 187.
80 Jeremy Stone, "Sexual Freedom in Denmark," *Adult Video News*, August 1986, 14.
81 Jennings, *Skinflicks*, chap. 11, Kindle edition.
82 Kleinhans, "The Change from Film to Video Pornography," 156, 159–60.
83 John Paone, "Combating the Adult Video Glut," *Adult Video News Confidential*, April 1986, 18; Paul Fishbein, "How to Sell Adult Tapes: Selling the Classics," *Adult Video News Confidential*, September 1986, 10–11; "Retail Feedback: Carrying Sub-genres" and "Consumer Feedback: Favorite Sub-genres," *Adult Video News Confidential*, February 1986, 6.
84 "Consumer Feedback: How Consumers Choose Their Video Rentals," *Adult Video News Confidential*, July 1986, 30; John Paone, "Combating the Adult Video Glut," *Adult Video News Confidential*, February 1986, 8–11; John Paone, "The Adult Film Industry: Waiting and Wondering," *Adult Video News Confidential*, September 1986, 8–10.
85 See Alilunas, "Smutty Little Movies," chap. 3.
86 Paul Fishbein, "Interview: Howard Farber of Video-X-Pictures," *Adult Video News Confidential*, June 1985, 22; "Top Sell-Through Adult Tapes," *Adult Video News*, February 1989, 29; Paul Fishbein, "69 Seminal Moments that Shaped the Adult Industry (1983–1998)," *Adult Video News*, Fifteenth Anniversary Issue supplement,

February 1998, 222. On the mainstream film industry's move into this two-tiered pricing strategy, see Frederick Wasser, *Veni, Vidi, Video: The Hollywood Empire and the VCR* (Austin: University of Texas Press, 2001), 132–35.

87 "Percentages of Adult Way Up for 1994," *Adult Video News*, February 1995, 74; Paul Fishbein, "The World's Biggest Glut," *Adult Video News*, October 1995, 144; Fishbein, "69 Seminal Moments," 222–28.

88 Jennings, *Skinflicks*, chap. 11, Kindle edition. Hustler Video subsequently acquired VCA in 2003.

89 Linda Williams, *Hard Core: Power, Pleasure, and the "Frenzy of the Visible"* (Berkeley: University of California Press, 1999), 269.

90 Justin Wyatt, "Selling 'Atrocious Sexual Behavior': Revising Sexualities in the Marketplace for Adult Film of the 1960s," in *Swinging Single: Representing Sexuality in the 1960s*, eds Hilary Radner and Moya Luckett (Minneapolis: University of Minnesota Press, 1999), 124.

91 Ziplow, *The Film Maker's Guide to Pornography*, 16; Rotsler, *Contemporary Erotic Cinema*, 29. The Danish label Color Climax, however, was an exception, as it did explicitly produce and export 8-mm loops featuring such illegal acts during the 1970s.

92 The fact that this scene was originally shot the previous year for *The Opening of Misty Beethoven*, and later recycled into *Barbara Broadcast* with little narrative pretense for its sudden appearance, merely exaggerates the abrupt cuts mutilating director Radley Metzger's otherwise meticulous editing. The uncut *Barbara Broadcast* with this scene intact was long out of print on home video until Distribpix's 2013 DVD/Blu-ray edition, as elaborated further in the next chapter.

93 Jennings, *Skinflicks*, chap. 4, Kindle edition. Legal concerns have also intermittently arisen over the participation of underage actors passing as legally adult, such as the infamous 1986 revelation that Traci Lords had already conducted a two-year hard-core career under false pretenses before reaching her eighteenth birthday, necessitating that over 100 films be withdrawn from circulation. Consequently, most films extensively starring Lords vanished almost entirely, while other films were withdrawn and later rereleased with Lords's scenes trimmed out.

94 O'Toole, *Pornotopia*, 207. Meanwhile, Tom Waugh usefully observes that rape, incest, and violence were "not uncommon" themes in gay male pornographic features as well, suggesting that the eroticization of power imbalances is not exclusive to pornographies organized around sexual difference. See Tom Waugh, "Men's Pornography: Gay vs. Straight," *Jump Cut*, no. 30 (1985): http://www.ejumpcut.org/archive/onlinessays/JC30folder/PornWaugh.html.

95 Holliday, *Only the Best*, 43, 218–19, 240. Quote at 43.

96 Jim Holliday, "Classic Video," *Adult Video News 1996 Adult Entertainment Buyer's Guide*, 226–29. Also see Jim Holliday, "Only the Best: The Long Lost Legendary Films and Videos," *Adult Video News*, December 1992, 90–91.

97 While not a unique strategy among major classics studios during the late 1980s and early 1990s, VCA's widespread editing of their films is particularly ironic since, unlike many competing studios that simply disposed of used film elements, VCA had a well-organized cold-storage vault for conserving its film library. Former VCA employee, personal communication, February 5, 2014.

98 Holliday, *Only the Best*, 58.

99 "Desires within Young Girls (1977)" Richard Kanter, *Vintage Classix* (blog), accessed October 2, 2014, http://www.vintageclassix.com/2014/06/desires-within-young-girls-1977-richard_16.html.
100 The U.S. Supreme Court ruled in *Ashcroft v. Free Speech Coalition* (2002) that fictional depictions of underage sex do not constitute obscenity or child pornography as long as they were made using legally adult actors.
101 Williams, *Hard Core*, 83.
102 Linda Williams, "Second Thoughts on *Hard Core*: American Obscenity Law and the Scapegoating of Deviance," in *More Dirty Looks: Gender, Pornography, and Power*, ed. Pamela Church Gibson (London: British Film Institute, 2004), 168.
103 See Holliday, *Only the Best*, 218–19; Lynne Huffer, *Are the Lips a Grave? A Queer Feminist on the Ethics of Sex* (New York: Columbia University Press, 2013), chap. 3.
104 On these more recent forms, see Linda Ruth Williams, *The Erotic Thriller in Contemporary Cinema* (Bloomington: Indiana University Press, 2005); David Andrews, *Soft in the Middle: The Contemporary Softcore Feature in Its Contexts* (Columbus: Ohio State University Press, 2006).
105 Whitney Strub, "The Clearly Obscene and the Queerly Obscene: Heteronormativity and Obscenity in Cold War Los Angeles," *American Quarterly* 60, no. 2 (2008): 389–92.
106 "Hardcore 'Joanna' to 'Class' Showcase," *Variety*, May 5, 1976, 7.
107 Joseph W. Slade, "The Porn Market and Porn Formulas: The Feature Film of the Seventies," *Journal of Popular Film* 6, no. 2 (1977): 169. Hard-core films have only appeared on *Variety*'s 1972 and 1973 annual lists of top-grossing films, indicating the peak years of "porno chic."
108 Ziplow, *The Film Maker's Guide to Pornography*, 7, 77–78, 143.
109 Robert H. Rimmer, *The X-Rated Videotape Guide* (New York: Arlington House, 1984); *Film World Magazine's Famous X-Rated Video Directory* (Los Angeles: Holloway House, 1985).
110 Holliday, *How to Build Your X-Rated Video Library*, 23–24; Holliday, *Only the Best*. Holliday's book, published by the Cal Vista porn studio, was accompanied by his popular *Only the Best* (1986) compilation video, containing his favorite scenes from the Cal Vista library.
111 Essex Video ad, *Adult Video News Confidential*, February 1986, 13; Lee Irving, "Adult Manufacturers Hedging Their Bets: General Release Tapes as Viable Alternatives," *Adult Video News Confidential*, June 1986, 22–23, 26.
112 Paone, "The Adult Film Industry," 10.
113 Gene Ross, "Overview: Oh Mama, How That 'Other' Market Has Changed," *Adult Video News* "Alternative Adult" supplement, Winter 1993, 3–4.
114 Gene Ross, "Sexploitation Films: The 60's Sexplosion!!!" *Adult Video News*, March 1987, 82 (quoted). Also see John Paone, "Consumer Interviews, Part 2: Gene Ross of Philadelphia, Pennsylvania," *Adult Video News Confidential*, May 1986, 22–23; Gene Ross, "Bell, Boobs, and Love Handles: Glamour Video," *Adult Video News*, May 1988, 57–59, 70, 76–77; Gene Ross, "Nudie Nostalgia," *Adult Video News*, May 1990, 58–59; Gene Ross, "Nudies and Roughies: The Exploitation Explosion," *Adult Video News*, July 1992, 120.
115 Gene Ross, "*Nudie-Cutie Shorts, Loops, and Peeps* (5 Volumes)," *Adult Video News*, October 1991, 74 (quoted); Gene Ross, "Take Off Your Clothes and Get Naked!!!" *Adult Video News* "Alternative Adult" supplement, Winter 1994, 4.

116 Mark Kernes, "Making Alternative Adult Video a Profit Center," *Adult Video News* "Alternative Adult" supplement, Winter 1993, 22.
117 Ross, "Sexploitation Films," 84–86; Ross, "Nudie Nostalgia," 58.
118 Gene Ross, "*Grindhouse Follies* (Volumes 1–3)," *Adult Video News*, December 1991, 80.
119 Gene Ross, "Monsters and Naked Maidens: Cult Director Frank Henenlotter and Something Weird Video Unearth 'Sexy Shockers from the Vault,'" *Adult Video News* "Alternative Adult" supplement, Summer 1993, 22–26; Gene Ross, "A Round-House Punch from the New York Art Houses—The Ruffies," *Adult Video News*, April 1994, 102–4; "Oh No!!! … Those Nice Clean-Cut, Wholesome Guys from Something Weird Video … into Bondage?" *Adult Video News* "A Special Look at Fetish" supplement, November 1994, 232; Gene Ross, "Harry Novak—Near to the Last of the Red Hot Papas," *Adult Video News* "Alternative Adult" supplement, Winter 1994, 8.
120 Scott, personal communication, January 24, 2014.
121 Ross, "Monsters and Naked Maidens," 25; Mike Vraney, interviewed in BigPoppaOnline, *Third Eye Cinema* podcast, May 6, 2012, http://www.blogtalkradio.com/bigpoppaonline/2012/05/06/third-eye-cinema-5612-with-mike-vraney.
122 Kernes, "Making Alternative Adult Video a Profit Center," 20.
123 Gene Ross, "The Bang You Hear Is the Sexploitation Film Explosion," *Adult Video News* "Alternative Adult" supplement, Winter 1993, 10; "Put Something Really Different in Your Store with Something Weird Video," *Adult Video News* "Alternative Adult" supplement, Summer 1994, 6, 23; Gene Ross, "Boogie Days and Nights Galore to Be Found in Something Weird Video's New Triple-X Blue Book," *Adult Video News*, January 1998, 378.
124 Something Weird Video ad, *Adult Video News*, June 1994, 112.
125 Ross, "Boogie Days and Nights Galore," 377–80.
126 Frick, *Saving Cinema*, 173–75, 178.
127 Fossati, *From Grain to Pixel*, 117–22.
128 Scott Aaron Stine, "Stags & Smokers: Collecting 8mm & Super 8 Films," *Filthy Habits: Hardcore & Sexploitation Fare from the 1960s & 1970s*, Fall 2002, 35.
129 Mary Desjardins, "Ephemeral Culture/eBay Culture: Film Collectibles and Fan Investments," in *Everyday eBay: Culture, Collecting, and Desire*, eds Ken Hillis, Michael Petit, and Nathan Scott Epley (New York: Routledge, 2006), 36–38.
130 Steedman, *Dust*, 77.
131 Geoff Nicholson, *Sex Collectors: The Secret World of Consumers, Connoisseurs, Curators, Creators, Dealers, Bibliographers, and Accumulators of "Erotica"* (New York: Simon & Schuster, 2006), 236.
132 Matt Hills, "Patterns of Surprise: The 'Aleatory Object' in Psychoanalytic Ethnography and Cyclical Fandom," *American Behavioral Scientist* 48, no. 7 (2005): 803–04, 812.
133 Ibid., 815–16, 818–19.
134 Brigid Cherry, "Subcultural Tastes, Genre Boundaries, and Fan Canons," in *The Shifting Definitions of Genre: Essays on Labeling Films, Television Shows, and Media*, eds Lincoln Geraghty and Mark Jancovich (Jefferson, NC: McFarland, 2008), 205.
135 C. Lee Harrington and Denise D. Bielby, "A Life Course Perspective on Fandom," *International Journal of Cultural Studies* 13, no. 5 (2010): 444. Original italics.

136 Gilles Deleuze and Felix Guattari, *A Thousand Plateaus: Capitalism and Schizophrenia*, trans. Brian Massumi (London: Continuum, 2004), 324–25. For a complimentary Deleuzoguattarian exploration of pornography as a genre invested in fragmented body parts contingently connected into unruly assemblages of affect and desire, see Berkeley Kaite, *Pornography and Difference* (Bloomington: Indiana University Press, 1995).
137 Annette Kuhn, *Dreaming of Fred and Ginger: Cinema and Cultural Memory* (New York: New York University Press, 2002), 68; Stephen Barber, *Abandoned Images: Film and Film's End* (London: Reaktion Books, 2010), 77.
138 Milly Buonanno, *The Age of Television: Experiences and Theories*, trans. Jennifer Radice (Bristol: Intellect Books, 2008), 119–32.
139 Amanda Ann Klein, *American Film Cycles: Reframing Genres, Screening Social Problems, and Defining Subcultures* (Austin: University of Texas Press, 2011), 61, 97. Quote at 61.
140 Mike Vraney, interviewed by Noel Murray, "Mike Vraney," A.V. Club, March 16, 2005, http://www.avclub.com/article/mike-vraney-13920.
141 Brief excerpts from the above discussion of self-narratives and cyclical fandom first appeared in a different generic context in my "Afterword: Memory, Genre, and Self-Narrativization; Or, Why I Should Be a More Content Horror Fan," in *American Horror Film: The Genre at the Turn of the Millennium*, ed. Steffen Hantke (Jackson: University Press of Mississippi, 2010), 235–42.
142 Steedman, *Dust*, 164. Original emphasis.
143 Ibid., 166–67.

Chapter 4

1 Jacy Catlin, "Jacy's new Alpha Blue Archives thread," AV Maniacs, posted June 11, 2008, accessed December 14, 2013, http://www.avmaniacs.com/forums/showthread.php?t=30910&page=18.
2 Steven Morowitz, interviewed by Timothy Snarr, "Exclusive: Steven Morowitz of Video-X-Pix on the First Classic HD Porn Transfer," *AEBN Official Blog*, posted October 2, 2010, accessed November 23, 2013, http://blog.aebn.net/interviews/exclusive-steven-morowitz-of-video-x-pix-on-the-first-classic-hd-porn-transfer/.
3 TVXCreative, "TVX/VCX Story of Joanna DVD," Adult DVD Talk, posted December 14, 2005, http://forum.adultdvdtalk.com/tvxvcx-story-of-joanna-dvd. As the above quote implies, these obscenity concerns were especially acute during the George W. Bush administration, since US Attorney General John Ashcroft began more aggressively prosecuting pornographers, including high-profile obscenity convictions against "extreme porn" purveyors Max Hardcore and Rob Black.
4 Janna Jones, *The Past Is a Moving Picture: Preserving the Twentieth Century on Film* (Gainesville: University Press of Florida, 2012), 78–80.
5 Caroline Frick, *Saving Cinema: The Politics of Preservation* (Oxford: Oxford University Press, 2011), 173–75, 178.
6 See "Code of Ethics," FIAF: International Federation of Film Archives, accessed December 6, 2013, http://www.fiafnet.org/uk/members/ethics.html; and "AMIA Code of Ethics," AMIA: The Association of Moving Image Archivists, accessed December 6, 2013, http://www.amianet.org/sites/all/files/Code%20of%20

Ethics%20-%20100101.pdf. Also see Ray Edmondson, *Audiovisual Archiving: Philosophy and Principles* (Paris: UNESCO, 2004), accessed December 6, 2013, http://ulis3.hq.int.unesco.org/images/0013/001364/136477e.pdf.
7   Giovanna Fossati, *From Grain to Pixel: The Archival Life of Film in Transition* (Amsterdam: Amsterdam University Press, 2009), 99–100.
8   Karen F. Gracy, *Film Preservation: Competing Definitions of Value, Use, and Practice* (Chicago, IL: Society of American Archivists, 2007), 22, 141–67.
9   Fossati, *From Grain to Pixel*, 72–73, 117. Quote at 72–73.
10 Also see Raiford Guins, "Blood and Black Gloves on Shiny Discs: New Media, Old Tastes, and the Remediation of Italian Horror Films in the United States," in *Horror International*, eds Steven Jay Schneider and Tony Williams (Detroit: Wayne State University Press, 2005), 15–32.
11 See, for example, the discussion of *Anna Obsessed* (1977) in the thread "TVX/VCX Story of Joanna DVD," Adult DVD Talk.
12 Jacques Boyreau, *Sexytime: The Post-porn Rise of the Pornoisseur* (Seattle: Fantagraphics Books, 2012).
13 See the thread "Are movies just movies? (or—where does XXX fit in your collection!)," Rock! Shock! Pop!, posted August 3, 2011, http://www.rockshockpop.com/forums/showthread.php?2038-Are-movies-just-movies-%28or-where-does-XXX-fit-in-your-collection!%29.
14 See the thread "Porn for Skeptics," Adult DVD Talk, posted December 10, 2010, http://forum.adultdvdtalk.com/porn-for-skeptics.
15 See the thread "Top Ten Rules for Porn Beginners," Adult DVD Talk, posted December 13, 2010, accessed January 12, 2014, http://forum.adultdvdtalk.com/top-ten-rules-for-porn-beginners.
16 "Porn for Skeptics," Adult DVD Talk.
17 David Andrews, *Theorizing Art Cinemas: Foreign, Cult, Avant-Garde, and Beyond* (Austin: University of Texas Press, 2013), 94.
18 Matt Hills, *The Pleasures of Horror* (London: Continuum, 2005), 74–78.
19 Martin Barker, "Embracing Rape: Understanding the Attractions of Exploitation Movies," in *Controversial Images: Media Representations on the Edge*, eds Feona Attwood, Vincent Campbell, I. Q. Hunter, and Sharon Lockyer (New York: Palgrave Macmillan, 2013), 217–38.
20 Cf. Nathan Scott Epley, "Pin-ups, Retro-chic, and the Consumption of Irony," in *Pornification: Sex and Sexuality in Media Culture*, eds Susanna Paasonen, Kaarina Nikunen, and Laura Saarenmaa (Oxford: Berg, 2007), 51–56.
21 See the thread "Classic XXX Features on DVD," AV Maniacs, posted September 20, 2005, accessed January 12, 2014, http://www.avmaniacs.com/forums/showthread.php?t=15370.
22 Gore Gore Girl, "Should adult films feature less pornography?" discussion thread, Adult DVD Talk, posted August 1, 2011, http://forum.adultdvdtalk.com/should-adult-films-feature-less-pornography. Also see her blog, *The Gore-Gore Girl: XXX Through a Feminist Lens*, accessed September 30, 2014, http://www.goregoregirl.com/.
23 David Jennings, *Skinflicks: The Inside Story of the X-Rated Video Industry* (Bloomington, IN: AuthorHouse, 2000), chap. 5, Kindle edition.
24 See Barbara Klinger, *Beyond the Multiplex: Cinema, New Technologies, and the Home* (Berkeley: University of California Press, 2006).

25 For a representative list, see "Appendix 2: DVD Releases by Company," in Jason S. Martinko, *The XXX Filmography, 1968–1988* (Jefferson, NC: McFarland, 2013), 342–47.
26 Jacy Catlin, "Femmes De Sade," AV Maniacs, posted July 8, 2007, accessed January 12, 2014, http://www.avmaniacs.com/forums/showthread.php?t=23071&page=3.
27 See, for example, "*Joanna* Enjoys Revival," *Adult Video News*, April 24, 2005, accessed January 12, 2014, http://business.avn.com/articles/video/i-Joanna-i-Enjoys-Revival-43326.html.
28 See "Classic XXX Features on DVD," AV Maniacs.
29 See the thread "1976 Classic THROUGH THE LOOKING GLASS," Adult DVD Talk, accessed January 8, 2014, http://forum.adultdvdtalk.com/1976-classic-through-the-looking-glass.
30 "Classic XXX Features on DVD" thread, AV Maniacs.
31 It is worth noting that Something Weird, Vinegar Syndrome, and several other video companies discussed in this chapter also distribute a handful of Golden Age all-male porn films, so these companies do not promote wholly heterocentrist selections—even if their gay titles remain a minority.
32 Eric Schaefer, "The Inside Story of Storefront Theaters," in *Something Weird Video Blue Book* (Seattle: Something Weird Video, 1997), 2–6. The inclusion of such edifying articles in the *Blue Book* would also help legally defend SWV's move into hard-core territory by asserting these films' "redeeming" historical value.
33 For a related discussion of DVD releases that deliberately recall downscale exhibition contexts, also see David Church, *Grindhouse Nostalgia: Memory, Home Video, and Exploitation Film Fandom* (Edinburgh: Edinburgh University Press, 2015), chaps. 1–2.
34 Mike Vraney, interviewed by Noel Murray, "Mike Vraney," A.V. Club, March 16, 2005, accessed January 10, 2014, http://www.avclub.com/article/mike-vraney-13920.
35 Mike Vraney, interviewed in BigPoppaOnline, *Third Eye Cinema* podcast, May 6, 2012, accessed January 10, 2014, http://www.blogtalkradio.com/bigpoppaonline/2012/05/06/third-eye-cinema-5612-with-mike-vraney. Unless otherwise noted, subsequent quotes attributed to Vraney in this section derive from this same interview.
36 Paul McDonald, *Video and DVD Industries* (London: British Film Institute, 2007), 93.
37 See Bradley Schauer, "The Warner Archive and DVD Collecting in the New Home Video Market," *The Velvet Light Trap*, no. 70 (2012): 35–48.
38 Chris Anderson, *The Long Tail: Why the Future of Business Is Selling Less of More* (New York: Hyperion, 2006).
39 Jeffrey Sconce, "'Trashing' the Academy: Taste, Excess, and an Emerging Politics of Cinematic Style," *Screen* 36, no. 4 (1995): 371–93. Indeed, whereas non-fans might readily mock Golden Age adult films instead of taking them seriously as a genre, SWV distributes a handful of hard-core feature films that have become subculturally notorious among even vintage porn fans for their mockable "badness," including *Necromania* (1971), *Bat Pussy* (1973), and *Hardgore* (1976). This tendency belies Sconce's attempted exclusion of hard-core cinema from the "paracinema" corpus (see Chapter 1).
40 See, for example, Zach Clark, "The Criterion Collection of Exploitation Cinema: Mike Vraney and Something Weird Video," *The L Magazine*, January 6, 2014, http://www.thelmagazine.com/TheMeasure/archives/2014/01/06/the-criterion-collection-of-exploitation-cinema-mike-vraney-and-something-weird-video.

41 James Kendrick, "What Is the Criterion? The Criterion Collection as an Archive of Film as Culture," *Journal of Film and Video* 53, no. 2–3 (2001): 124–39. Kendrick suggests that "beneath the Criterion banner one is still more likely to find a more eclectic collection of world cinema than in any other single home video collection" (137)—a considerably shortsighted observation, given the label's predominant focus on "reputable" cinema.
42 See David F. Friedman with Don de Nevi, *A Youth in Babylon: Confessions of a Trash-Film King* (Buffalo, NY: Prometheus Books, 1990).
43 On this latter category, see Charles R. Acland and Haidee Wasson, eds, *Useful Cinema* (Durham, NC: Duke University Press, 2011).
44 Casey Scott, "The Alpha Blue Archives Feature Film Collection (2004)," DVD Drive-In, accessed December 8, 2013, http://www.dvddrive-in.com/reviews/a-d/alphabluearchives74757904.htm.
45 Jacy Catlin, "Jacy's new Alpha Blue Archives thread," AV Maniacs, posted July 11, 2007, accessed January 12, 2014, http://www.avmaniacs.com/forums/showthread.php?t=30910. Unless otherwise noted, subsequent quotes from Catlin derive from this same discussion thread.
46 Bill Landis and Michelle Clifford, "The Avon Dynasty," Alpha Blue Archives, accessed December 8, 2013, http://alphabluearchives.com/store/the-avon-dynasty/.
47 Catlin, "Femmes De Sade," AV Maniacs.
48 See Catlin's partial list in "Jacy's new Alpha Blue Archives thread," AV Maniacs, posted July 12, 2007, accessed January 12, 2014, http://www.avmaniacs.com/forums/showthread.php?t=30910&page=2.
49 Scott, "The Alpha Blue Archives Feature Film Collection."
50 Leo Enticknap, *Film Restoration: The Culture and Science of Audiovisual Heritage* (New York: Palgrave Macmillan, 2013), 40.
51 Lucas Hilderbrand, *Inherent Vice: Bootleg Histories of Videotape and Copyright* (Durham, NC: Duke University Press, 2009), 6, 13, 61–67. Quote at 6.
52 My cue here comes from Kate Egan's discussion of Vipco's déclassé DVD releases of previously censored "video nasties" in Britain. See Egan, *Trash or Treasure? Censorship and the Changing Meanings of the Video Nasties* (Manchester: Manchester University Press, 2007), chap. 7.
53 A. J. Hall, "Selling Classic Content in Modern Formats," *Adult Video News*, January 28, 2014, accessed January 17, 2014, http://business.avn.com/articles/technology/A-J-Hall-Column-Selling-Classic-Content-in-Modern-Formats-545756.html. Many of the largest tube sites are partially populated by short promotional clips deliberately uploaded by younger studios and paysites, so most tube sites actually exist in a far-from-oppositional relationship to content producers, despite some of the old guard's anti-piracy rhetoric.
54 Hilderbrand, *Inherent Vice*, 22–23.
55 Jones, *The Past Is a Moving Picture*, 144–45, 148; Fossati, *From Grain to Pixel*, 234.
56 See "The Story of Joanna (XXX)—DVD comparison" thread, AV Maniacs, posted January 12, 2005, accessed January 12, 2014, http://www.avmaniacs.com/forums/showthread.php?t=10931.
57 Catlin, "Jacy's new Alpha Blue Archives thread," AV Maniacs, posted July 11, 2007, accessed January 12, 2014, http://www.avmaniacs.com/forums/showthread.php?t=30910.
58 Casey Scott, personal communication, January 24, 2014.
59 Ramon Lobato, *Shadow Economies of Cinema: Mapping Informal Film Distribution* (London: British Film Institute, 2012), 114.

60 See David Andrews, *Soft in the Middle: The Contemporary Softcore Feature in Its Contexts* (Columbus: Ohio State University Press, 2006), chap. 8. Quote at 196.
61 Joe Rubin, personal communication, November 14, 2013, and January 9, 2014. Unless otherwise noted, statements attributed to Rubin derive from these conversations.
62 Erik Piepenburg, "Smut, Refreshed for a New Generation," *New York Times*, January 23, 2014, accessed November 12, 2013, http://www.nytimes.com/2014/01/26/movies/smut-refreshed-for-a-new-generation.html.
63 Of course, Rubin's willingness to be interviewed for an academic readership is also another part of his label's larger legitimization strategy—so this book is itself a partial extension of his efforts to court a broader viewership.
64 Robert Harris, "A few words about … ™ The Telephone Book—in Blu-ray," Home Theater Forum, posted April 24, 2013, accessed November 12, 2013, http://www.hometheaterforum.com/topic/323106-a-few-words-about%E2%84%A2-the-telephone-book-in-blu-ray/#entry3950576. The description of Harris as a "starchivist" comes from Enticknap, *Film Restoration*, 69.
65 Ashley West, April Hall, and Robert Kerman, "R. Bolla: Adult Film's Method Actor," *The Rialto Report* (podcast), June 2, 2013, http://www.therialtoreport.com/2013/06/02/r-bolla-adult-films-method-actorpodcast-12/.
66 West, quoted in George Pacheco, "An Interview with The Rialto Report," *10K Bullets* (blog), November 11, 2013, accessed February 1, 2014, http://10kbullets.com/features/articles/an-interview-with-the-rialto-report/. Contrast West's respectful and intelligent approach with that of 42nd Street Pete, a self-proclaimed grindhouse film expert who hosts a line of 1970s-era hard-core films through Alternative Cinema's after Hours Cinema shingle. Like a third-rate Joe Bob Briggs imitator (swap the redneck attire and drive-in nostalgia for raincoat crowd attire and storefront porn theater nostalgia), minus the paracinematic humor and genre-literate insight, 42nd Street Pete's sleazeball shtick glorifies the stereotype of the vintage porn fan as crude masturbator concerned with little more than "hot" scenes and bad taste.
67 On 1970s porno chic as an influential moment in film criticism, see Raymond J. Haberski, Jr., "Critics and the Sex Scene," in *Sex Scene: Media and the Sexual Revolution*, ed. Eric Schaefer (Durham, NC: Duke University Press, 2014), 383–406. Although a cultural arbiter like the *New York Times* only rarely offered (largely dismissive) reviews of hard-core films (e.g., Vincent Canby, "What Are We to Think of 'Deep Throat'?" January 21, 1973; Walter Goodman, "The New Porno Movies: From X to Zzzzzzzz," November 23, 1975), *Variety* routinely reviewed hard-core features before phasing out such coverage around 1976. Another factor in this shift was the September 1977 murder of *Variety*'s in-house specialist for hard-core film reviews, Addison Verrill, one of the victims in the serial killing case that later inspired the film *Cruising* (1980).
68 Lynda Nead, "'Above the Pulp-Line': The Cultural Significance of Erotic Art," in *More Dirty Looks: Gender, Pornography, and Power*, ed. Pamela Church Gibson (London: British Film Institute, 2004), 219–20. Also see, among others, Dian Hanson, ed., *Vanessa Del Rio: Fifty Years of Slightly Slutty Behavior* (Cologne: TASCHEN Books, 2007).
69 "Classic XXX Features on DVD," AV Maniacs.
70 Joshua M. Greenberg, *From Betamax to Blockbuster: Video Stores and the Invention of Movies on Video* (Cambridge, MA: MIT Press, 2008), 64–65. In addition to Distribpix's own in-house line of Video-X-Pix tapes, the company also distributed tapes for several other adult labels, including Quality-X and Red Light Video,

through its New Jersey-based sales arm, A&H Video, and its regional Metro Distributors warehouses.
71 Morowitz, interviewed by Snarr, "Exclusive: Steven Morowitz of Video-X-Pix."
72 Ibid.
73 Jon Houghton, "DEEP INSIDE ANNIE SPRINKLE—PLATINUM ELITE COLLECTION" thread, AV Maniacs, posted September 25, 2010, accessed January 12, 2014, http://www.avmaniacs.com/forums/showthread.php?t=43048&page=4.
74 Morowitz, interviewed by Jeremy Richey, "A Moon in the Gutter Q&A with Distribpix's Steven Morowitz," *Moon in the Gutter* (blog), posted May 5, 2012, http://mooninthegutter.blogspot.com/2012/05/moon-in-gutter-q-with-distribpixs.html.
75 Steven Morowitz, personal communication, April 24, 2014, and October 16, 2014. Unless otherwise noted, information attributed to Morowitz comes from these interviews.
76 Morowitz, interviewed by Richey, "A Moon in the Gutter Q&A."
77 Morowitz, interviewed by Snarr, "Exclusive: Steven Morowitz of Video-X-Pix." Also see Steven Morowitz, "The Henry Paris Collection—new singles out on DVD and MORE!!" *The Distribpix Blog*, posted September 12, 2014, accessed November 12, 2013, http://distribpixblog.wordpress.com/2014/09/12/the-films-of-henry-paris-update/.
78 Kevin Heffernan, "Seen as a Business: Adult Film's Historical Framework and Foundations," in *New Views on Pornography: Sexuality, Politics, and the Law*, eds Lynn Comella and Shira Tarrant (Santa Barbara, CA: Praeger, 2015), 48–49.
79 Linda Williams, *Hard Core: Power, Pleasure, and the "Frenzy of the Visible"* (Berkeley: University of California Press, 1999), 136–38, 144–45.
80 Chuck Tryon, *On-Demand Culture: Digital Delivery and the Future of Movies* (New Brunswick, NJ: Rutgers University Press, 2013), 147.
81 See, for example, Matt Hills, "Para-Paracinema: The *Friday the 13th* Film Series as Other to Trash and Legitimate Film Cultures," in *Sleaze Artists: Cinema at the Margins of Taste, Style, and Politics*, ed. Jeffrey Sconce (Durham, NC: Duke University Press, 2007), 220–22; Andrews, *Soft in the Middle*, chap. 2; Andrews, *Theorizing Art Cinemas*.
82 In 1988, Sprinkle adapted the term "post-porn modernism" from Dutch artist Wink van Kempen to describe a "new genre of sexually explicit material that is perhaps more visually experimental, political, humorous, 'arty,' and eclectic than the rest." Annie Sprinkle, *Post-porn Modernist: My 25 Years as a Multimedia Whore* (San Francisco: Cleis Press, 1998), 160.
83 Linda Williams, "A Provoking Agent: The Pornography and Performance Art of Annie Sprinkle," *Social Text*, no. 37 (1993): 122–23, 124–26. Also see Chris Straayer, "The Seduction of Boundaries: Feminist Fluidity in Annie Sprinkle's Art/Education/Sex," in *More Dirty Looks*, 228–35.
84 See Adair Rounthwaite, "From This Body to Yours: Porn, Affect, and Performance Art Documentation," *Camera Obscura* 26, no. 3 (2011): 67–69.
85 Direct quotes from *Herstory of Porn* come from the script published in Annie Sprinkle, *Hardcore from the Heart: The Pleasures, Profits, and Politics of Sex in Performance*, ed. Gabrielle Cody (London: Continuum, 2001), 45–64. A performance of the show was preserved as a self-released 1999 video of the same name (codirected by Sprinkle and Scarlot Harlot).
86 Williams, "A Provoking Agent," 128.
87 Marla Carlson, "Performative Pornography: Annie Sprinkle Reads Her Movies," *Text and Performance Quarterly* 19, no. 3 (1999): 238, 241 (original emphasis).

88 Sprinkle, *Post-porn Modernist*, 34 (quoted). Also see the editorial commentaries by Gabrielle Cody in Sprinkle, *Hardcore from the Heart* (17, 66).
89 Annie Sprinkle, personal communication, September 27 and October 29, 2014.
90 "Sprinkle Shop," Anniesprinkle.org(asm), accessed March 23, 2014, https://anniesprinkle.org/shop/.
91 Sprinkle, personal communication, January 18, 2014.
92 Carlson, "Performative Pornography," 237, 239, 243, 246. Quote at 243.
93 Sprinkle, "My Brushes and Crushes with the Law," in *Hardcore from the Heart*, 74.
94 Sprinkle, *Post-porn Modernist*, 57.
95 Boyreau, *Sexytime*, 4–5.
96 Also see Tim Stüttgen, ed., *Post/Porn/Politics* (Berlin: b_books, 2009); Virginie Despentes, *King Kong Theory*, trans. Stéphanie Benson (New York: The Feminist Press, 2010); Anne G. Sabo, *After Pornified: How Women Are Transforming Pornography & Why It Matters* (London: Zero Books, 2012); Tristan Taormino, Celine Parreñas Shimizu, Constance Penley, and Mireille Miller-Young, eds, *The Feminist Porn Book* (New York: The Feminist Press, 2013); Enrico Biasin, Giovanna Maina, and Federico Zecca, eds, *Porn After Porn: Contemporary Alternative Pornographies* (Milano-Udine: Mimesis International, 2014).
97 Tryon, *On-Demand Culture*, 4–5, 20, 60–61, 70, 114. Also see Daniel Herbert, *Videoland: Movie Culture at the American Video Store* (Berkeley: University of California Press, 2014), 179–82.
98 Tryon, *On-Demand Culture*, 177.
99 Chris Morris, "Porn Studios Look for Better 2014 after Rough Year," NBC News, accessed January 14, 2014, http://www.nbcnews.com/business/porn-studios-look-better-2014-after-rough-year-2D11923847.
100 Morowitz, personal communication, April 24, 2014. Whether the future of 3-D printing as a consumer-grade technology will allow such toys to be commonly bootlegged as well remains to be seen.
101 Susanna Paasonen, *Carnal Resonance: Affect and Online Pornography* (Cambridge, MA: MIT Press, 2011), 102.
102 Jones, *The Past Is a Moving Picture*, 53.
103 Hilderbrand, *Inherent Vice*, 232–34.
104 See Tryon, *On-Demand Culture*, 31–32.
105 See David Bordwell, *Pandora's Digital Box: Films, Files, and the Future of Movies* (Madison, WI: Irvington Way Institute Press, 2012).
106 Enticknap, *Film Restoration*, 149–50, 156–57.
107 Adam Baran, "Talking 'Straight vs. Gay' with New York's Gay Curator of Straight Porn," *The Sword* (blog), posted May 19, 2014, accessed June 8, 2014, http://thesword.com/straight-talk-talking-straight-vs-gay-with-new-yorks-gay-straight-porn-guru.html.
108 Unless otherwise noted, information on the series comes from Casey Scott, personal communication, January 24, 2014.
109 Casey Scott, "'In the Flesh'—my first curated series," *Movies in the City* (blog), posted December 10, 2013, accessed June 8, 2014, http://nycmovieboy.blogspot.com/2013/12/in-flesh-my-first-curated-series.html.
110 For his own review of the series, see Steven Morowitz, "In the Flesh—A Powerhouse Film Series," *The Distribpix Blog*, posted December 22, 2013, accessed June 8, 2014, http://distribpixblog.wordpress.com/2013/12/22/in-the-flesh-a-powerhouse-film-series/.
111 See Lawrence W. Levine, *Highbrow/Lowbrow: The Emergence of Cultural Hierarchy in America* (Cambridge, MA: Harvard University Press, 1988).

Conclusion

1. Kenneth Turan and Stephen F. Zito, *Sinema: American Pornographic Films and the People Who Make Them* (New York: Praeger, 1974), 148.
2. Lovelace, quoted in Legs McNeil and Jennifer Osbourne with Peter Pavia, *The Other Hollywood: The Uncensored Oral History of the Porn Film Industry* (New York: HarperCollins, 2005), 439.
3. Spelvin, quoted in Ibid., 42.
4. Mireille Miller-Young, *A Taste for Brown Sugar: Black Women in Pornography* (Durham, NC: Duke University Press, 2014), chaps. 5–6. Also see Steven Ziplow, *The Film Maker's Guide to Pornography* (New York: Drake, 1977), 45; Jeffrey Escoffier, *Bigger Than Life: The History of Gay Porn Cinema from Beefcake to Hardcore* (Philadelphia: Running Press, 2009), 214; Robert J. Stoller and I. S. Levine, *Coming Attractions: The Making of an X-Rated Video* (New Haven, CT: Yale University Press, 1996), 214.
5. Noah Berlatsky, "Ex Porn Stars Are the 99 Percent," *The Atlantic*, September 13, 2012, accessed June 9, 2014, http://www.theatlantic.com/entertainment/archive/2012/09/ex-porn-stars-are-the-99-percent/262349/. On feminist attempts to equitably improve the working conditions for sex workers in the porn industry, see the many essays by porn practitioners in Tristan Taormino, Celine Parreñas Shimizu, Constance Penley, and Mireille Miller-Young, eds, *The Feminist Porn Book: The Politics of Producing Pleasure* (New York: The Feminist Press, 2013). Begun in 2013, the nonprofit Golden Age Appreciation Fund (http://tgaafund.blogspot.com) also runs periodic fundraisers for Golden Age porn stars who have fallen on hard times, allowing fans to monetarily give back to them.
6. Steve Green, "Settlement Reached in Wage Case Involving Las Vegas Adult Clubs," *Las Vegas Sun*, October 28, 2010, accessed June 9, 2014, http://www.lasvegassun.com/news/2010/oct/28/settlement-reached-wage-case-involving-las-vegas-a/; Tom Horgen and Jennifer Bjorhus, "The King of Clubs," *Star Tribune* (Minneapolis), July 19, 2011, accessed June 9, 2014, http://www.startribune.com/entertainment/dining/124498918.html (quoted).
7. Ralph Blumenthal, "Sex Museum Says It Is Here to Educate," *New York Times*, September 19, 2002, http://www.nytimes.com/2002/09/19/arts/sex-museum-says-it-is-here-to-educate.html.
8. Steve Green, "Sex Industry Figure Sues over Donations to Erotic Heritage Museum," *Vegas Inc*, November 4, 2011, accessed June 9, 2014, http://www.vegasinc.com/business/legal/2011/nov/04/sex-industry-figure-sues-over-donations-las-vegas-/.
9. Ken Miller, "Las Vegas' Erotic Heritage Museum Closes Its Doors," *Las Vegas Weekly*, February 19, 2014, accessed June 9, 2014, http://www.lasvegasweekly.com/as-we-see-it/2014/feb/19/las-vegas-erotic-heritage-museum-closes-its-doors/; Wesley Juhl, "Las Vegas Sex Museum Goes Dormant after Operators' Relationship Sours," *Las Vegas Review-Journal*, February 20, 2014, accessed June 9, 2014, http://www.reviewjournal.com/news/las-vegas-sex-museum-goes-dormant-after-operators-relationship-sours (quoted).
10. Wesley Juhl, "After Melodramatic Closing, Erotic Museum Set to Reopen Saturday," *Las Vegas Review-Journal*, June 6, 2014, accessed June 9, 2014, http://www.reviewjournal.com/news/las-vegas/after-melodramatic-closing-erotic-museum-set-reopen-Saturday.
11. Eithne Johnson, "The 'Sexarama': Or Sex Education as an Environmental Multimedia Experience," in *Sex Scene: Media and the Sexual Revolution*, ed. Eric Schaefer (Durham, NC: Duke University Press, 2014), 265–96.

12 Distribpix did, however, curate a temporary 2008 exhibit of *Deep Inside Annie Sprinkle* ephemera, which prominently displayed her feature-length on-screen commentary, to commemorate their Platinum Elite reissue. See Steven Morowitz, "Annie Sprinkle Museum Exhibit—Needs a home!!" *The Distribpix Blog*, posted March 7, 2011, accessed June 9, 2014, http://distribpixblog.wordpress.com/2011/03/07/annie-sprinkle-museum-exhibit-needs-a-home/.
13 Jim Holliday, *Only the Best: Jim Holliday's Adult Video Almanac and Trivia Treasury* (Van Nuys, CA: Cal Vista Publications, 1986), 111.
14 For a discussion of *Deep Inside Porn Stars* and Club 90, which first developed from a baby shower held for Hamilton, see Annette Fuentes and Margaret Schrage, "Deep Inside Porn Stars: Veronica Hart, Gloria Leonard, Kelly Nichols, Candida Royalle, Annie Sprinkle, and Veronica Vera Interviewed," *Jump Cut*, no. 32 (1987), accessed February 1, 2014, http://www.ejumpcut.org/archive/onlinessays/JC32folder/PornWomenInt.html; Shannon Bell, *Reading, Writing, and Rewriting the Prostitute Body* (Bloomington: Indiana University Press, 1994), 143–47.
15 Jane Hamilton, personal communication, January 31, 2014.
16 Escoffier, *Bigger than Life*, 198.
17 Gregory Storms, "Bare-ing Witness: Bareback Porn and the Ethics of Watching," in *New Views on Pornography: Sexuality, Politics, and the Law*, eds Lynn Comella and Shira Tarrant (Santa Barbara, CA: Praeger, 2015), 376–79. Quote at 376, 369–81.
18 Richard Verrier, "Porn Production Plummets in Los Angeles," *Los Angeles Times*, August 6, 2014, http://www.latimes.com/entertainment/envelope/cotown/la-et-ct-onlocation-la-porn-industry-20140806-story.html.
19 For earlier, VHS-era examples of these more diverse appropriations, written by a sex-positive queer woman for the largely hetero-male *Penthouse Forum* readership, see Susie Bright's collection of early porn criticism, *Susie Bright's Erotic Screen, Volume I: 1967–1989: The Golden Hardcore & Shimmering Dyke-Core* (Santa Cruz, CA: Bright Stuff, 2011), Kindle edition. On the queer pleasures of straight porn viewership, also see Jane Ward, "Queer Feminist Pigs: A Spectator's Manifesta," in *The Feminist Porn Book*, 130–39.
20 My cue here comes from Elizabeth Freeman, *Time Binds: Queer Temporalities, Queer Histories* (Durham, NC: Duke University Press, 2010), 95–96, 120, 123; Tim Dean, *Unlimited Intimacy: Reflections on the Subculture of Barebacking* (Chicago: University of Chicago Press, 2009), 149.
21 Jacy Catlin, "Jacy's new Alpha Blue Archives thread," AV Maniacs, comment posted on August 3, 2007, accessed January 12, 2014, http://www.avmaniacs.com/forums/showthread.php?t=30910&page=8. *Sic* throughout.
22 Peter Alilunas, "Smutty Little Movies: The Creation and Regulation of Adult Video, 1976–1986" (Ph.D. diss., University of Michigan, 2013), 30–47.
23 Giuliana Bruno, *Streetwalking on a Ruined Map: Cultural Theory and the City Films of Elvira Notari* (Princeton, NJ: Princeton University Press, 1993).
24 Jacqueline Stewart, "Discovering Black Film History: Tracing the Tyler, Texas Black Film Collection," *Film History* 23, no. 2 (2011): 151–55, 165–66. Consider as well that, alongside its exploitation/adult offerings, Something Weird Video distributes a number of these same race films in an "All Black Cast Classics" category of its catalogue.

25 Giovanna Fossati, *From Grain to Pixel: The Archival Life of Film in Transition* (Amsterdam: Amsterdam University Press, 2009), 128; Janna Jones, *The Past Is a Moving Picture: Preserving the Twentieth Century on Film* (Gainesville: University Press of Florida, 2012), 155.
26 Caitlin Shanley, "Clandestine Catalogs: A Bibliography of Porn Research Collections," in *Porn Archives*, eds Tim Dean, Steven Ruszczycky, and David Squires (Durham, NC: Duke University Press, 2014), 441–55.
27 Linda Williams, "Pornography, Porno, Porn: Thoughts on a Weedy Field," *Porn Studies* 1, no. 1–2 (2014): 30.

Selected Bibliography

Acland, Charles R., and Haidee Wasson, eds. *Useful Cinema*. Durham, NC: Duke University Press, 2011.
Alilunas, Peter. "Smutty Little Movies: The Creation and Regulation of Adult Video, 1976–1986." Ph.D. diss., University of Michigan, 2013.
Alilunas, Peter. "Ephemerata: *Ginger's Private Party* Flyer (circa 1985)." *Film History* 26, no. 3 (2014): 144–55.
"AMIA Code of Ethics." AMIA: The Association of Moving Image Archivists. Accessed December 6, 2013. http://www.amianet.org/sites/all/files/Code%20of%20Ethics%20-%20100101.pdf.
Anderson, Chris. *The Long Tail: Why the Future of Business Is Selling Less of More*. New York: Hyperion, 2006.
Andrews, David. *Soft in the Middle: The Contemporary Softcore Feature in Its Contexts*. Columbus: Ohio State University Press, 2006.
Andrews, David. "What Soft-Core Can Do for Porn Studies." *The Velvet Light Trap* no. 59 (2007): 51–61.
Andrews, David. "Toward a More Valid Definition of 'Pornography.'" *Journal of Popular Culture* 45, no. 3 (2012): 457–77.
Andrews, David. *Theorizing Art Cinemas: Foreign, Cult, Avant-Garde, and Beyond*. Austin: University of Texas Press, 2013.
Assmann, Aleida. "Canon and Archive." In *Cultural Memory Studies: An International and Interdisciplinary Handbook*, edited by Astrid Erll and Ansgar Nünnung, 97–107. Berlin: Walter de Gruyter, 2008.
Attwood, Feona. "No Money Shot? Commerce, Pornography, and New Sex Taste Cultures." *Sexualities* 10, no. 4 (2007a): 441–56.
Attwood, Feona. "'Other' or 'One of Us'? The Porn User in Public and Academic Discourse." *Participations: Journal of Audience and Reception Studies* 4, no. 1 (2007b). Accessed April 8, 2013. http://www.participations.org/Volume%204/Issue%201/4_01_attwood.htm.
Attwood, Feona, and Clarissa Smith. "Emotional Truths and Thrilling Slide Shows: The Resurgence of Antiporn Feminism." In *The Feminist Porn Book: The Politics of Producing Pleasure*, edited by Tristan Taormino, Celine Parreñas Shimizu, Constance Penley, and Mireille Miller-Young, 41–57. New York: The Feminist Press, 2013.
Barber, Stephen. *Abandoned Images: Film and Film's End*. London: Reaktion Books, 2010.
Barker, Jennifer M. *The Tactile Eye: Touch and the Cinematic Experience*. Berkeley: University of California Press, 2009.
Barker, Martin. "Embracing Rape: Understanding the Attractions of Exploitation Movies." In *Controversial Images: Media Representations on the Edge*, edited by Feona Attwood, Vincent Campbell, I. Q. Hunter, and Sharon Lockyer, 217–38. New York: Palgrave Macmillan, 2013.
Barker, Martin. "The 'Problem' of Sexual Fantasies." *Porn Studies* 1, no. 1–2 (2014): 143–60.
Barthes, Roland. *Image/Music/Text*. Translated by Stephen Heath. New York: Hill and Wang, 1977.

Barthes, Roland. *Camera Lucida: Reflections on Photography*. Translated by Richard Howard. New York: Hill and Wang, 1981.
Baudrillard, Jean. "The System of Collecting." In *The Cultures of Collecting*, edited by John Elsner and Roger Cardinal, 7–24. Cambridge, MA: Harvard University Press, 1994.
Bazin, André. "The Ontology of the Photographic Image." Translated by Hugh Gray. *Film Quarterly* 13, no. 4 (1960): 4–9.
Bell, Shannon. *Reading, Writing, and Rewriting the Prostitute Body*. Bloomington: Indiana University Press, 1994.
Betz, Mark. "Art, Exploitation, Underground." In *Defining Cult Movies: The Cultural Politics of Oppositional Taste*, edited by Mark Jancovich, Antonio Lázaro Reboll, Julian Stringer, and Andy Willis, 202–22. Manchester: Manchester University Press, 2003.
Biasin, Enrico, Giovanna Maina, and Federico Zecca, eds. *Porn after Porn: Contemporary Alternative Pornographies*. Milano-Udine: Mimesis International, 2014.
Blake, Roger. *The Porno Movies*. Cleveland: Century Books, 1970.
Bolter, Jay David, and Richard Grusin. *Remediation: Understanding New Media*. Cambridge, MA: MIT Press, 2000.
Bordwell, David. *Pandora's Digital Box: Films, Files, and the Future of Movies*. Madison, WI: Irvington Way Institute Press, 2012.
Boyreau, Jacques. *Sexytime: The Post-porn Rise of the Pornoisseur*. Seattle: Fantagraphics Books, 2012.
Bright, Susie. *Susie Bright's Erotic Screen, Volume I: 1967–1989: The Golden Hardcore & Shimmering Dyke-Core*. Santa Cruz, CA: Bright Stuff, 2011.
Brinkmann, Tom. *Bad Mags: The Strangest, Sleaziest, Most Unusual Periodicals Ever Published!, Volume 1*. London: Headpress, 2008.
Bruno, Giuliana. *Streetwalking on a Ruined Map: Cultural Theory and the City Films of Elvira Notari*. Princeton, NJ: Princeton University Press, 1993.
Bruno, Giuliana. *Atlas of Emotion: Journeys in Art, Architecture, and Film*. New York: Verso, 2002.
Buonanno, Milly. *The Age of Television: Experiences and Theories*. Translated by Jennifer Radice. Bristol: Intellect Books, 2008.
Burns Bright, Jennifer, and Ronan Crowley. "'A Quantity of Offensive Matter': Private Cases in Public Places." In *Porn Archives*, edited by Tim Dean, Steven Ruszczycky, and David Squires, 103–26. Durham, NC: Duke University Press, 2014.
Buszek, Maria Elena. *Pin-Up Grrrls: Feminism, Sexuality, Popular Culture*. Durham, NC: Duke University Press, 2006.
Capino, José B. "Seminal Fantasies: Wakefield Poole, Pornography, Independent Cinema, and the Avant-Garde." In *Contemporary American Independent Film: From the Margins to the Mainstream*, edited by Chris Holmlund and Justin Wyatt, 155–73. New York: Routledge, 2005.
Carlson, Marla. "Performative Pornography: Annie Sprinkle Reads Her Movies." *Text and Performance Quarterly* 19, no. 3 (1999): 236–47.
Chappell, Fred. "Twenty-Six Propositions about Skin Flicks." In *Man and the Movies*, edited by W. R. Robinson with George Garrett, 53–59. Baton Rouge: Louisiana State University Press, 1967.
Cherchi Usai, Paolo. *The Death of Cinema: History, Cultural Memory, and the Digital Dark Age*. London: British Film Institute, 2001.
Cherry, Brigid. "Subcultural Tastes, Genre Boundaries, and Fan Canons." In *The Shifting Definitions of Genre: Essays on Labeling Films, Television Shows, and Media*, edited by Lincoln Geraghty and Mark Jancovich, 201–15. Jefferson, NC: McFarland, 2008.

Church, David. "Afterword: Memory, Genre, and Self-Narrativization; or, Why I Should Be a More Content Horror Fan." In *American Horror Film: The Genre at the Turn of the Millennium*, edited by Steffen Hantke, 235–42. Jackson: University Press of Mississippi, 2010.

Church, David. "'This Thing of Ours': Heterosexuality, Recreational Sex, and the Survival of Adult Movie Theaters." *Media Fields Journal* no. 8 (2014). Accessed November 16, 2014. http://mediafieldsjournal.squarespace.com/this-thing-of-ours/.

Church, David. *Grindhouse Nostalgia: Memory, Home Video, and Exploitation Film Fandom*. Edinburgh: Edinburgh University Press, 2015.

"Code of Ethics." FIAF: International Federation of Film Archives. Accessed December 6, 2013. http://www.fiafnet.org/uk/members/ethics.html.

Cohen, Emily. "The Orphanista Manifesto: Orphan Films and the Politics of Reproduction." *American Anthropologist* 106, no. 4 (2004): 719–31.

Connerton, Paul. "Seven Types of Forgetting." *Memory Studies* 1, no. 1 (2008): 59–71.

Coopersmith, Jonathan. "Pornography, Technology, and Progress." *ICON* 4 (1998): 94–125.

Crafton, Donald. "McCay and Keaton: Colligating, Conjecturing, and Conjuring." *Film History* 25, no. 1–2 (2013): 31–44.

Dean, Tim. *Unlimited Intimacy: Reflections on the Subculture of Barebacking*. Chicago: University of Chicago Press, 2009.

Dean, Tim. "Introduction: Pornography, Technology, Archive." In *Porn Archives*, edited by Tim Dean, Steven Ruszczycky, and David Squires, 1–26. Durham, NC: Duke University Press, 2014.

Deleuze, Gilles, and Felix Guattari. *A Thousand Plateaus: Capitalism and Schizophrenia*. Translated by Brian Massumi. London: Continuum, 2004.

D'Emilio, John, and Estelle B. Freedman. *Intimate Matters: A History of Sexuality in America*, 2nd ed. Chicago: University of Chicago Press, 1997.

Desjardins, Mary. "Systematizing Scandal: *Confidential* Magazine, Stardom, and the State of California." In *Headline Hollywood: A Century of Film Scandal*, edited by Adrienne L. McLean and David A. Cook, 206–31. New Brunswick, NJ: Rutgers University Press, 2001.

Desjardins, Mary. "Ephemeral Culture/eBay Culture: Film Collectibles and Fan Investments." In *Everyday eBay: Culture, Collecting, and Desire*, edited by Ken Hillis, Michael Petit, and Nathan Scott Epley, 31–43. New York: Routledge, 2006.

Despentes, Virginie. *King Kong Theory*. Translated by Stéphanie Benson. New York: The Feminist Press, 2010.

Di Lauro, Al, and Gerald Rabkin. *Dirty Movies: An Illustrated History of the Stag Film, 1915–1970*. New York: Chelsea House, 1976.

Downing, Lisa. *Desiring the Dead: Necrophilia and Nineteenth-Century French Literature*. Oxford: Legenda, 2003.

Earle, David M. *All Man! Hemingway, 1950s Men's Magazines, and the Masculine Persona*. Kent, OH: Kent State University Press, 2009a.

Earle, David M. *Re-covering Modernism: Pulps, Paperbacks, and the Prejudice of Form*. Burlington, VT: Ashgate, 2009b.

Edmondson, Ray. *Audiovisual Archiving: Philosophy and Principles*. Paris: UNESCO, 2004. Accessed December 6, 2013. http://www.fiafnet.org/images/tinyUpload/E-Resources/Official-Documents/Philosophy-of-Audiovisual-Archiving_UNESCO.pdf.

Edwards, Elizabeth. "Photographs as Objects of Memory." In *The Object Reader*, edited by Fiona Candlin and Raiford Guins, 331–42. London: Routledge, 2009.

Egan, Kate. *Trash or Treasure? Censorship and the Changing Meanings of the Video Nasties*. Manchester: Manchester University Press, 2007.

Ehrenreich, Barbara. *The Hearts of Men: American Dreams and the Flight from Commitment*. New York: Anchor, 1983.

Elsaesser, Thomas. "Cinephilia or the Uses of Disenchantment." In *Cinephilia: Movies, Love, and Memory*, edited by Marijke de Valck and Malte Hagener, 27–43. Amsterdam: Amsterdam University Press, 2005.

Enticknap, Leo. *Film Restoration: The Culture and Science of Audiovisual Heritage*. New York: Palgrave Macmillan, 2013.

Epley, Nathan Scott. "Pin-Ups, Retro-chic, and the Consumption of Irony." In *Pornification: Sex and Sexuality in Media Culture*, edited by Susanna Paasonen, Kaarina Nikunen, and Laura Saarenmaa, 45–57. Oxford: Berg, 2007.

Escoffier, Jeffrey. *Bigger Than Life: The History of Gay Porn Cinema from Beefcake to Hardcore*. Philadelphia: Running Press, 2009.

Felleman, Susan. *Art in the Cinematic Imagination*. Austin: University of Texas Press, 2006.

Ferreday, Debra. "'Showing the Girl': The New Burlesque." *Feminist Theory* 9, no. 1 (2008): 47–65.

Film World Magazine's Famous X-Rated Video Directory. Los Angeles: Holloway House, 1985.

Fossati, Giovanna. *From Grain to Pixel: The Archival Life of Film in Transition*. Amsterdam: Amsterdam University Press, 2009.

Foucault, Michel. *The History of Sexuality, Vol. 1: An Introduction*. Translated by Robert Hurley. New York: Vintage, 1990.

Fraterrigo, Elizabeth. Playboy *and the Making of the Good Life in Modern America*. New York: Oxford University Press, 2009.

Freeman, Elizabeth. *Time Binds: Queer Temporalities, Queer Histories*. Durham, NC: Duke University Press, 2010.

Frick, Caroline. *Saving Cinema: The Politics of Preservation*. Oxford: Oxford University Press, 2011.

Friedman, David F., with Don de Nevi. *A Youth in Babylon: Confessions of a Trash-Film King*. Buffalo, NY: Prometheus Books, 1990.

Fuentes, Annette, and Margaret Schrage. "Deep Inside Porn Stars: Veronica Hart, Gloria Leonard, Kelly Nichols, Candida Royalle, Annie Sprinkle, and Veronica Vera Interviewed." *Jump Cut* no. 32 (1987). Accessed February 1, 2014. http://www.ejumpcut.org/archive/onlinessays/JC32folder/PornWomenInt.html.

Fuller, Kathryn. *At the Picture Show: Small-Town Audiences and the Creation of Movie Fan Culture*. Washington, DC: Smithsonian Institution Press, 1996.

Gaines, Jane M. "Machines That Make the Body Do Things." In *More Dirty Looks: Gender, Pornography, and Power*, edited by Pamela Church Gibson, 31–44. London: British Film Institute, 2004.

Gaines, Jane M. "Early Cinema's Heyday of Copying: The Too Many Copies of *L'Arroseur arrosé* (*The Waterer Watered*)." *Cultural Studies* 20, no. 2–3 (2006): 227–44.

Geraghty, Lincoln. *Cult Collectors: Nostalgia, Fandom, and Collecting Popular Culture*. London: Routledge, 2014.

Gifford, Justin. *Pimping Fictions: African American Crime Literature and the Untold Story of Black Pulp Publishing*. Philadelphia: Temple University Press, 2013.

Giles, Dennis. "Pornographic Space: The Other Place." In *The 1977 Film Studies Annual: Part 2*, 52–66. Pleasantville, NY: Redgrave, 1977.

Gorfinkel, Elena. "Radley Metzger's 'Elegant Arousal': Taste, Aesthetic Distinction, and Sexploitation." In *Underground U.S.A.: Filmmaking beyond the Hollywood Canon*, edited by Xavier Mendik and Steven Jay Schneider, 26–39. London: Wallflower Press, 2002.

Gorfinkel, Elena. "The Future of Anachronism: Todd Haynes and the Magnificent Andersons." In *Cinephilia: Movies, Love, and Memory*, edited by Marijke de Valck and Malte Hagener, 153–67. Amsterdam: Amsterdam University Press, 2005.

Gorfinkel, Elena. "'Indecent Desires': Sexploitation Cinema, 1960s Film Culture, and the Adult Film Audience." Ph.D. diss., New York University, 2008.

Gorfinkel, Elena. "Arousal in Ruins: *The Color of Love* and the Haptic Object of Film History." *World Picture* no. 4 (2010). Accessed March 17, 2012. http://www.worldpicturejournal.com/WP_4/Gorfinkel.html.

Gorfinkel, Elena. "'Dated Sexuality': Anna Biller's *Viva* and the Retrospective Life of Sexploitation Cinema." *Camera Obscura* 26, no. 3 (2011): 95–135.

Gorfinkel, Elena. "The Body's Failed Labor: Performance Work in Sexploitation Cinema." *Framework* 53, no. 1 (2012): 79–98.

Gracy, Karen F. *Film Preservation: Competing Definitions of Value, Use, and Practice.* Chicago: Society of American Archivists, 2007.

Gray, Jonathan. *Show Sold Separately: Promos, Spoilers, and Other Media Paratexts.* New York: New York University Press, 2010.

Greenberg, Joshua M. *From Betamax to Blockbuster: Video Stores and the Invention of Movies on Video.* Cambridge, MA: MIT Press, 2008.

Guins, Raiford. "Blood and Black Gloves on Shiny Discs: New Media, Old Tastes, and the Remediation of Italian Horror Films in the United States." In *Horror International*, edited by Steven Jay Schneider and Tony Williams, 15–32. Detroit: Wayne State University Press, 2005.

Gunning, Tom. "The Cinema of Attractions: Early Film, Its Spectator, and the Avant-Garde." In *Early Cinema: Space, Frame, Narrative*, edited by Thomas Elsaesser, 56–62. London: British Film Institute, 1990.

Haberski, Jr., Raymond J. "Critics and the Sex Scene." In *Sex Scene: Media and the Sexual Revolution*, edited by Eric Schaefer, 383–406. Durham, NC: Duke University Press, 2014.

Hanson, Dian, ed. *Vanessa Del Rio: Fifty Years of Slightly Slutty Behavior.* Cologne: TASCHEN Books, 2007.

Harrington, C. Lee, and Denise D. Bielby. "A Life Course Perspective on Fandom." *International Journal of Cultural Studies* 13, no. 5 (2010): 429–50.

Harrison, John. *Hip Pocket Sleaze: The Lurid World of Vintage Adult Paperbacks.* London: Headpress, 2011.

Harvey, James. *Pornography for Fun and Profit.* Los Angeles: Edka Books, 1967.

Hastie, Amelie. *Cupboards of Curiosity: Women, Recollection, and Film History.* Durham, NC: Duke University Press, 2007.

Hawkins, Joan. *Cutting-Edge: Art-Horror and the Horrific Avant-Garde.* Minneapolis: University of Minnesota Press, 2000.

Heffernan, Kevin. "Seen as a Business: Adult Film's Historical Framework and Foundations." In *New Views on Pornography: Sexuality, Politics, and the Law*, edited by Lynn Comella and Shira Tarrant, 37–55. Santa Barbara, CA: Praeger, 2015.

Herbert, Daniel. *Videoland: Movie Culture at the American Video Store*. Berkeley: University of California Press, 2014.
Herzog, Amy. "In the Flesh: Space and Embodiment in the Pornographic Peep Show Arcade." *The Velvet Light Trap* no. 62 (2008): 29–43.
Hilderbrand, Lucas. *Inherent Vice: Bootleg Histories of Videotape and Copyright*. Durham, NC: Duke University Press, 2009.
Hilderbrand, Lucas. "Historical Fantasies: 1970s Gay Pornography in the Archives." In *Porno Chic and the Sex Wars: American Sexual Representation in the 1970s.*, edited by Carolyn Bronstein and Whitney Strub. Amherst: University of Massachusetts Press, 2016.
Hills, Matt. *Fan Cultures*. London: Routledge, 2002.
Hills, Matt. "Patterns of Surprise: The 'Aleatory Object' in Psychoanalytic Ethnography and Cyclical Fandom." *American Behavioral Scientist* 48, no. 7 (2005a): 801–21.
Hills, Matt. *The Pleasures of Horror*. London: Continuum, 2005b.
Hills, Matt. "Para-Paracinema: The *Friday the 13th* Film Series as Other to Trash and Legitimate Film Cultures." In *Sleaze Artists: Cinema at the Margins of Taste, Style, and Politics*, edited by Jeffrey Sconce, 219–39. Durham, NC: Duke University Press, 2007.
Holliday, Jim. *How to Build Your X-Rated Video Library*. Beverly Hills, CA: Skull Mountain Publishing, 1980.
Holliday, Jim. *Only the Best: Jim Holliday's Adult Video Almanac and Trivia Treasury*. Van Nuys, CA: Cal Vista Publications, 1986.
Hollows, Joanne. "The Masculinity of Cult." In *Defining Cult Movies: The Cultural Politics of Oppositional Taste*, edited by Mark Jancovich, Antonio Lázaro Reboll, Julian Stringer, and Andy Willis, 35–53. Manchester: Manchester University Press, 2003.
Hoyt, Eric. "The Future of Selling the Past: Studio Libraries in the 21st Century." *Jump Cut* no. 52 (2010). Accessed May 22, 2014. http://www.ejumpcut.org/archive/jc52.2010/hoytStudioLibraries/index.html.
Huffer, Lynne. *Are the Lips a Grave? A Queer Feminist on the Ethics of Sex*. New York: Columbia University Press, 2013.
Huyssen, Andreas. *After the Great Divide: Modernism, Mass Culture, Postmodernism*. Bloomington: Indiana University Press, 1986.
Huyssen, Andreas. "Present Pasts: Media, Politics, Amnesia." *Public Culture* 12, no. 1 (2000): 21–38.
Jancovich, Mark. "Naked Ambitions: Pornography, Taste, and the Problem of the Middlebrow." *Scope* (June 2001). Accessed March 17, 2011. http://www.scope.nottingham.ac.uk/article.php?issue=jun2001&id=274&section=article.
Jancovich, Mark. "Cult Fictions: Cult Movies, Subcultural Capital, and the Production of Cultural Distinctions." *Cultural Studies* 16, no. 2 (2002): 306–22.
Jenkins, Henry. *Textual Poachers: Television Fans & Participatory Culture*. New York: Routledge, 1992.
Jennings, David. *Skinflicks: The Inside Story of the X-Rated Video Industry*. Bloomington, IN: AuthorHouse, 2000.
Johnson, Eithne. "The 'Sexarama': Or Sex Education as an Environmental Multimedia Experience." In *Sex Scene: Media and the Sexual Revolution*, edited by Eric Schaefer, 265–96. Durham, NC: Duke University Press, 2014.
Jones, Janna. *The Past is a Moving Picture: Preserving the Twentieth Century on Film*. Gainesville: University Press of Florida, 2012.
Jones, William E. *Halsted Plays Himself*. Los Angeles: Semiotext(e), 2011.

Juffer, Jane. *At Home with Pornography: Women, Sex, and Everyday Life*. New York: New York University Press, 1998.
Juffer, Jane. "There's No Place Like Home: Further Developments on the Domestic Front." In *More Dirty Looks: Gender, Pornography, and Power*, edited by Pamela Church Gibson, 45–58. London: British Film Institute, 2004.
Kaite, Berkeley. *Pornography and Difference*. Bloomington: Indiana University Press, 1995.
Kakoudaki, Despina. "Pinup: The American Secret Weapon in World War II." In *Porn Studies*, edited by Linda Williams, 335–69. Durham, NC: Duke University Press, 2004.
Keathley, Christian. *Cinephilia and History, or the Wind in the Trees*. Bloomington: Indiana University Press, 2006.
Kendrick, James. "What Is the Criterion? The Criterion Collection as an Archive of Film as Culture." *Journal of Film and Video* 53, no. 2–3 (2001): 124–39.
Kendrick, James. "Phantom Cinema: Illuminating the Structuring Absences of Film History." *Quarterly Review of Film and Video* 30, no. 1 (2013): 62–73.
Kendrick, Walter. *The Secret Museum: Pornography in Modern Culture*. New York: Viking, 1987.
Kipnis, Laura. *Bound and Gagged: Pornography and the Politics of Fantasy in America*. New York: Grove Press, 1996.
Kipnis, Laura. "She-Male Fantasies and the Aesthetics of Pornography." In *More Dirty Looks: Gender, Pornography, and Power*, edited by Pamela Church Gibson, 204–15. London: British Film Institute, 2004.
Klein, Amanda Ann. *American Film Cycles: Reframing Genres, Screening Social Problems, and Defining Subcultures*. Austin: University of Texas Press, 2011.
Kleinhans, Chuck. "The Change from Film to Video Pornography: Implications for Analysis." In *Pornography: Film and Culture*, edited by Peter Lehman, 154–67. New Brunswick, NJ: Rutgers University Press, 2006.
Kleinhans, Chuck. "Pornography and Documentary: Narrating the Alibi." In *Sleaze Artists: Cinema at the Margins of Taste, Style, and Politics*, edited by Jeffrey Sconce, 96–120. Durham, NC: Duke University Press, 2007.
Klinger, Barbara. *Beyond the Multiplex: Cinema, New Technologies, and the Home*. Berkeley: University of California Press, 2006.
Koch, Gertrud. "The Body's Shadow Realm." Translated by Jan-Christopher Horak and Joyce Rheuban. *October* no. 50 (1989): 3–29.
Kuhn, Annette. *Dreaming of Fred and Ginger: Cinema and Cultural Memory*. New York: New York University Press, 2002.
Landis, Bill, and Michelle Clifford. *Sleazoid Express: A Mind-Twisting Tour through the Grindhouse Cinema of Times Square*. New York: Fireside, 2002.
Lane III, Frederick S. *Obscene Profits: The Entrepreneurs of Pornography in the Cyber Age*. New York: Routledge, 2000.
Larson, Randall D. *Films into Books: An Analytical Bibliography of Film Novelizations, Movie and TV Tie-Ins*. Metuchen, NJ: Scarecrow Press, 1995.
Levine, Lawrence W. *Highbrow/Lowbrow: The Emergence of Cultural Hierarchy in America*. Cambridge, MA: Harvard University Press, 1988.
Lewis, Jon. *Hollywood v. Hard Core: How the Struggle over Censorship Saved the Modern Film Industry*. New York: New York University Press, 2000.
Lindgren, Simon. "Widening the Glory Hole: The Discourse of Online Porn Fandom." In *Porn.com: Making Sense of Online Pornography*, edited by Feona Attwood, 171–85. New York: Peter Lang, 2010.

Lithgow, James, and Colin Heard. "Underground U.S.A. and the Sexploitation Market." *Films and Filming*, August 1969, 18–29.
Lobato, Ramon. *Shadow Economies of Cinema: Mapping Informal Film Distribution*. London: British Film Institute, 2012.
Lowenthal, David. *The Past Is a Foreign Country*. Cambridge, UK: Cambridge University Press, 1985.
Lucas, Tim. *Throat Sprockets*. New York: Dell, 1994.
Marks, Laura U. *The Skin of the Film: Intercultural Cinema, Embodiment, and the Senses*. Durham, NC: Duke University Press, 2000.
Marks, Laura U. *Touch: Sensuous Theory and Multisensory Media*. Minneapolis: University of Minnesota Press, 2002.
Martin, Adrian. "What's Cult Got to Do with It? In Defense of Cinephile Elitism." *Cineaste* 34, no. 1 (2008): 39–42.
Martin, Adrian. "Beyond the Fragments of Cinephilia: Towards a Synthetic Analysis." In *Cinephilia in the Age of Digital Reproduction, Vol. 1*, edited by Scott Balcerzak and Jason Sperb, 30–53. London: Wallflower Press, 2009.
Martinko, Jason S. *The XXX Filmography, 1968–1988*. Jefferson, NC: McFarland, 2013.
McCarty, John. *The Sleaze Merchants: Adventures in Exploitation Filmmaking*. New York: St. Martin's Griffin, 1995.
McDonald, Paul. *Video and DVD Industries*. London: British Film Institute, 2007.
McDonough, Jimmy. *The Ghastly One: The Sex-Gore Netherworld of Filmmaker Andy Milligan*. Chicago: A Cappella Books, 2001.
McKee, Alan. "The Fans of Cultural Theory." In *Fandom: Identities and Communities in a Mediated World*, edited by Jonathan Gray, Cornel Sandvoss, and C. Lee Harrington, 88–97. New York: New York University Press, 2007.
McKee, Alan, Katherine Albury, and Catharine Lumby. *The Porn Report*. Carlton: Melbourne University Press, 2008.
McLean, Adrienne L. "'New Films in Story Form': Movie Story Magazines and Spectatorship." *Cinema Journal* 42, no. 3 (2003): 3–26.
McNair, Brian. *Porno? Chic! How Pornography Changed the World and Made It a Better Place*. New York: Routledge, 2013.
McNeil, Legs, and Jennifer Osbourne with Peter Pavia. *The Other Hollywood: The Uncensored Oral History of the Porn Film Industry*. New York: HarperCollins, 2005.
Miller-Young, Mireille. *A Taste for Brown Sugar: Black Women in Pornography*. Durham, NC: Duke University Press, 2014.
Moretti, Franco. "The Slaughterhouse of Literature." *Modern Language Quarterly* 61, no. 1 (2000): 207–27.
Morrison, James. "After the Revolution: On the Fate of Cinephilia." *Michigan Quarterly Review* 44, no. 3 (2005): 393–413.
Muller, Eddie, and Daniel Faris. *Grindhouse: The Forbidden World of "Adults Only" Cinema*. New York: St. Martin's Griffin, 1996.
Mulvey, Laura. "Visual Pleasure and Narrative Cinema." *Screen* 16, no. 3 (1975): 6–18.
Naremore, James. *More than Night: Film Noir in Its Contexts*. Berkeley: University of California Press, 2008.
Nash, Hester. "On How a Longtime Interest in Vintage Porn Launched a Unique Site on the Internet." In *Naked Ambition: Women Who Are Changing Pornography*, edited by Carly Milne, 207–20. New York: Carroll & Graf, 2005.

Nash, Jennifer C. *The Black Body in Ecstasy: Reading Race, Reading Pornography*. Durham, NC: Duke University Press, 2014.
Nead, Lynda. "'Above the Pulp-Line': The Cultural Significance of Erotic Art." In *More Dirty Looks: Gender, Pornography, and Power*, edited by Pamela Church Gibson, 216–23. London: British Film Institute, 2004.
Nelson, Jill C. *Golden Goddesses: 25 Legendary Women of Classic Erotic Cinema, 1968–1985*. Duncan, OK: BearManor Media, 2012.
Nicholson, Geoff. *Sex Collectors: The Secret World of Consumers, Connoisseurs, Curators, Creators, Dealers, Bibliographers, and Accumulators of "Erotica."* New York: Simon & Schuster, 2006.
Nishikawa, Kinohi. "Reading the Street: Iceberg Slim, Donald Goines, and the Rise of Black Pulp Fiction." Ph.D. diss., Duke University, 2010.
Nobus, Dany. "Over My Dead Body: On the Histories and Cultures of Necrophilia." In *Inappropriate Relationships: The Unconventional, the Disapproved, and the Forbidden*, edited by Robin Goodwin and Duncan Cramer, 173–92. Mahwah, NJ: Lawrence Erlbaum Associates, 2002.
O'Donoghue, Darragh. "Paradise Regained: *Queen Kelly* and the Lure of the 'Lost' Film." *Senses of Cinema* no. 27 (2003): http://sensesofcinema.com/2003/27/queen_kelly/.
O'Toole, Laurence. *Pornotopia: Porn, Sex, Technology, and Desire*. London: Serpent's Tail, 1998.
Orgeron, Marsha. "Making *It* in Hollywood: Clara Bow, Fandom, and Consumer Culture." *Cinema Journal* 42, no. 4 (2003): 76–97.
Orgeron, Marsha. "'You Are Invited to Participate': Interactive Fandom in the Age of the Movie Magazine." *Journal of Film and Video* 61, no. 3 (2009): 3–23.
Osgerby, Bill. *Playboys in Paradise: Masculinity, Youth, and Leisure-Style in Modern America*. New York: Berg, 2001.
Paasonen, Susanna. *Carnal Resonance: Affect and Online Pornography*. Cambridge, MA: MIT Press, 2011.
Paasonen, Susanna, and Laura Saarenmaa. "The Golden Age of Porn: Nostalgia and History in Cinema." In *Pornification: Sex and Sexuality in Media Culture*, edited by Susanna Paasonen, Kaarina Nikunen, and Laura Saarenmaa, 23–32. Oxford: Berg, 2007.
Patterson, Zabet. "Going On-Line: Consuming Pornography in the Digital Era." In *Porn Studies*, edited by Linda Williams, 104–23. Durham, NC: Duke University Press, 2004.
Patton, Cindy. *L.A. Plays Itself/Boys in the Sand*. Queer Film Classics. Vancouver: Arsenal Pulp Press, 2014.
Peterson, Richard A., and Roger M. Kern. "Changing Highbrow Taste: From Snob to Omnivore." *American Sociological Review* 61, no. 5 (1996): 900–07.
Pierce, David. "Forgotten Faces: Why Some of Our Cinema Heritage Is Part of the Public Domain." *Film History* 19, no. 2 (2007): 125–43.
Pierce, David. *The Survival of American Silent Feature Films: 1912–1929*. Washington, DC: Council on Library and Information Resources and the Library of Congress, 2013.
Pitzulo, Carrie. *Bachelors and Bunnies: The Sexual Politics of Playboy*. Chicago: University of Chicago Press, 2011.
Powell, Ryan. "Man Country: A Social History of Seventies Gay Cinema." Ph.D. diss., King's College London, 2010.
Read, Jacinda. "The Cult of Masculinity: From Fan-Boys to Academic Bad-Boys." In *Defining Cult Movies: The Cultural Politics of Oppositional Taste*, edited by

Mark Jancovich, Antonio Lázaro Reboll, Julian Stringer, and Andy Willis, 54–70. Manchester: Manchester University Press, 2003.
The Report of the Commission on Obscenity and Pornography. New York: Bantam Books, 1970.
Rimmer, Robert H. *The X-Rated Videotape Guide*. New York: Arlington House, 1984.
Robinson, Sally. "Feminized Men and Inauthentic Women." *Genders* no. 53 (2011). Accessed March 17, 2011. http://www.genders.org/g53/g53_robinson.html.
Ross, Andrew. *No Respect: Intellectuals and Popular Culture*. New York: Routledge, 1989.
Rotsler, William. *Contemporary Erotic Cinema*. New York: Penthouse/Ballantine, 1973.
Rounthwaite, Adair. "From This Body to Yours: Porn, Affect, and Performance Art Documentation." *Camera Obscura* 26, no. 3 (2011): 63–93.
Rubin, Roger H. "Alternative Lifestyles Revisited, or Whatever Happened to Swingers, Group Marriages, and Communes?" *Journal of Family Issues* 22, no. 6 (2001): 711–26.
Sabo, Anne G. *After Pornified: How Women Are Transforming Pornography & Why It Matters*. London: Zero Books, 2012.
Sandvoss, Cornel. *Fans: The Mirror of Consumption*. Cambridge, UK: Polity Press, 2005.
Schaefer, Eric. "The Inside Story of Storefront Theaters." In *Something Weird Video Blue Book*, 2–6. Seattle: Something Weird Video, 1997.
Schaefer, Eric. *"Bold! Daring! Shocking! True!" A History of Exploitation Films, 1919–1959*. Durham, NC: Duke University Press, 1999.
Schaefer, Eric. "Gauging a Revolution: 16 mm Film and the Rise of the Pornographic Feature." *Cinema Journal* 41, no. 3 (2002): 3–26.
Schaefer, Eric. "Dirty Little Secrets: Scholars, Archivists, and Dirty Movies." *The Moving Image* 5, no. 2 (2005): 79–105.
Schaefer, Eric. "Pandering to the 'Goon Trade': Framing the Sexploitation Audience through Advertising." In *Sleaze Artists: Cinema at the Margins of Taste, Style, and Politics*, edited by Jeffrey Sconce, 19–46. Durham, NC: Duke University Press, 2007a.
Schaefer, Eric. "Plain Brown Wrapper: Adult Films for the Home Market, 1930–1969." In *Looking Past the Screen: Case Studies in American Film History and Method*, edited by Jon Lewis and Eric Smoodin, 201–26. Durham, NC: Duke University Press, 2007b.
Schauer, Bradley. "The Warner Archive and DVD Collecting in the New Home Video Market." *The Velvet Light Trap* no. 70 (2012): 35–48.
Sconce, Jeffrey. "'Trashing' the Academy: Taste, Excess, and an Emerging Politics of Cinematic Style." *Screen* 36, no. 4 (1995): 371–93.
Sconce, Jeffrey. "Introduction." In *Sleaze Artists: Cinema at the Margins of Taste, Style, and Politics*, edited by Jeffrey Sconce, 1–16. Durham, NC: Duke University Press, 2007.
Shanley, Caitlin. "Clandestine Catalogs: A Bibliography of Porn Research Collections." In *Porn Archives*, edited by Tim Dean, Steven Ruszczycky, and David Squires, 441–55. Durham, NC: Duke University Press, 2014.
Sheaffer, Russell. "Smut, Novelty, Indecency: Reworking a History of the Early-Twentieth-Century 'Stag Film.'" *Porn Studies* 1, no. 4 (2014): 346–59.
Shelby, H. C. *Stag Movie Review*. Canoga Park, CA: Viceroy Books, 1970.
Shelton, Emily. "A Star Is Porn: Corpulence, Comedy, and the Homosocial Cult of Adult Film Star Ron Jeremy." *Camera Obscura* 17, no. 3 (2002): 115–46.
Slade, Joseph W. "The Porn Market and Porn Formulas: The Feature Film of the Seventies." *Journal of Popular Film* 6, no. 2 (1977): 168–86.
Slade, Joseph W. "Eroticism and Technological Regression: The Stag Film." *History and Technology* 22, no. 1 (2006): 27–52.

Slide, Anthony. *Nitrate Won't Wait: Film Preservation in the United States*. Jefferson, NC: McFarland, 1992.
Slide, Anthony. *Inside the Hollywood Fan Magazine: A History of Star Makers, Fabricators, and Gossip Mongers*. Jackson: University Press of Mississippi, 2011.
Smith, Clarissa. *One for the Girls! The Pleasures and Practices of Reading Women's Porn*. Bristol: Intellect Books, 2007.
Sobchack, Vivian. "Chasing the Maltese Falcon: On the Fabrications of a Film Prop." *Journal of Visual Culture* 6, no. 2 (2007): 219–46.
Sontag, Susan. "Notes on 'Camp.'" In *The Cult Film Reader*, edited by Ernest Mathijs and Xavier Mendik, 41–52. Maidenhead, UK: Open University Press-McGraw-Hill Education, 2008.
Sperb, Jason, and Scott Balcerzak. "Introduction: Presence of Pleasure." In *Cinephilia in the Age of Digital Reproduction, Vol. 1*, edited by Scott Balcerzak and Jason Sperb, 7–29. London: Wallflower Press, 2009.
Sperb, Jason. "Be Kind … Rewind/or, the A–Zs of an American *Off-Modern Cinephilia*." In *Cinephilia in the Age of Digital Reproduction, Vol. 2*, edited by Scott Balcerzak and Jason Sperb, 71–107. London: Wallflower Press, 2012.
Sprinkle, Annie. *Post-porn Modernist: My 25 Years as a Multimedia Whore*. San Francisco: Cleis Press, 1998.
Sprinkle, Annie. *Hardcore from the Heart: The Pleasures, Profits, and Politics of Sex in Performance*. Edited by Gabrielle Cody. London: Continuum, 2001.
Squires, David. "Pornography in the Library." In *Porn Archives*, edited by Tim Dean, Steven Ruszczycky, and David Squires, 78–99. Durham, NC: Duke University Press, 2014.
Staiger, Janet. *Perverse Spectators: The Practices of Film Reception*. New York: New York University Press, 2000.
Stamp, Shelley. *Movie-Struck Girls: Women and Motion Picture Culture after the Nickelodeon*. Princeton, NJ: Princeton University Press, 2000.
Stanfield, Peter. *Maximum Movies—Pulp Fictions: Film Culture and the Worlds of Samuel Fuller, Mickey Spillane, and Jim Thompson*. New Brunswick, NJ: Rutgers University Press, 2011.
Steedman, Carolyn. *Dust: The Archive and Cultural History*. New Brunswick, NJ: Rutgers University Press, 2002.
Stewart, Jacqueline. "Discovering Black Film History: Tracing the Tyler, Texas Black Film Collection." *Film History* 23, no. 2 (2011): 147–73.
Stine, Scott Aaron. "Stags & Smokers: Collecting 8mm & Super 8 Films." *Filthy Habits: Hardcore & Sexploitation Fare from the 1960s & 1970s* (Fall 2002).
Stine, Scott Aaron. "Index & Current Market Values for *Adam* Magazine (1956–1979)." *Filthy Habits: Hardcore & Sexploitation Fare from the 1960s & 1970s* (Spring 2003): 34–41.
Stoller, Robert J., and I. S. Levine. *Coming Attractions: The Making of an X-Rated Video*. New Haven, CT: Yale University Press, 1993.
Storms, Gregory. "Bare-ing Witness: Bareback Porn and the Ethics of Watching." In *New Views on Pornography: Sexuality, Politics, and the Law*, edited by Lynn Comella and Shira Tarrant, 369–81. Santa Barbara, CA: Praeger, 2015.
Straayer, Chris. "The Seduction of Boundaries: Feminist Fluidity in Annie Sprinkle's Art/Education/Sex." In *More Dirty Looks: Gender, Pornography, and Power*, edited by Pamela Church Gibson, 228–35. London: British Film Institute, 2004.

Strub, Whitney. "The Clearly Obscene and the Queerly Obscene: Heteronormativity and Obscenity in Cold War Los Angeles." *American Quarterly* 60, no. 2 (2008): 373–98.
Stüttgen, Tim, ed. *Post/Porn/Politics*. Berlin: b_books, 2009.
Taormino, Tristan, Celine Parreñas Shimizu, Constance Penley, and Mireille Miller-Young, eds. *The Feminist Porn Book*. New York: The Feminist Press, 2013.
Tashiro, Charles. "Videophilia: What Happens When You Wait for It on Video." *Film Quarterly* 45, no. 1 (1991): 7–17.
Thompson, Dave. *Black and White and Blue: Adult Cinema from the Victorian Age to the VCR*. Toronto: ECW Press, 2007.
Thornton, Sarah. *Club Cultures: Music, Media, and Subcultural Capital*. Middletown, CT: Wesleyan University Press, 1996.
Tryon, Chuck. *On-Demand Culture: Digital Delivery and the Future of Movies*. New Brunswick, NJ: Rutgers University Press, 2013.
Turan, Kenneth, and Stephen F. Zito. *Sinema: American Pornographic Films and the People Who Make Them*. New York: Praeger, 1974.
Vogel, Amos. *Film as a Subversive Art*. New York: Random House, 1974.
Waller, Gregory A. "An Annotated Filmography of R-Rated Sexploitation Films Released during the 1970s." *Journal of Popular Film and Television* 9, no. 2 (1981): 98–112.
Ward, Jane. "Queer Feminist Pigs: A Spectator's Manifesta." In *The Feminist Porn Book*, edited by Tristan Taormino, Celine Parreñas Shimizu, Constance Penley, and Mireille Miller-Young, 130–39. New York: The Feminist Press, 2013.
Wasser, Frederick. *Veni, Vidi, Video: The Hollywood Empire and the VCR*. Austin: University of Texas Press, 2001.
Waugh, Thomas. "Men's Pornography: Gay vs. Straight." *Jump Cut* no. 30 (1985). Accessed July 16, 2015. http://www.ejumpcut.org/archive/onlinessays/JC30folder/PornWaugh.html.
Waugh, Thomas. *Hard to Imagine: Gay Male Eroticism in Photography and Film from Their Beginnings to Stonewall*. New York: Columbia University Press, 1996.
Waugh, Thomas. *The Fruit Machine: Twenty Years of Writings on Queer Cinema*. Durham, NC: Duke University Press, 2000.
Waugh, Thomas. "Homosociality in the Classical American Stag Film: Off-Screen, On-Screen." *Sexualities* 4, no. 3 (2001): 275–92.
Wicke, Jennifer. "Through a Gaze Darkly: Pornography's Academic Market." In *More Dirty Looks: Gender, Pornography, and Power*, edited by Pamela Church Gibson, 176–87. London: British Film Institute, 2004.
Wickham, Phil. "Scrapbooks, Soap Dishes, and Screen Dreams: Ephemera, Everyday Life, and Cinema History." *New Review of Film and Television Studies* 8, no. 3 (2010): 315–30.
Willemen, Paul. *Looks and Frictions: Essays in Cultural Studies and Film Theory*. Bloomington: Indiana University Press, 1994.
Williams, Linda. "A Provoking Agent: The Pornography and Performance Art of Annie Sprinkle." *Social Text* no. 37 (1993): 117–33.
Williams, Linda. *Hard Core: Power, Pleasure, and the "Frenzy of the Visible."* Berkeley: University of California Press, 1999.
Williams, Linda. "Second Thoughts on *Hard Core*: American Obscenity Law and the Scapegoating of Deviance." In *More Dirty Looks: Gender, Pornography, and Power*, edited by Pamela Church Gibson, 165–75. London: British Film Institute, 2004.
Williams, Linda. "'White Slavery' versus the Ethnography of 'Sexworkers': Women in Stag Films at the Kinsey Archive." *The Moving Image* 5, no. 2 (2005): 107–34.

Williams, Linda. *Screening Sex*. Durham, NC: Duke University Press, 2008.
Williams, Linda. "Pornography, Porno, Porn: Thoughts on a Weedy Field." *Porn Studies* 1, no. 1–2 (2014): 24–40.
Williams, Linda Ruth. *The Erotic Thriller in Contemporary Cinema*. Bloomington: Indiana University Press, 2005.
Wyatt, Justin. "Selling 'Atrocious Sexual Behavior': Revising Sexualities in the Marketplace for Adult Film of the 1960s." In *Swinging Single: Representing Sexuality in the 1960s*, edited by Hilary Radner and Moya Luckett, 105–31. Minneapolis: University of Minnesota Press, 1999.
Ziplow, Steven. *The Film Maker's Guide to Pornography*. New York: Drake, 1977.

Index

A&H Video. *See* Distribpix Inc.
academia 10, 15, 17–19, 25, 56–7, 109, 154, 172, 176, 182, 201, 214–15, 246 n.63
Acid Eaters, The 105
action films 114
Adam 74, 78–83, 94–5, 227 n.3, 229 n.35
Adam Film Quarterly/World 65, 70, 80–2, 84–5, 88–96, 98–101, 105, 108, 128, 158, 205
Adam Film World's X-Rated Video Directory 139
Adult Art Films 71
adult bookstores 33, 69, 95, 108, 133, 202. *See also* peepshow arcades
Adult DVD Talk 158
Adult Film Association of America 91–2
Adult Film Critics Awards 206
adult films. *See* pornography
Adult Loop Database 144
Adult Movies Illustrated 67, 73, 75–6, 87
Adult Version of Jekyll & Hide, The 78
Adult Video News (*AVN*) 70, 128–31, 134, 136, 139–42, 153, 158, 165, 201
Adventure 71
Advocate, The 5
AEBN 165
After Hours Cinema. *See* Alternative Cinema
ageplay 187
Agony of Love 80
Ahlberg, Mac 11
Ahwesh, Peggy 50
AIDS/HIV 188–9, 207, 210
Alice in Wonderland 138
Alilunas, Peter 125, 213, 215
All America Distributors Corporation 80
Alpha Blue Archives 141, 151, 153, 164–72, 174, 177, 186–7, 212
Alternative Cinema 141, 170–1, 177, 246 n.66

Amanda by Night 205–6
Amazon.com 174, 177–8
Amazon Prime 191
American Dream, An 82
American Film Institute Catalog of Motion Pictures 109
American Genre Film Archive 123
American Sexual Revolution 50
American Stag 39, 220 n.13
Amero, John 197
Amero, Lem 105, 197
AMG Story, The 221 n.31
Anal Openings and Face Soakings 28
Anatomy of Hell 11
Anderson, Chris 163
Anderson, Paul Thomas 11, 218 n.27
...And God Created Woman 139
Andrews, David 6–7, 25, 28, 58, 68, 83, 156, 171
Anger, Kenneth 55
Animal, The 91
Annie Sprinkle's Herstory of Porn: Reel to Real 183–9, 212
Ann-Margret 79
Anthology Film Archives 171, 196–9, 207
antiporn rhetoric 6, 10, 12, 15, 17, 19, 47, 131, 133, 154–6, 186, 201, 210, 215
Anyone But My Husband 166, 169
Apostolof, Stephen C. 82
Aqua-Nudes, The 74
Aquarius Releasing 114
archives 4, 19–21, 40, 45, 54, 61, 103, 106–7, 109–15, 118, 121–4, 141, 143–5, 147, 149, 152, 164, 170, 175, 187, 192, 194, 202, 204, 213–16, 235 n.19
Arrow Film and Video 113, 131, 134, 141, 165, 182
Ashcroft, John 242 n.3
Ashcroft v. Free Speech Coalition 240 n.100

art cinema 5–6, 8, 11, 24–5, 57, 68, 80–5, 88, 114, 116, 156, 163, 173, 194, 207
Art Films Review 71, 76, 84, 87, 90
ARTISEX 90–1, 116, 158, 232 n.99, 236 n.40
Assmann, Aleida 4
Association of Moving Image Archivists 152, 215
Astral Trip 99–100, 108
Audubon Films 180
auteurism 13, 24, 154–7, 172, 181–2, 187–90, 194, 205, 213
authenticity 13–14, 23, 26, 31, 39, 42, 45–6, 49–50, 54, 58, 143, 146, 148, 153, 180, 183–4, 187
autoeroticism 1–3, 7, 10, 15–18, 24–5, 28, 32–3, 35, 44, 46, 49, 51, 56, 58, 63–5, 72, 74, 155–7, 171, 173, 175–6, 182–5, 187, 190–3, 198–9, 203, 208, 211, 219 n.40, 246 n.66
Auto Focus 56
Avalon, James 205
avant-gardism 5, 24, 40, 45, 49–50, 57, 163, 172, 184, 190, 196
AV Maniacs 158
AVN Awards 202
Avon Dynasty series (Alpha Blue Archives) 166–7, 174
Avon theaters 166
Avon Video 166

Babiole, Cécile 225 n.87
Babyface 169
Babylon Pink 28
Bad Girls Go to Hell 104
Baker, Carroll 79
Bang My White Tight Ass 17 28
Banned (film) 98
Banned (magazine) 71, 81, 83
Barbara Broadcast 24, 133–4, 239 n.92
Barbara Broadcast Too! 205
Barker, Martin 156
Barr, Candy 37
Barred 71
Barrington, Pat 11
Barthes, Roland 31, 58–9, 74

Bataille, Georges 149
Bat Pussy 244 n.39
Baudrillard, Jean 64
Bazin, André 31
B. B. Sales Company 76–7
BDSM 42, 47, 67, 74, 85, 87, 99, 103, 108, 133–6, 161, 166, 181, 223 n.64
Beach Blanket Bingo 87
behaviorism. *See* media effects
Behind the Green Door 10, 34, 139, 204, 229 n.40
Bell, Bare, and Beautiful 74
Bénazéraf, José 82
Bennett, Darlene 104
Bergman, Ingmar 82, 84
bestiality 133, 144, 239 n.91
Bettie Page: Dark Angel 12
Big Apple Releasing 114
Bijou Video 5
Black Love 182
Black, Rob 242 n.3
blaxploitation 93
Blaze Starr Goes Nudist 141
Bloch, Robert 78
blogs. *See* Internet
Blonde Ambition 177–8, 198
Blow-Up 80
Blue Book (magazine) 71
Blue Underground 158
Blue Vanities 37, 140–1
Body of a Female 67, 116
Bogart, Humphrey 208
Bonnie and Clyde 82
Boogie Nights 11, 13, 55–6, 143, 205, 218 n.27
bootlegs 18, 21, 46, 58, 126–7, 135, 140, 142–3, 153, 159, 167–9, 192–3
Bowen, Michael J. 109
Boxoffice International Pictures 80
Boyreau, Jacques 154, 189
Boys in the Sand 10
Bradbury, Ray 78
Brass, Tinto 139
Braun, Lasse 11
Briggs, Joe Bob 246 n.66
Bright, Jennifer Burns 122
Bright, Susie 250 n.19
Bruno, Giuliana 27, 213

Buckalew, Bethel 7, 139
Bucky Beaver's series (Something Weird) 143, 155, 159–60
Buñuel, Luis 82
Buonanno, Milly 147
burlesque 26, 33, 37, 47, 64, 66, 116, 140, 223 n.64
Burning Angel 44, 224 n.66
Bush, George W. 242 n.3
Buszek, Maria Elena 43
Byron, Tom 11

Caballero Control Corporation 128, 131, 135, 151, 153, 157, 168, 206
Cad 78
Calga Publishers 78
California v. Freeman 13, 127
Cal Vista Video 130, 165, 240 n.110
Camille 2000 24
camp 15, 43, 46, 48, 83, 155, 187. *See also* irony; paracinema
Candy Stripers 133
Cannes Film Festival 47
canons 4, 71, 100, 139, 163, 179, 182, 199, 204, 207
Cardinale, Claudia 79
Caribbean Films 202
Carlson, Marla 184, 186–7
Carmen, Baby 24
Casting Call 69
Casting Couch, The 55
Catlin, Jacy 151, 165–6, 168–9, 212
CAV Distributing Corporation 174, 177–8, 180
Censored 98
censorship 2–4, 9–10, 12, 20–1, 33–4, 55, 59–60, 65, 68–9, 71, 80–6, 88, 90–4, 98, 116, 131–8, 151, 153–4, 164–8, 170, 172, 177, 187, 190, 195, 209–10, 239 n.93, 239 n.97, 245 n.52. *See also* obscenity
Center Spread Girls 205
Chained Girls 76
chain of title. *See* copyright
Chambers, Marilyn 8, 11
Chaplin, Charlie 47
Chappell, Fred 57
Cherchi Usai, Paolo 106–7, 145

child pornography 133, 144, 239 n.93, 239 n.91, 240 n.100
Chinn, Bob 172
Cinderfella 78
Cindy and Donna 93
Cine-Arts 72
Cinemageddon 193
cinema of attractions 31, 48
Cinema Video 126
Cinema-X 93
cinephilia 18, 20, 24–8, 31, 49–54, 56–60, 74, 110, 157, 162–3, 171, 173, 181–2, 193, 195–7
class 2, 14, 23–4, 32–3, 45, 47, 57, 66, 70–1, 78, 161, 170, 178, 180–1, 190, 201–2, 220 n.1, 229 n.31, 249 n.5. *See also* taste
Classic Publications 72
Classic Stags 35
Classix Video 36
Cleopatra 78
Clifford, Michelle 166
Climax of Blue Power, A, 151
Climb It, Tarzan! 43
Clockwork Orange, A, 91
Club 90 205, 250 n.14
collecting 2, 4, 7–9, 17–18, 20–1, 35, 37, 40, 45, 47, 49, 54, 61–5, 69–70, 74, 76, 100–1, 111, 118, 124, 129–31, 137, 140–8, 151–2, 162–5, 171, 190–3, 195, 199, 207, 214–16, 227 n.3, 228 n.12, 236 n.46. *See also* fandom
Collection Series 128
Color Climax 144, 239 n.91
Color of Love, The 50
Colt, Zebedy 135–6
comedy 13, 19, 29, 43, 46–8, 66, 78, 83, 85, 99, 101, 109, 135, 180, 194, 207–8, 210, 232 n.104
Command Video 125
compilations 34–5, 37, 39, 41, 47, 50, 53–4, 66, 72, 86–7, 98, 122, 127–9, 131, 137, 140–1, 143, 165, 166, 187, 205, 224 n.72, 225 n.87, 240 n.110
Conde, Manuel 144
Confidential 55, 69, 71, 90
Conner, Bruce 49

connoisseurship 2–3, 6, 8, 14, 17, 26, 45, 49, 129, 131, 141, 145, 153–9, 162–3, 186, 189, 199. *See also* fandom; taste
Consenting Adults 183
conservation 114, 124, 152, 239 n.97. *See also* preservation
Contemporary Erotic Cinema 94–5, 139
Cool Hand Luke 82
copyright 18, 21, 78, 91, 112–13, 116, 122, 125–7, 132, 135, 141–4, 152, 158, 161, 165, 168–70, 172, 178, 193, 203, 210, 212. *See also* bootlegs; piracy
Copyright Act of 1976 112
Corman, Roger 57
Costello, Shaun 137, 165
counterculture 34, 40, 82, 95, 208–9
Crawford, Joan 55, 86
crime films 86, 208
Criterion Collection The, 8, 151, 163–4, 171–2, 175–8, 182, 190–1, 195, 245 n.41
crowd-funding 171, 182, 194, 197
Crowley, Ronan 122
Crown International Pictures 93
Cruising 246 n.67
Cuban Rebel Girls 86
Cubeiro, Emilio 183
Cult Epics 46, 174, 180
cultism 11, 18, 21, 25, 29, 45–7, 50, 55, 58, 110, 118, 137, 140–3, 145, 153, 158, 161–3, 165, 169–74, 176–7, 182, 191, 196
Cult 70s Porno Directors series (Alpha Blue Archives) 165
cultural memory 3–4, 8–9, 21–2, 24, 26–8, 31, 47, 50–2, 54, 58–9, 107, 111, 118, 121, 123, 137, 144, 146–9, 151, 214–16
Currier, Althea 78–9
Curse of Her Flesh, The 103–5
cycles (film) 7, 76, 78, 145–8

Damiano, Gerard 13, 164–5, 169, 183
Daring Films & Books 71
Darlene, Gigi 104–8, 110
Daughter of the Sun 74

Davis, Don 77
Dean, Tim 235 n.19
Debbie Does Dallas 113, 130
Deep Inside Annie Sprinkle 182–90, 199, 203, 212, 250 n.12
Deep Inside Porn Stars 183, 205, 250 n.14
Deep Throat 8, 10, 13, 34, 93, 113, 129–30, 138–9, 201, 204, 215, 229 n.40
Deep Throat Part II 138
Deep Throat Sex Scandal, The 205
Defilers, The 74, 84, 88, 141
Déjà Vu clubs 202
Deleuze, Gilles 242 n.136
Delta of Venus 45
Denberg, Susan 82
De Renzy, Alex 30, 34–5, 165, 169, 172, 204–5
Desires within Young Girls 135
Desjardins, Mary 90, 144
Despentes, Virginie 190
Deutsch, Gustav 50
Devil in Miss Jones, The 139, 175, 201
Devil Inside Her, The 184
Diamond Films 74
Digital Cinema Initiative 196, 198
Digital Cinema Package (DCP) 118, 196
Di Lauro, Al 29, 34, 226 n.114
Dirty Western A, 134
discussion forums. *See* Internet
Disney, Walt 83
Distribpix Archive Collection series 178
Distribpix Inc. 131, 141, 151, 171, 175–83, 186–91, 194, 196–9, 203, 208–9, 212, 239 n.92, 246 n.70, 250 n.12
documentary 1, 15, 30, 34–5, 39, 47, 50, 53, 55, 66, 76, 78, 83, 115, 172, 183, 190, 218 n.27, 220 n.13, 221 n.31, 222 n.46
Dominion Publishing 72
Downing, Lisa 51
Drive-In Collection series (Vinegar Syndrome) 174
Dworkin, Andrea 201

eBay 61, 144, 236 n.46
Edge of Night, The 210
edgeplay 187
educational films 113, 164, 204

Edwards, Elizabeth 62
Egan, Kate 245 n.52
800 Fantasy Lane 133
8MM 55
8-mm (format) 29, 32–4, 41, 49–50, 54, 61, 72, 74–6, 80, 93, 100, 108, 128, 132–3, 144, 151, 166, 229 n.40
Elgin Films 74
Elite Visuals 140
Ellison, Harlan 78, 80
Elsaesser, Thomas 50
Emerson, Ryan 171
Entertainment Ventures, Inc. 85
Entertainment World International 202
Enticknap, Leo 196
ephemera 2–3, 5, 8, 11, 19–21, 29, 50, 53, 61–5, 100, 103, 111, 115, 144, 149, 164, 168, 194–5, 198, 203, 208, 213, 215–16, 236 n.46, 250 n.12
Epley, Nathan Scott 15
erotica 2, 5–6, 25, 27, 45–8, 56, 62, 92, 175, 202–4, 207, 221 n.31. *See also* pornography
Erotic Heritage Museum (Las Vegas) 202–5, 207, 215, 250 n.12
Erotic Past 45
Erotikus: A History of the Gay Movie 221 n.31
erotohistoriography 52, 211
Escoffier, Jeffrey 210
Esquire 70
Essex Video 130–1, 140
Etiquette Pictures 172, 194
Evart Enterprises. *See* Distribpix Inc.
Eve and the Handyman 82
Evil Angel 158
exercise videos 128, 155
Exhausted: John C. Holmes, The Real Story 218 n.27
Exodus Trust 202, 204, 207. *See also* Institute for the Advanced Study of Human Sexuality
exploitation cinema 2, 5, 7, 14, 25, 46, 55, 57–9, 61, 66, 83, 85, 92, 109, 114–16, 121, 137–40, 164–5, 169, 171–2, 174, 194–5, 250 n.24. *See also* sexploitation

Exploitation.tv 194–5
Expose Me, Lovely 28
EYE (archive) 147

Famous Smokers of the Past series 129
fandom 2–4, 6–9, 13–18, 20–1, 24–9, 35, 37, 39, 45–6, 48–52, 54, 56–9, 65, 72, 76, 83–4, 88, 98–100, 105–6, 109, 111, 115, 118, 121, 123, 127–8, 131–2, 137, 140–1, 143, 145–9, 151, 153–63, 165–6, 169–77, 182, 190–9, 201–2, 204–5, 207–8, 211–14, 216, 219 n.47, 223 n.61, 228 n.12, 244 n.39
  cyclical fandom 145–9, 242 n.141
  fan studies 15–18
  fan magazines 16, 18, 20, 44, 61–2, 65, 68–76, 79–101, 103, 108, 116, 141–2, 144, 158, 228 n.15, 236 n.40
Fanny Hill 71
Felicia 181
Felleman, Susan 50
feminism 6, 10, 12–15, 18, 43–4, 47, 56, 63, 67–8, 86, 133, 156–7, 182, 186–8, 190, 201, 205, 210, 213, 223 n.64, 249 n.5
Femmes de Sade 133–4, 205
Filthy Habits 16
Filmfare Video Labs 140
Film Ist: A Girl and a Gun 50
film preservation movement 21, 109, 152, 166, 196, 213–14
Film Threat 141
Findlay, Michael 103–4, 106, 110, 142
Findlay, Roberta 103–4, 106, 110, 127, 142, 165–6, 169
Firestorm 125
first-sale doctrine 169, 190–1
Fishbein, Paul 128
fisting 133–6, 164–6
Flynn, Errol 86
Forced Entry 137
For Love and Money (film) 77
For Love or Money (book) 77
Fossati, Giovanna 122, 143, 153, 169
Foucault, Michel 4, 17, 19, 41, 66
42nd Street (New York City). *See* Times Square

42nd Street Pete 246 n.66
Franco, Jesús (Jess) 11, 57, 139
Freeman, Elizabeth 52
FreeOnes 37, 158
Free Ride, A 204
Frick, Caroline 143, 152, 164
Friedman, David F. 11, 59, 74, 92, 106, 142, 161, 164, 237 n.64
Frost, Lee 84, 91, 139
Fuses 49

Gable, Clark 55, 86, 226 n.114
Gaines, Jane 17, 46, 125
Gamelink 165
Game People Play, The 89
Gang Bang Bitches 13, 28
Garbo, Greta, 55
gay liberation 5, 12, 14, 43, 52
gender 14–15, 19–20, 25, 27–8, 32, 41–5, 47–8, 51, 58, 69–71, 86, 95, 115, 171, 181–2, 189, 201. *See also* heterosexism
genre 1, 10, 19, 21–2, 24–5, 35, 37, 44, 65, 74, 81, 83, 85–6, 109, 114, 116, 130–2, 137, 139, 146, 153–5, 159, 163–4, 170–1, 174, 177–8, 190–4, 198–9, 202, 204–5, 208, 210–16, 224 n.77, 242 n.136
Gentlemen II Productions 69
Giles, Dennis 51
Gillette, Paul J. 78
Gillis, Jamie 11, 133–6
Girl with the Hungry Eyes, The 80
Girls on F Street, The 74, 79, 87
Global Media International 140
Goines, Donald 93
Golden State News 72
Goldilocks and the Three Bares 67
Goldstein, Al 11
Good Luck, Miss Wyckoff 193
Good Old Naughty Days, The 47, 53, 225 n.87
Good Old Naughty Days [deconstructed], The 225 n.87
Good Old XXX 41
Gore Gore Girl, The 157
Gorfinkel, Elena 6, 53, 64, 68–9, 96

Gracy, Karen 113, 152
Grandpa Bucky's series (Something Weird) 46, 224 n.72
Grandpa's Hot Movies 41
Grindhouse Releasing 174
Guattari, Felix 242 n.136
Gunning, Tom 31

Halsted, Fred 221 n.31
Hamilton, Jane 197, 205–7, 250 n.14
Hampshire, Russ 134
Hanson, Dian 175
haptics 20, 46, 49, 51–2, 60–1, 65, 153, 168
Hardcore 55
Hardcore, Max 212, 242 n.3
Hardgore 244 n.39
Harlot, Scarlot 247 n.85
Harlow, Jean 55, 86, 226 n.114
Harmon, Joy 82
Harris, Robert A. 172
Hart, Veronica. *See* Hamilton, Jane
Hastie, Amelie 9, 64–5
Hawkins, Joan 24, 46
Heffernan, Kevin 181
Hefner, Hugh 71
Henenlotter, Frank 142
Herzog, Amy 49
heterosexism 5, 10, 12, 14–16, 19, 28–9, 32, 39–44, 48, 51–2, 60, 64, 67–8, 70, 74, 78, 86, 95, 103, 135–7, 151, 154, 156, 174, 180–2, 184, 186–7, 190, 211–13, 215, 239 n.94, 244 n.31
High Rise 28, 197
High Society 9, 93
Hilderbrand, Lucas 4, 168–9
Hill, Jack 139
Hills, Matt 145
Historic Erotica 140–1
historiography 4, 9–10, 12–13, 19–22, 52, 61–2, 64, 87, 101, 106–11, 115, 121, 123–5, 132, 137, 144–9, 164, 182, 188, 201, 208, 210–13, 215–16
History of Incest series (Alpha Blue Archives) 166
History of Rape series (Alpha Blue Archives) 166

History of the Blue Movie, A 30, 32–5, 55
Hitchcock, Alfred 172
Hodas, Martin J. 11, 33
Holliday, Jim 130, 134–6, 139
Holloway House 78, 80, 93. *See also*
    Knight Publishing
Hollywood Babylon 55
Hollywood Blue 55
Hollywood cinema 10, 20, 31, 39, 48,
    53–7, 65–6, 68–9, 72, 76, 78–9,
    81–8, 90–1, 96, 106, 113, 130–1,
    146, 155, 163, 169, 179, 190, 195–6,
    198, 201, 207–10, 239 n.86
Holmes, John C. 218 n.27
home film projection 13, 23–4, 32–3, 72,
    74–6, 151, 229 n.40. *See also* 8-mm
    (format); 16-mm (format)
home video 2, 4–5, 7, 11, 13–14, 18, 20–2,
    24–8, 34–5, 44, 46, 50, 53, 56, 58,
    61, 100, 104–6, 109–10, 112–13,
    118, 121–2, 124–44, 147, 151–5,
    157–83, 186–96, 198–9, 202, 206,
    208–10, 214, 216
  Beta (format) 137, 157–8, 166, 193
  Blu-ray (format) 2, 21, 141, 153, 157,
    162–4, 171, 174, 179–82, 191,
    193–6, 198, 239 n.92
  DVD (format) 2, 12, 20–1, 40, 45–6,
    50, 61, 100, 103, 122, 131, 133–5,
    137, 141, 151, 153–5, 157, 159–69,
    171, 174–8, 180, 182–3, 186–95,
    198–9, 201, 208–9, 216, 239 n.92,
    244 n.33, 245 n.52
  laser disc (format) 157
  manufactured-on-demand (MOD)
    discs 163, 175
  pay-per-view video. *See* video-on-
    demand
  streaming video. *See* Internet; video-
    on-demand
  VHS (format) 4, 7, 18, 35–6, 39, 41,
    58, 100, 103, 128, 133, 137, 157–9,
    161–2, 165, 166, 168–9, 172, 187,
    190, 193–5, 216
  video-on-demand (VOD) 2, 12, 14,
    141, 157, 159, 165, 168, 173, 177,
    191, 193–5, 199, 214

homophobia. *See* heterosexism
homosexuality. *See* pornography, gay,
    lesbian; queerness
homosociality 28–9, 31–3, 41–6, 48, 59,
    135, 173
Hookers, The 78
horror films 19, 86, 108, 114, 116, 137,
    156, 194
Horulu, Kemal 175
Hot Movies 165
Hot Skin and Cold Cash 89
Hot Spur 73, 76
House of Pain and Pleasure 94, 96
Howard, Cecil 125
Howard Mahler Films 114
How to Build Your X-Rated Video Library
    139
Hugo Awards 80
Hugo, Victor 78
Hulu Plus 195
Hustler 70
Huyssen, Andreas 227 n.129

I, a Woman 80
Image, The 180
Image Entertainment 161, 174, 176
Immoral Mr. Teas, The 66, 81–2, 139
incest 133, 154, 156, 161, 166, 187, 210,
    239 n.94
Indiana University Cinema 115
industrial films 80, 113, 164
Insatiable 130
inserts 7, 55, 81, 226 n.114
Inserts 55
Inside Deep Throat 13
Institute for the Advanced Study of
    Human Sexuality 202, 204, 207
International Federation of Film Archives
    (FIAF) 152, 172
International Video Distributors 175,
    177–8
Internet 2, 10–11, 13–14, 17–18, 20, 25–6,
    35, 37–8, 40, 44–8, 50, 61, 110,
    127, 154, 157–9, 161, 163, 165–6,
    168–9, 173, 177, 191, 193–5, 199,
    209–12, 214–16, 219 n.47, 238 n.78,
    245 n.53

Internet Adult Film Database 158
"In the Flesh" series (Anthology Film Archives) 196–9, 207, 210
Intimacy 156
Intrator, Jerald 116, 119
irony 14–15, 17, 44, 46, 48, 55, 57–9, 90, 129, 146, 156, 163–4, 171–2, 187, 210, 214, 232 n.104, 244 n.39
iTunes 191

Jack 'n' Jill 184
Jacobellis v. Ohio 81, 230 n.55
Jacques 43, 223 n.61
Jaeckin, Just 7, 139
Jancovich, Mark 45
Janus Films 179
Jenkins, Henry 15
Jennings, David 130–1, 133, 157
Johnsen, Sande N. 89
Johnson, Eithne 204
Jones, Janna 115, 123, 169
Jordan, Marsha 79

Kakoudaki, Despina 43
Kama Sutra 71
Karagarga 193
Keathley, Christian 31
Kendrick, James 110, 245 n.41
Kendrick, Walter 62, 111
Kickstarter 171, 182
King of Kings 78
Kinky Ladies of Bourbon Street, The 181
Kinky World of Annie Sprinkle, The 187
Kinsey, Alfred 78
Kinsey Institute for Research in Sex, Gender, and Reproduction 50, 61, 114–16, 118, 122–3, 127, 232 n.99, 236 n.49
Kipnis, Laura 2
Klaw, Irving 13
Klein, Amanda Ann 148
Kleinhans, Chuck 130
Kneel Before Me 184
Knight 74, 78, 80, 94, 97
Knight Publishing 72, 80, 93–4
Koch, Gertrud 54
Kristel, Sylvia 11

Lady Chatterley's Lover 71
Lady in the Lake 100
Lamont, Charles 110
Lampert, Andrew 196
Landis, Bill 166
Lease, Maria 101
legality. *See* censorship; copyright; obscenity
Leigh, Janet 82
Leisure Time Booking 114
Leonard, Gloria 11, 205
Leslie, John 11
Lewis, Herschell Gordon 59, 67, 142, 171, 182
Lewis, Jerry 78
libraries (books) 62, 112–14, 118, 122–3, 202, 204, 215
Library of Congress 112, 118, 123
Lickerish Quartet, The 23–4, 31, 59, 180, 207
Like It Is 94
Lincoln, Fred J. 11
Lincoln, Marv 72
Linda and Abilene 86, 99
Linda/Les & Annie: The First Female-to-Male Transsexual Love Story 183
Lindgren, Simon 18
Lloyd, Harold 47
Lobato, Ramon 3, 127, 170
Lockwood, Dee 99
loops 13, 32–4, 74–5, 92–3, 112, 127–33, 139, 143–4, 164, 166, 229 n.40. *See also* 8-mm (format); 16-mm (format)
Lords, Traci 239 n.93
Lorna 67
lost films 21, 100–1, 106–7, 109–11, 114, 116, 121, 123–4, 140–1, 143, 145, 147, 149, 154, 162, 213–14
Love Camp 7 230 n.48
Love-Ins, The 82
Lovelace 13
Lovelace, Linda 93, 201
Lowenthal, David 62
Lucas, Tim 1, 18
Lumet, Sidney 83
Lustful Feelings 175

Lusting Hours, The 76
Lust of the Eyes 107–8, 114
Lynn, Amber 11
Lynn, Ginger 11, 237 n.66

Mabe, Byron 99
McIlvenna, Ted 202–4
MacKinnon, Catherine 201
McNair, Brian 9, 12
Mahon, Barry 82, 86, 89, 104, 139
Mailer, Norman 82
Mail Order Confidential 74
Man & Wife 92
Mankind 78
Mansfield, Jayne 71
Mantis in Lace 80
Maraschino Cherry 28, 198
Marilyn Times Five 49–50
Marins, José Mojica 57
Marks, Laura U. 46
Martha's Girls 43
martial arts films 114
Martin, Adrian 56
Martin, Dean 82
Mashon, Mike 118
Maslon, Jimmy 142
masturbation. *See* autoeroticism
media effects 15, 17, 19, 154, 210–11
Meese Commission on Pornography 12, 133, 140
Melton Viewer 32–3
Memoirs of Casanova 78
men's magazines 43, 62, 66, 69–71, 78–80, 93–4, 227 n.3
metasites. *See* Internet
Metro Distributors 247 n.70
Metzger, Radley 7, 23–4, 139, 177–82, 190, 220 n.1
Meyer, Russ 66, 81–2, 139–40, 196
Midnight Cowboy 91
Miller v. California 81, 132, 136, 153
Miller-Young, Mireille 202
Millett, Kate 43
Milligan, Andy 116
Miranda, Vince 161
Mishkin, Lewis 116, 123, 236 n.40
Mishkin, William 116, 123

misogyny. *See* heterosexism
Misty Beethoven: The Musical! 11, 205
Mitchell, Jim and Artie 96, 184
Mitchell, Sharon 202
Mizer, Bob 221 n.31
Modern Screen 65
modularity 69, 72, 88–90, 98, 116, 127, 146
Mohney, Harry 202–4
Monarch Releasing Corporation 114
Mona: The Virgin Nymph 34, 91, 93
Mondo Freudo 76
Mondo Oscenità 98
Money, Constance 133–4
Monogram Pictures 85
Monroe, Marilyn 50, 55, 95
Moody, Titus 72
Morowitz, Arthur 142, 175–6, 178, 184, 191
Morowitz, Steven 151, 175–8, 180, 182, 186, 192, 198
Morrison, James 58
Morriss, Bentley 80
Motel Confidential 88
Motion Picture 65
Motion Picture Association of America 81, 91, 139
Motion Picture Producers and Distributors of America 68–9
Movielab 142
Movies Unlimited 128
Mulvey, Laura 31
Museum of Sex (New York City) 112, 203
Mutantes (Punk, Porn, Feminism) 190
My Brother's Wife 87
My Fair Lady 180–1
Mystery Science Theater 3000 187

Naked Lunch 71
Nash, Hester 40
Nash, Jennifer C. 129
National Film Registry 215
National Film Preservation Act 113
National Sex Forum. *See* Institute for the Advanced Study of Human Sexuality
Naylor, David 164, 166
Nead, Lynda 175

Necromania 244 n.39
necrophilia 20, 28, 49–52, 54, 56, 64
Neon Nights 125
Nero, Sue 205
New Behind the Green Door, The 11
New, Bill 77
new cinema history 109
New Devil in Miss Jones, The 11
New Link Publications 72, 80
Newman, Paul 82
New World Pictures 93
New York Releasing 114
New York Times 172, 246 n.67
Nichols, Kelly 11, 205
Nichols, Wade 207–11
Nicholson, Geoff 144
Night of Submission 184
Nin, Anaïs 45
9 Songs 11
nitrate films 109, 196
Nixon, Richard 12
Nobus, Dany 52
nostalgia 6, 8–10, 12–14, 22, 27–8, 39–40, 42, 44–5, 47–9, 54, 56, 58–9, 106, 109, 129, 132, 140–1, 153, 157, 165, 168, 186–7, 194, 210–12, 246 n.66
Nostalgia Blue 35–6, 129
Nostalgia Sex 35
Nothing to Hide 28
Notorious Bettie Page, The 12, 55
Notorious Daughter of Fanny Hill, The 78, 80
Notte Erotique 82
Novak, Harry 11, 59, 80, 142, 144, 162
Nudie Classics 129
Nun's Story, The 30
Nymphomaniac 11, 156

obscenity 4–5, 9–10, 12, 24, 26, 28, 34, 45, 52, 55, 68–9, 71, 74, 81–2, 92, 98, 100, 112, 125, 132–4, 136, 138, 154, 170, 172, 187, 193, 209, 229 n.35, 242 n.3. *See also* censorship
OCN Digital Labs. *See* Process Blue
O'Donoghue, Darragh 110
Odyssey: The Ultimate Trip 13
Old, Borrowed, and Stag 35, 129

Old-Time Blue 35
Olympic International Pictures 101
"one-day wonders" 93, 161, 180–1
101 Acts of Love 92
One Naked Night 120
Only the Best 136, 139, 240 n.110
On Our Backs 44
Opening of Misty Beethoven, The 24, 135, 139, 179–83, 187, 190, 239 n.92
Orbit Publications 72–3
O'Ree, Mal 188
organized crime 112–13, 125, 152
Orgeron, Marsha 96
Orgy at Lil's Place, The 116–23, 143, 147, 237 n.58
Original Classic Stags, The 151
Orleans Theatre 184–5, 188, 199
orphan films 3, 49, 108, 110–11, 113–14, 118, 123–4, 142–3, 161, 168, 170, 193
Orphan Film Symposium 118, 123
Osco, Bill 34
Osgerby, Bill 66
O'Toole, Laurence 129, 133

Paasonen, Susanna 12–13, 15, 19, 31, 52, 193
Page, Bettie 12–13, 44, 223 nn.64–5
Pandora's Mirror 205
paperback books 20, 34–5, 61–3, 72, 74, 76–8, 92, 95–6, 98, 120–1
paracinema 15–16, 57–9, 163, 171–2, 187, 190, 244 n.39, 246 n.66. *See also* irony
paratexts 20, 29, 50, 59, 61, 64–5, 68–9, 74, 100, 116–18, 120–1, 130, 146, 157–9, 163–4, 175–6, 180, 188, 191, 193–4, 198
Paris, Henry. *See* Metzger, Radley
Parker, Eleanor 82
Passions of Carol, The 177
Patron of the Arts 98
Patterson, Zabet 25
Pawnbroker, The 83–4
paysites. *See* Internet
Peekarama series (Vinegar Syndrome) 174, 178

peepshow arcades 9, 13, 33–4, 133
Penthouse 78
Penthouse Forum 250 n.19
performance art 183–7, 190, 223 n.61
Perry, Peter 99
Persona 80
Pervert! 43
phantom films 110
Photoplay 65
physique magazines 71, 221 n.31
Picture of Dorian Gray, The 207, 211
Pigkeeper's Daughter, The 7
pink films 82
pin-ups 15, 37, 43–4, 47, 63, 223 n.64
piracy 3, 112, 124–8, 135, 137, 143, 157, 159, 168–9, 177, 192–3, 195–6
Pirandello, Luigi 24
Pitzulo, Carrie 70
Planet of the Apes 98
Platinum Elite series (Distribpix) 176–8, 180, 182, 186–91, 198, 203, 250 n.12
Playboy, 10–11, 43, 69–71, 78, 209, 223 n.64
Players 93
Police Gazette 71
Poole, Wakefield 221 n.31
Porn Archives 215
Porn Inspector 38, 42, 49
porno chic 9–12, 14, 34, 39, 132, 139, 161, 173, 179–80, 182, 190, 201, 205, 212, 215, 229 n.40, 240 n.107, 246 n.67. *See also* pornography, Golden Age of
pornography
    alternative 19, 22, 44, 130, 132, 138, 140–2, 224 n.66
    amateur 13, 27, 29, 31–2, 38, 46, 49, 54, 100, 211–12, 221 n.37
    bareback 210
    couples' market for 28, 35, 68, 88, 135, 161, 167, 188
    female viewers of 19, 26–8, 42–4, 48, 52, 54, 56, 60, 63, 111, 211, 250 n.19
    feminist 56, 186–7, 212, 249 n.5
    fetish. *See* pornography, niche
    gay (all-male) 4–5, 109, 122, 138, 207, 210–11, 221 n.31, 239 n.94, 244 n.31
    Golden Age of 12–13, 21, 25–6, 28, 56, 125, 129–31, 152, 154–6, 158–9, 165, 168–9, 172, 174, 179, 186–7, 189–90, 193–4, 196, 198–9, 201, 207, 210–12, 244 n.31, 244 n.39, 249 n.5
    gonzo 31, 130, 174, 212
    lesbian 189, 212
    mainstream industry 21, 45, 127, 131–2, 135–6, 141, 151, 153–4, 158–9, 161, 166, 171, 187, 189, 192–3, 207, 212, 237 n.66
    niche 5, 9, 11, 14, 18, 26, 28, 35, 37–41, 44–5, 47–8, 50–2, 56, 59–60, 130–2, 136, 140, 153, 163, 170, 205, 215
    online. *See* Internet
    shot-on-video 13, 31, 129–32, 137, 153, 174, 183, 190, 211–12
    Silver Age of 129–30, 155, 212, 238 n.78
    specialty. *See* pornography, niche
    soft core. *See* sexploitation
    stars 11, 13, 17, 26, 34, 37, 42, 55, 105–6, 128, 131, 165, 182–3, 192, 194, 196–7, 201–2, 205, 207, 211, 216, 222 n.54, 237 n.66, 249 n.5
    vintage 2–6, 9–11, 14–15, 17–22, 25–9, 37–56, 59–60, 62, 106, 109, 111, 113, 118, 121–2, 127–9, 131–2, 135, 137–8, 140, 143–5, 148, 151–60, 162, 164–6, 171–4, 193, 195, 198–9, 202, 204–5, 207–8, 211–14, 216, 246 n.66
    wall-to-wall 28, 31, 174
    websites. *See* Internet
Pornography in Denmark: A New Approach 34
porn studies. *See* academia
postfeminism 44
post-porn 21, 154–5, 159, 171, 183, 187, 189–90, 247 n.82
Post-Porn Modernist 183–4, 186
Powell, Ryan 5
preservation 21, 40, 45, 50, 108–9, 112–13, 115–18, 122, 152–4, 159, 164, 170, 172, 178, 207, 212–16, 236 n.49, 237 n.58

preservational ethics 152–4, 164, 166, 168–70, 172, 178, 180, 186, 196, 199
Preservation of Orphan Works Act 113
President's Commission on Obscenity and Pornography 12, 71, 85
Pretty Peaches 133
Private Afternoons of Pamela Mann, The 24
Process Blue 171, 180
Production Code Administration 65, 68–9, 81–3, 86
ProQuest 109
prostitution 13, 32, 35, 43, 69, 89, 127, 180, 183, 207
Psychotronic Video 141
public domain. *See* copyright
pulps. *See* paperback books
punctum 31, 58–9, 74
punk 39, 44, 190
Pussycat Theaters 161, 187
Pygmalion 180

Quality-X 246 n.70
queerness 19, 32, 34, 39, 42–3, 47–8, 52, 54, 56, 71, 86, 88, 95, 122, 135–7, 183, 187, 189–90, 197, 211–12, 221 n.21, 250 n.19. *See also* pornography, gay, lesbian

Rabkin, Gerald 29, 34, 226 n.114
race films 164, 213, 250 n.24
rape 6, 10, 12, 15, 51, 67, 78, 83–6, 88, 95, 133–4, 151, 154, 156, 161, 184, 187, 205, 207, 210, 239 n.94. *See also* sexploitation, roughies
Rated X 56
Reagan, Ronald 12, 55
reception studies 19
Red Dust 55
Red Light Video 246 n.70
Reems, Harry 11
Reflections in a Golden Eye 82
remediation 3, 8, 12, 14, 20–1, 26–7, 37, 44–5, 50, 52, 54, 58–9, 62, 105–6, 110–11, 113, 118, 121, 124, 127–9, 133, 137–8, 144, 151–3, 157–9, 161–2, 166, 168–70, 172, 198, 202, 212–13, 215–16. *See also* home video

Rent-a-Girl 120
restoration 45, 143, 152–3, 158, 161, 163–4, 166, 169, 172, 187, 194, 213–14. *See also* preservation
Retro Porn Archive 25
RetroRaunch 38–40, 45
retrosploitation 43
Revene, Larry 197
Rexroth, Mary 92
Rhino Video 140
Rialto Report, The 110, 173
Riley, Patrick 139
Rimmer, Robert H. 139
RM Films 139
Roberts, June 104–5
Rocco and His Brothers 81
Rock! Shock! Pop! 158
Romance 156
Romeo and Juliet 82
Roommates 205
Ross, Gene 140–2, 167
Roth v. United States 71
Rotsler, William 8–9, 70, 72, 80, 84, 88–90, 93–101, 104, 108, 139
Royalle, Candida 11, 205
Rubin, Joe 109, 171–4, 176–7, 193–4, 197, 199

Saarenmaa, Laura 12–13
Sade, Marquis de 78
Sadistic Seventies series (Alpha Blue Archives) 166
St. Vincent, Julia 218 n.27
Sandvoss, Cornel 51
Sari Publishing 72
Sarno, Joe 11, 183
Satan in High Heels 116
Satisfiers of Alpha Blue, The 164
Satyricon 78
Scent of Heather, A 205
Schaefer, Eric 5, 34, 40, 83, 91, 109, 111, 118, 123–4, 161, 172, 215
Schneemann, Carolee 49
science fiction 80, 96, 98–9, 101, 164
Sconce, Jeffrey 15, 57–8, 163, 244 n.39
Score 180
Scott, Casey 112, 166, 169, 196–8, 202

Screening Room, The 34
Screen Stories 87
Scum of the Earth 67, 74, 116, 119
Searchers, The 78
Seasoned Players 11
Secret Sex Lives of Romeo and Juliet, The 78, 99
Sensations 181
serials 86, 147
Seven Daring Girls 81
Seven Seventy Publishers 72
Sex by Advertisement 78
sexploitation 5–8, 10, 18, 20–1, 24–5, 34, 43, 57–9, 61–2, 64–101, 103–10, 114, 116, 118–21, 123–5, 133, 138–43, 146, 153, 156, 161, 164–5, 171, 175, 178, 180, 182–3, 194, 196, 205, 212, 214, 218 n.16, 230 n.48, 230 n.63
   beaver films 34, 92
   nudie cuties 66–7, 74–5, 78, 80–5, 89–90, 92, 94, 100, 116, 119, 141
   kinkies 67, 74, 79, 84–5, 87–8, 119–20, 145
   roughies 8, 67, 73–4, 83–6, 88, 91, 99, 116, 119, 121, 133–4, 137, 145, 156, 161, 166–7, 186, 228 n.15
   simulation films 34
Sexploitation Nation 194
Sexploiters, The 74, 120, 124
Sexual Freedom in Denmark 130
Sexual Freedom in Marriage 92
Sexual Freedom League 91
Sexual Freedom: The Journal of the Sexual Freedom League 91
sexual revolution 9–14, 21, 26, 40, 52, 64–7, 69–70, 74, 82–3, 89–91, 94–6, 98–9, 101, 173
sexual violence. See rape
sex work 69, 104, 124, 127–8, 180, 201–3, 210–11, 216, 234 n.3, 237 n.66, 249 n.5. See also prostitution
Shannon's Women. 96
Shaw, George Bernard 180
Sheaffer, Russell 25
Shearer, Norma 86

Shelton, Emily 46
Sher, Louis 142
Sherman, Cindy 43, 223 n.61
Shortbus 11
Silverstein Films 114
Six Characters in Search of an Author 24
16-mm (format) 29, 32–4, 40–1, 49, 54, 74–5, 91–2, 96, 100, 128–9, 132–3, 159–62, 166, 181, 203–4
Skin-Flicks 13
Slade, Joseph 9, 29, 31–2, 55
Sleazoid Express 103, 106
Slide, Anthony 112
Slifkin, I. L. 128
Slim, Iceberg 93
Slippery When Wet 184
slow cinema 57, 226 n.124
Smalley, Sean 115
Smart Alec 37
Smith, C. Davis 88
Society for Cinema and Media Studies 215
Space Thing 99
Spelvin, Georgina 201
Spinelli, Anthony 165
Sobchack, Vivian 64–5
Something Weird Video 46, 103, 140–5, 147, 153, 155, 159–66, 168, 170–2, 174, 176, 178, 196, 244 nn.31–2, 250 n.24
Sonney, Dan 142
Sontag, Susan 48
Sperb, Jason 57
Sprinkle, Annie 182–90, 202–3, 205, 250 n.12
Squires, David 122
stag films 5–6, 8, 10, 19–20, 23–55, 59–61, 74, 78, 83, 91, 122, 128–30, 132, 135, 139, 143–5, 151, 155, 180, 204–5, 207–9, 212, 216, 220 n.13, 224 n.72, 225 n.87, 225 n.100, 236 n.50
Starlet! 85
Starr, Blaze 11
Star Trek 98
Steedman, Carolyn 61, 103, 115, 123, 148–9

Stevens, Kirdy 11
Stevenson, Robert Louis 78
Stewart, Jacqueline 123, 213
Stewart, Potter 1
Stine, Scott Aaron 16
Storms, Gregory 210
Story of Joanna, The 13, 133, 135–6, 138, 169
Stranger by the Lake 11
Street of a Thousand Pleasures 80, 96, 234 n.7
Striporama 116
striptease 26, 33–4, 47, 66, 78, 88, 92, 106, 108, 140, 164, 202
Student Nurses, The 93
Sturman, Reuben 33
subculture 3, 11, 14–15, 17–18, 21, 26, 37, 44–8, 50–1, 62, 109, 124, 140, 145–8, 153, 159, 161, 165, 170–2, 189–90, 201, 213–14, 223 n.64. See also fandom; taste, cultural
Suburban Pagans 94
SuicideGirls 44, 224 n.66
Sullivan, Edward S. 95
Sunset Software 140
Superior Video 130
Surfside 6 83
Surftide 77 83, 141
Sutton, Laird 204
Swedish Erotica series (Caballero) 128, 131
Sweetheart Theatres 175–6, 178, 184
Swingers, The 89
Swingers World 94, 97
swinging 94–8
Synapse Films 174, 177, 180

Taboo 133
Taboo Triples series (Alpha Blue Archives) 166
Take Off 197, 207–11, 216
TASCHEN 175
taste, cultural 3, 5–7, 9–11, 14–16, 21, 24–5, 27, 29, 38–9, 43, 45, 47–8, 50–1, 54, 56–60, 62, 68, 70–1, 78, 82–5, 91, 100, 107, 112–14, 121, 124, 129, 131, 136, 138–40, 152–66, 169–84, 186–99, 205, 207, 212–15, 220 n.1, 229 n.31, 230 n.63, 246 nn.66–7
Teaserama 66, 141
Teenage Deviate 184, 187
teenpics 82, 87, 93–4
television 83, 85, 116, 128, 138, 140, 147, 168, 210
theatrical exhibition 7, 9–10, 20, 24–5, 27–8, 34, 40, 56–7, 65–6, 70, 72, 75–6, 81, 83, 85, 87, 90, 92, 98, 100, 109, 112–14, 116, 125, 128–30, 132–3, 135, 137–9, 157, 159, 161, 165, 174–6, 183–4, 194–9, 244 n.33
  adults-only 1, 5, 56, 65, 94, 109, 125, 128–9, 161, 180, 199, 238 n.77
  art/repertory 7, 27, 50, 55, 65, 71, 74, 83, 109, 152, 171, 196–9
  drive-in 7, 138, 174, 183, 246 n.66
  storefront 27, 33–4, 92–3, 141, 143, 160–1, 166, 174, 246 n.66. See also peepshow arcades
Thompson, Dave 39, 54
Thornton, Sarah 3
Throat Sprockets 1, 18
Through the Looking Glass 197
Tijuana bibles 55
Times Square (New York City) 107–8, 116, 166, 175–6
torrent websites 37, 127, 135, 193–5. See also Internet
To the Land of the Electric Angel 98
Touch of Her Flesh, The 103
Toushin, Steven 5
Tower Records 161
transgenderism 43, 64, 71, 183, 190
Trip, The 82
Tropic of Cancer 71
Tryon, Chuck 182, 190–1, 195
tube websites 12, 127, 157, 168, 177, 192–4, 245 n.53. See also Internet
Turan, Kenneth 106
Two Women 81, 84
TVX 125–6, 130, 141, 151, 157, 165, 168, 237 n.64

underage characters 135, 161, 166, 187, 210, 239 n.93, 240 n.100
underground cinema 40, 57, 81–2, 230 n.63
Universal Pictures 172
Unreleased Blazing Films 98
Unreleased Dynamic Films 98
Untitled Centerfolds 43
Untitled Film Stills 43
urolagnia 133–5, 151, 164, 183, 187–8, 190

Vadim, Roger 82
Valentino, Rudolph 86
Van Doren, Mamie 79
Van Kempen, Wink 247 n.82
Varietease 66
Variety 116, 138, 240 n.107, 246 n.67
VCA Pictures 36, 131, 133–4, 151, 153, 157, 168, 177, 205, 239 n.97
VCX 113, 130, 141, 151, 157–8, 165
Velvet's Erotic Film Guide 93, 158
Vera, Veronica 205
Verne, Jules 78
Verrill, Addison 246 n.67
Video Dimensions 140
"video nasties" 245 n.52
Video Shack 175–6, 191–2
video stores 111, 125, 128, 130–2, 138, 140, 142, 174–6, 191
Video Watchdog 18
Video-X 158
Video-X-Pix. *See* Distribpix Inc.
Vincent, Chuck 197, 205
"vinegar syndrome" (decay) 114, 170
Vinegar Syndrome (label) 141, 153, 170–4, 177–8, 182, 190, 193–7, 244 n.31
Vintage Classic Porn 38
Vintage Cuties 25, 42
Vintage Erotica Forums 37, 62, 158, 212, 219 n.47
Vintage Erotica series (Cult Epics) 46, 224 n.72
Vintage Porn Review 38, 43
Vintage Queens 43
Vintage Taboo 25, 49

Violated 116
Vipco 245 n.52
Virgin Spring, The 81, 84
Visconti, Luchino 82
Viva (film) 43
Vivid Entertainment 130–1, 192, 212, 237 n.66
Vogel, Amos 35
voyeurism 29, 31, 52, 56, 61, 66, 70, 78, 88, 92
Vraney, Mike 11, 141–3, 148, 159, 161–3, 168, 171, 176

Wallace, Vincene 79
Wanda Whips Wall Street 197, 207
war movies 86
Warm, Warm Bed, The 89
Warner Archive series 163
Warner Bros. 82
Waterpower 137
watersports. *See* urolagnia
Waugh, Thomas 32, 42–3, 48
Weinstock, Ralph 80
West, Ashley 110, 173, 189, 246 n.66
westerns 73, 86
Weston, Armand 207
Wet Rainbow 139
When Sex Was Dirty 39
white coaters 34–5, 50, 92, 116, 145, 182, 232 n.104
White Slaves of Chinatown 116
Whittington, Ralph 112
Wicked Pictures 158
Wicke, Jennifer 58
Wild Bunch, The 86
Wilde, Oscar 207–8, 211
Wildest Films 76, 80, 83, 88
Wild World of Video 202
Wilkinson, June 79
Willemen, Paul 50, 57
Williams, Kathy 79
Williams, Linda 2, 18, 22, 31, 37, 42, 47, 51, 69, 132, 136, 172, 181, 183, 215, 225 n.100
Wilson, Chelly 166
Wishman, Doris 7–8, 104, 139, 142, 165
Wonderland 56

Wood, Edward D. 77
Wrangler, Jack 11

X-Caliber Awards 100
X-Rated Videotape Guide, The 139
X rating 7, 86, 91, 138–9, 142, 173, 198, 205

Yeager, Bunny 11
You 100–01

Young Dillinger 135
Young Sinners 81

Zeffirelli, Franco 82
Zero Tolerance 192
Ziehm, Howard 34
Ziplow, Steven 93, 138
Zito, Stephen 106